ART
SAVES

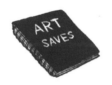

THE PLAIN JANES
Published by Titan Books,
A division of Titan Publishing Group Ltd.
144 Southwark Street
London SE1 0UP

ISBN-10: 1 84576 551 6
ISBN-13: 9781845765514

Printed in Lithuania.

A CIP catalogue record for this book is available from the British Library.

This edition first published: July 2007
10 9 8 7 6 5 4 3 2 1

COVER BY JIM RUGG
Special thanks to the Manhattan and Maplewood MINX Collectives.

Also available from Titan Books:
Re-Gifters (ISBN-13: 9781845765798)

What did you think of this book? We love to hear from our readers.
Please email us at: readerfeedback@titanemail.com, or write to us
at the above address.

To subscribe to our regular newsletter for up-to-the-minute news, great
offers and competitions, email: booksezine@titanemail.com

www.titanbooks.com

THE PLAIN JANES

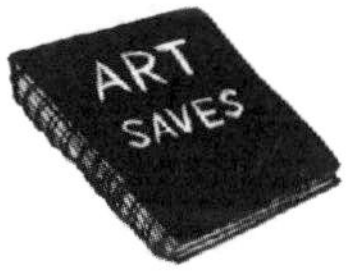
ART
SAVES

by CECIL CASTELLUCCI

and JIM RUGG

with lettering by

Jared K. Fletcher

minx

To all you Dandelions.

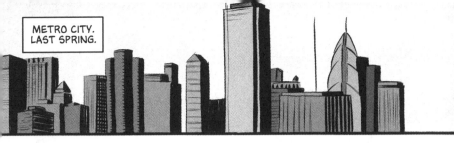

METRO CITY.
LAST SPRING.

WHEN IT HAPPENED, I FELL.

Cafe

THERE WAS A POP AND THEN NOTHING.

I DIDN'T KNOW WHAT WAS HAPPENING.

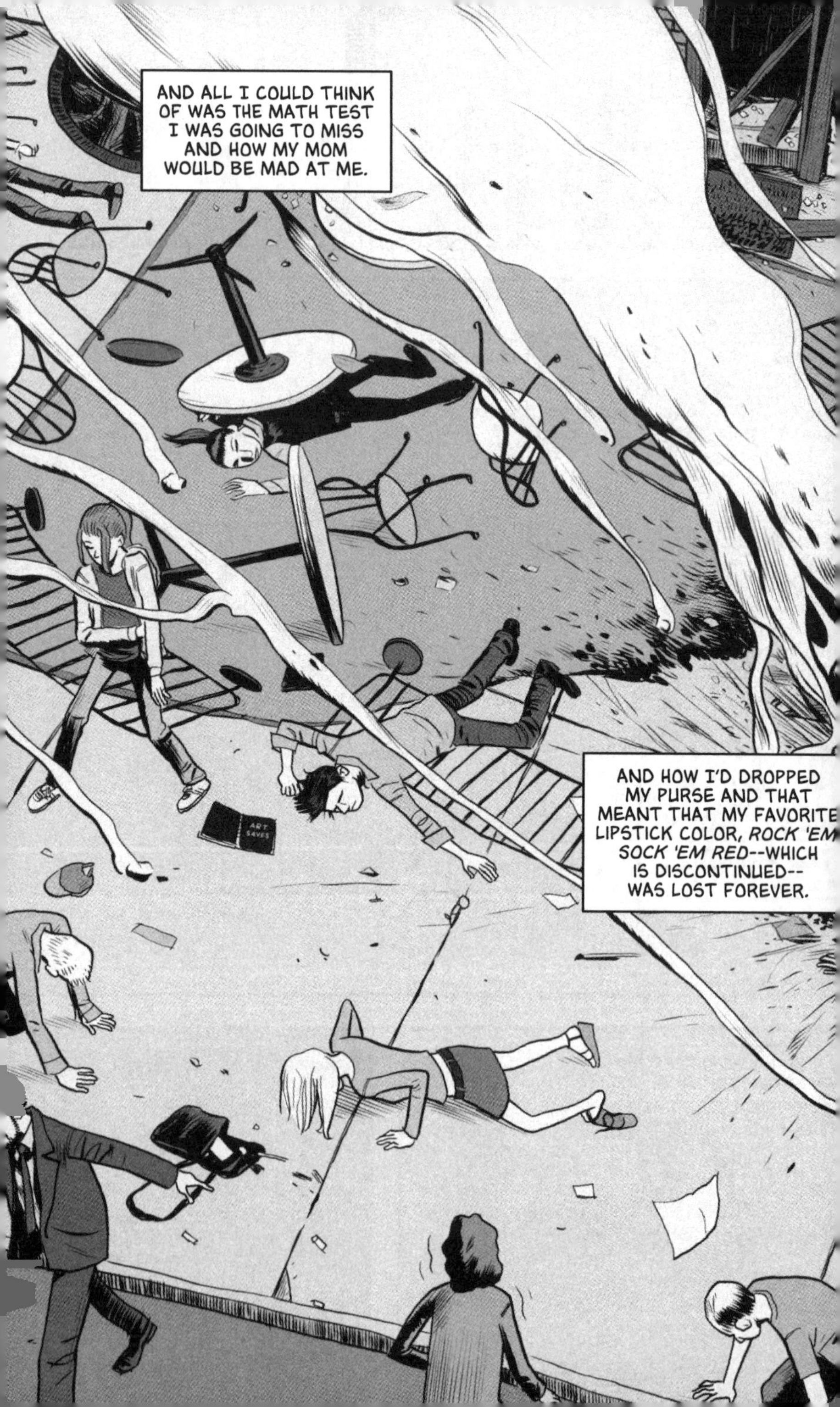
AND ALL I COULD THINK OF WAS THE MATH TEST I WAS GOING TO MISS AND HOW MY MOM WOULD BE MAD AT ME.
ART SAVES
AND HOW I'D DROPPED MY PURSE AND THAT MEANT THAT MY FAVORITE LIPSTICK COLOR, *ROCK 'EM SOCK 'EM RED*--WHICH IS DISCONTINUED--WAS LOST FOREVER.

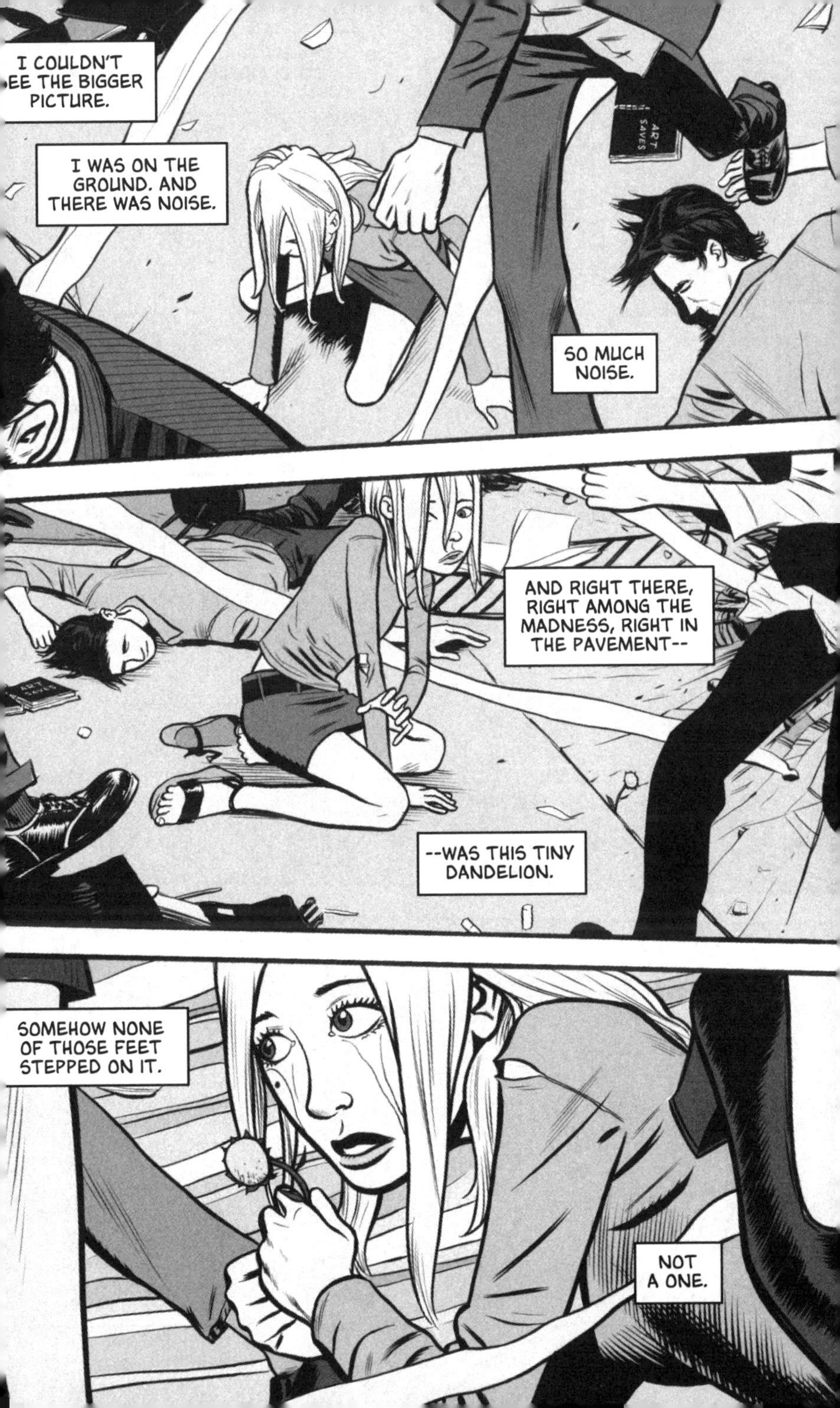

I COULDN'T
EE THE BIGGER
PICTURE.
I WAS ON THE GROUND. AND THERE WAS NOISE.
ART SAVES
SO MUCH NOISE.
AND RIGHT THERE, RIGHT AMONG THE MADNESS, RIGHT IN THE PAVEMENT--
--WAS THIS TINY DANDELION.
SOMEHOW NONE OF THOSE FEET STEPPED ON IT.
NOT A ONE.

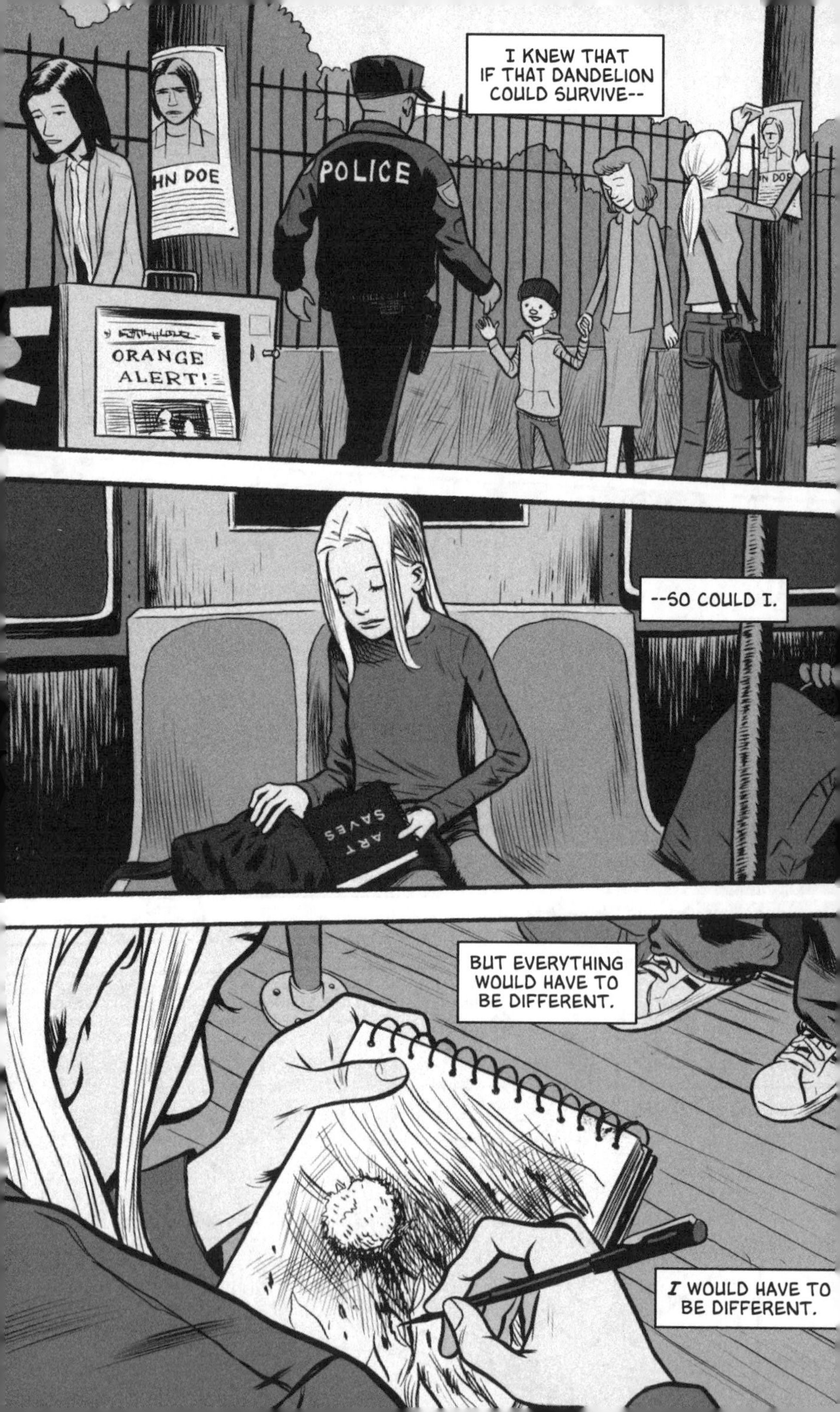
HN DOE
POLICE
ORANGE ALERT!
I KNEW THAT IF THAT DANDELION COULD SURVIVE--
--SO COULD I.
ART SAVES
BUT EVERYTHING WOULD HAVE TO BE DIFFERENT.
I WOULD HAVE TO BE DIFFERENT.

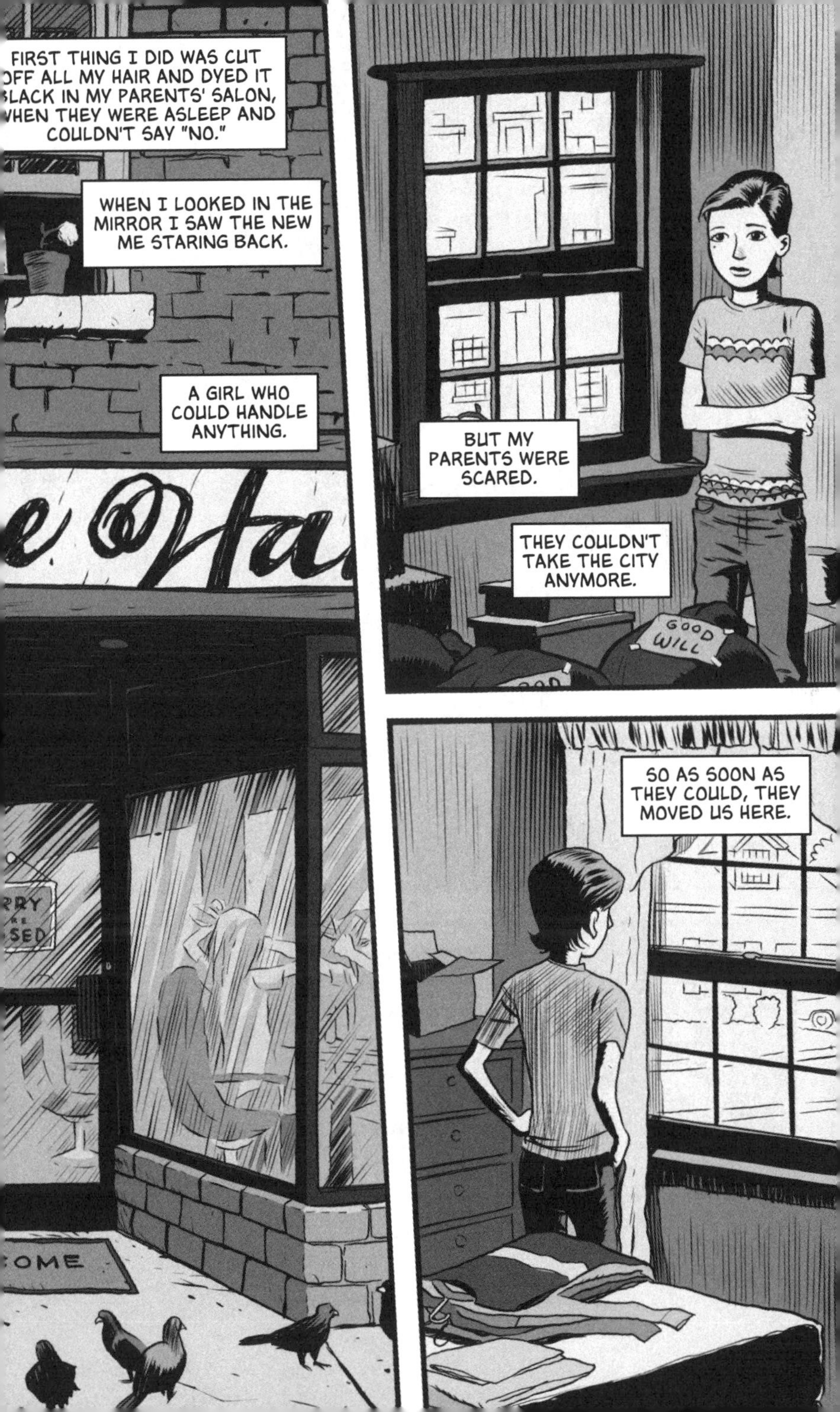
FIRST THING I DID WAS CUT OFF ALL MY HAIR AND DYED IT BLACK IN MY PARENTS' SALON, WHEN THEY WERE ASLEEP AND COULDN'T SAY "NO."
WHEN I LOOKED IN THE MIRROR I SAW THE NEW ME STARING BACK.
A GIRL WHO COULD HANDLE ANYTHING.
BUT MY PARENTS WERE SCARED.
THEY COULDN'T TAKE THE CITY ANYMORE.
GOOD WILL
SO AS SOON AS THEY COULD, THEY MOVED US HERE.

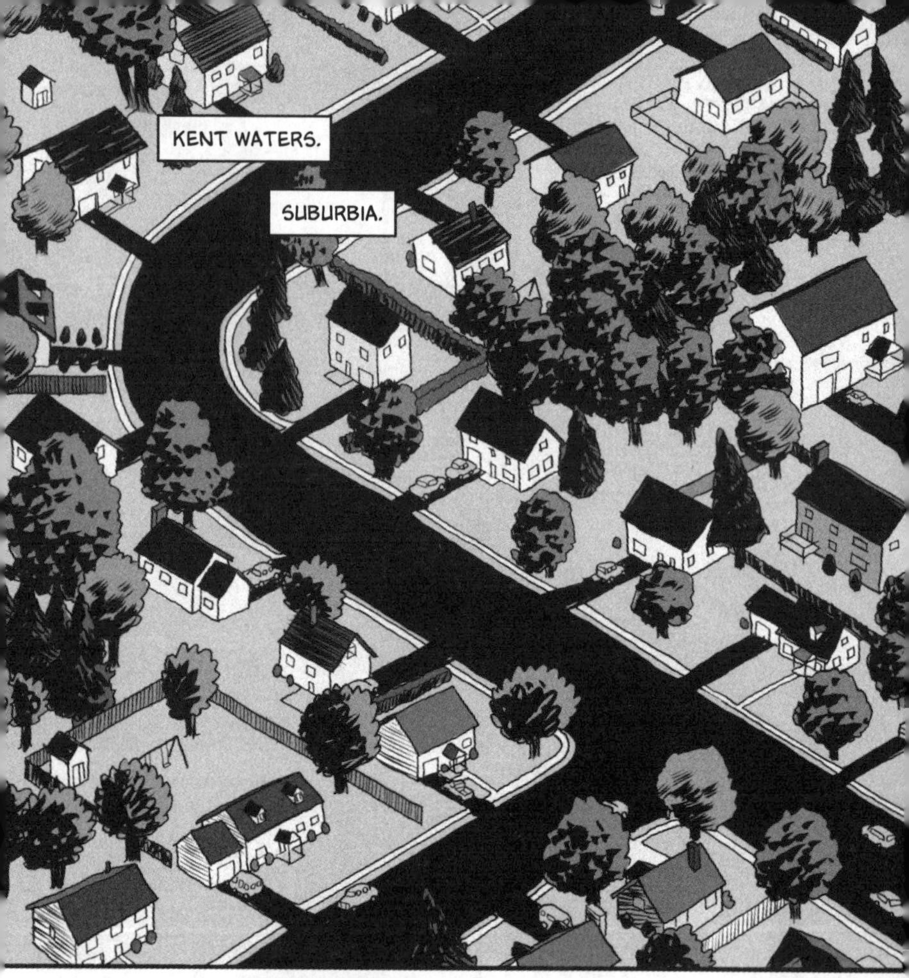
KENT WATERS.
SUBURBIA.

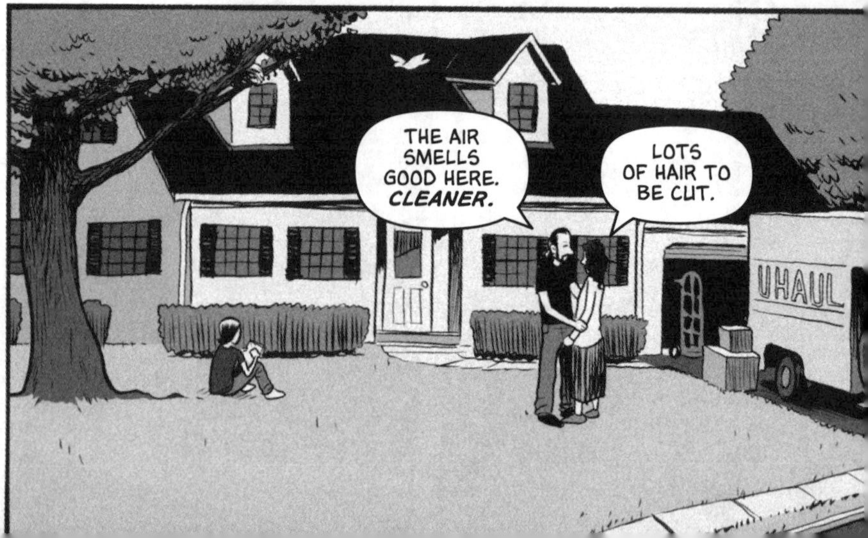
THE AIR SMELLS GOOD HERE. *CLEANER.*
LOTS OF HAIR TO BE CUT.
UHAUL

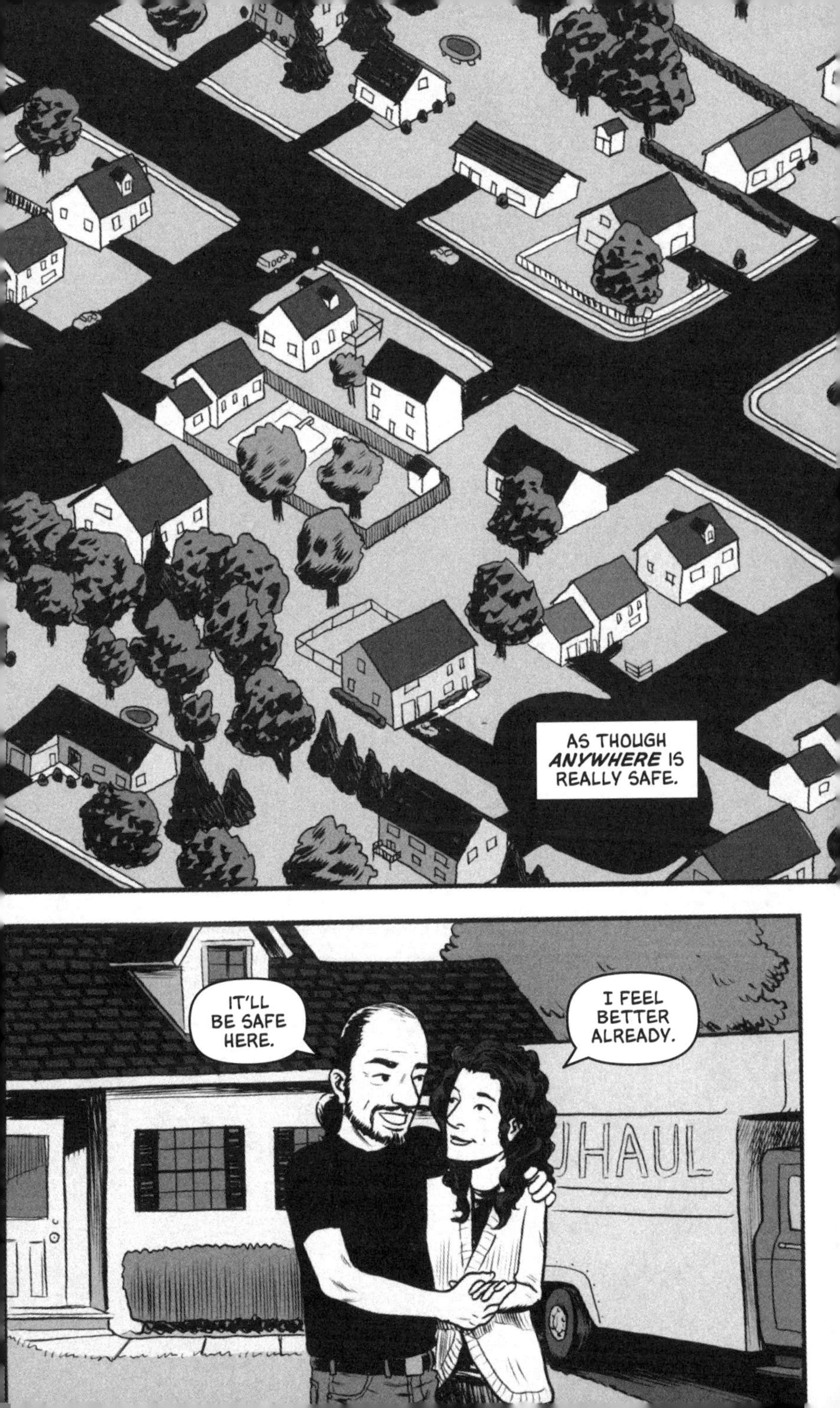
AS THOUGH *ANYWHERE* IS REALLY SAFE.
IT'LL BE SAFE HERE.
I FEEL BETTER ALREADY.
UHAUL

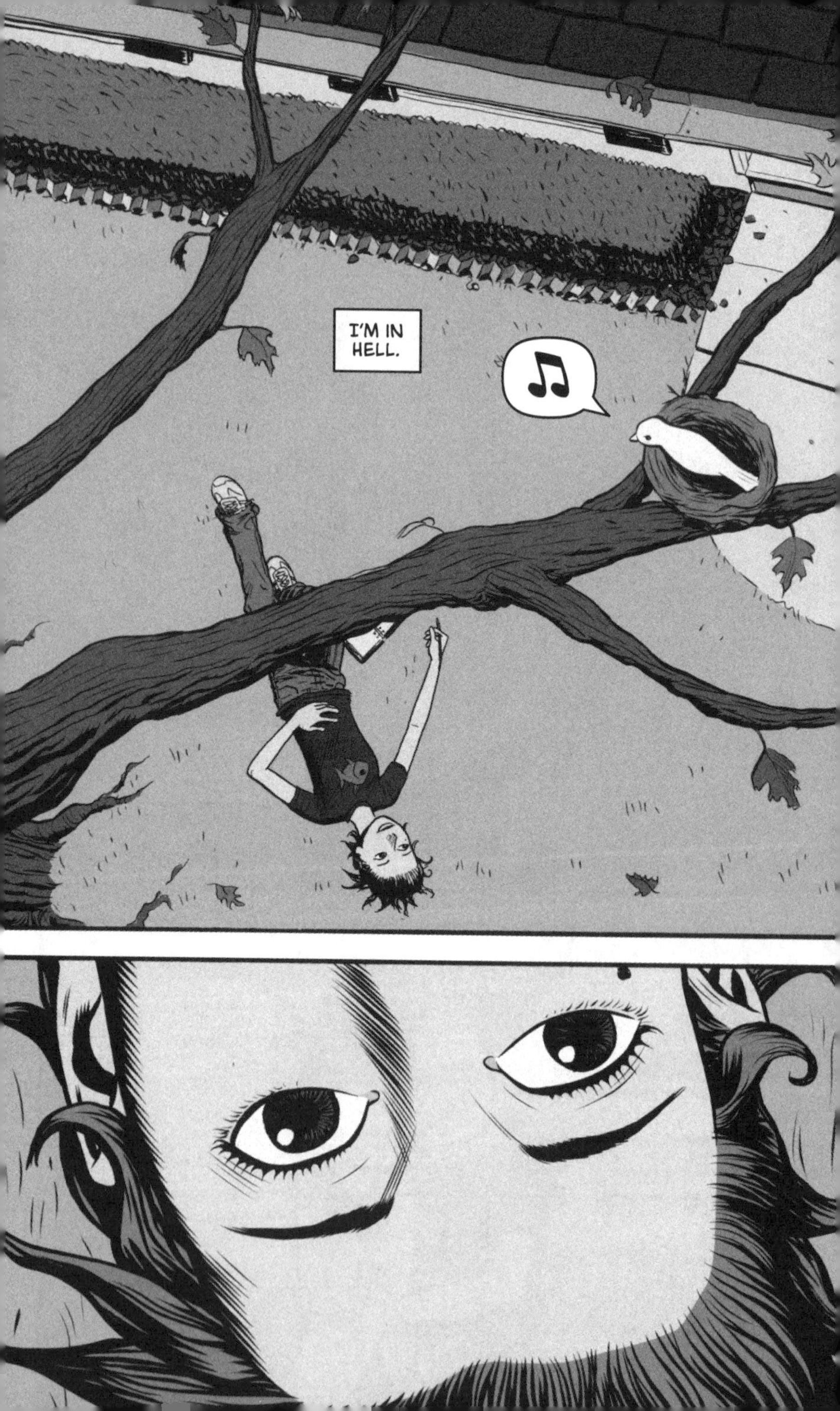
I'M IN HELL.
♫

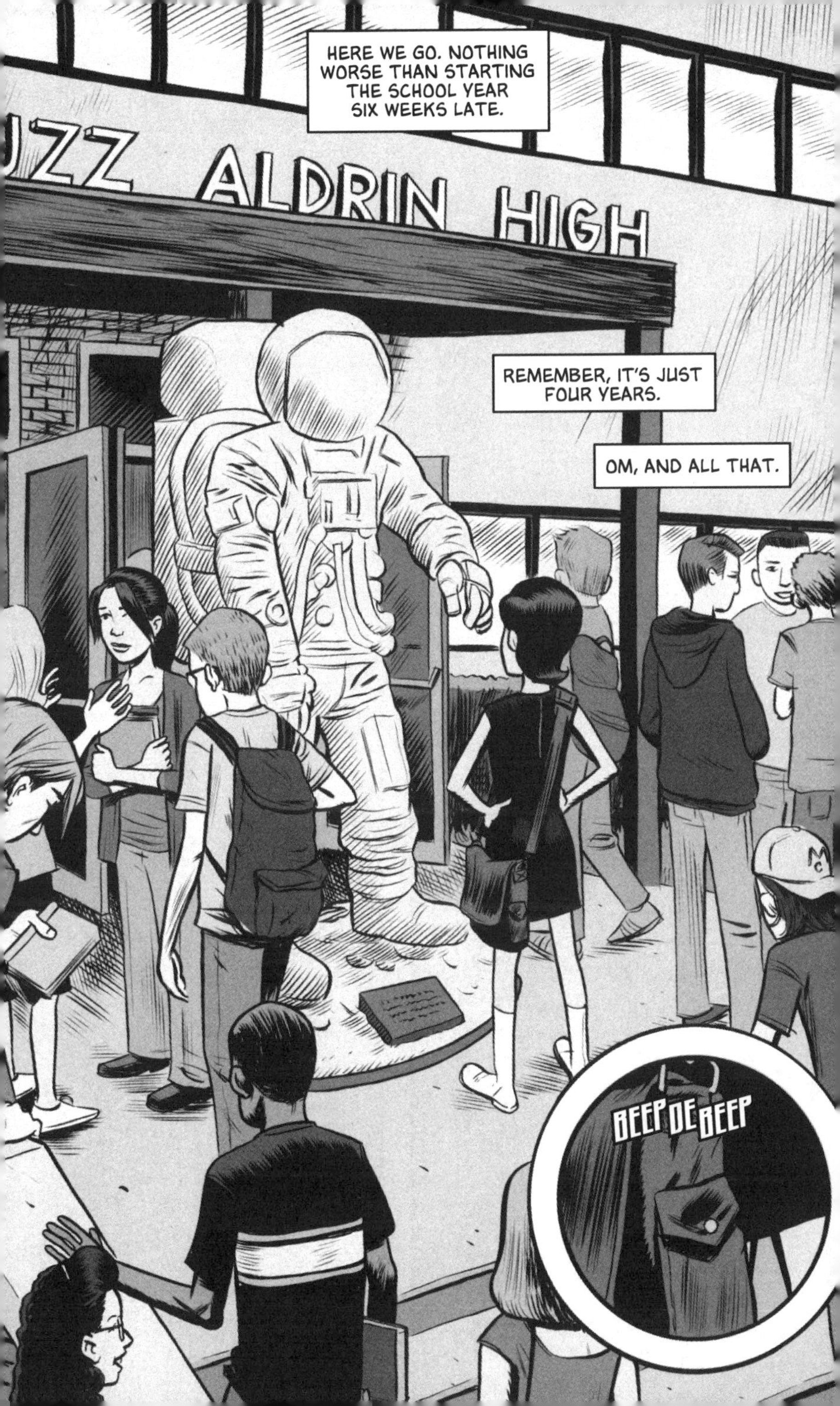
HERE WE GO. NOTHING WORSE THAN STARTING THE SCHOOL YEAR SIX WEEKS LATE.
UZZ ALDRIN HIGH
REMEMBER, IT'S JUST FOUR YEARS.
OM, AND ALL THAT.
BEEP DE BEEP

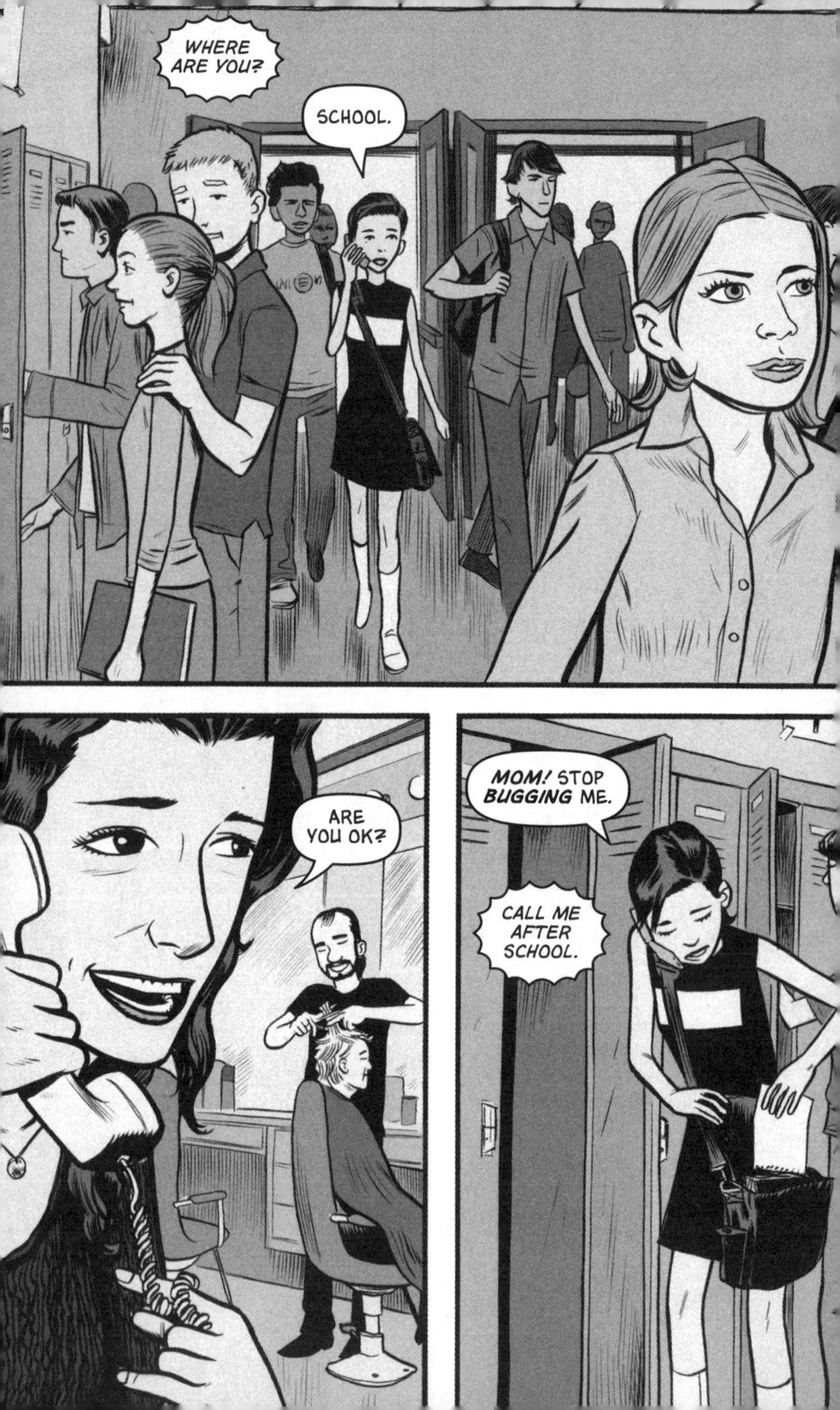
WHERE ARE YOU?
SCHOOL.
ARE YOU OK?
MOM! STOP BUGGING ME.
CALL ME AFTER SCHOOL.

IT'S HARD TO BE A REBEL WITH A LEASH.
SLAM

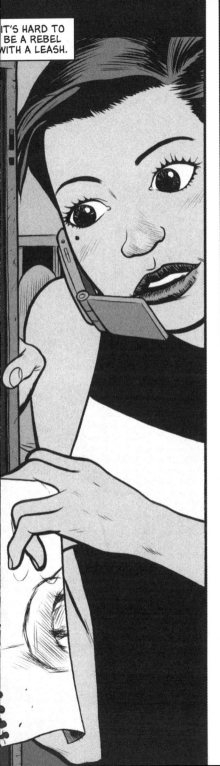

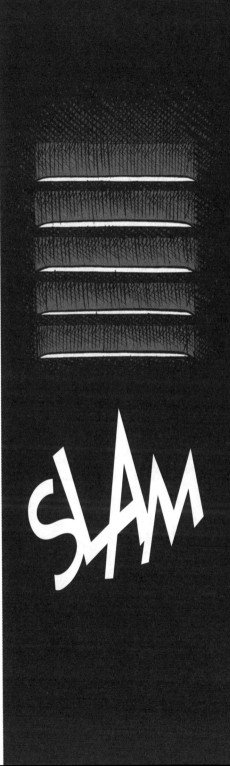

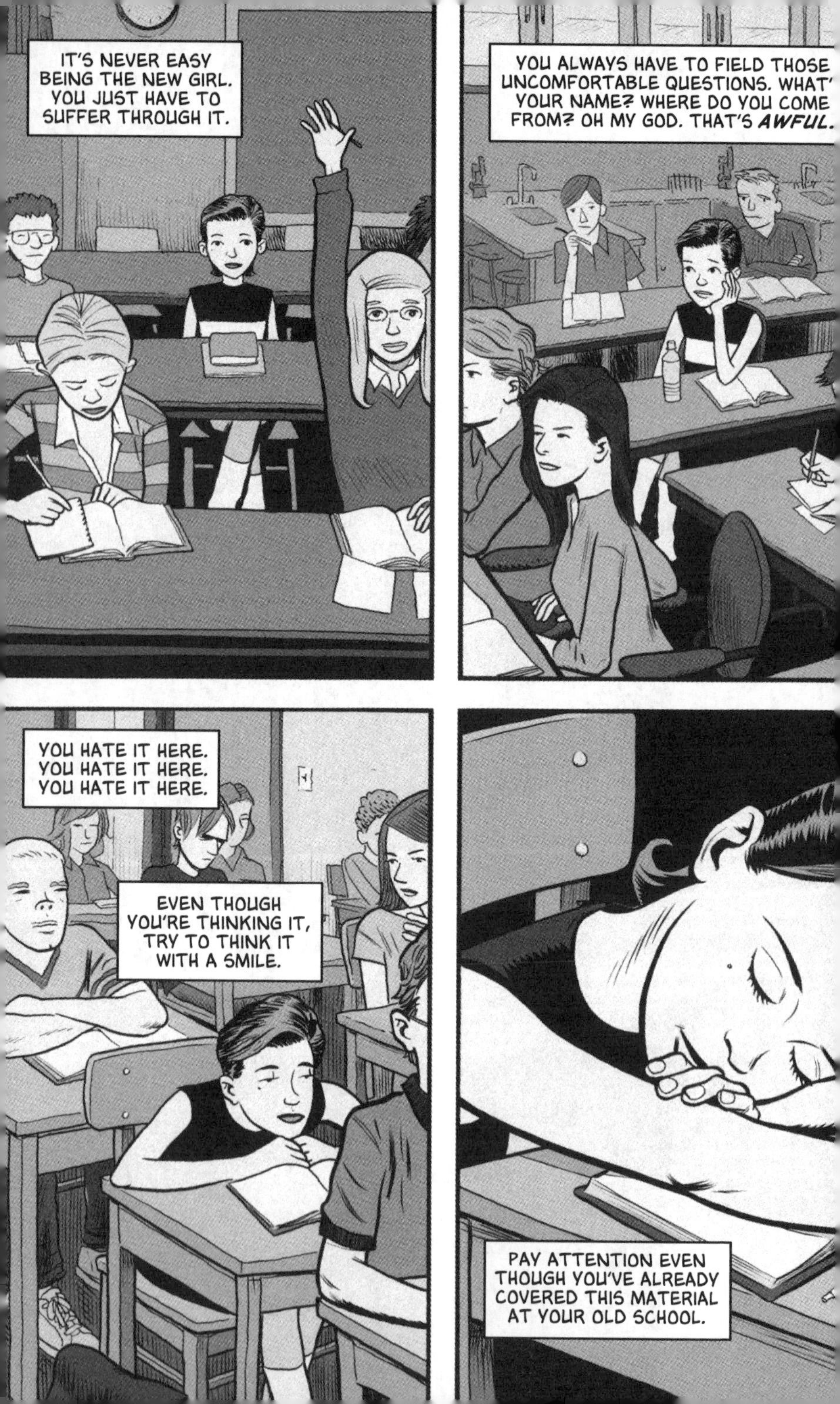
IT'S NEVER EASY BEING THE NEW GIRL. YOU JUST HAVE TO SUFFER THROUGH IT.
YOU ALWAYS HAVE TO FIELD THOSE UNCOMFORTABLE QUESTIONS. WHAT' YOUR NAME? WHERE DO YOU COME FROM? OH MY GOD. THAT'S AWFUL.
YOU HATE IT HERE. YOU HATE IT HERE. YOU HATE IT HERE.
EVEN THOUGH YOU'RE THINKING IT, TRY TO THINK IT WITH A SMILE.
PAY ATTENTION EVEN THOUGH YOU'VE ALREADY COVERED THIS MATERIAL AT YOUR OLD SCHOOL.

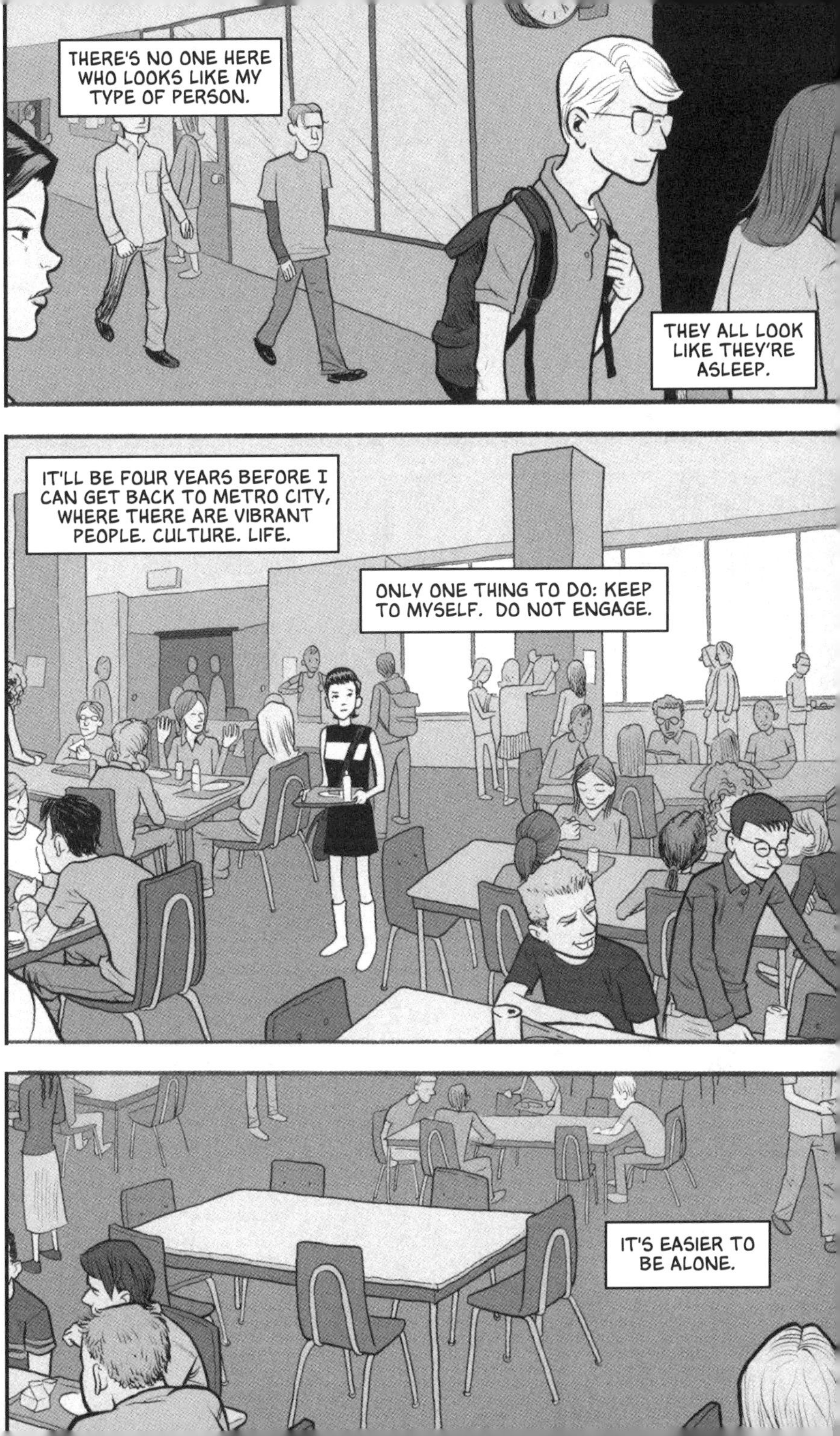
THERE'S NO ONE HERE WHO LOOKS LIKE MY TYPE OF PERSON.
THEY ALL LOOK LIKE THEY'RE ASLEEP.
IT'LL BE FOUR YEARS BEFORE I CAN GET BACK TO METRO CITY, WHERE THERE ARE VIBRANT PEOPLE. CULTURE. LIFE.
ONLY ONE THING TO DO: KEEP TO MYSELF. DO NOT ENGAGE.
IT'S EASIER TO BE ALONE.

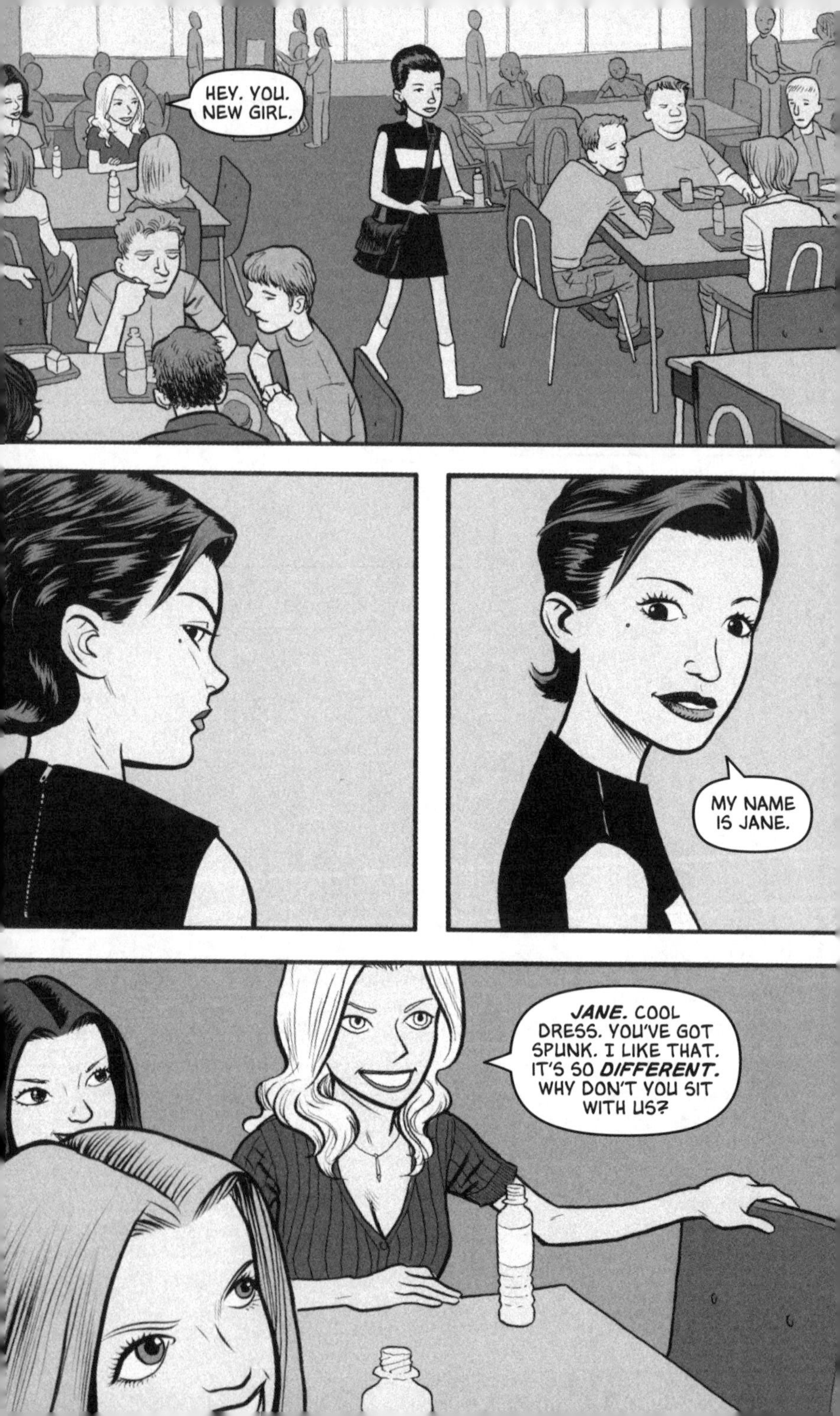
HEY. YOU. NEW GIRL.
MY NAME IS JANE.
JANE. COOL DRESS. YOU'VE GOT SPUNK. I LIKE THAT. IT'S SO DIFFERENT. WHY DON'T YOU SIT WITH US?

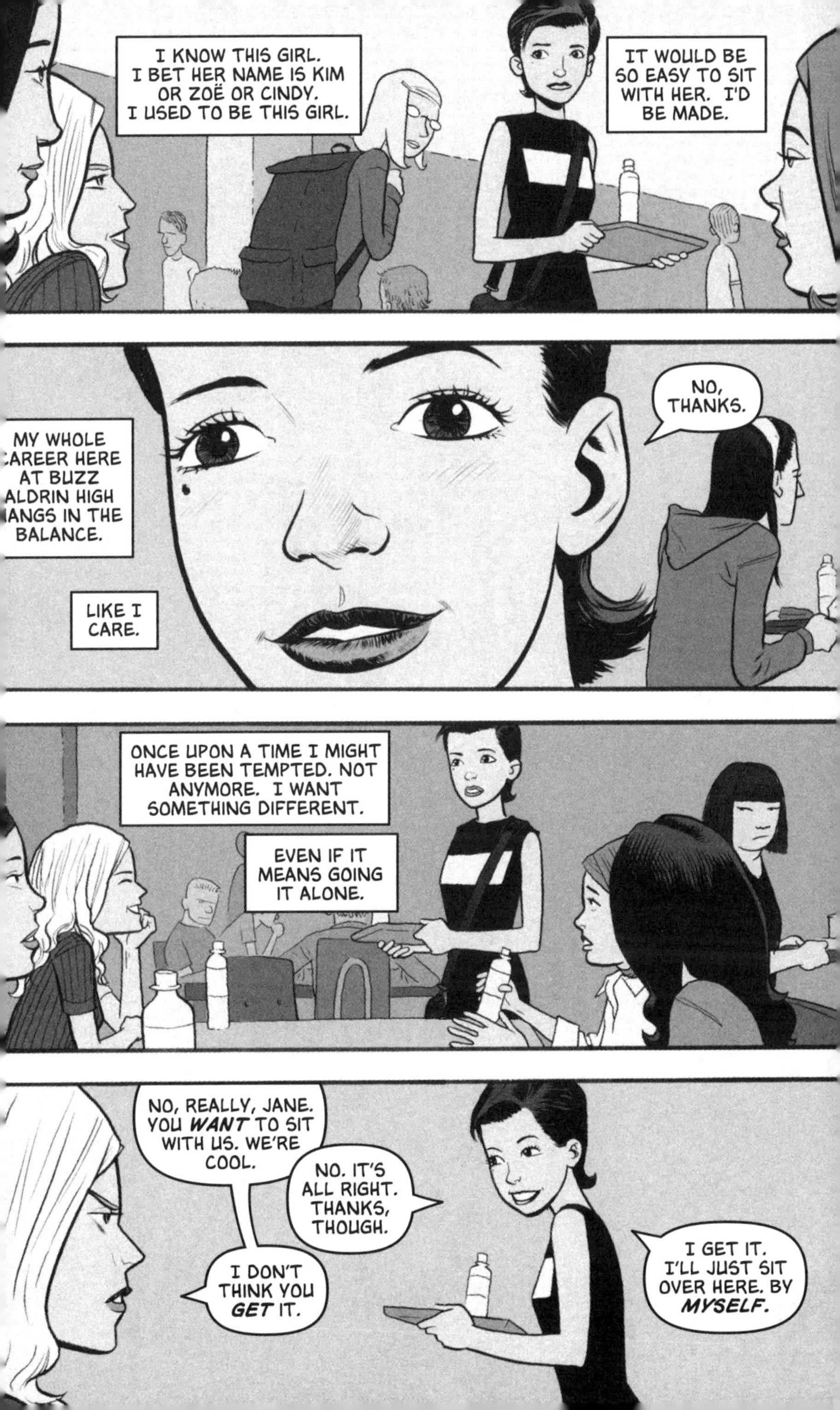
I KNOW THIS GIRL. I BET HER NAME IS KIM OR ZOË OR CINDY. I USED TO BE THIS GIRL.
IT WOULD BE SO EASY TO SIT WITH HER. I'D BE MADE.
MY WHOLE AREER HERE AT BUZZ ALDRIN HIGH ANGS IN THE BALANCE.
NO, THANKS.
LIKE I CARE.
ONCE UPON A TIME I MIGHT HAVE BEEN TEMPTED. NOT ANYMORE. I WANT SOMETHING DIFFERENT.
EVEN IF IT MEANS GOING IT ALONE.
NO, REALLY, JANE. YOU *WANT* TO SIT WITH US. WE'RE COOL.
NO. IT'S ALL RIGHT. THANKS, THOUGH.
I DON'T THINK YOU *GET* IT.
I GET IT. I'LL JUST SIT OVER HERE. BY *MYSELF*.

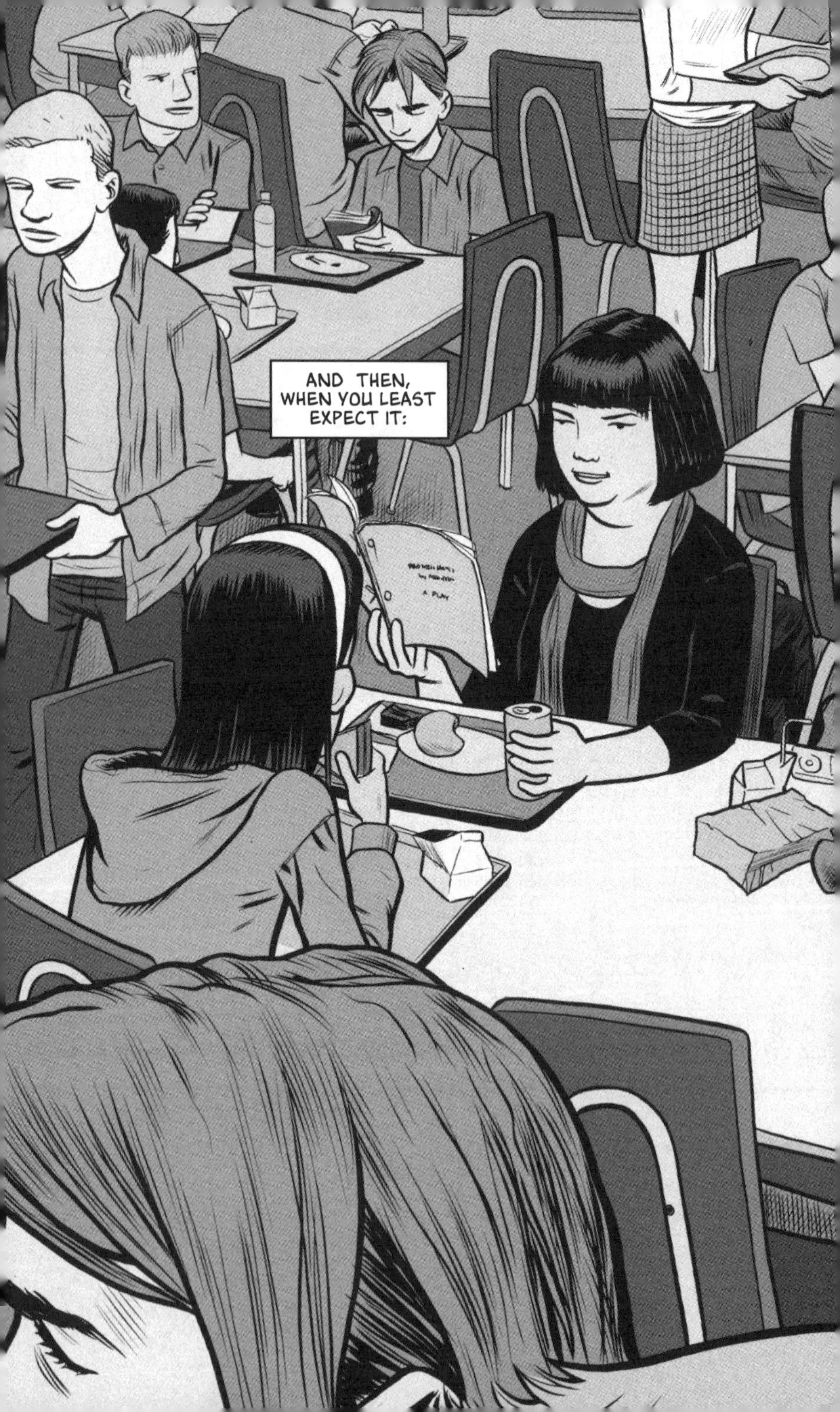
AND THEN, WHEN YOU LEAST EXPECT IT:

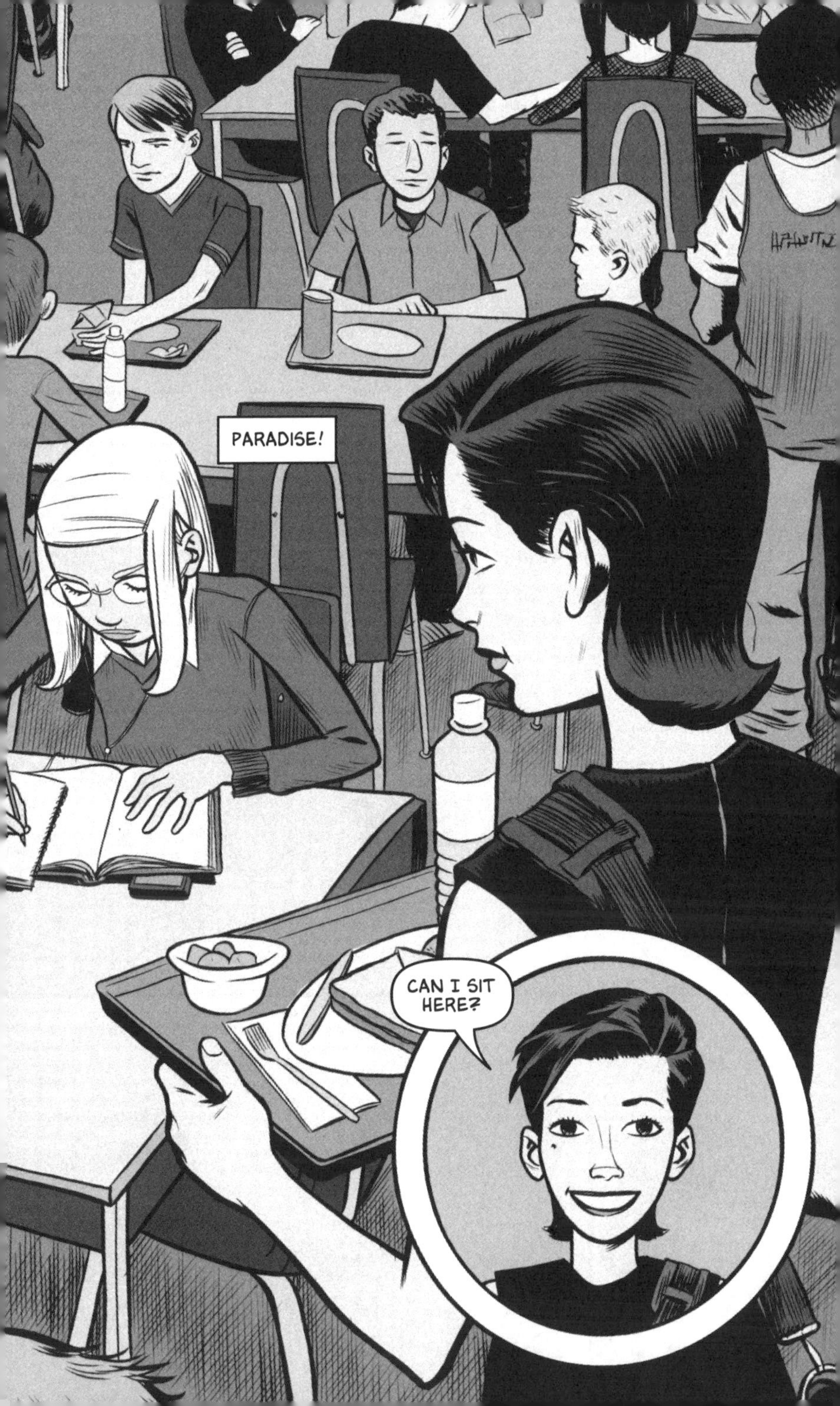
PARADISE!
CAN I SIT HERE?

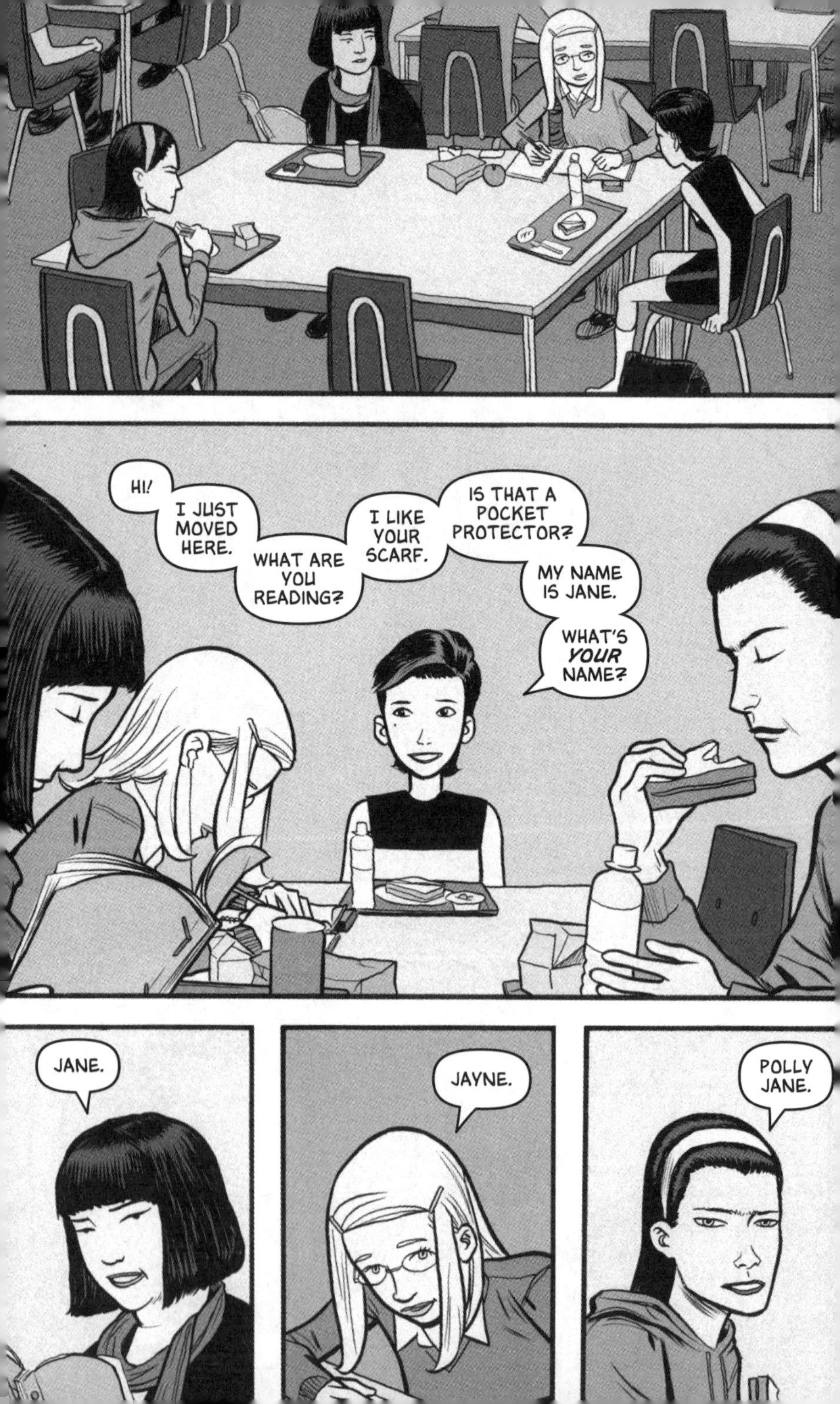

HI!
I JUST MOVED HERE.
WHAT ARE YOU READING?
I LIKE YOUR SCARF.
IS THAT A POCKET PROTECTOR?
MY NAME IS JANE.
WHAT'S *YOUR* NAME?
JANE.
JAYNE.
POLLY JANE.

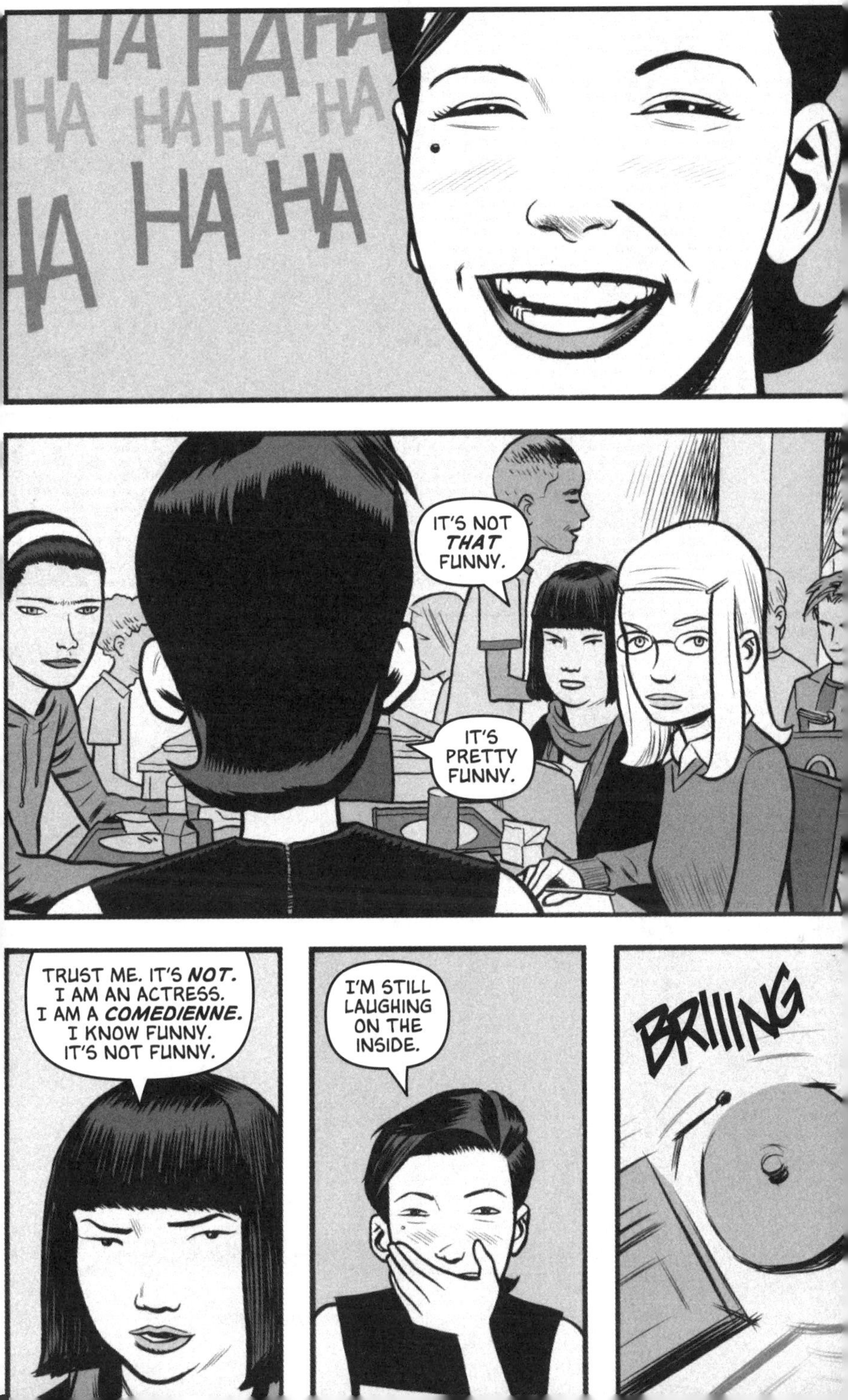
HA HA HA HA HA HA HA HA HA HA HA
IT'S NOT THAT FUNNY.
IT'S PRETTY FUNNY.
TRUST ME. IT'S NOT. I AM AN ACTRESS. I AM A COMEDIENNE. I KNOW FUNNY. IT'S NOT FUNNY.
I'M STILL LAUGHING ON THE INSIDE.
BRIIING

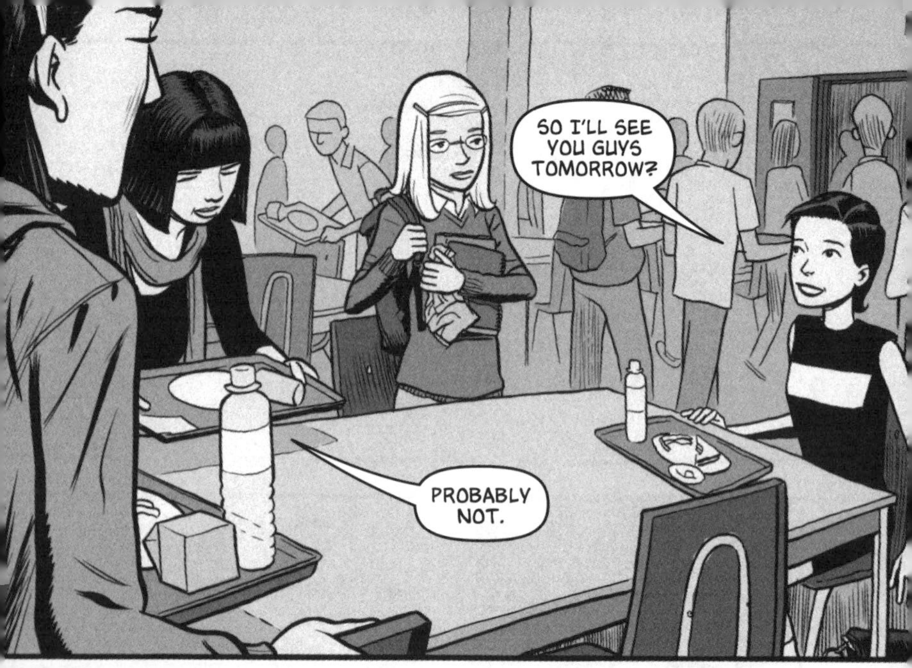
SO I'LL SEE YOU GUYS TOMORROW?
PROBABLY NOT.

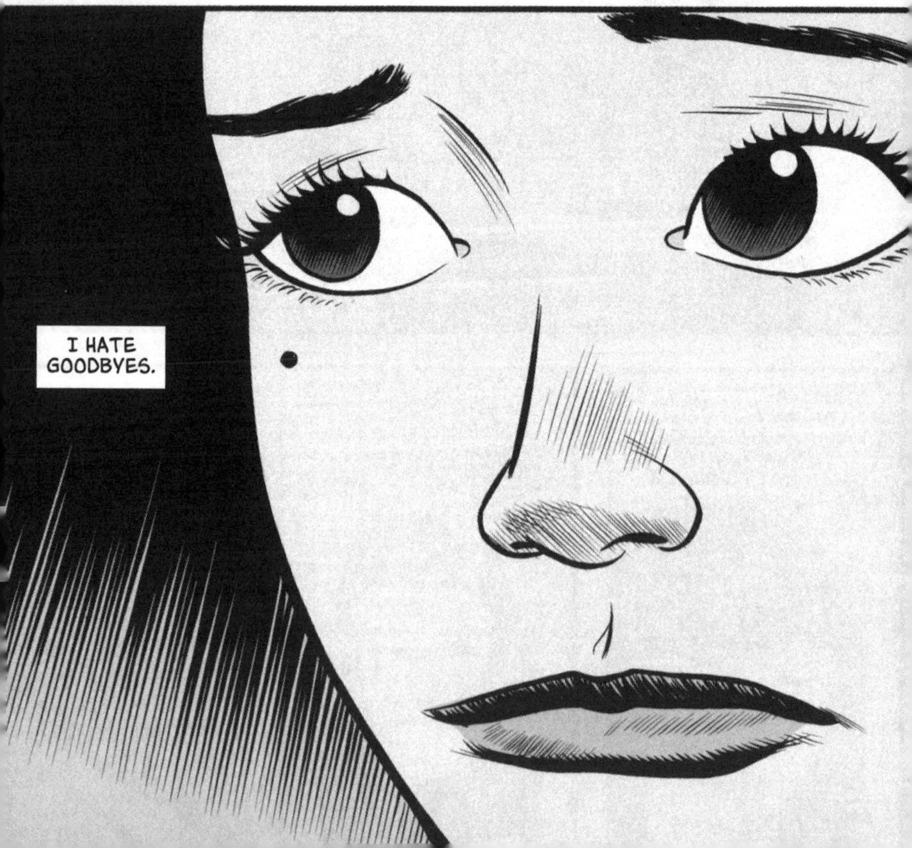
I HATE GOODBYES.

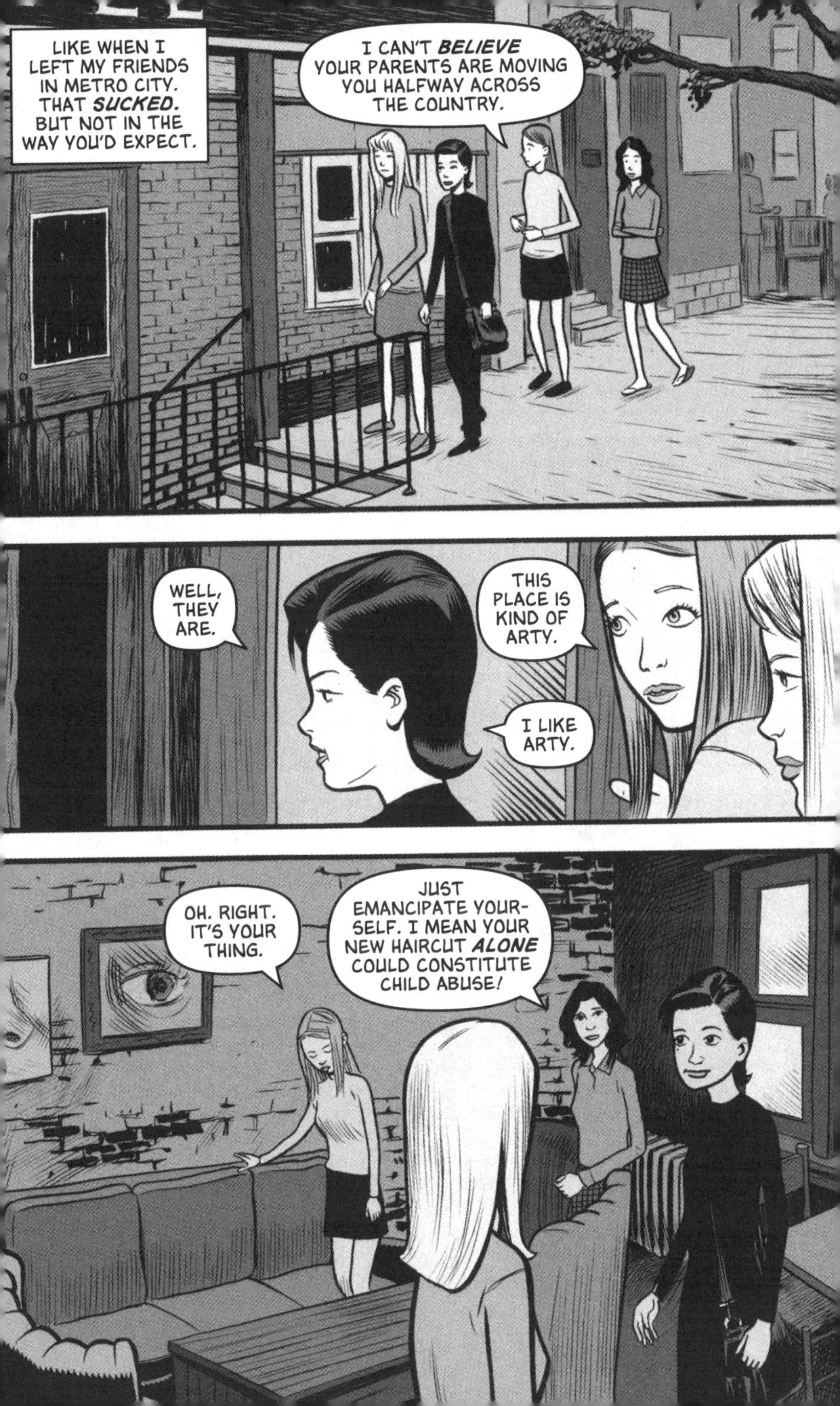
LIKE WHEN I LEFT MY FRIENDS IN METRO CITY. THAT SUCKED. BUT NOT IN THE WAY YOU'D EXPECT.
I CAN'T BELIEVE YOUR PARENTS ARE MOVING YOU HALFWAY ACROSS THE COUNTRY.
WELL, THEY ARE.
THIS PLACE IS KIND OF ARTY.
I LIKE ARTY.
OH. RIGHT. IT'S YOUR THING.
JUST EMANCIPATE YOUR-SELF. I MEAN YOUR NEW HAIRCUT ALONE COULD CONSTITUTE CHILD ABUSE!

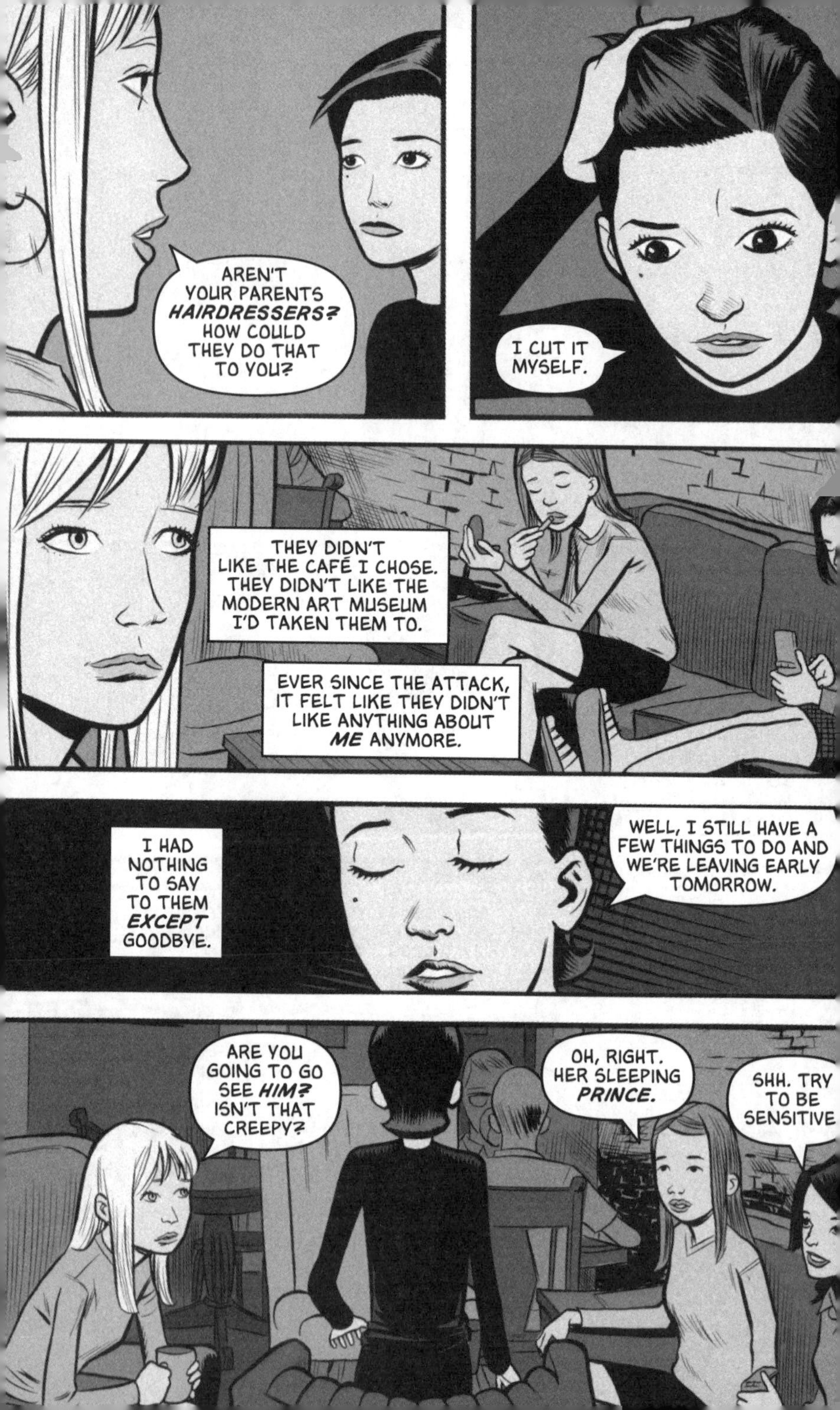
AREN'T YOUR PARENTS HAIRDRESSERS? HOW COULD THEY DO THAT TO YOU?
I CUT IT MYSELF.
THEY DIDN'T LIKE THE CAFÉ I CHOSE. THEY DIDN'T LIKE THE MODERN ART MUSEUM I'D TAKEN THEM TO.
EVER SINCE THE ATTACK, IT FELT LIKE THEY DIDN'T LIKE ANYTHING ABOUT ME ANYMORE.
I HAD NOTHING TO SAY TO THEM EXCEPT GOODBYE.
WELL, I STILL HAVE A FEW THINGS TO DO AND WE'RE LEAVING EARLY TOMORROW.
ARE YOU GOING TO GO SEE HIM? ISN'T THAT CREEPY?
OH, RIGHT. HER SLEEPING PRINCE.
SHH. TRY TO BE SENSITIVE

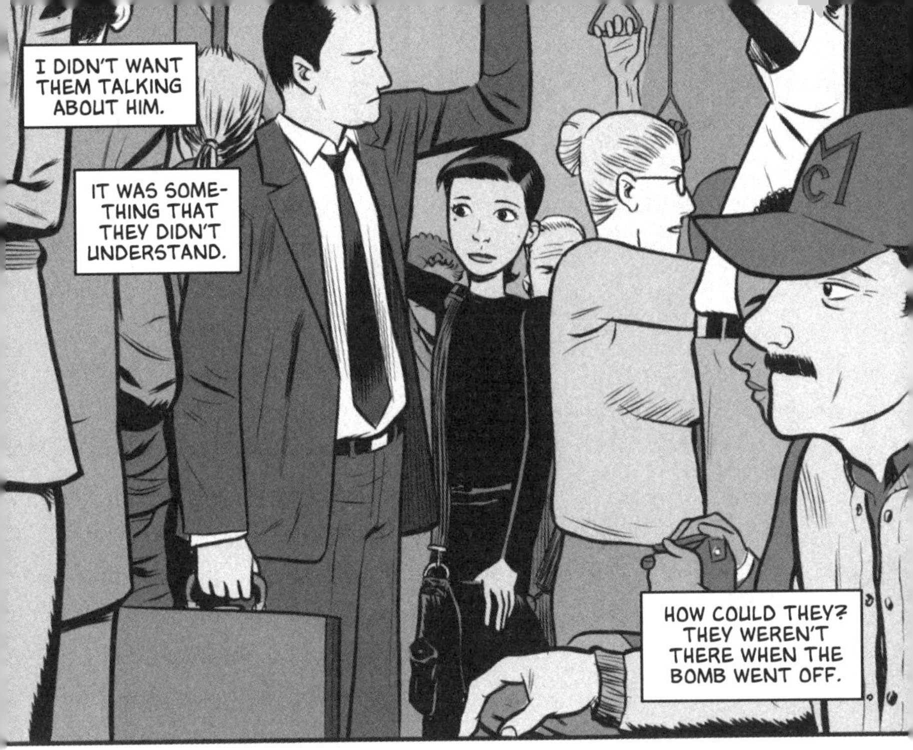
I DIDN'T WANT THEM TALKING ABOUT HIM.
IT WAS SOME-THING THAT THEY DIDN'T UNDERSTAND.
HOW COULD THEY? THEY WEREN'T THERE WHEN THE BOMB WENT OFF.

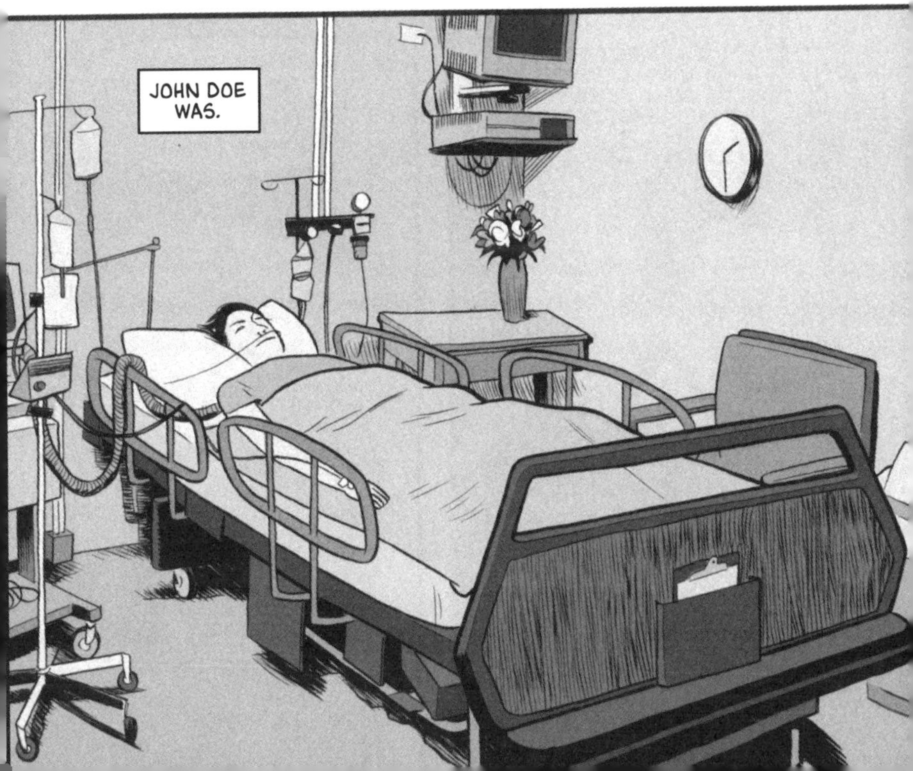
JOHN DOE WAS.

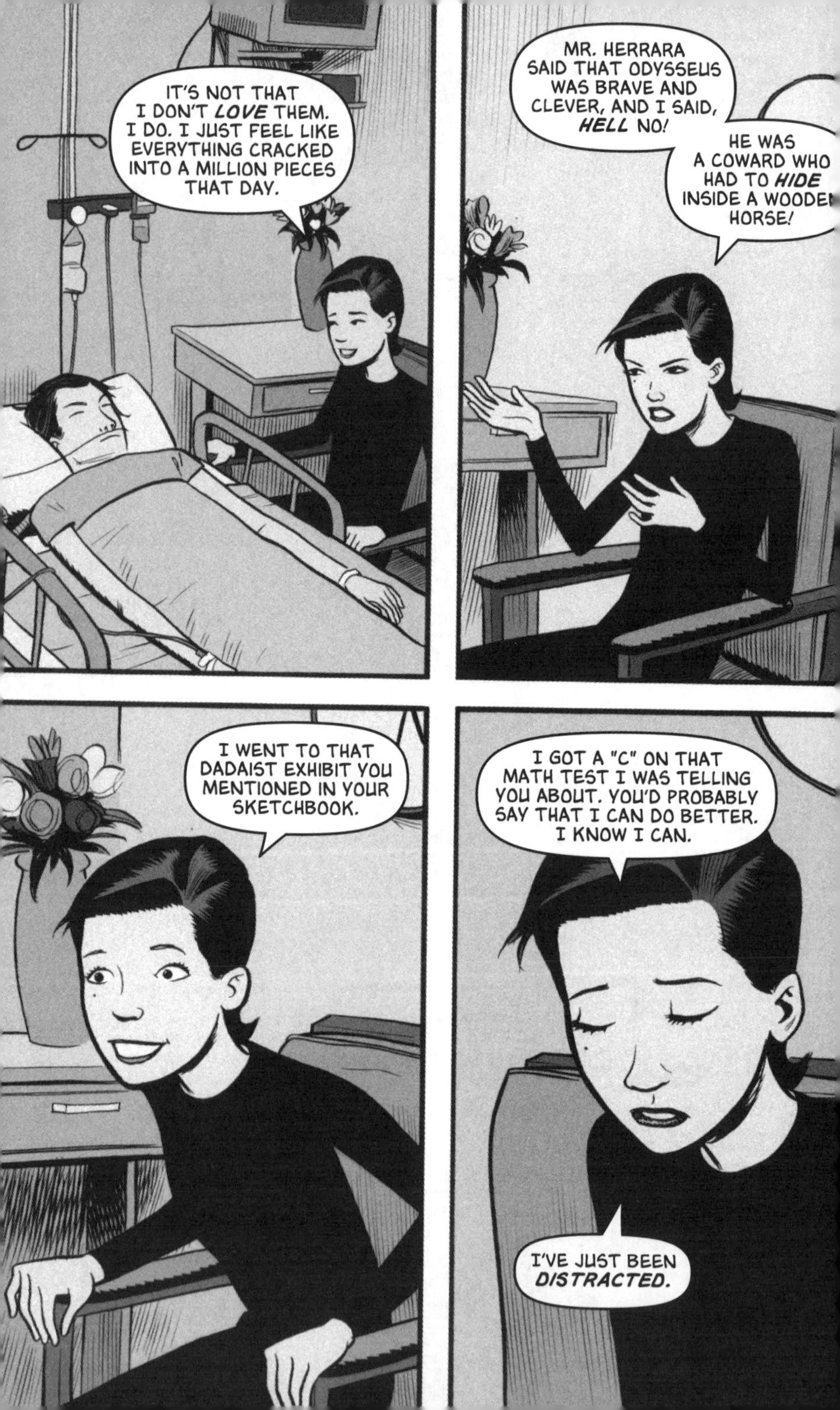
IT'S NOT THAT I DON'T LOVE THEM. I DO. I JUST FEEL LIKE EVERYTHING CRACKED INTO A MILLION PIECES THAT DAY.
MR. HERRARA SAID THAT ODYSSEUS WAS BRAVE AND CLEVER, AND I SAID, HELL NO!
HE WAS A COWARD WHO HAD TO HIDE INSIDE A WOODEN HORSE!
I WENT TO THAT DADAIST EXHIBIT YOU MENTIONED IN YOUR SKETCHBOOK.
I GOT A "C" ON THAT MATH TEST I WAS TELLING YOU ABOUT. YOU'D PROBABLY SAY THAT I CAN DO BETTER. I KNOW I CAN.
I'VE JUST BEEN DISTRACTED.

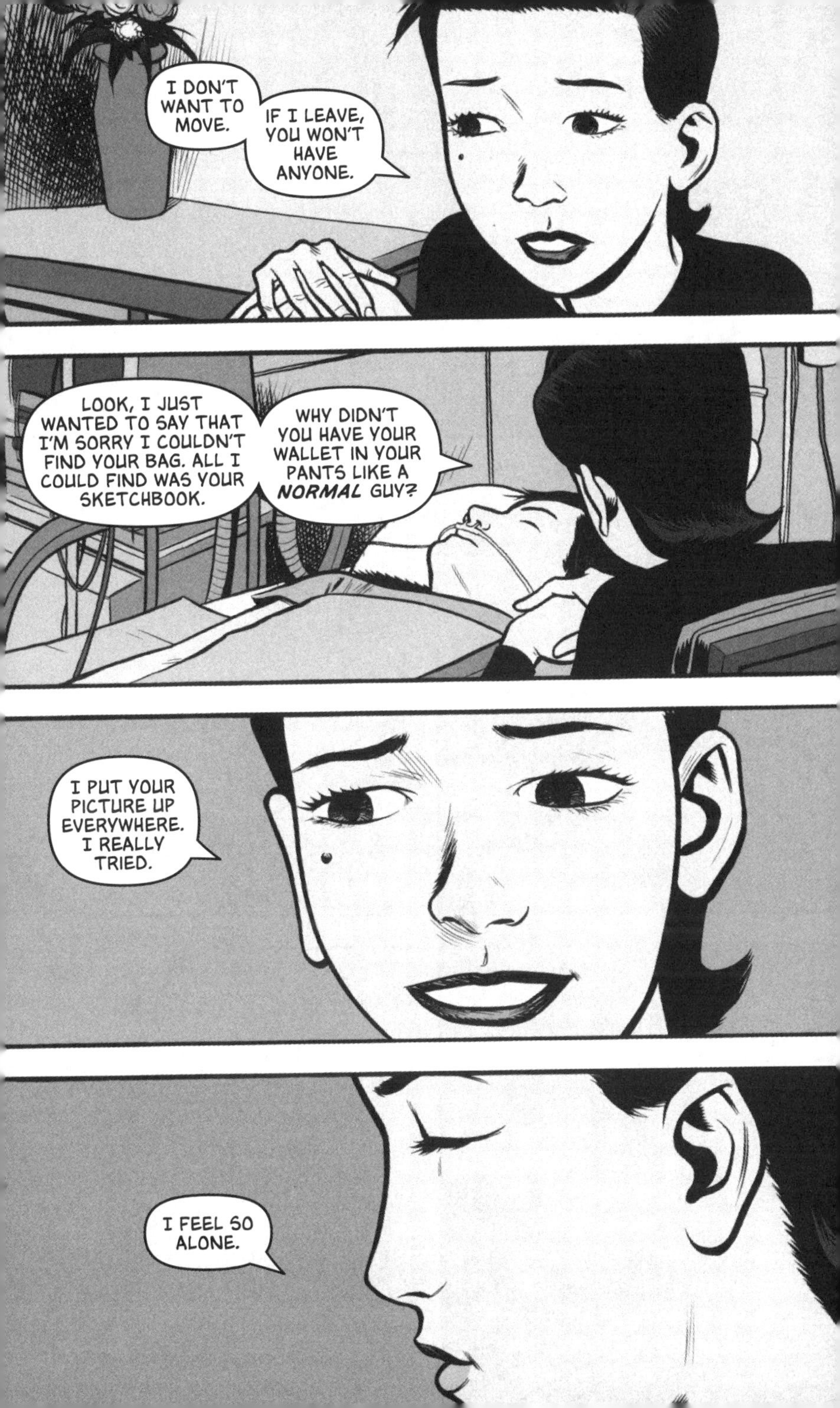
I DON'T WANT TO MOVE.
IF I LEAVE, YOU WON'T HAVE ANYONE.
LOOK, I JUST WANTED TO SAY THAT I'M SORRY I COULDN'T FIND YOUR BAG. ALL I COULD FIND WAS YOUR SKETCHBOOK.
WHY DIDN'T YOU HAVE YOUR WALLET IN YOUR PANTS LIKE A *NORMAL* GUY?
I PUT YOUR PICTURE UP EVERYWHERE. I REALLY TRIED.
I FEEL SO ALONE.

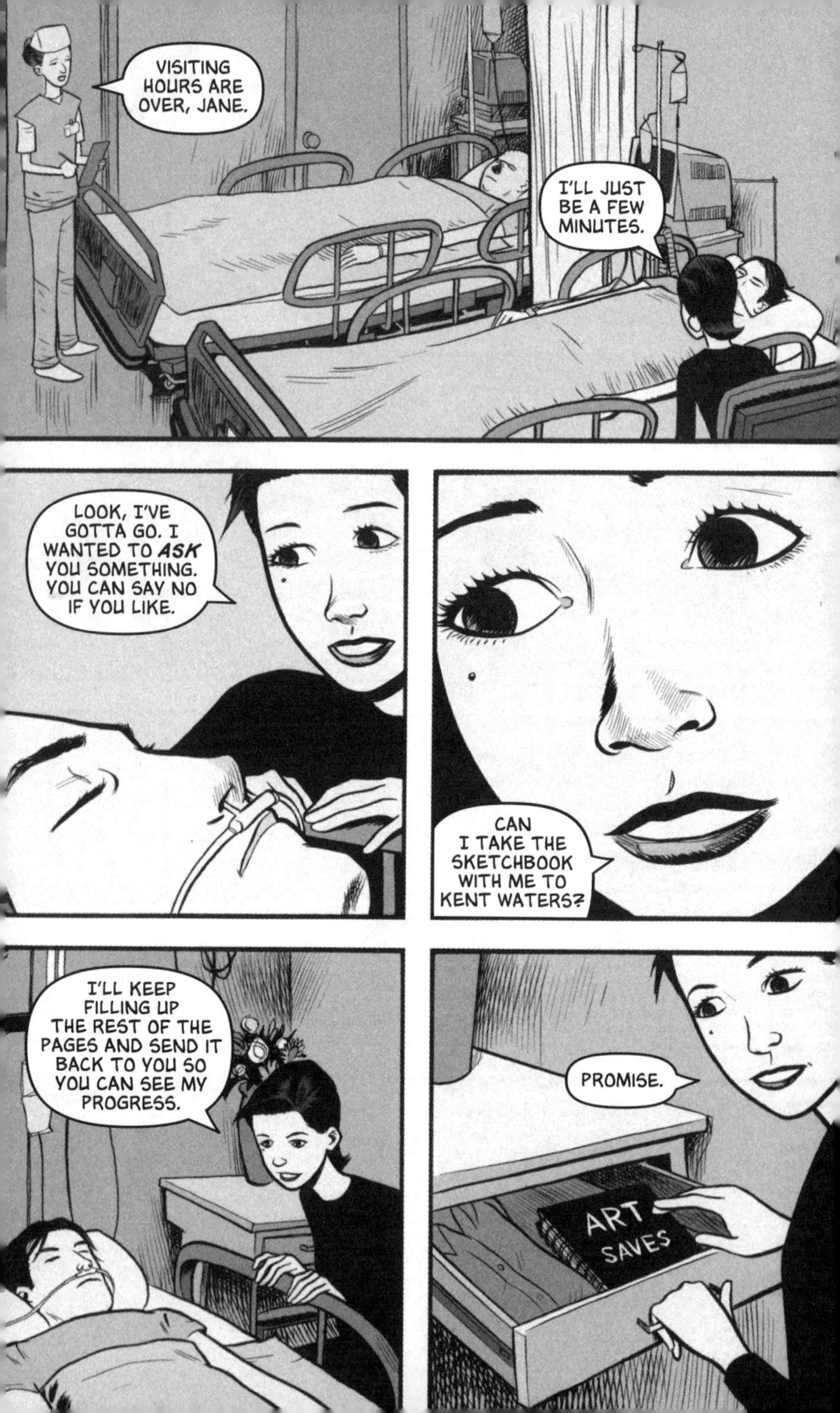
VISITING HOURS ARE OVER, JANE.
I'LL JUST BE A FEW MINUTES.
LOOK, I'VE GOTTA GO. I WANTED TO ASK YOU SOMETHING. YOU CAN SAY NO IF YOU LIKE.
CAN I TAKE THE SKETCHBOOK WITH ME TO KENT WATERS?
I'LL KEEP FILLING UP THE REST OF THE PAGES AND SEND IT BACK TO YOU SO YOU CAN SEE MY PROGRESS.
PROMISE.
ART SAVES

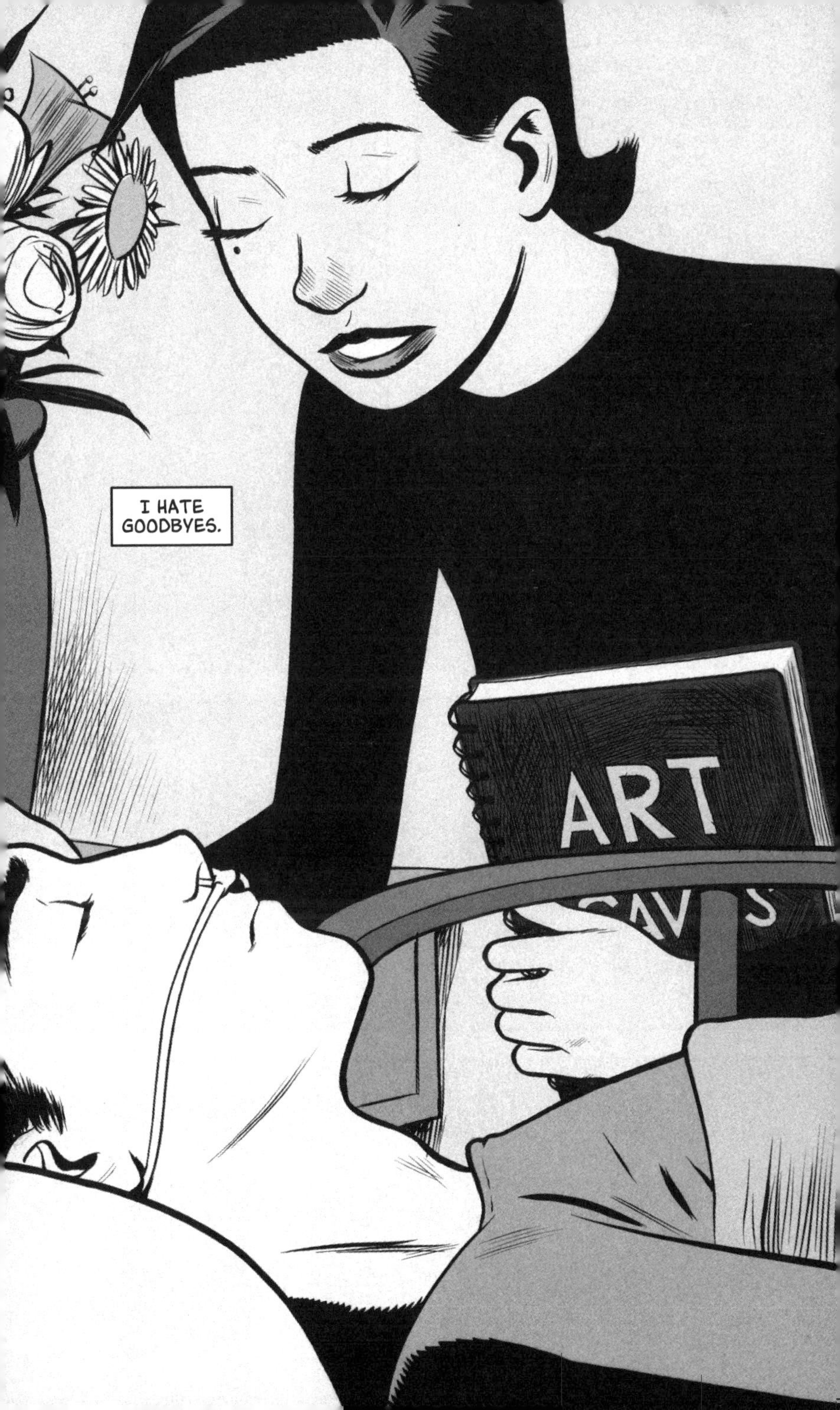
I HATE GOODBYES.
ART

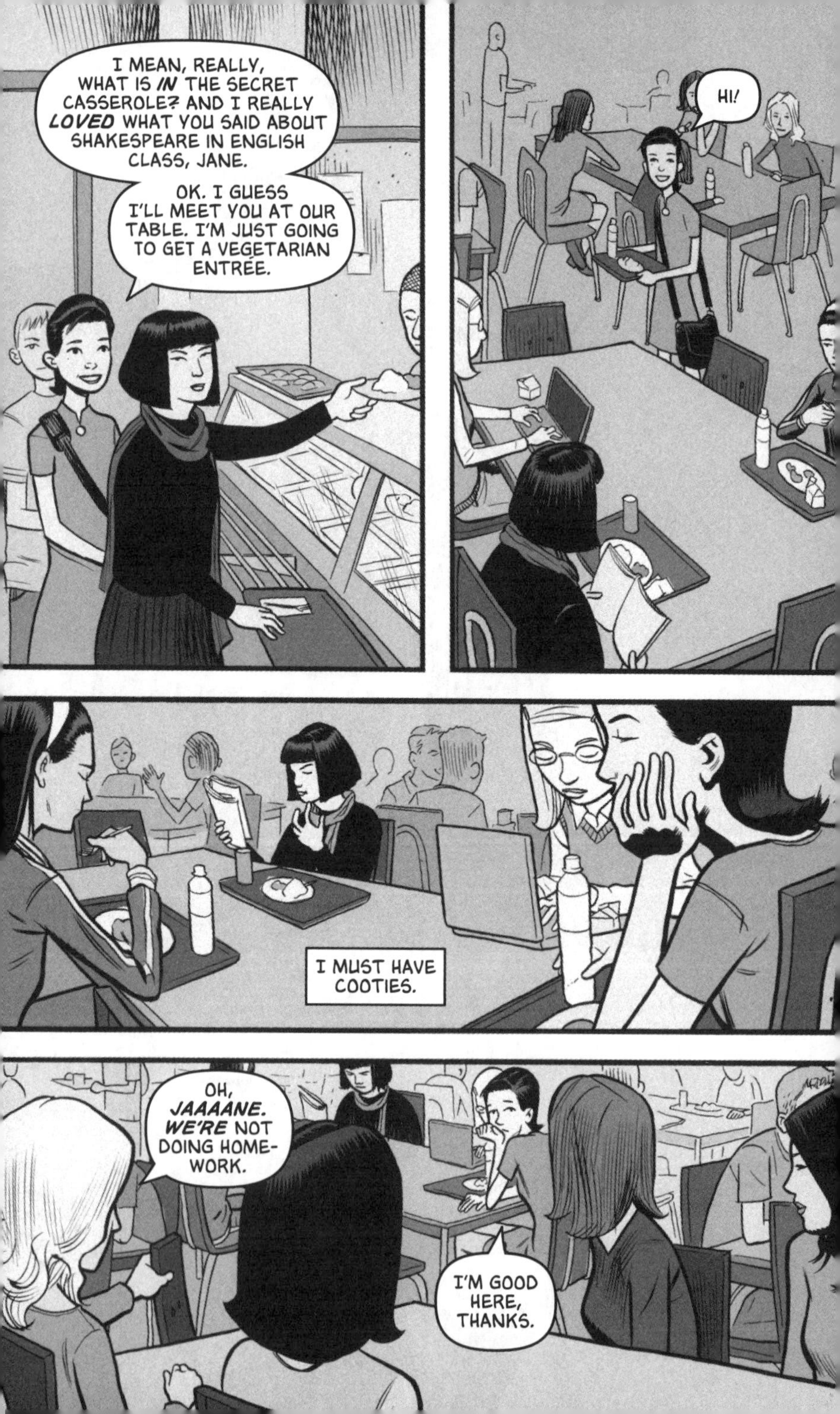

I MEAN, REALLY, WHAT IS *IN* THE SECRET CASSEROLE? AND I REALLY *LOVED* WHAT YOU SAID ABOUT SHAKESPEARE IN ENGLISH CLASS, JANE.
OK. I GUESS I'LL MEET YOU AT OUR TABLE. I'M JUST GOING TO GET A VEGETARIAN ENTRÉE.
HI!
I MUST HAVE COOTIES.
OH, *JAAAANE. WE'RE* NOT DOING HOME-WORK.
I'M GOOD HERE, THANKS.

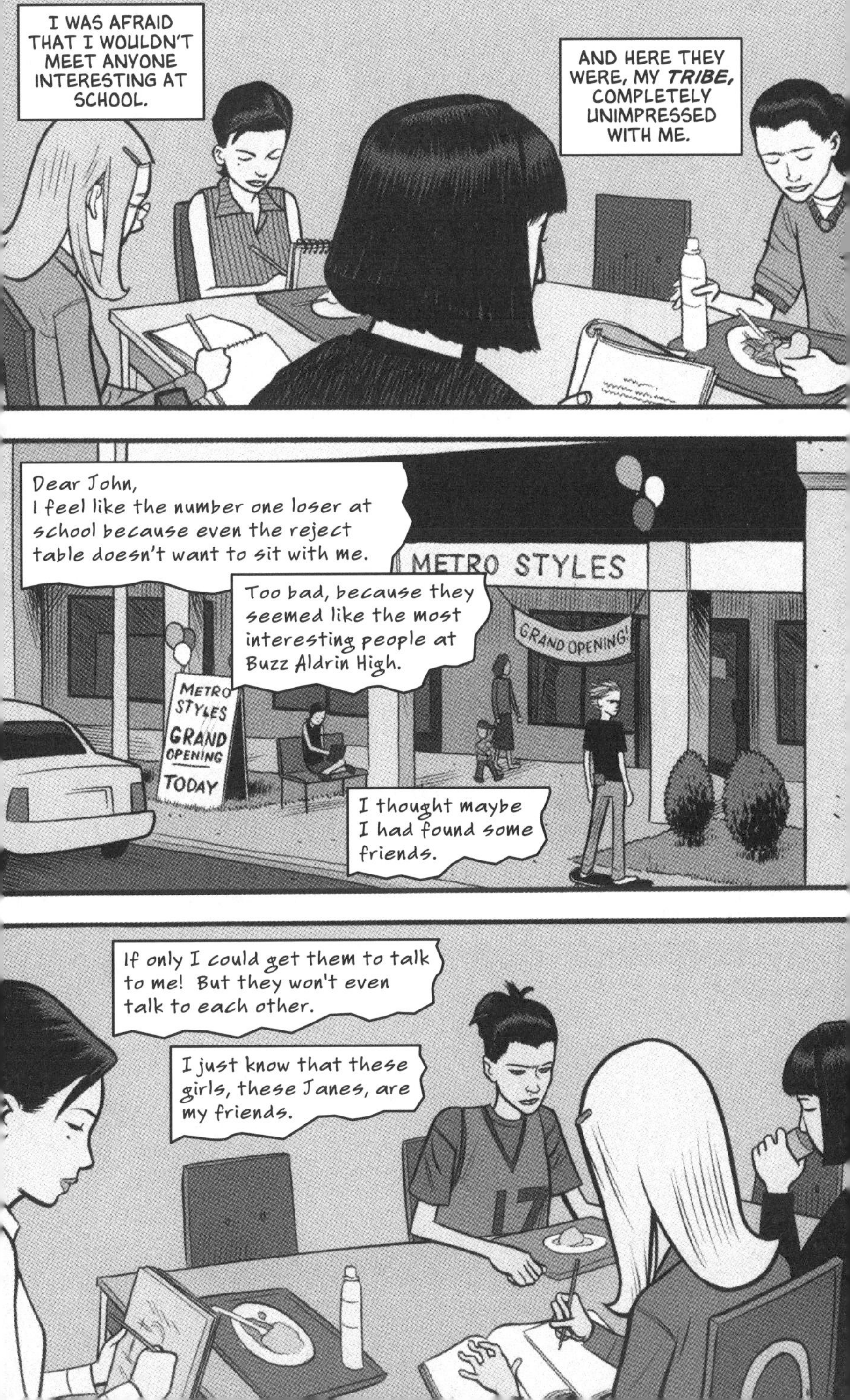
I WAS AFRAID THAT I WOULDN'T MEET ANYONE INTERESTING AT SCHOOL.
AND HERE THEY WERE, MY *TRIBE,* COMPLETELY UNIMPRESSED WITH ME.
Dear John,
I feel like the number one loser at school because even the reject table doesn't want to sit with me.
METRO STYLES
Too bad, because they seemed like the most interesting people at Buzz Aldrin High.
GRAND OPENING!
METRO STYLES GRAND OPENING TODAY
I thought maybe I had found some friends.
If only I could get them to talk to me! But they won't even talk to each other.
I just know that these girls, these Janes, are my friends.
17

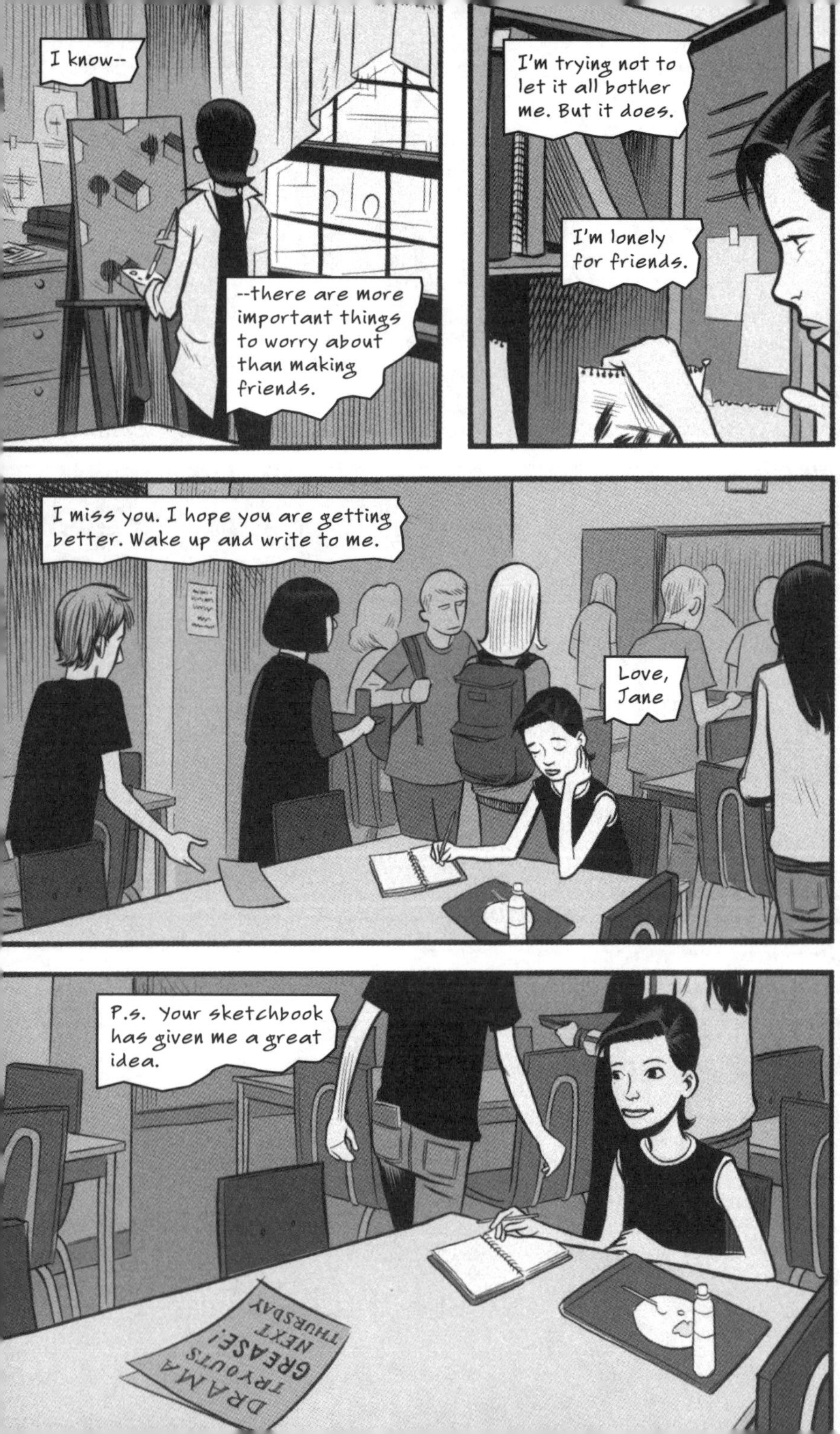
I know--
--there are more important things to worry about than making friends.
I'm trying not to let it all bother me. But it does.
I'm lonely for friends.
I miss you. I hope you are getting better. Wake up and write to me.
Love, Jane
P.s. Your sketchbook has given me a great idea.
DRAMA TRYOUTS GREASE! NEXT THURSDAY

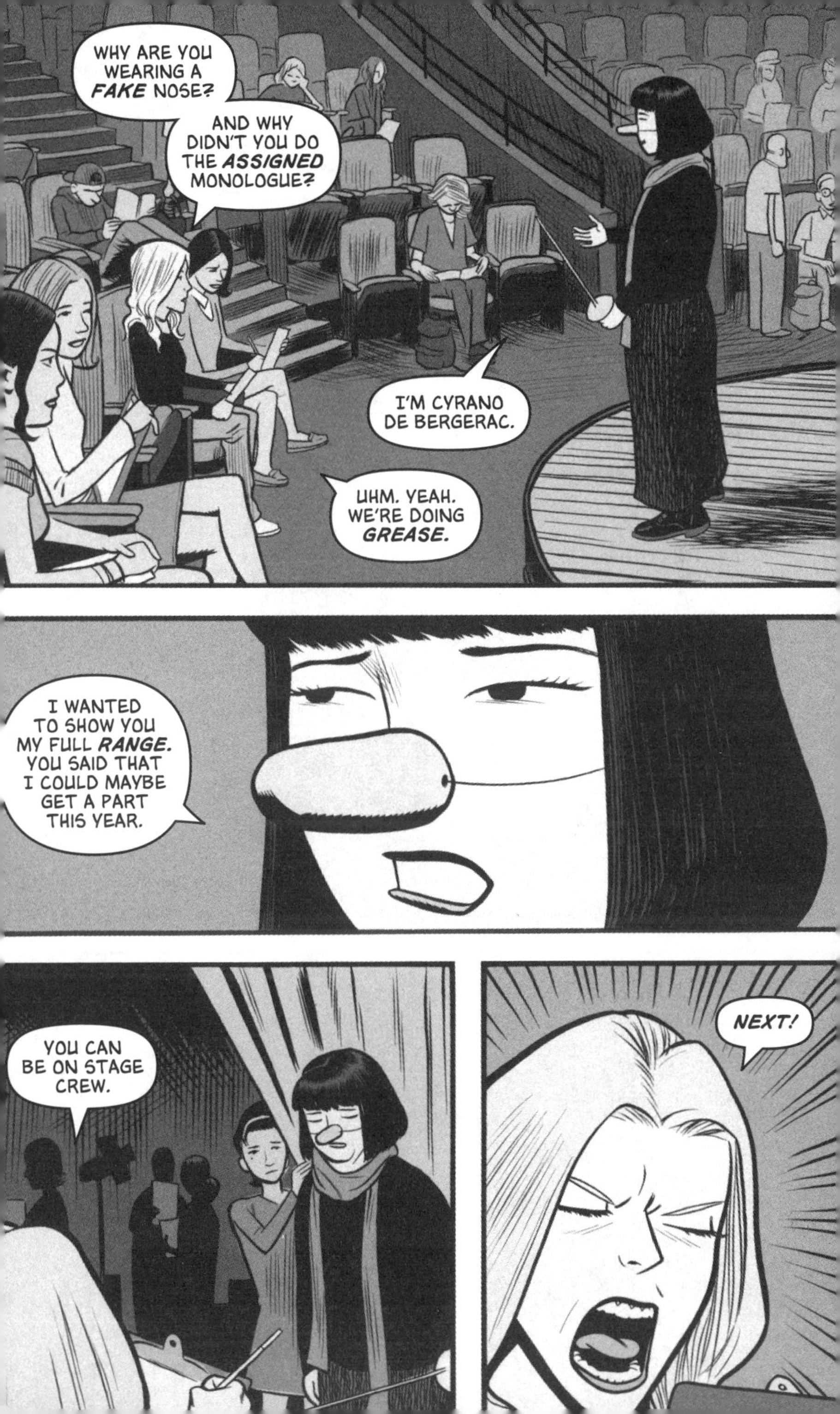
WHY ARE YOU WEARING A FAKE NOSE?
AND WHY DIDN'T YOU DO THE ASSIGNED MONOLOGUE?
I'M CYRANO DE BERGERAC.
UHM. YEAH. WE'RE DOING GREASE.
I WANTED TO SHOW YOU MY FULL RANGE. YOU SAID THAT I COULD MAYBE GET A PART THIS YEAR.
YOU CAN BE ON STAGE CREW.
NEXT!

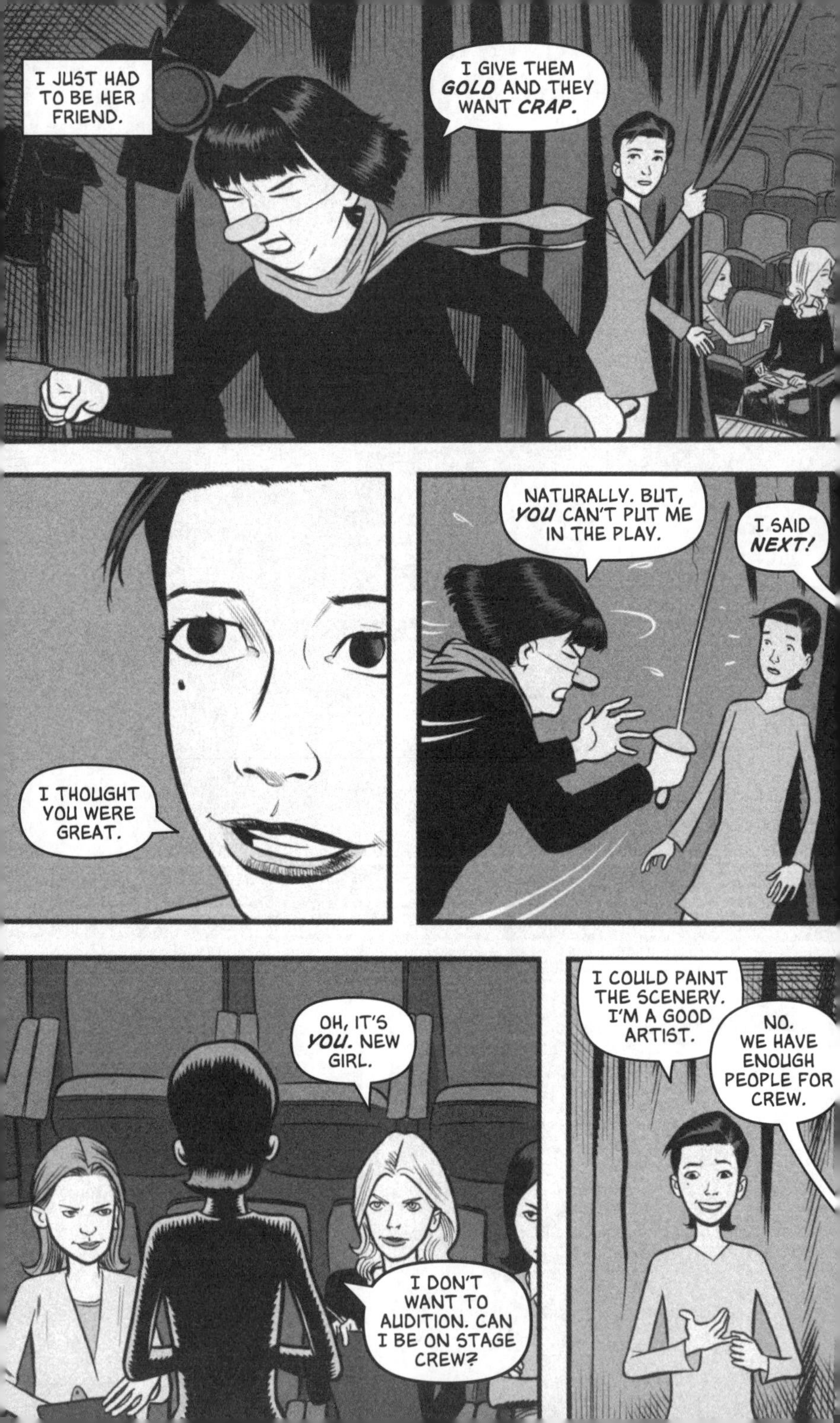
I JUST HAD TO BE HER FRIEND.
I GIVE THEM GOLD AND THEY WANT CRAP.
I THOUGHT YOU WERE GREAT.
NATURALLY. BUT, YOU CAN'T PUT ME IN THE PLAY.
I SAID NEXT!
OH, IT'S YOU. NEW GIRL.
I DON'T WANT TO AUDITION. CAN I BE ON STAGE CREW?
I COULD PAINT THE SCENERY. I'M A GOOD ARTIST.
NO. WE HAVE ENOUGH PEOPLE FOR CREW.

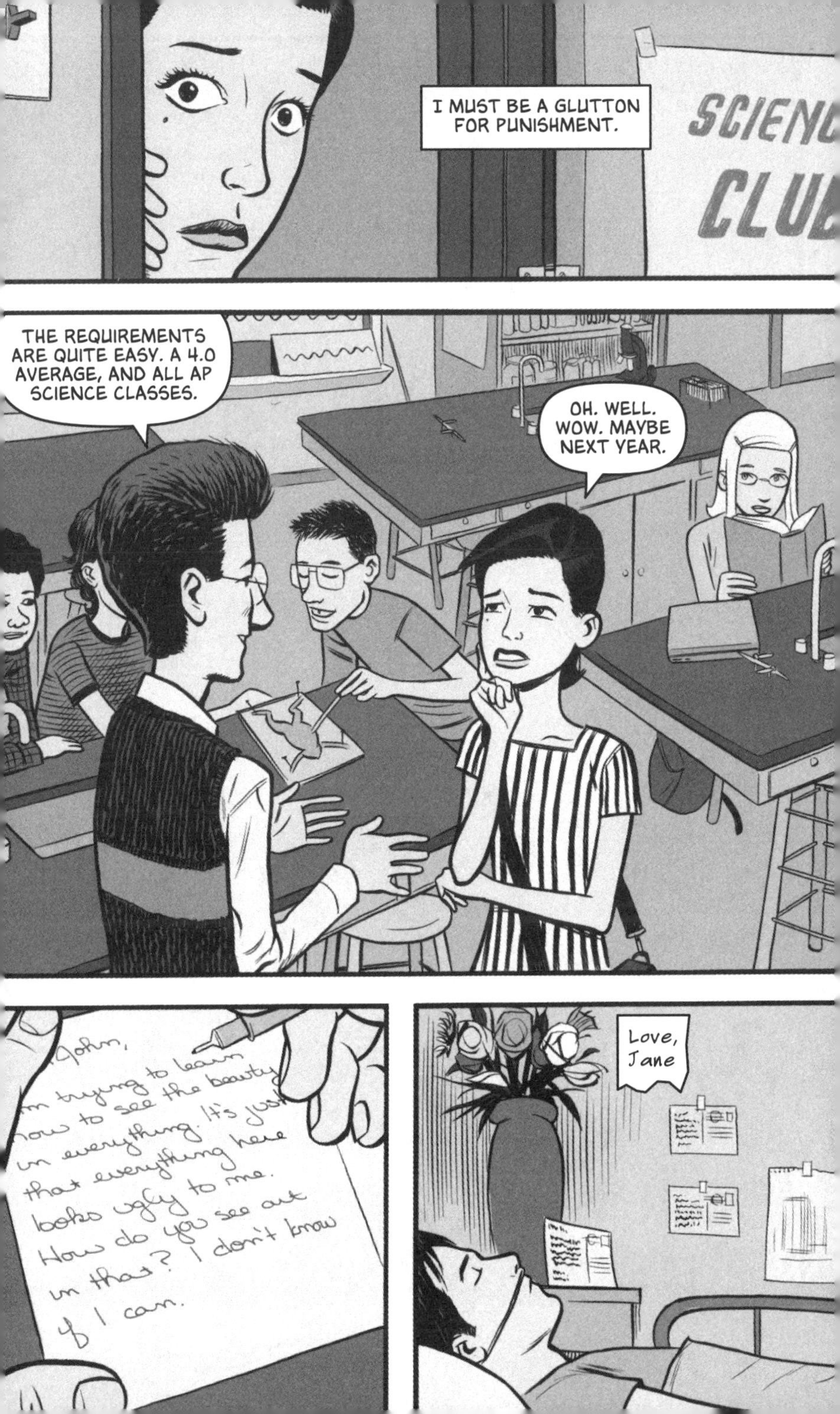
I MUST BE A GLUTTON FOR PUNISHMENT.
THE REQUIREMENTS ARE QUITE EASY. A 4.0 AVERAGE, AND ALL AP SCIENCE CLASSES.
OH. WELL. WOW. MAYBE NEXT YEAR.
John,
m trying to learn
ow to see the beauty
n everything. It's just
that everything here
looks ugly to me.
How do you see art
in that? I don't know
if I can.
Love, Jane

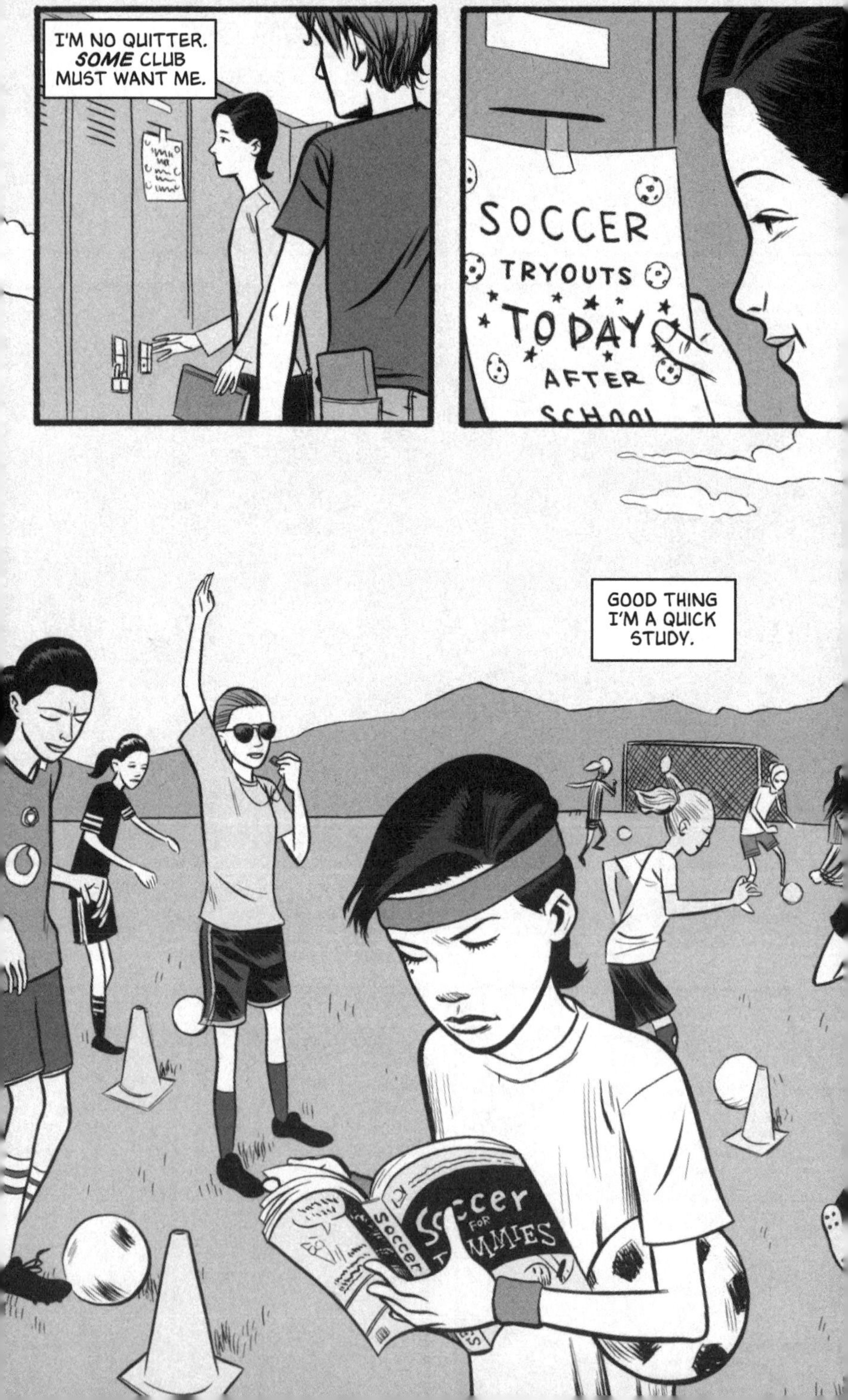
I'M NO QUITTER. SOME CLUB MUST WANT ME.
SOCCER TRYOUTS TODAY AFTER
GOOD THING I'M A QUICK STUDY.
Soccer
Soccer FOR DUMMIES

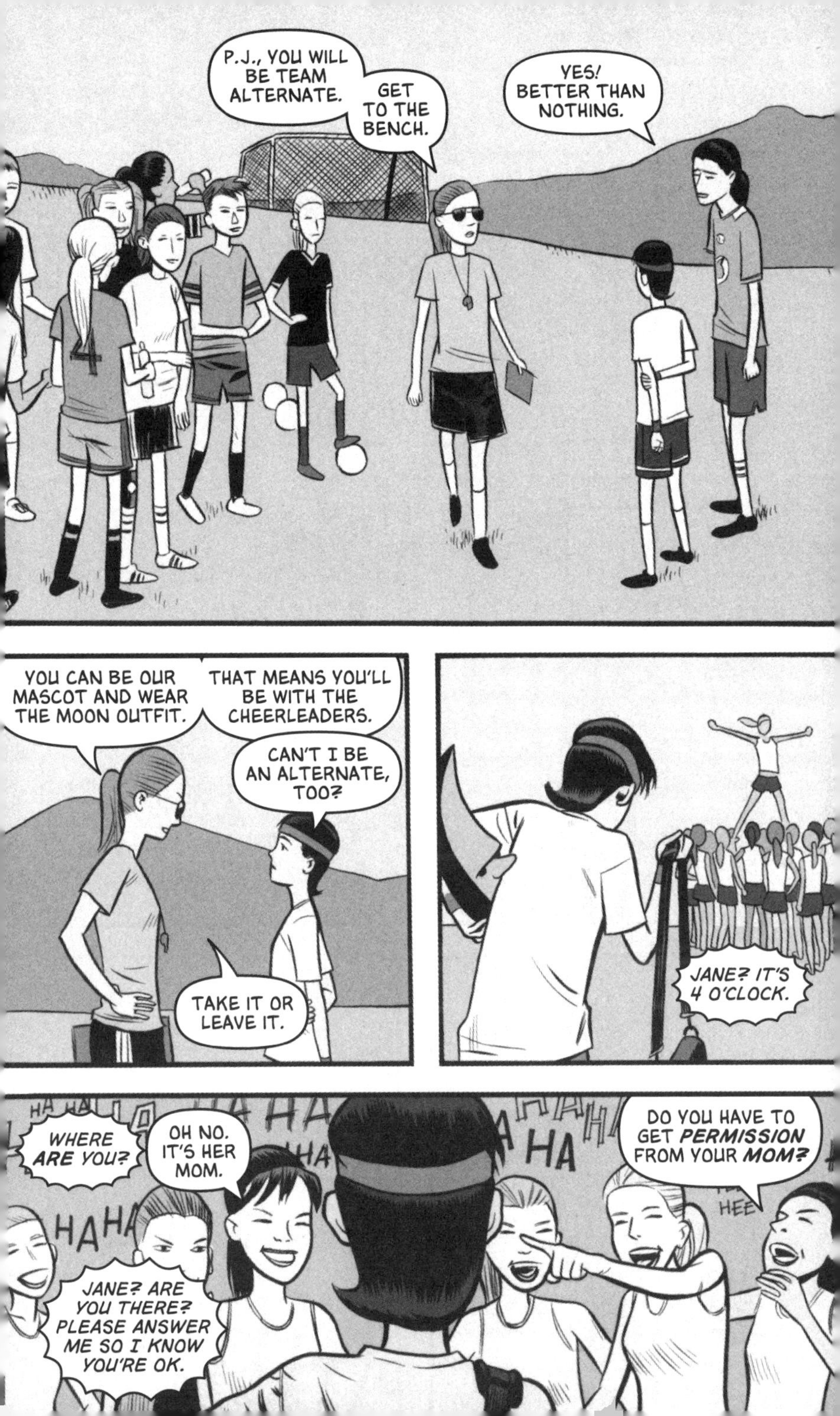
P.J., YOU WILL BE TEAM ALTERNATE.
GET TO THE BENCH.
YES! BETTER THAN NOTHING.
YOU CAN BE OUR MASCOT AND WEAR THE MOON OUTFIT.
THAT MEANS YOU'LL BE WITH THE CHEERLEADERS.
CAN'T I BE AN ALTERNATE, TOO?
TAKE IT OR LEAVE IT.
JANE? IT'S 4 O'CLOCK.
HA HA
HA HA
WHERE ARE YOU?
OH NO. IT'S HER MOM.
HA HA
DO YOU HAVE TO GET PERMISSION FROM YOUR MOM?
HEE
HAHA
JANE? ARE YOU THERE? PLEASE ANSWER ME SO I KNOW YOU'RE OK.

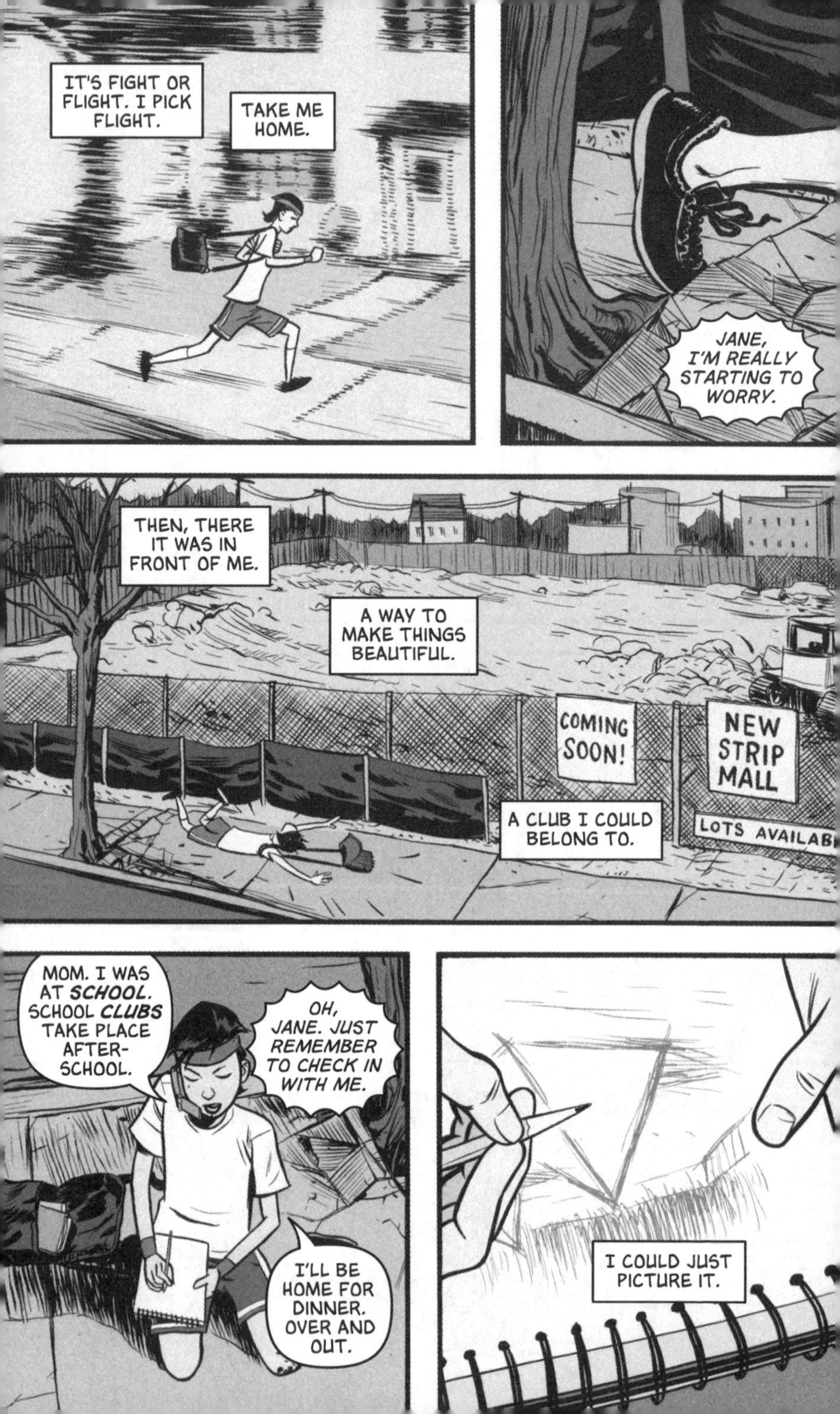
IT'S FIGHT OR FLIGHT. I PICK FLIGHT.
TAKE ME HOME.
JANE, I'M REALLY STARTING TO WORRY.
THEN, THERE IT WAS IN FRONT OF ME.
A WAY TO MAKE THINGS BEAUTIFUL.
COMING SOON!
NEW STRIP MALL
LOTS AVAILAB
A CLUB I COULD BELONG TO.
MOM. I WAS AT SCHOOL. SCHOOL CLUBS TAKE PLACE AFTER-SCHOOL.
OH, JANE. JUST REMEMBER TO CHECK IN WITH ME.
I'LL BE HOME FOR DINNER. OVER AND OUT.
I COULD JUST PICTURE IT.

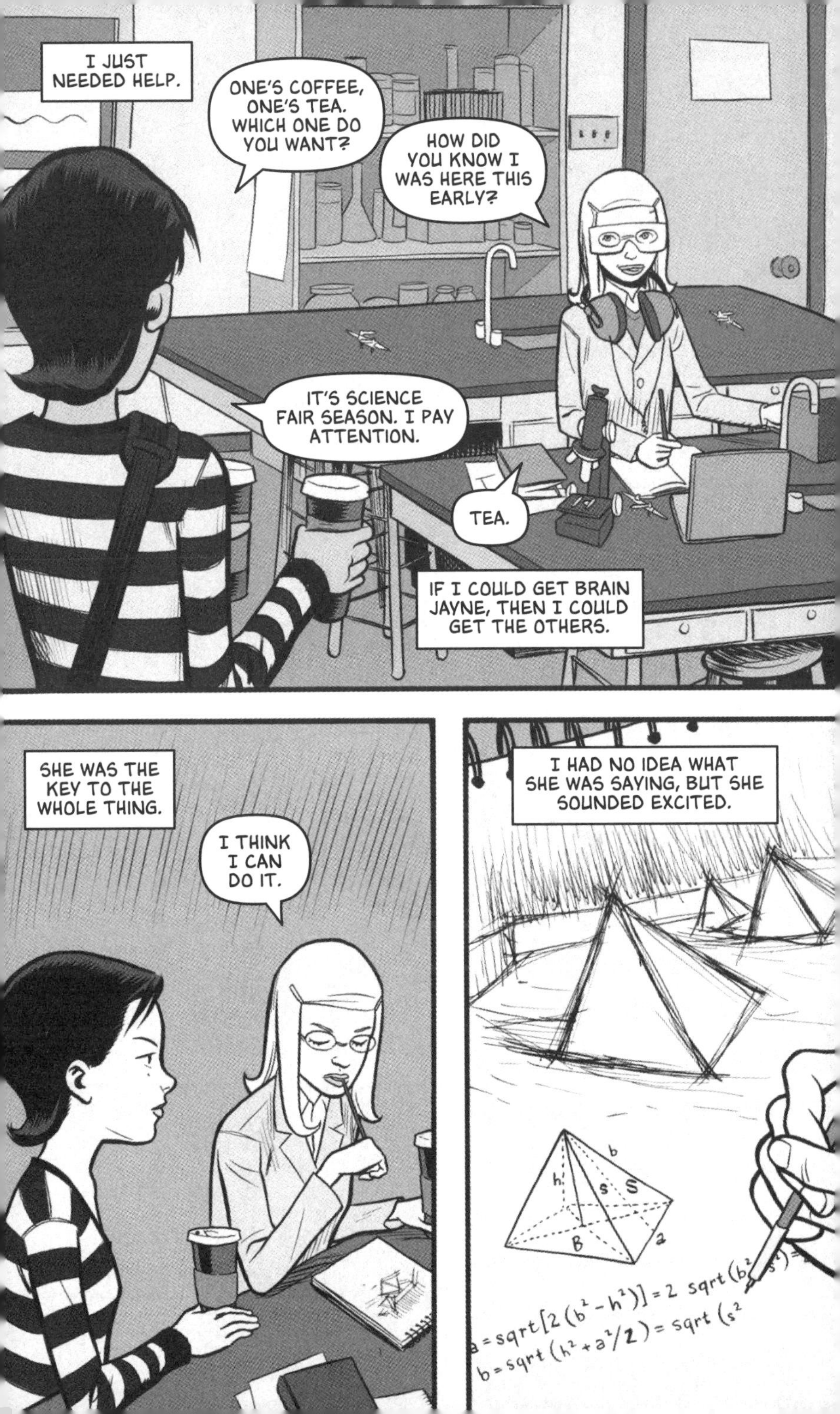
I JUST NEEDED HELP.
ONE'S COFFEE, ONE'S TEA. WHICH ONE DO YOU WANT?
HOW DID YOU KNOW I WAS HERE THIS EARLY?
IT'S SCIENCE FAIR SEASON. I PAY ATTENTION.
TEA.
IF I COULD GET BRAIN JAYNE, THEN I COULD GET THE OTHERS.
SHE WAS THE KEY TO THE WHOLE THING.
I THINK I CAN DO IT.
I HAD NO IDEA WHAT SHE WAS SAYING, BUT SHE SOUNDED EXCITED.
b
h
s
S
B
a
= sqrt[2(b² – h²)] = 2 sqrt (b²
a = sqrt (h² + a²/2) = sqrt (s²
b = sqrt

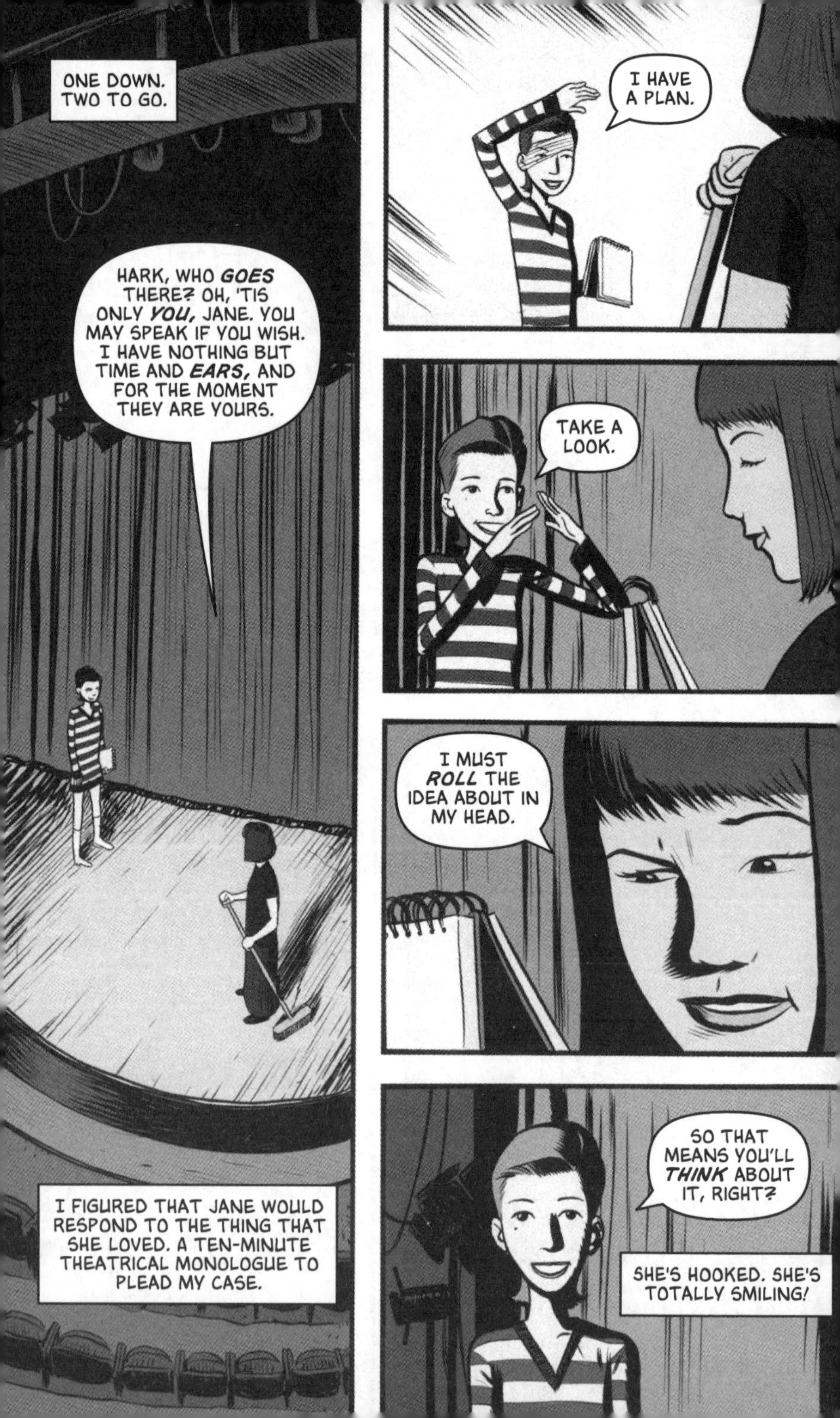
ONE DOWN. TWO TO GO.
HARK, WHO GOES THERE? OH, 'TIS ONLY YOU, JANE. YOU MAY SPEAK IF YOU WISH. I HAVE NOTHING BUT TIME AND EARS, AND FOR THE MOMENT THEY ARE YOURS.
I FIGURED THAT JANE WOULD RESPOND TO THE THING THAT SHE LOVED. A TEN-MINUTE THEATRICAL MONOLOGUE TO PLEAD MY CASE.
I HAVE A PLAN.
TAKE A LOOK.
I MUST ROLL THE IDEA ABOUT IN MY HEAD.
SO THAT MEANS YOU'LL THINK ABOUT IT, RIGHT?
SHE'S HOOKED. SHE'S TOTALLY SMILING!

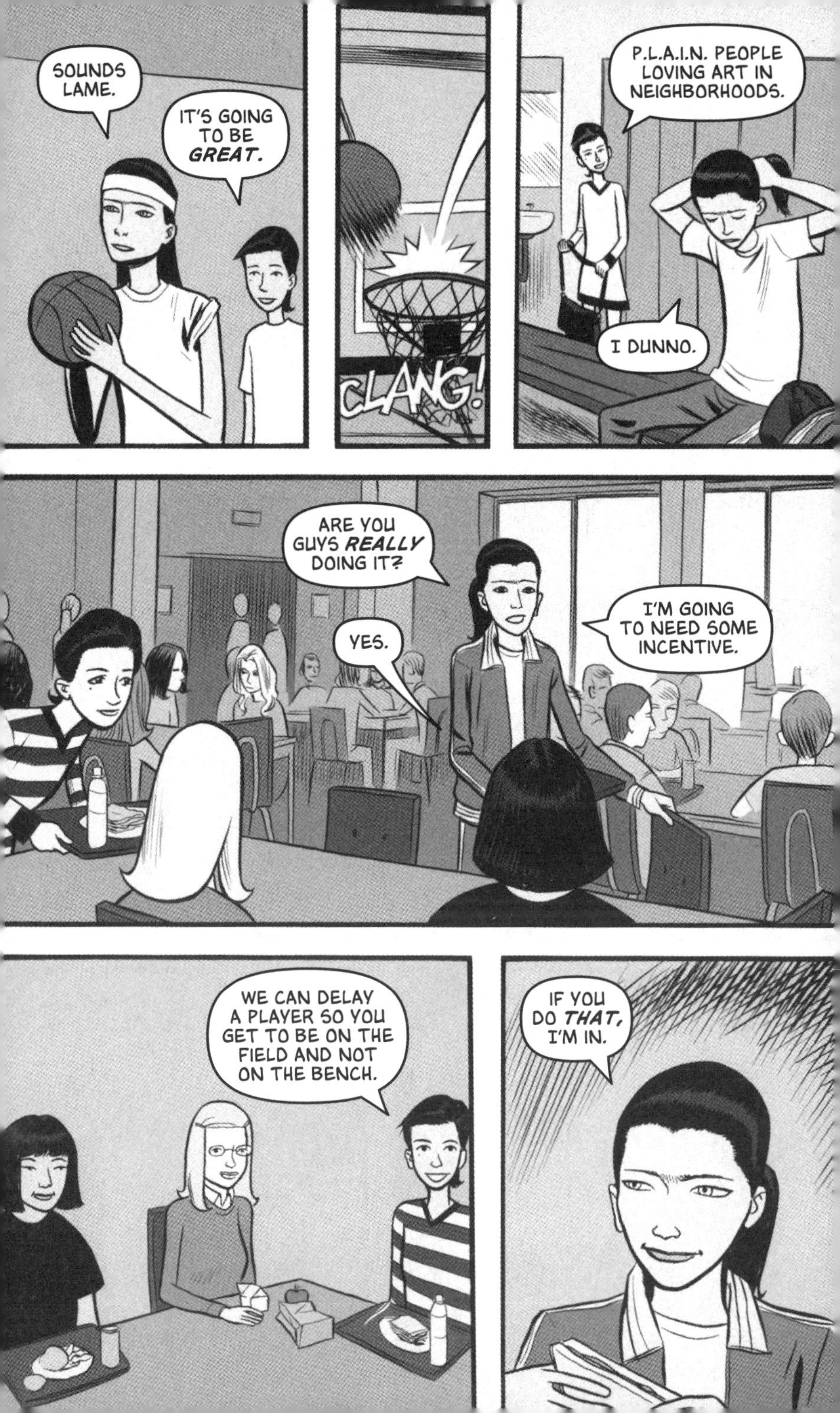

SOUNDS LAME.
IT'S GOING TO BE *GREAT.*
CLANG!
P.L.A.I.N. PEOPLE LOVING ART IN NEIGHBORHOODS.
I DUNNO.
ARE YOU GUYS *REALLY* DOING IT?
YES.
I'M GOING TO NEED SOME INCENTIVE.
WE CAN DELAY A PLAYER SO YOU GET TO BE ON THE FIELD AND NOT ON THE BENCH.
IF YOU DO *THAT,* I'M IN.

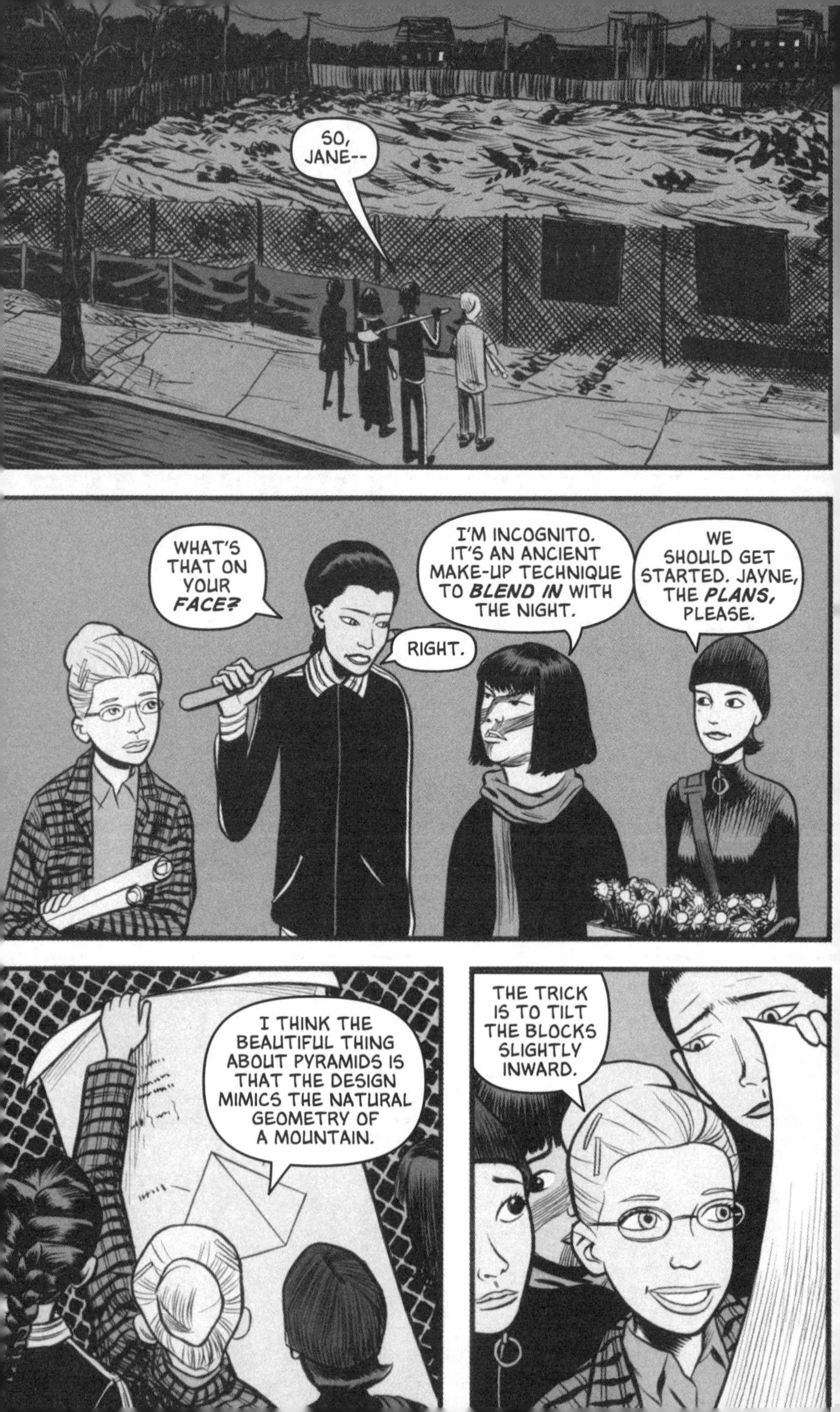

SO, JANE--
WHAT'S THAT ON YOUR *FACE?*
I'M INCOGNITO. IT'S AN ANCIENT MAKE-UP TECHNIQUE TO *BLEND IN* WITH THE NIGHT.
RIGHT.
WE SHOULD GET STARTED. JAYNE, THE *PLANS,* PLEASE.
I THINK THE BEAUTIFUL THING ABOUT PYRAMIDS IS THAT THE DESIGN MIMICS THE NATURAL GEOMETRY OF A MOUNTAIN.
THE TRICK IS TO TILT THE BLOCKS SLIGHTLY INWARD.

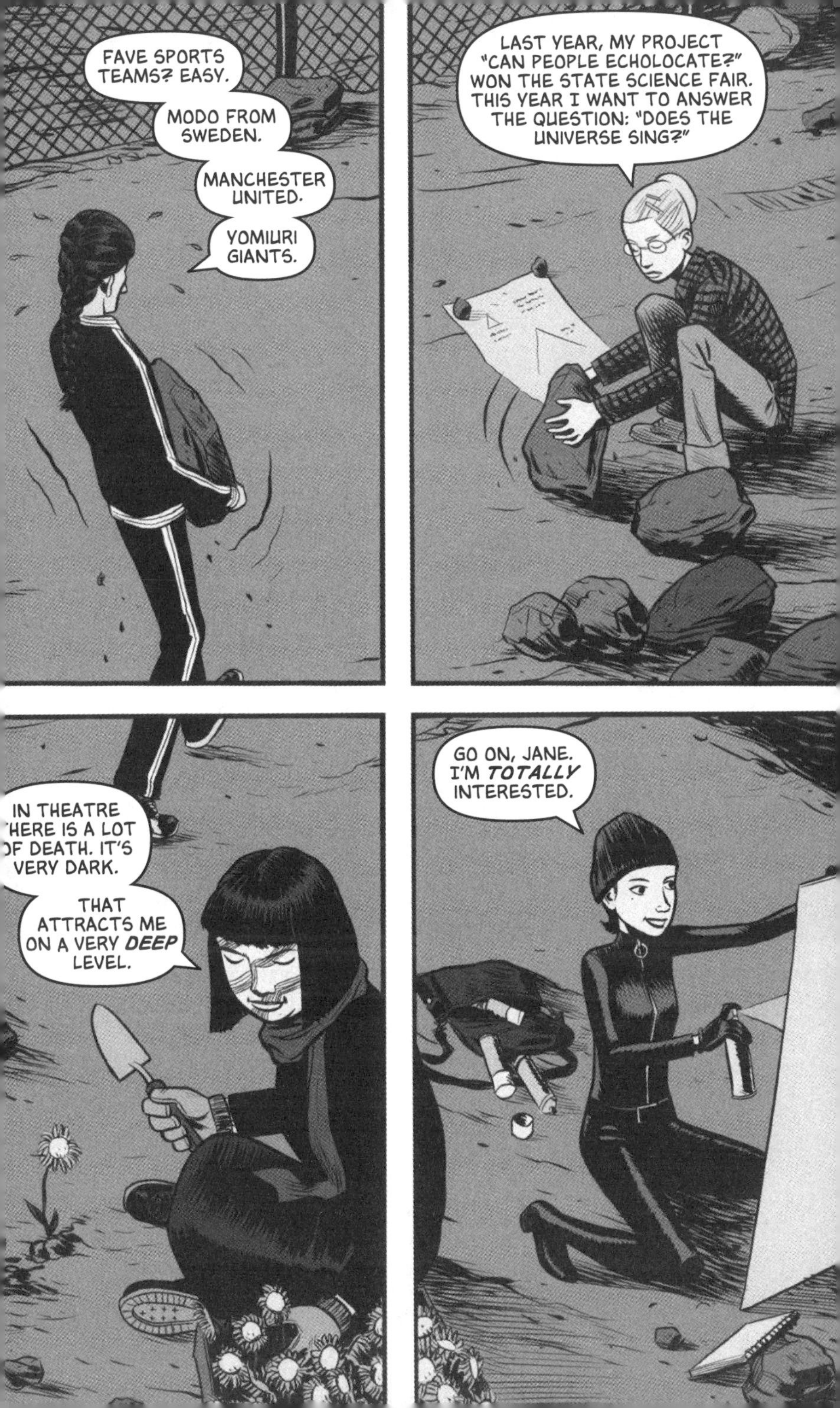
FAVE SPORTS TEAMS? EASY.
MODO FROM SWEDEN.
MANCHESTER UNITED.
YOMIURI GIANTS.
LAST YEAR, MY PROJECT "CAN PEOPLE ECHOLOCATE?" WON THE STATE SCIENCE FAIR. THIS YEAR I WANT TO ANSWER THE QUESTION: "DOES THE UNIVERSE SING?"
IN THEATRE THERE IS A LOT OF DEATH. IT'S VERY DARK.
THAT ATTRACTS ME ON A VERY DEEP LEVEL.
GO ON, JANE. I'M TOTALLY INTERESTED.

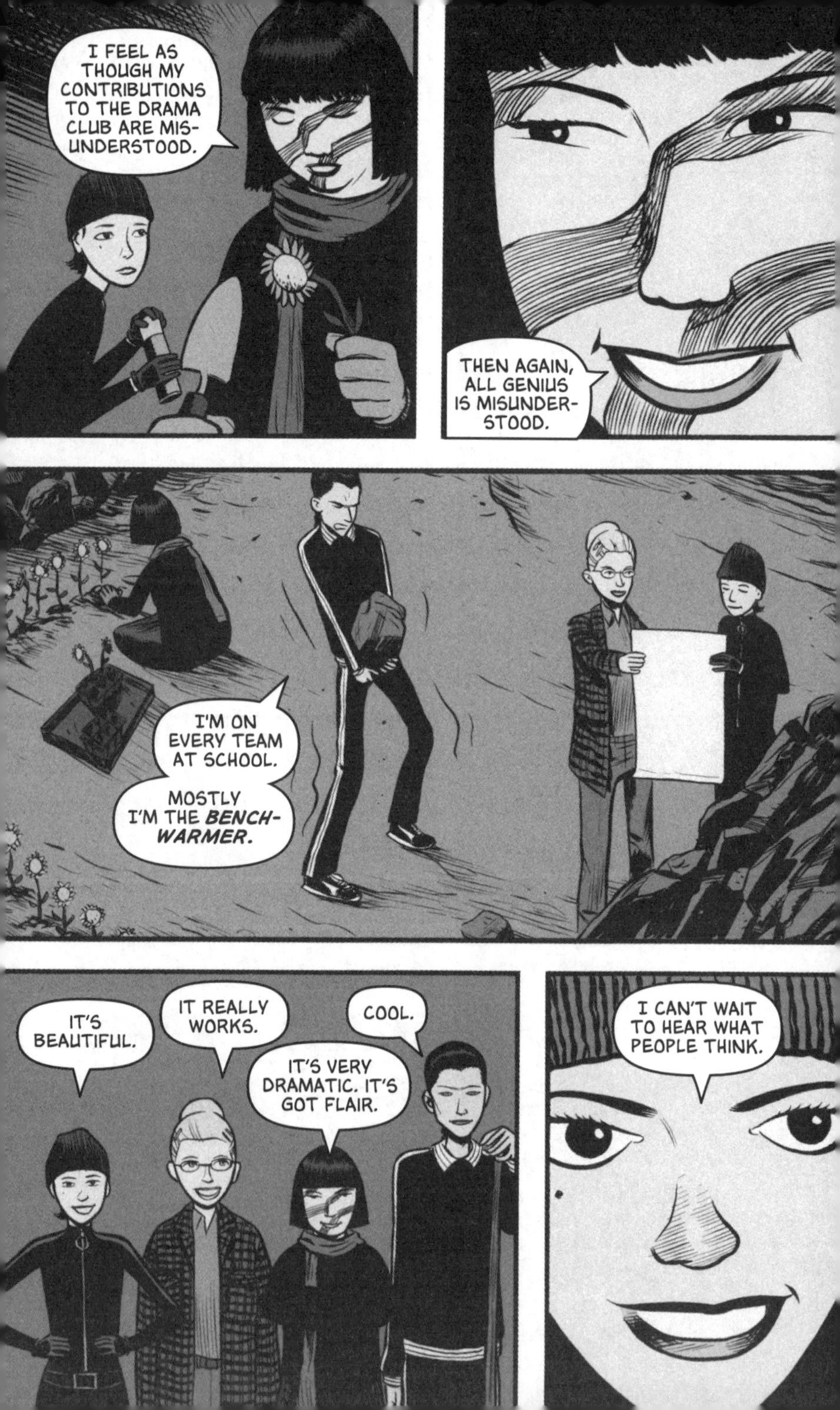
I FEEL AS THOUGH MY CONTRIBUTIONS TO THE DRAMA CLUB ARE MIS-UNDERSTOOD.
THEN AGAIN, ALL GENIUS IS MISUNDER-STOOD.
I'M ON EVERY TEAM AT SCHOOL.
MOSTLY I'M THE ***BENCH-WARMER.***
IT'S BEAUTIFUL.
IT REALLY WORKS.
COOL.
IT'S VERY DRAMATIC. IT'S GOT FLAIR.
I CAN'T WAIT TO HEAR WHAT PEOPLE THINK.

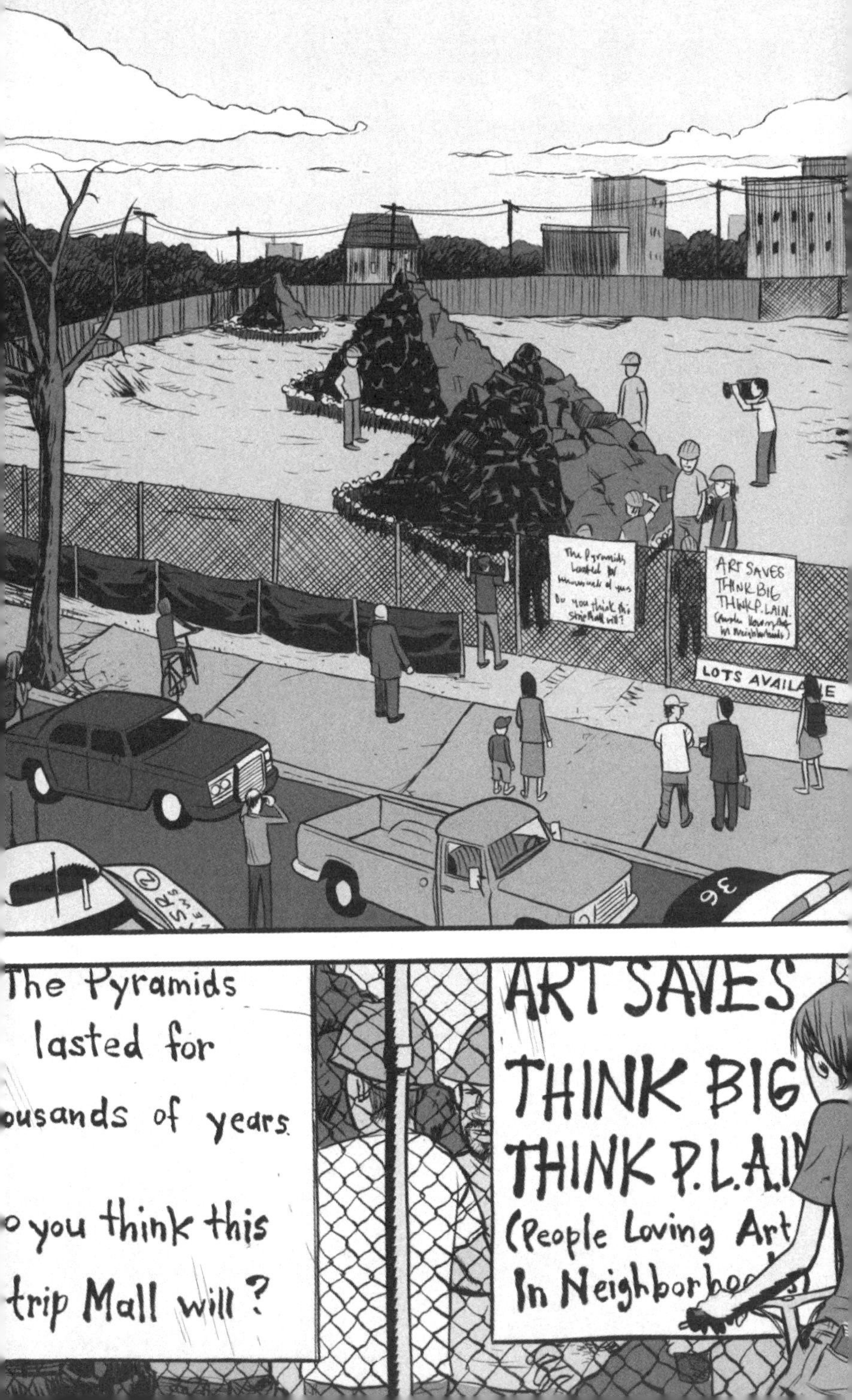
The Pyramids lasted for
ART SAVES
THINK BIG
THINK P.L.AIN.
LOTS AVAILA E
36
The Pyramids
lasted for
ousands of years.
o you think this
trip Mall will?
ART SAVES
THINK BIG
THINK P.L.A.I
(People Loving Art
In Neighborho

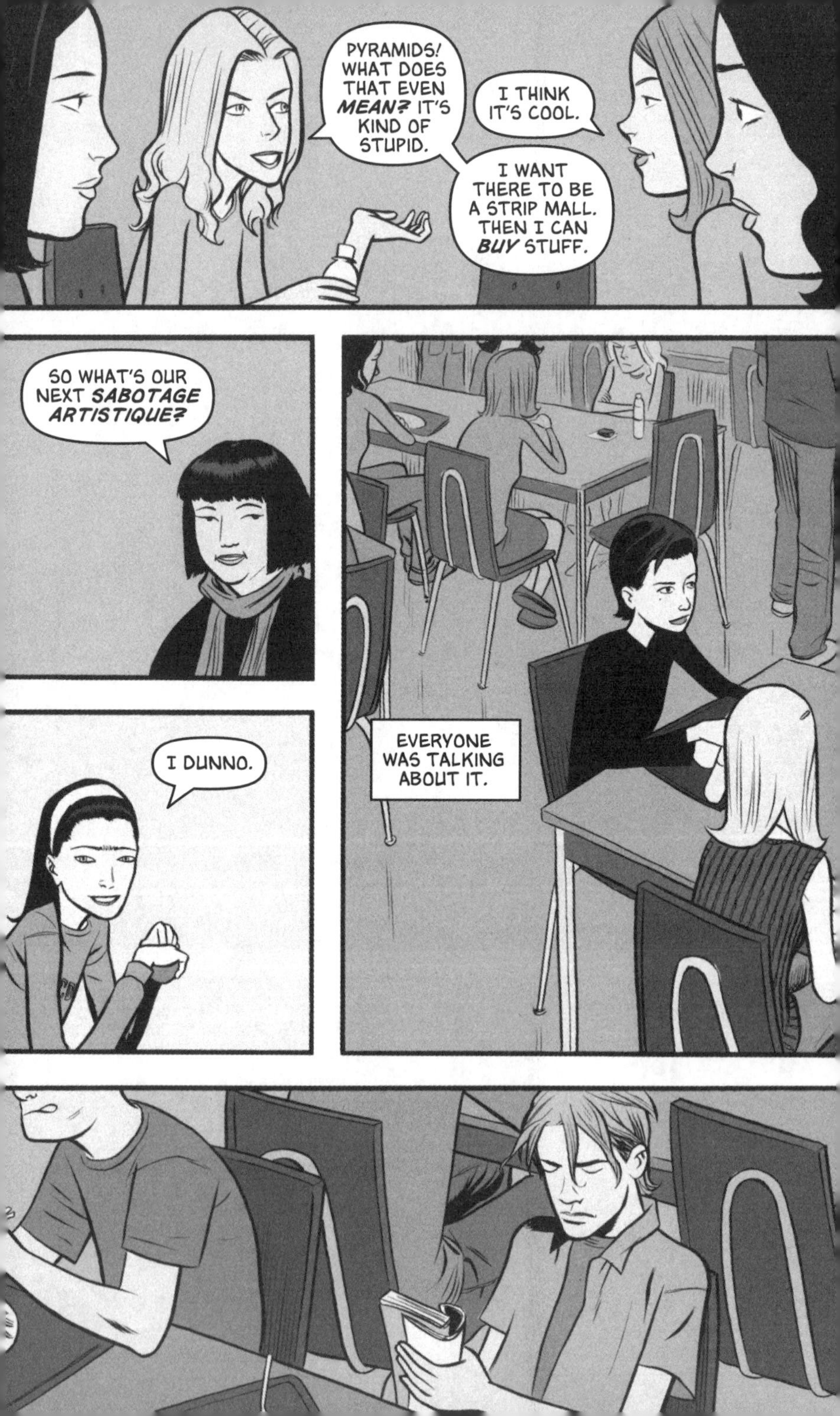
PYRAMIDS! WHAT DOES THAT EVEN *MEAN?* IT'S KIND OF STUPID.
I THINK IT'S COOL.
I WANT THERE TO BE A STRIP MALL. THEN I CAN *BUY* STUFF.
SO WHAT'S OUR NEXT *SABOTAGE ARTISTIQUE?*
I DUNNO.
EVERYONE WAS TALKING ABOUT IT.

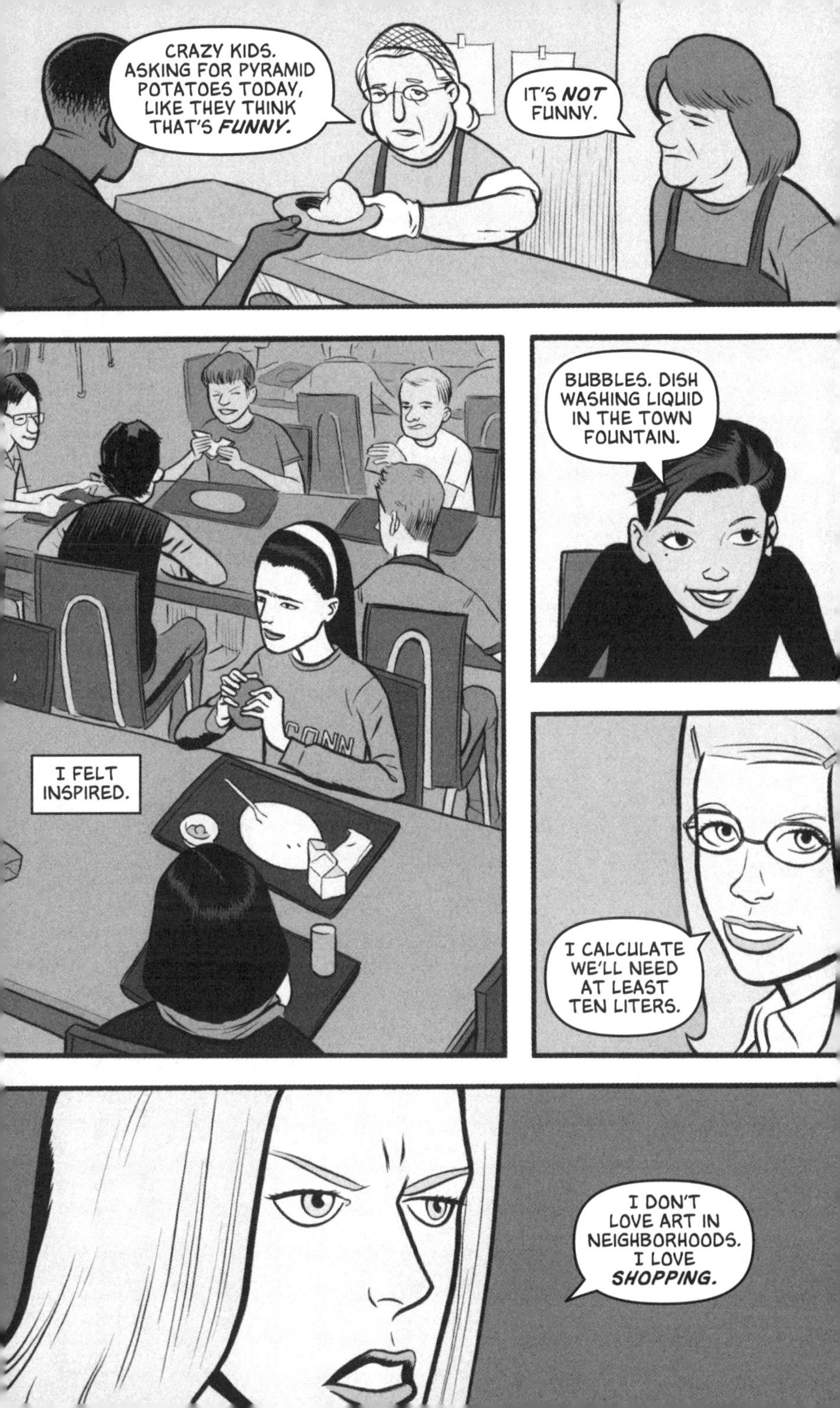
CRAZY KIDS. ASKING FOR PYRAMID POTATOES TODAY, LIKE THEY THINK THAT'S *FUNNY.*
IT'S *NOT* FUNNY.
CONN
I FELT INSPIRED.
BUBBLES. DISH WASHING LIQUID IN THE TOWN FOUNTAIN.
I CALCULATE WE'LL NEED AT LEAST TEN LITERS.
I DON'T LOVE ART IN NEIGHBORHOODS. I LOVE *SHOPPING.*

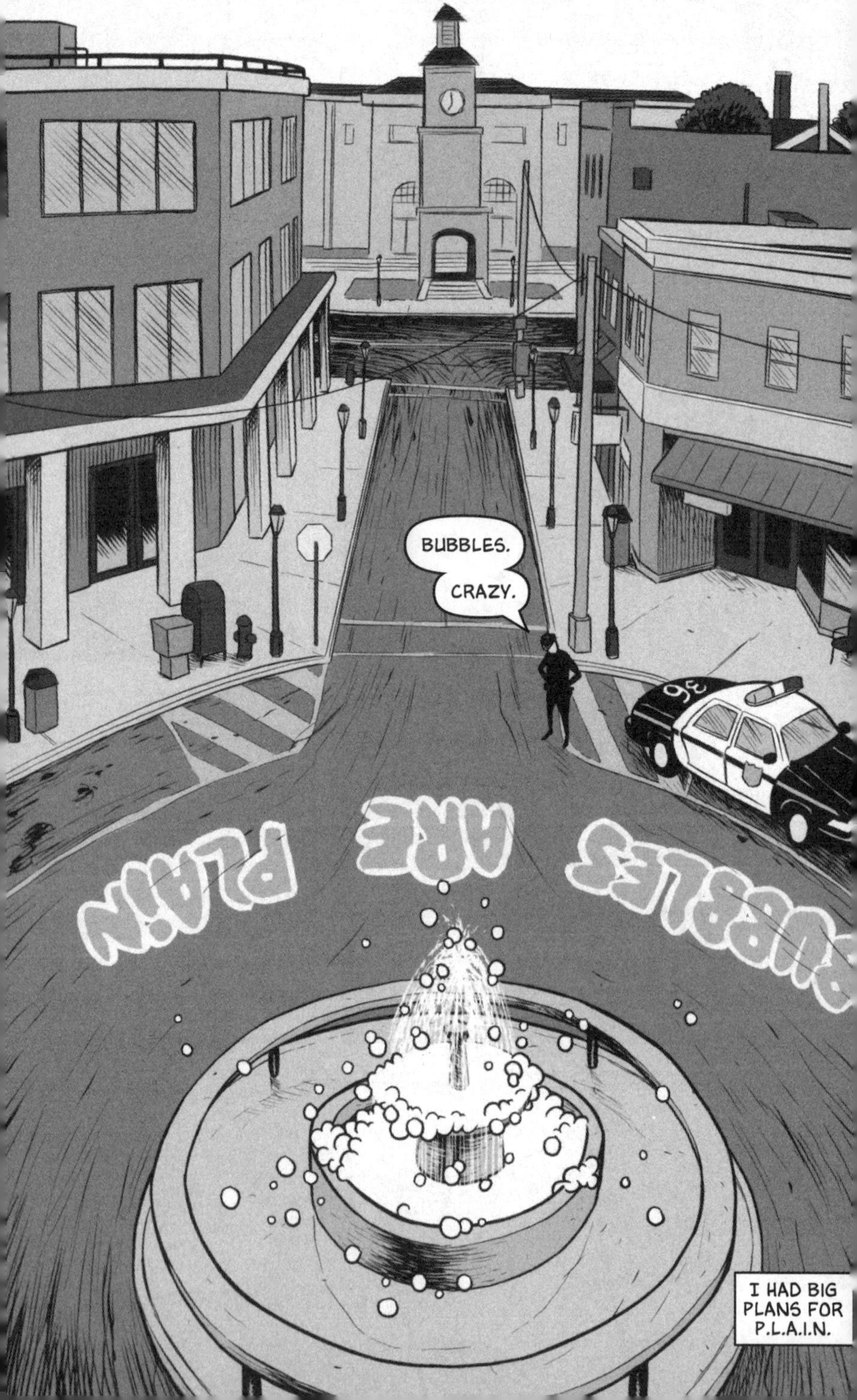
BUBBLES.
CRAZY.
I HAD BIG PLANS FOR P.L.A.I.N.

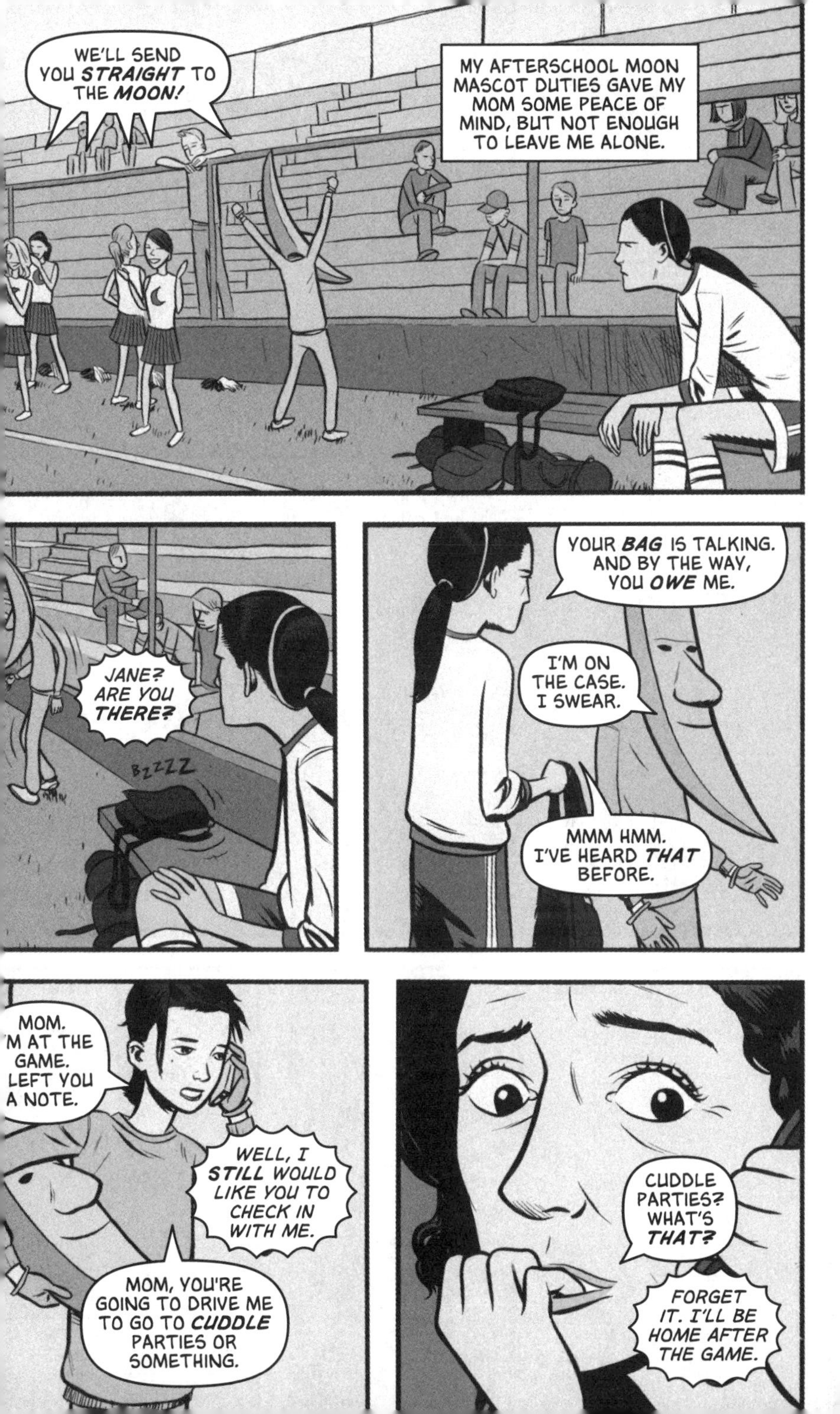
WE'LL SEND YOU STRAIGHT TO THE MOON!
MY AFTERSCHOOL MOON MASCOT DUTIES GAVE MY MOM SOME PEACE OF MIND, BUT NOT ENOUGH TO LEAVE ME ALONE.
JANE? ARE YOU THERE?
BZZZZ
YOUR BAG IS TALKING. AND BY THE WAY, YOU OWE ME.
I'M ON THE CASE. I SWEAR.
MMM HMM. I'VE HEARD THAT BEFORE.
MOM. 'M AT THE GAME. LEFT YOU A NOTE.
WELL, I STILL WOULD LIKE YOU TO CHECK IN WITH ME.
MOM, YOU'RE GOING TO DRIVE ME TO GO TO CUDDLE PARTIES OR SOMETHING.
CUDDLE PARTIES? WHAT'S THAT?
FORGET IT. I'LL BE HOME AFTER THE GAME.

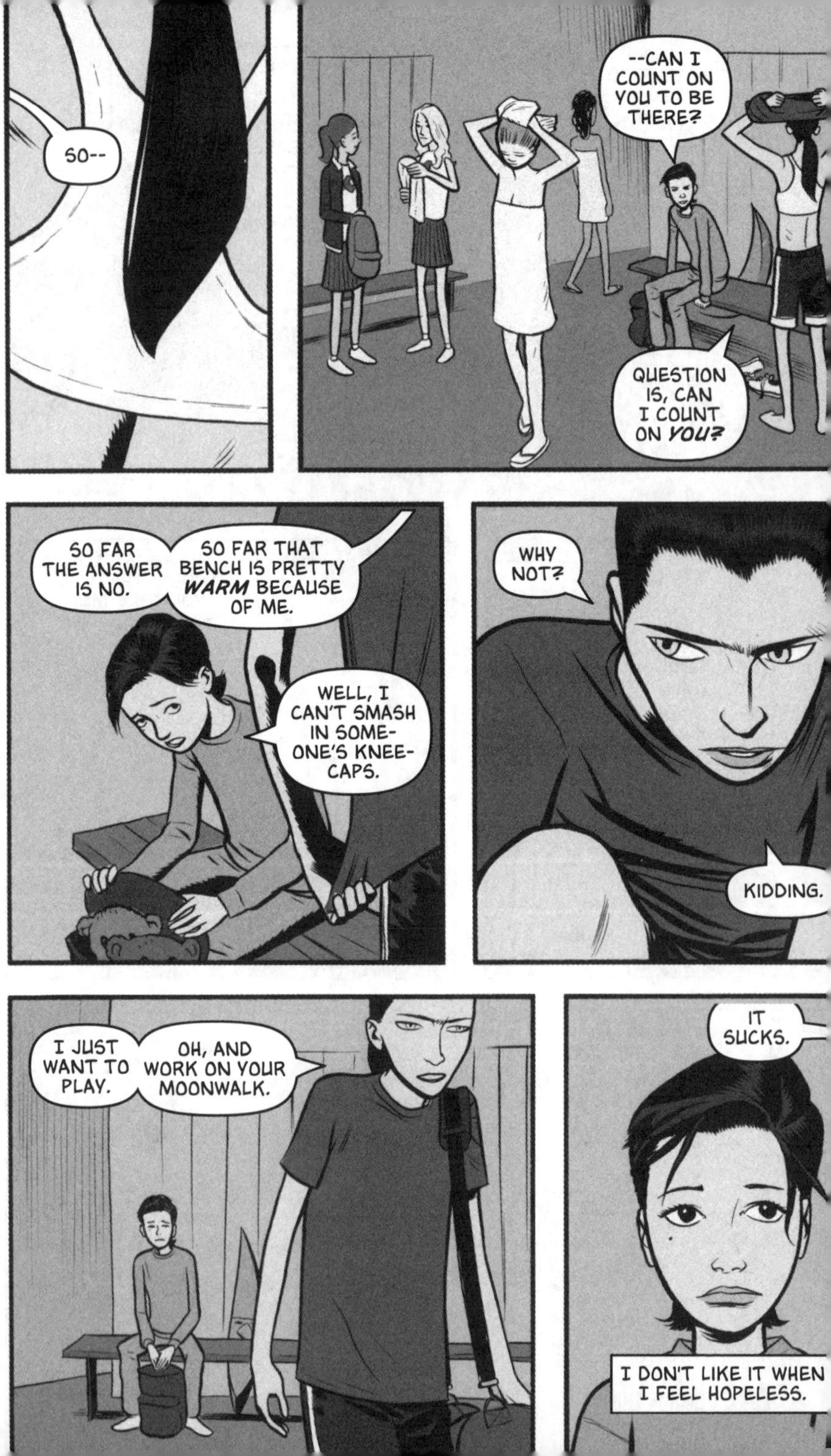
SO--
--CAN I COUNT ON YOU TO BE THERE?
QUESTION IS, CAN I COUNT ON *YOU?*
SO FAR THE ANSWER IS NO.
SO FAR THAT BENCH IS PRETTY *WARM* BECAUSE OF ME.
WELL, I CAN'T SMASH IN SOME-ONE'S KNEE-CAPS.
WHY NOT?
KIDDING.
I JUST WANT TO PLAY.
OH, AND WORK ON YOUR MOONWALK.
IT SUCKS.
I DON'T LIKE IT WHEN I FEEL HOPELESS.

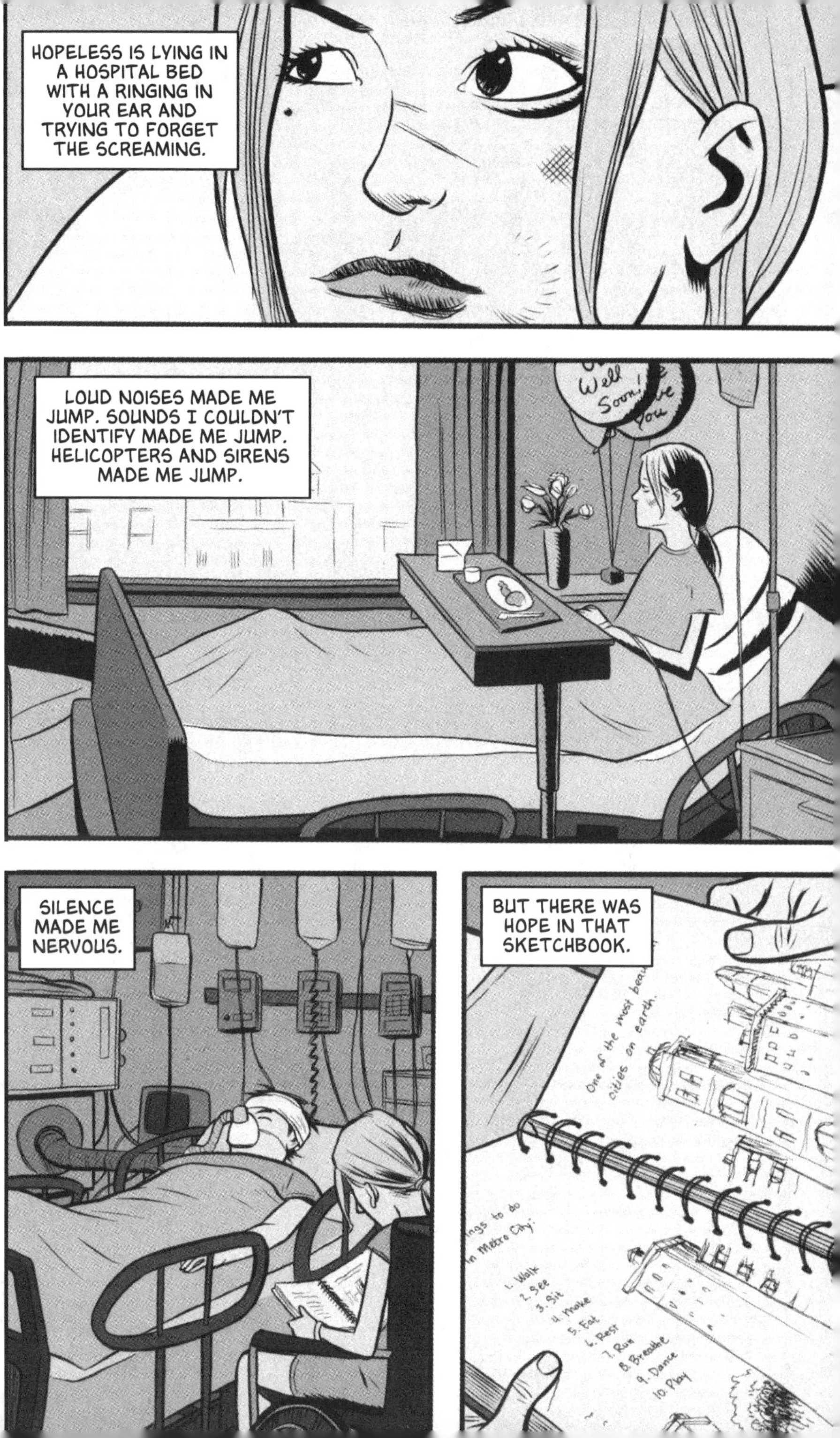
HOPELESS IS LYING IN A HOSPITAL BED WITH A RINGING IN YOUR EAR AND TRYING TO FORGET THE SCREAMING.
LOUD NOISES MADE ME JUMP. SOUNDS I COULDN'T IDENTIFY MADE ME JUMP. HELICOPTERS AND SIRENS MADE ME JUMP.
Well Soon!
SILENCE MADE ME NERVOUS.
BUT THERE WAS HOPE IN THAT SKETCHBOOK.
cities on earth.
1. Walk
2. See
3. Sit
4. Make
5. Eat
6. Rest
7. Run
8. Breathe
9. Dance
10. Play

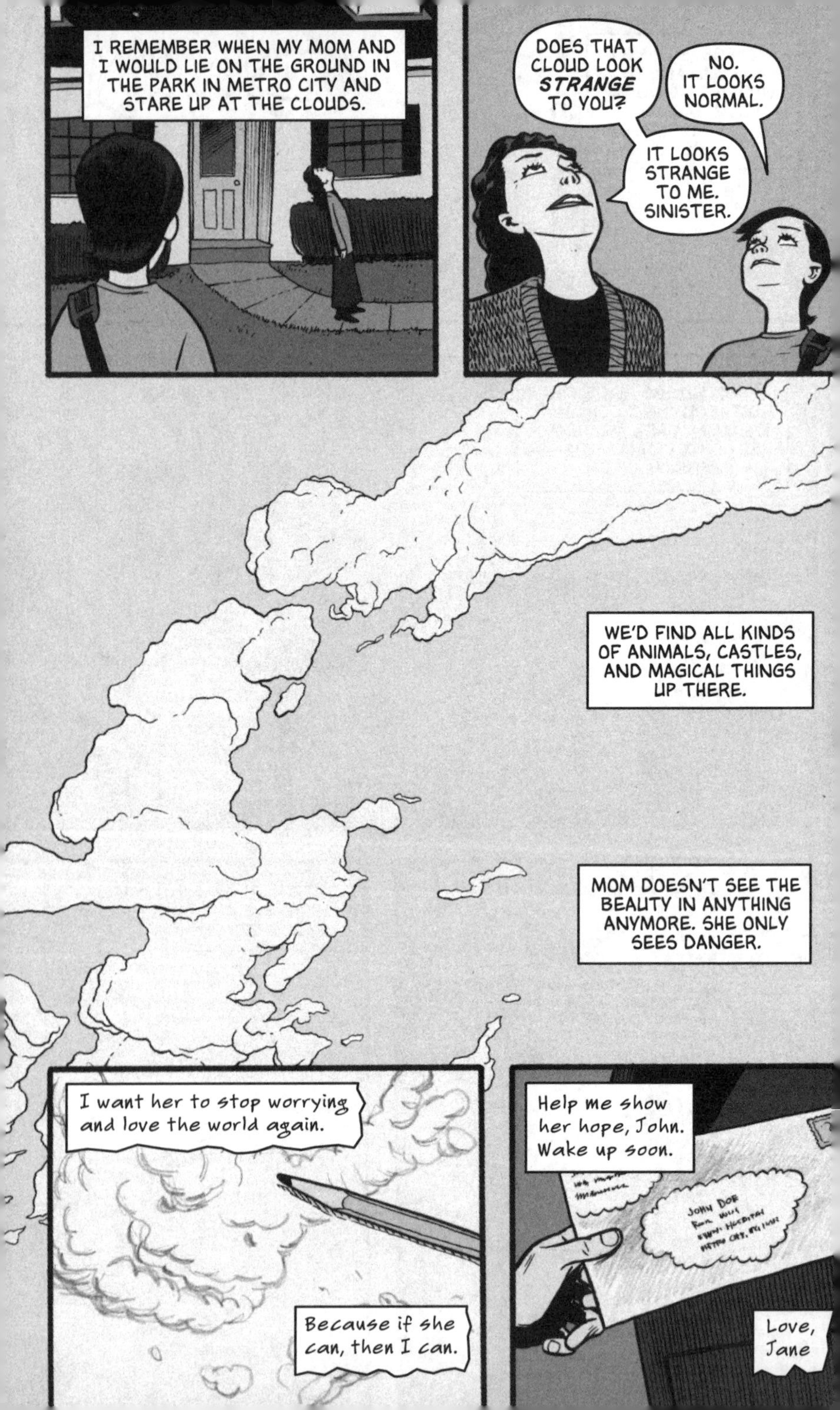
I REMEMBER WHEN MY MOM AND I WOULD LIE ON THE GROUND IN THE PARK IN METRO CITY AND STARE UP AT THE CLOUDS.
DOES THAT CLOUD LOOK *STRANGE* TO YOU?
NO. IT LOOKS NORMAL.
IT LOOKS STRANGE TO ME. SINISTER.
WE'D FIND ALL KINDS OF ANIMALS, CASTLES, AND MAGICAL THINGS UP THERE.
MOM DOESN'T SEE THE BEAUTY IN ANYTHING ANYMORE. SHE ONLY SEES DANGER.
I want her to stop worrying and love the world again.
Because if she can, then I can.
Help me show her hope, John. Wake up soon.
JOHN DOE
Love, Jane

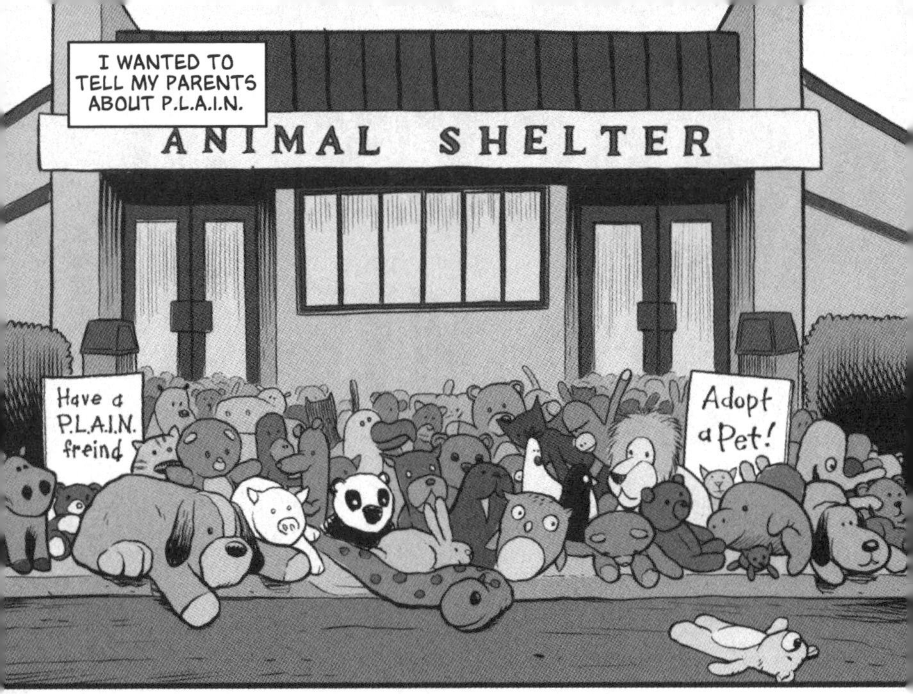
I WANTED TO TELL MY PARENTS ABOUT P.L.A.I.N.
ANIMAL SHELTER
Have a P.L.A.I.N. freind
Adopt a Pet!

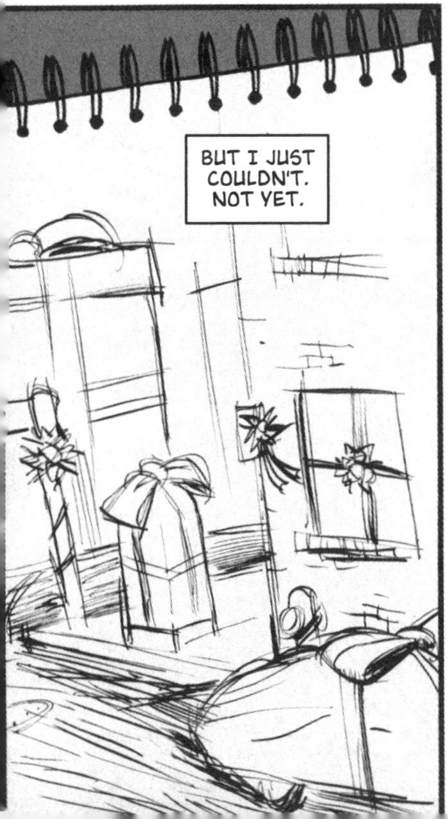
BUT I JUST COULDN'T. NOT YET.

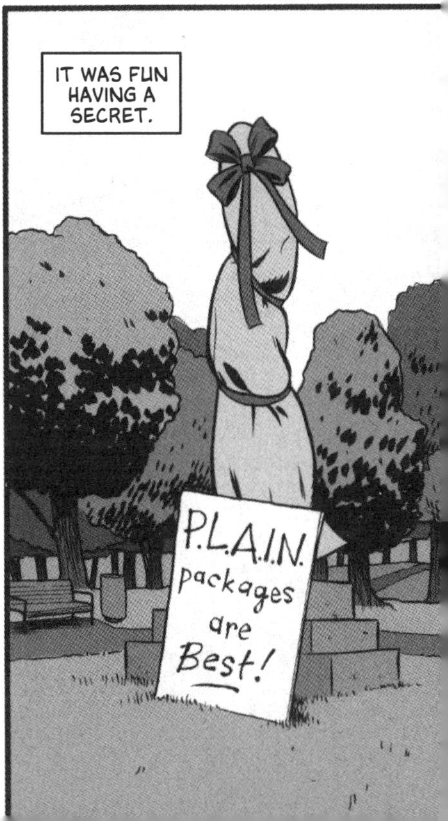
IT WAS FUN HAVING A SECRET.
P.L.A.I.N. packages are Best!

Attacks in plain view!!!

Yet another art attack, this time hitting Main and Elm, where various objects were wrapped up like a present.

Who are these artists and what do they want?

"The scariest part of this whole incident, is that they could be anyone."

Chilling words from the Chief of Police offers little hope that attacks can .... happy ending.

THE WHOLE TOWN WAS TALKING ABOUT P.L.A.I.N. EVERYONE HAD AN OPINION ABOUT WHAT WE WERE DOING.

EXTRA CREDIT

$s(\omega t + \phi) = A_1 \cos(\omega t + \phi_1) + A_2 \cos(\omega t + \phi_2$

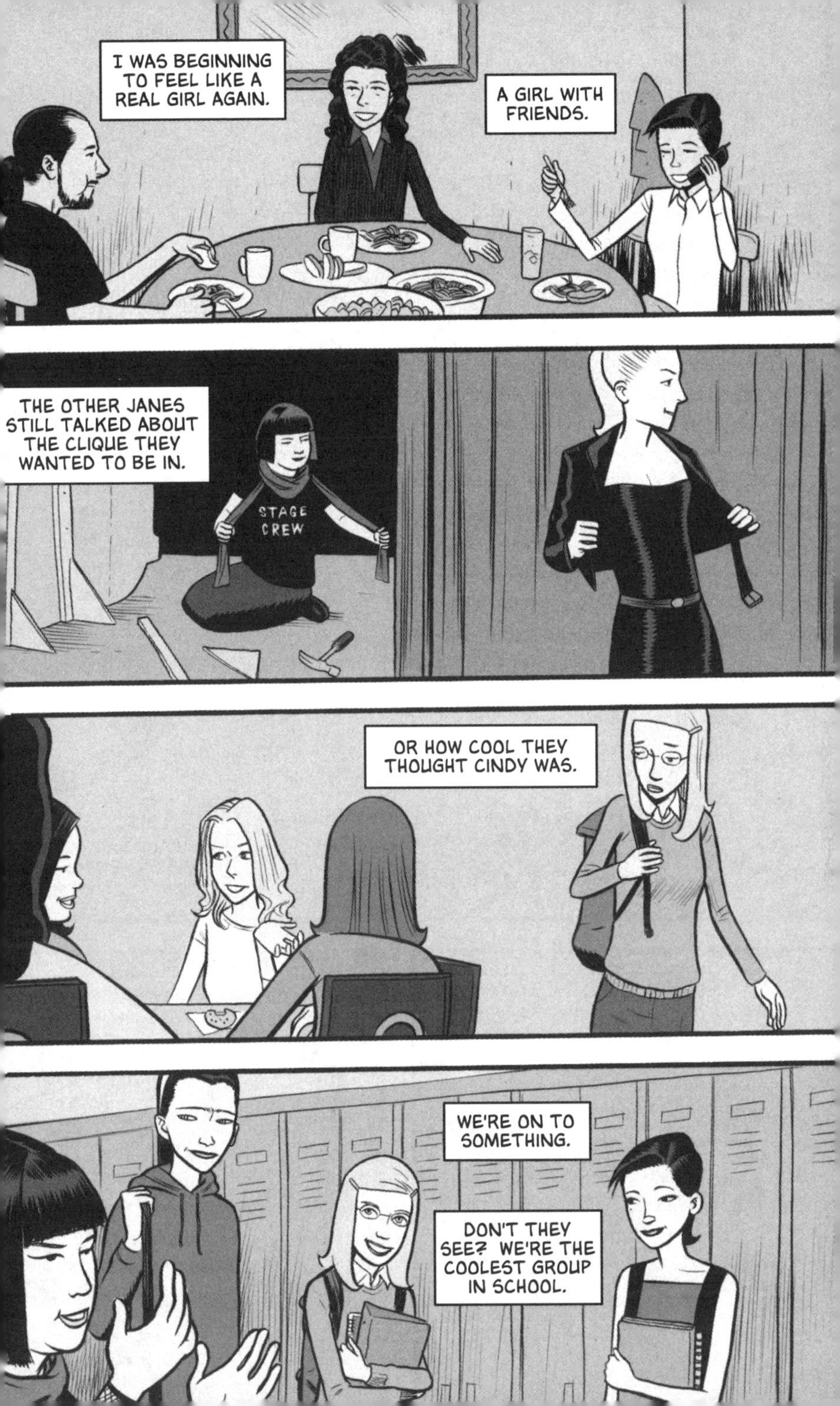
I WAS BEGINNING TO FEEL LIKE A REAL GIRL AGAIN.
A GIRL WITH FRIENDS.
THE OTHER JANES STILL TALKED ABOUT THE CLIQUE THEY WANTED TO BE IN.
STAGE CREW
OR HOW COOL THEY THOUGHT CINDY WAS.
WE'RE ON TO SOMETHING.
DON'T THEY SEE? WE'RE THE COOLEST GROUP IN SCHOOL.

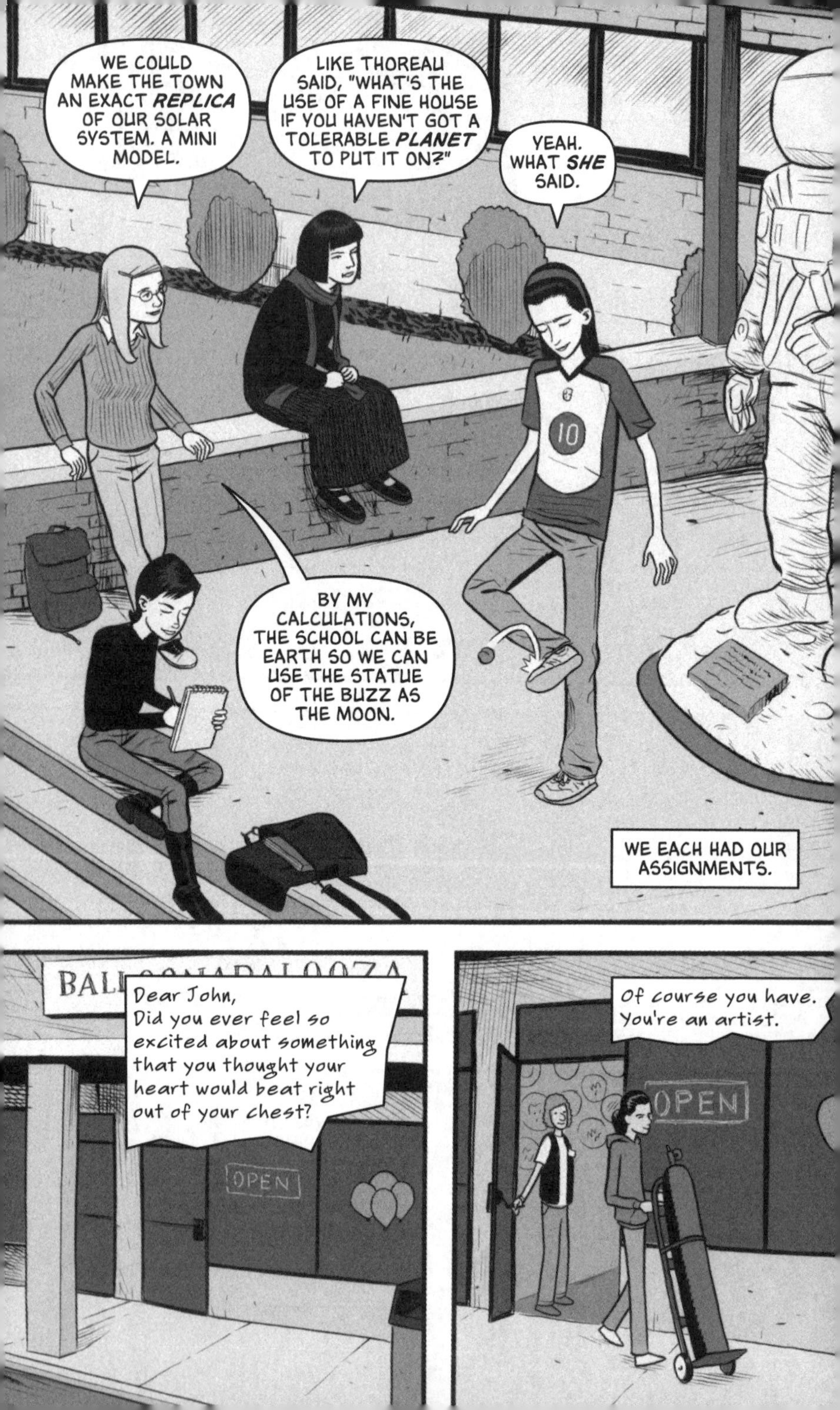
WE COULD MAKE THE TOWN AN EXACT *REPLICA* OF OUR SOLAR SYSTEM. A MINI MODEL.
LIKE THOREAU SAID, "WHAT'S THE USE OF A FINE HOUSE IF YOU HAVEN'T GOT A TOLERABLE *PLANET* TO PUT IT ON?"
YEAH. WHAT *SHE* SAID.
BY MY CALCULATIONS, THE SCHOOL CAN BE EARTH SO WE CAN USE THE STATUE OF THE BUZZ AS THE MOON.
WE EACH HAD OUR ASSIGNMENTS.
Dear John,
Did you ever feel so excited about something that you thought your heart would beat right out of your chest?
OPEN
Of course you have. You're an artist.
OPEN

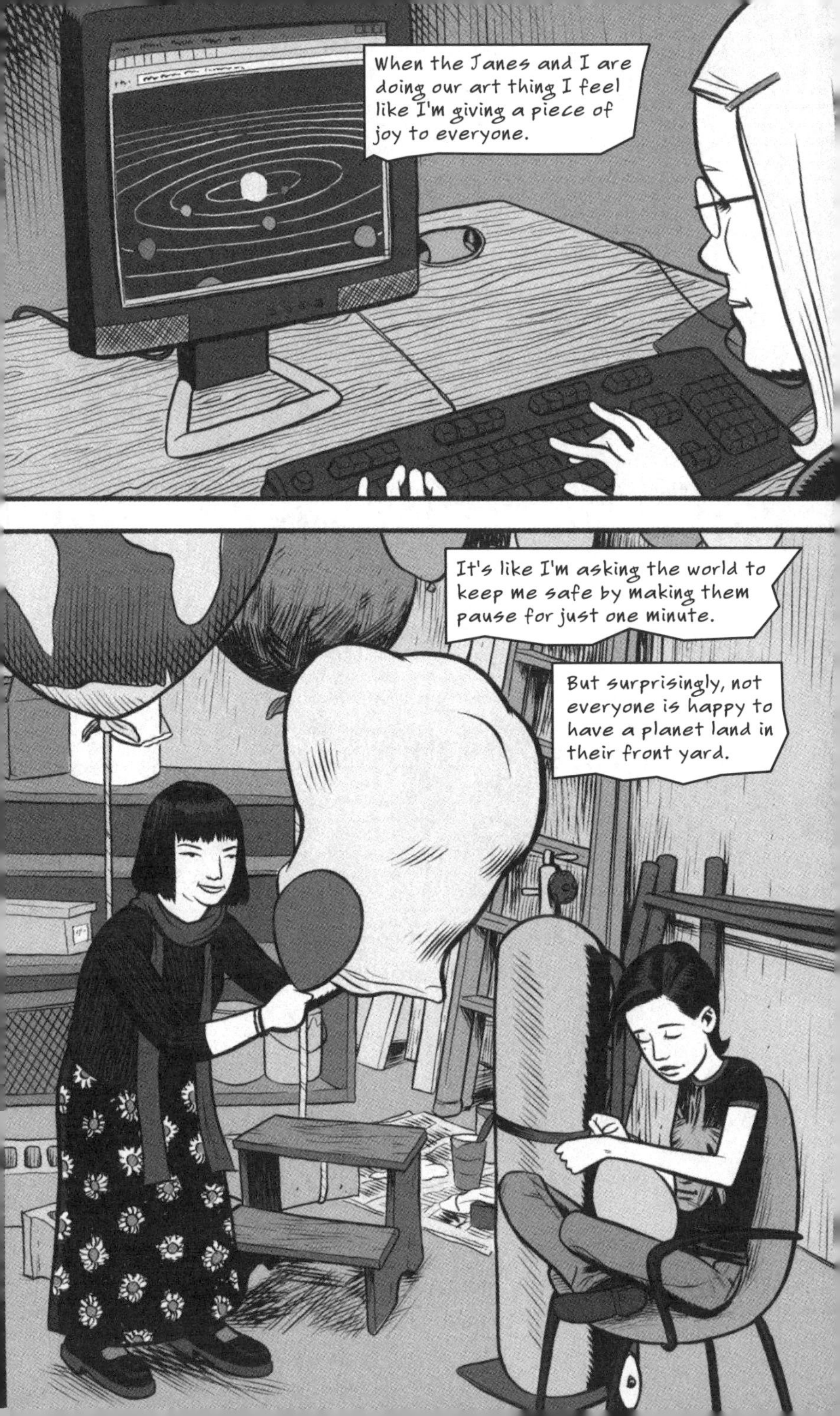
When the Janes and I are doing our art thing I feel like I'm giving a piece of joy to everyone.
It's like I'm asking the world to keep me safe by making them pause for just one minute.
But surprisingly, not everyone is happy to have a planet land in their front yard.

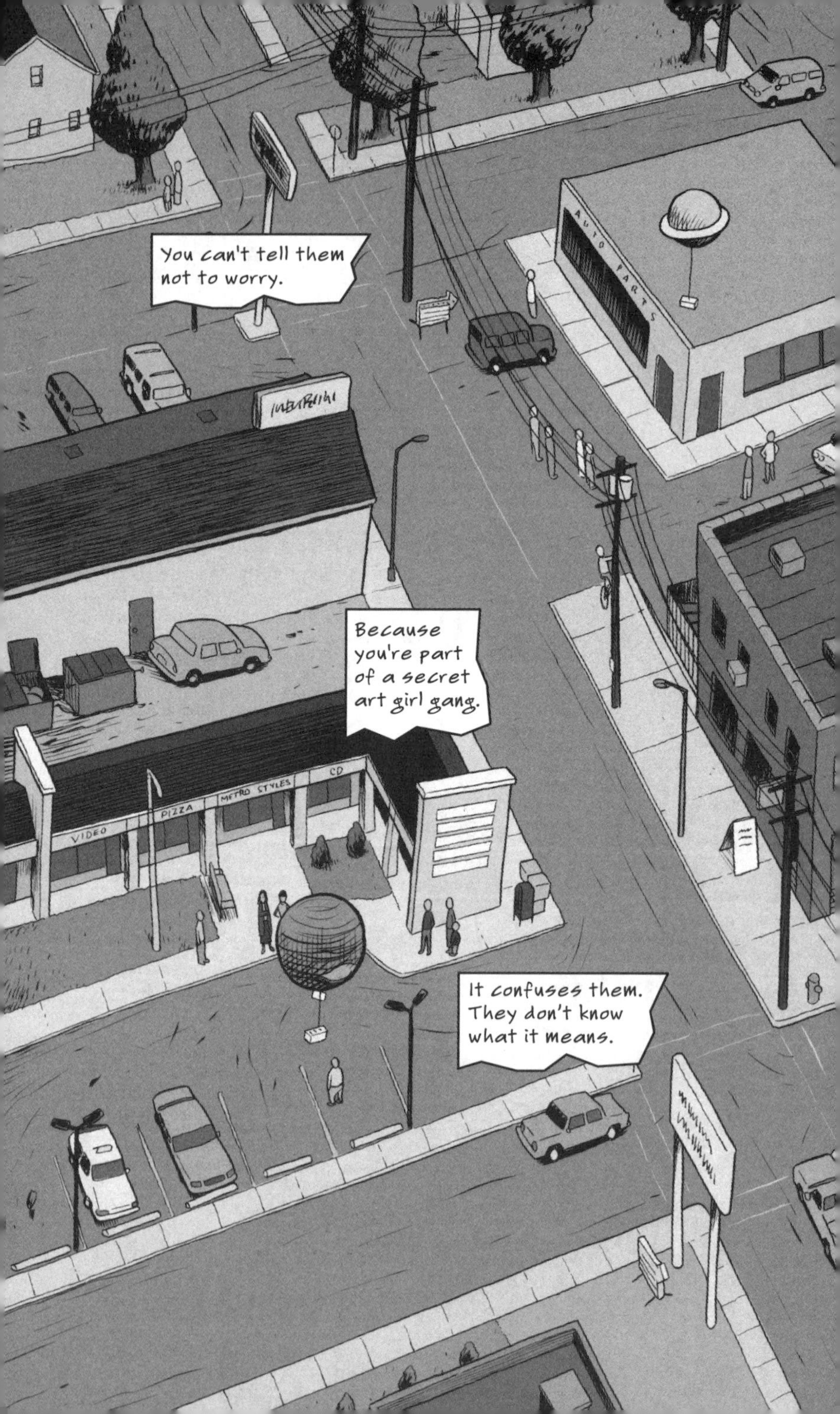
You can't tell them not to worry.
AUTO PARTS
Because you're part of a secret art girl gang.
VIDEO
PIZZA
METRO STYLES
CD
It confuses them. They don't know what it means.

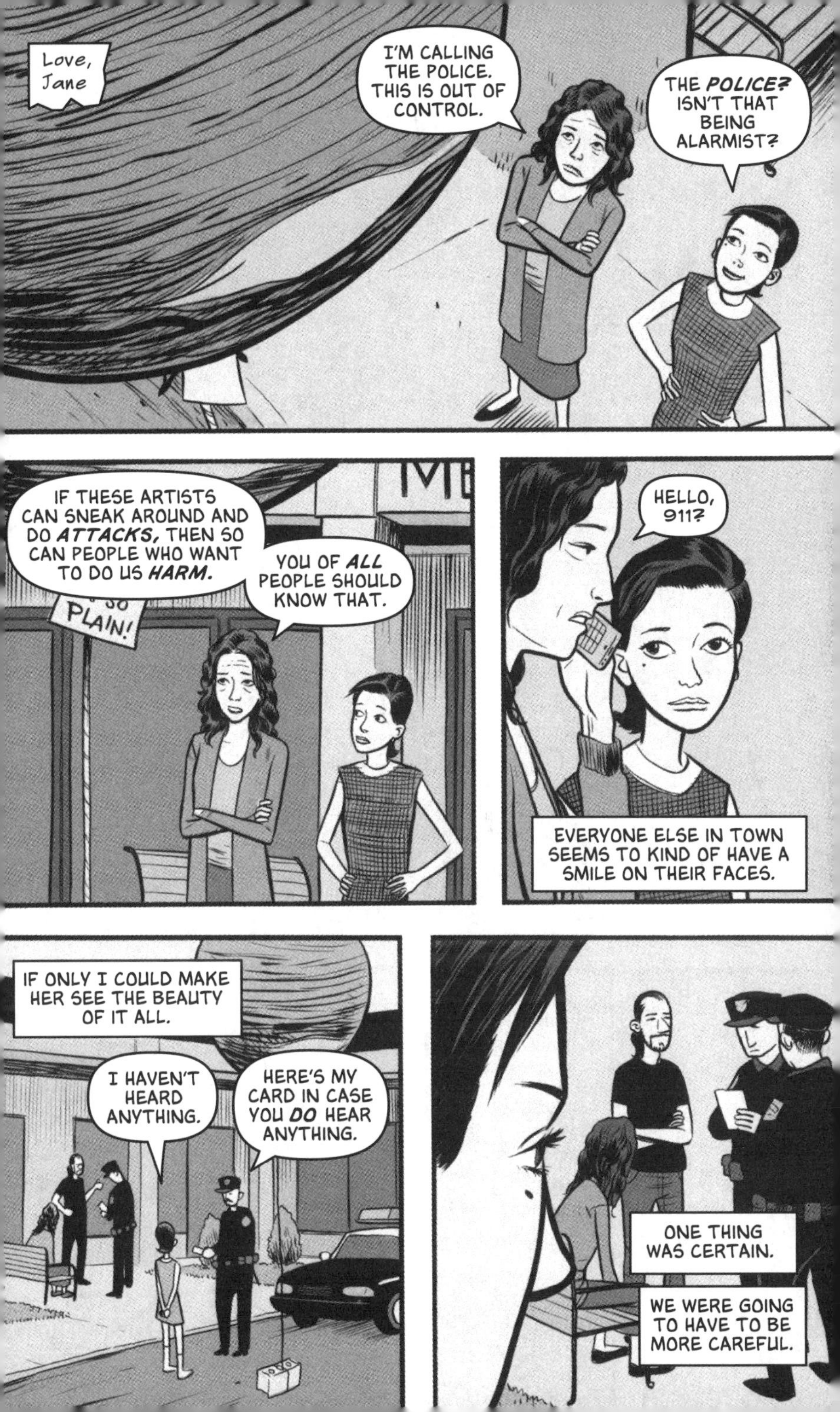
Love, Jane
I'M CALLING THE POLICE. THIS IS OUT OF CONTROL.
THE POLICE? ISN'T THAT BEING ALARMIST?
IF THESE ARTISTS CAN SNEAK AROUND AND DO ATTACKS, THEN SO CAN PEOPLE WHO WANT TO DO US HARM.
YOU OF ALL PEOPLE SHOULD KNOW THAT.
PLAIN!
HELLO, 911?
EVERYONE ELSE IN TOWN SEEMS TO KIND OF HAVE A SMILE ON THEIR FACES.
IF ONLY I COULD MAKE HER SEE THE BEAUTY OF IT ALL.
I HAVEN'T HEARD ANYTHING.
HERE'S MY CARD IN CASE YOU DO HEAR ANYTHING.
ONE THING WAS CERTAIN.
WE WERE GOING TO HAVE TO BE MORE CAREFUL.

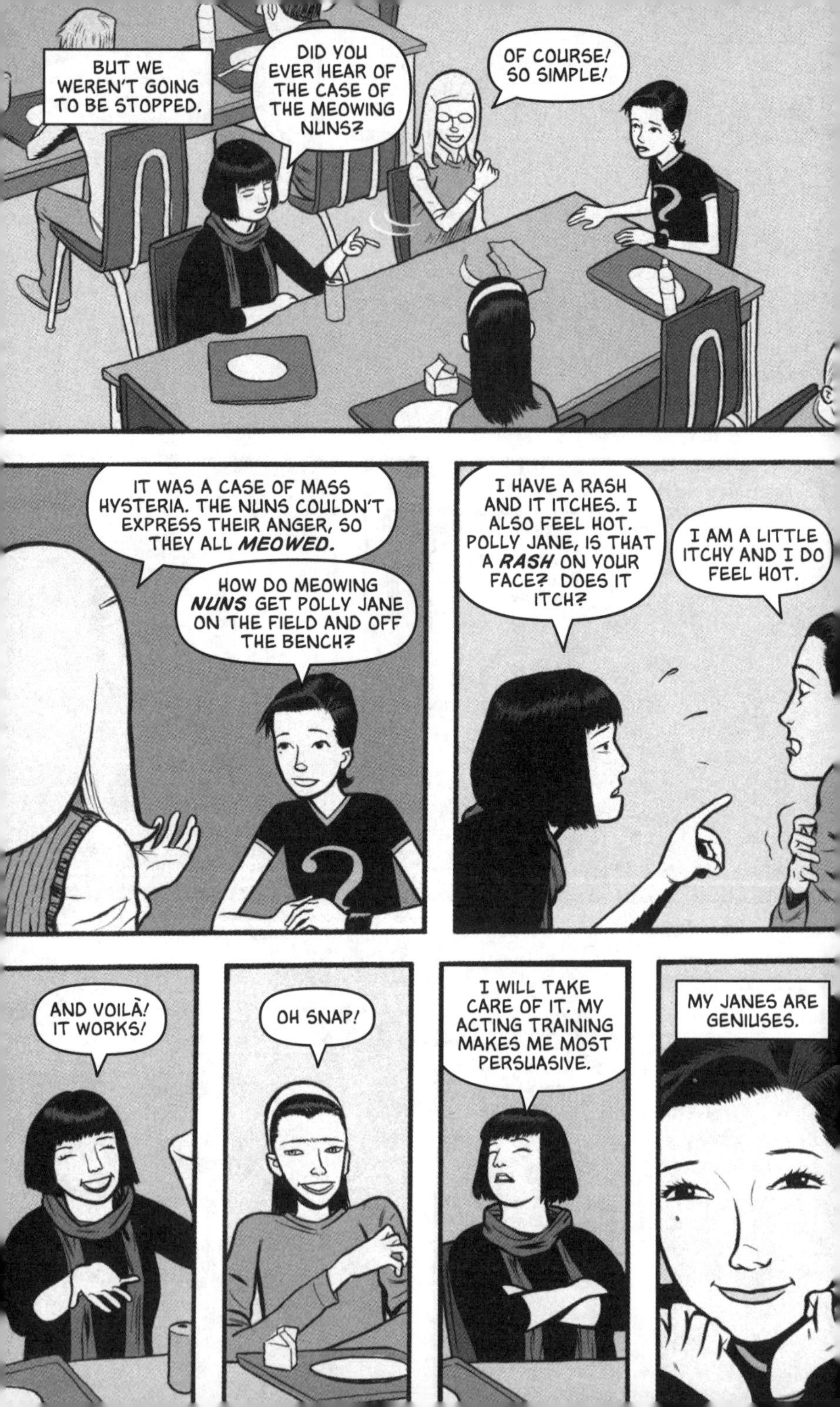

BUT WE WEREN'T GOING TO BE STOPPED.
DID YOU EVER HEAR OF THE CASE OF THE MEOWING NUNS?
OF COURSE! SO SIMPLE!
IT WAS A CASE OF MASS HYSTERIA. THE NUNS COULDN'T EXPRESS THEIR ANGER, SO THEY ALL *MEOWED.*
HOW DO MEOWING *NUNS* GET POLLY JANE ON THE FIELD AND OFF THE BENCH?
I HAVE A RASH AND IT ITCHES. I ALSO FEEL HOT. POLLY JANE, IS THAT A *RASH* ON YOUR FACE? DOES IT ITCH?
I AM A LITTLE ITCHY AND I DO FEEL HOT.
AND VOILÀ! IT WORKS!
OH SNAP!
I WILL TAKE CARE OF IT. MY ACTING TRAINING MAKES ME MOST PERSUASIVE.
MY JANES ARE GENIUSES.

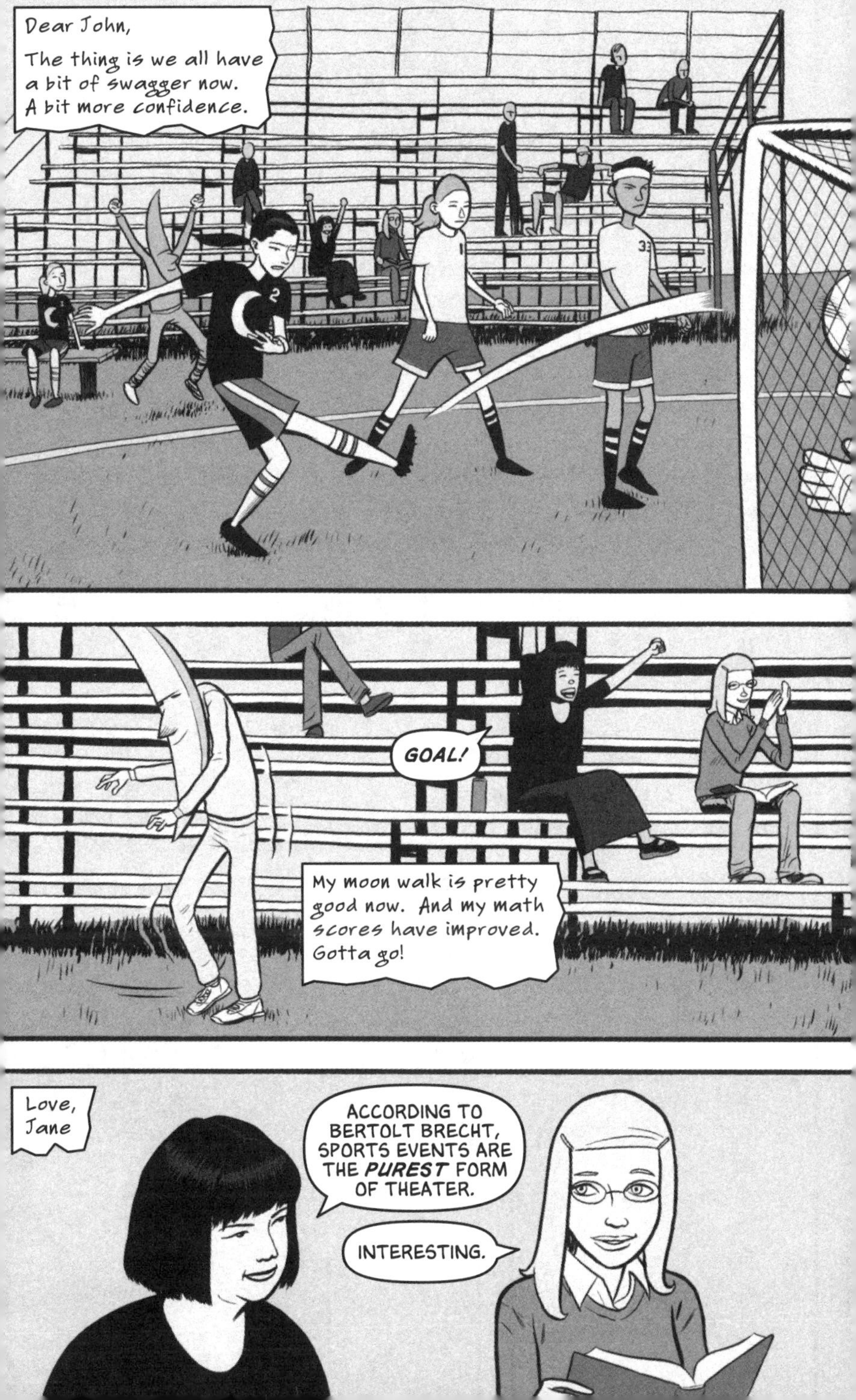
Dear John,
The thing is we all have a bit of swagger now. A bit more confidence.
GOAL!
My moon walk is pretty good now. And my math scores have improved. Gotta go!
Love, Jane
ACCORDING TO BERTOLT BRECHT, SPORTS EVENTS ARE THE PUREST FORM OF THEATER.
INTERESTING.

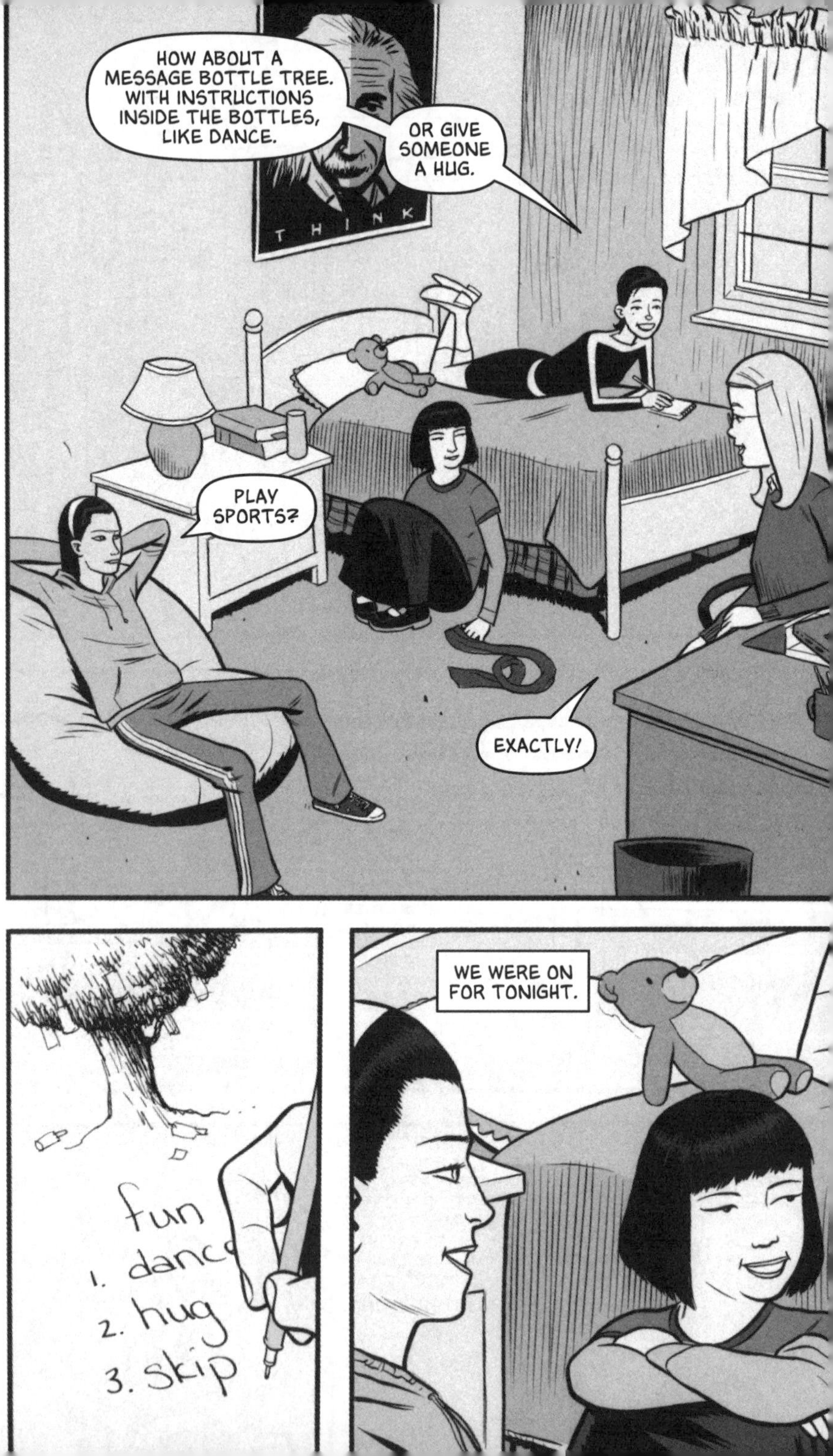

THINK
HOW ABOUT A MESSAGE BOTTLE TREE. WITH INSTRUCTIONS INSIDE THE BOTTLES, LIKE DANCE.
OR GIVE SOMEONE A HUG.
PLAY SPORTS?
EXACTLY!
fun
1. danc
2. hug
3. skip
WE WERE ON FOR TONIGHT.

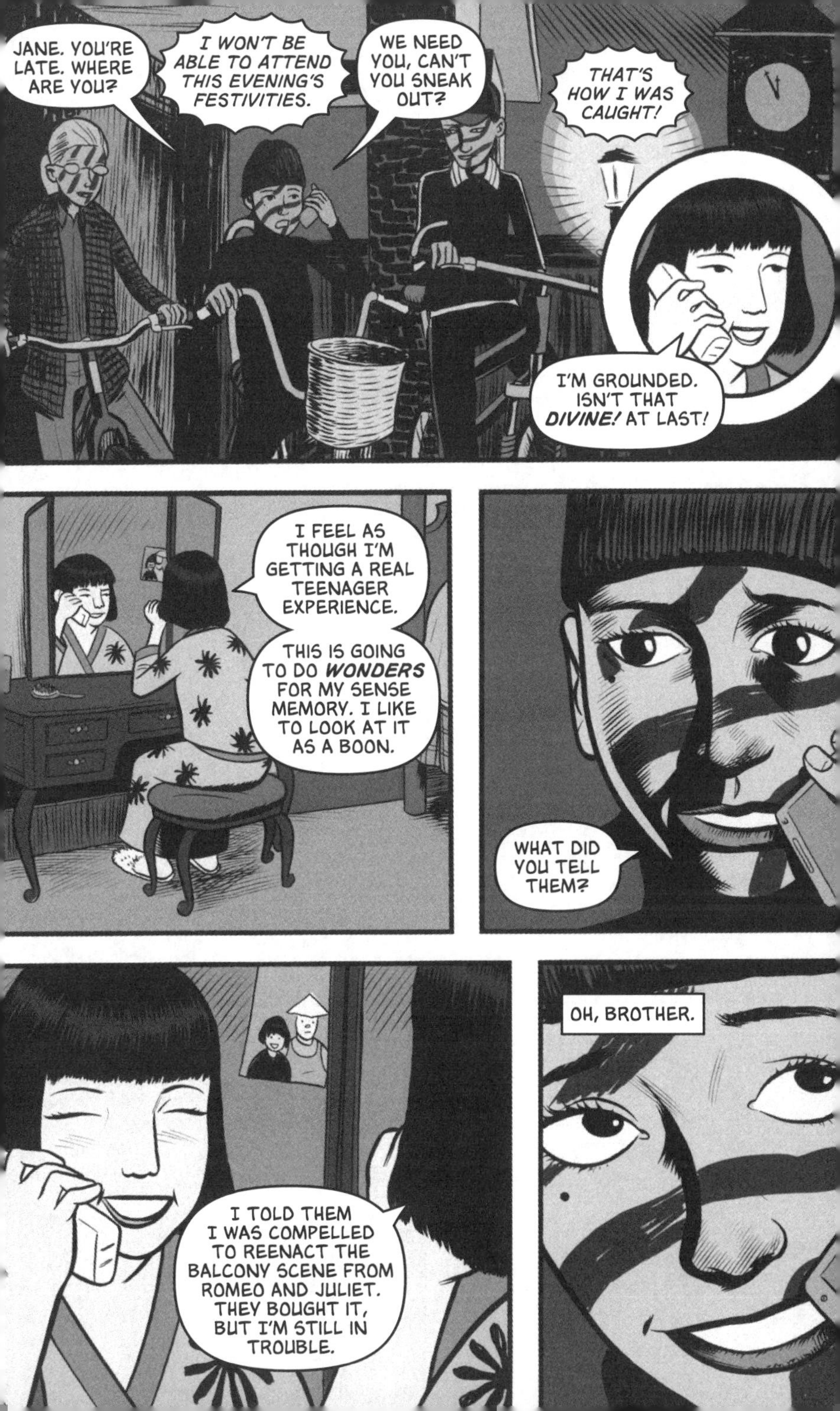
JANE. YOU'RE LATE. WHERE ARE YOU?
I WON'T BE ABLE TO ATTEND THIS EVENING'S FESTIVITIES.
WE NEED YOU, CAN'T YOU SNEAK OUT?
THAT'S HOW I WAS CAUGHT!
I'M GROUNDED. ISN'T THAT DIVINE! AT LAST!
I FEEL AS THOUGH I'M GETTING A REAL TEENAGER EXPERIENCE.
THIS IS GOING TO DO WONDERS FOR MY SENSE MEMORY. I LIKE TO LOOK AT IT AS A BOON.
WHAT DID YOU TELL THEM?
I TOLD THEM I WAS COMPELLED TO REENACT THE BALCONY SCENE FROM ROMEO AND JULIET. THEY BOUGHT IT, BUT I'M STILL IN TROUBLE.
OH, BROTHER.

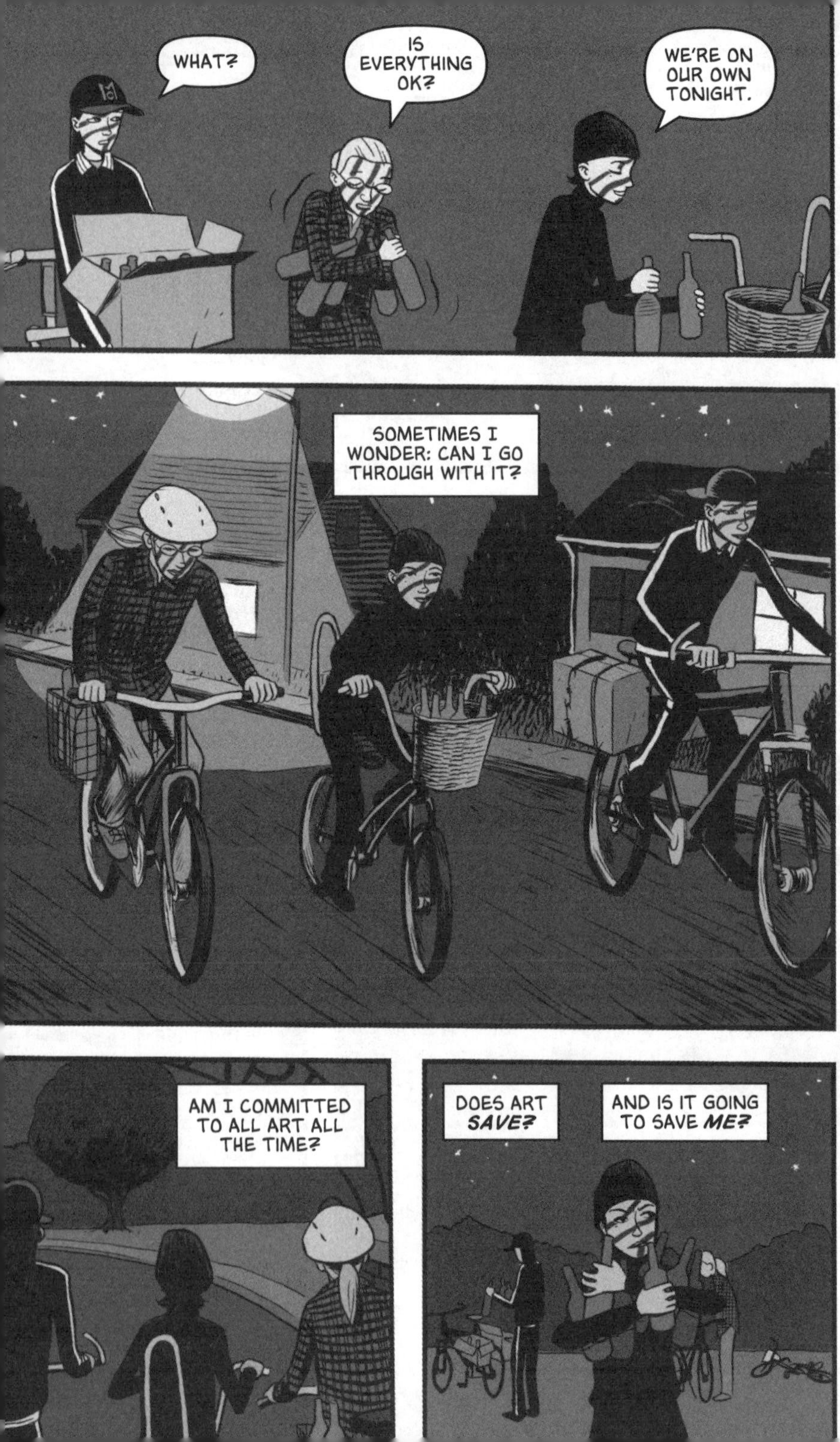
WHAT?
IS EVERYTHING OK?
WE'RE ON OUR OWN TONIGHT.
SOMETIMES I WONDER: CAN I GO THROUGH WITH IT?
AM I COMMITTED TO ALL ART ALL THE TIME?
DOES ART *SAVE?*
AND IS IT GOING TO SAVE *ME?*

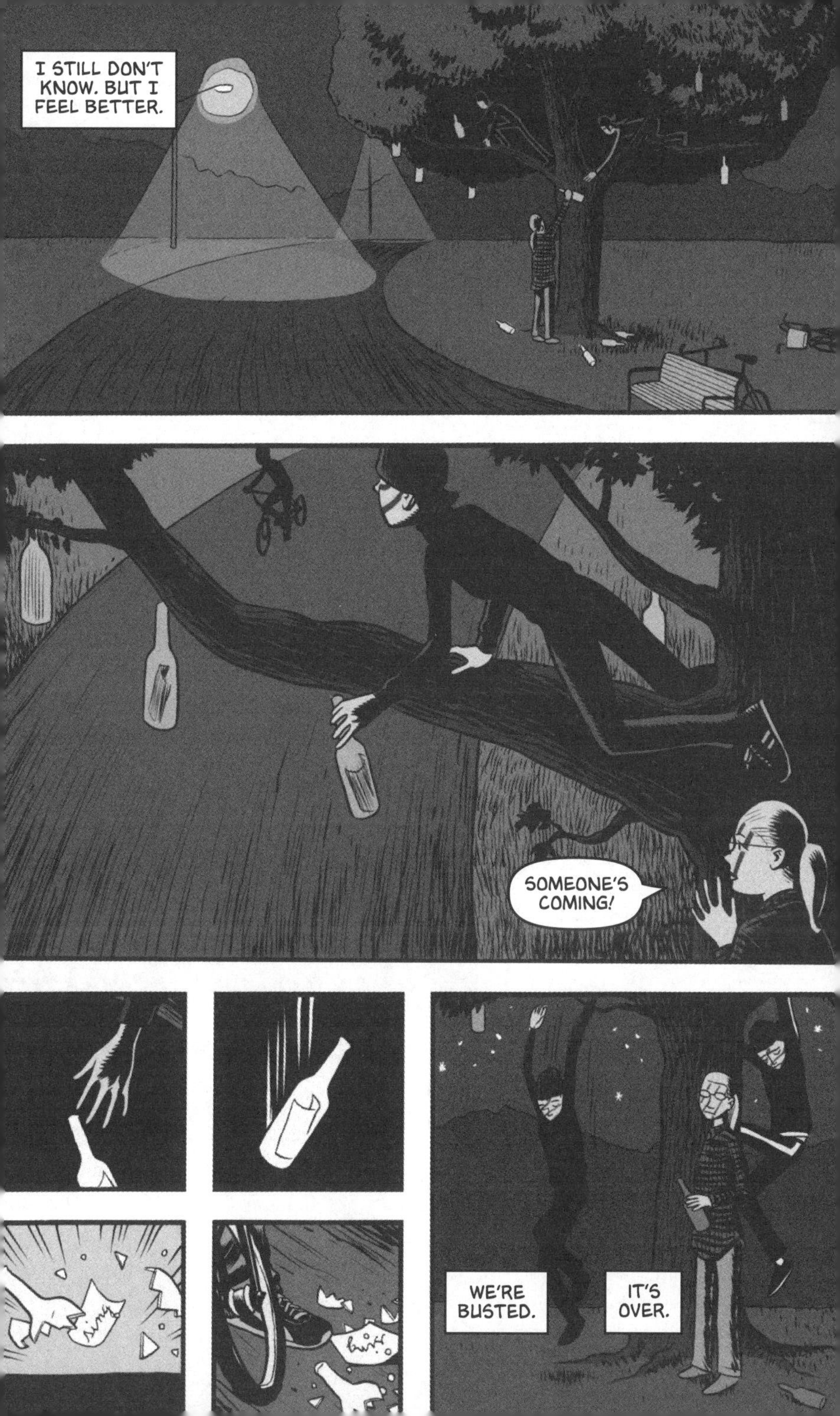
I STILL DON'T KNOW. BUT I FEEL BETTER.
SOMEONE'S COMING!
WE'RE BUSTED.
IT'S OVER.

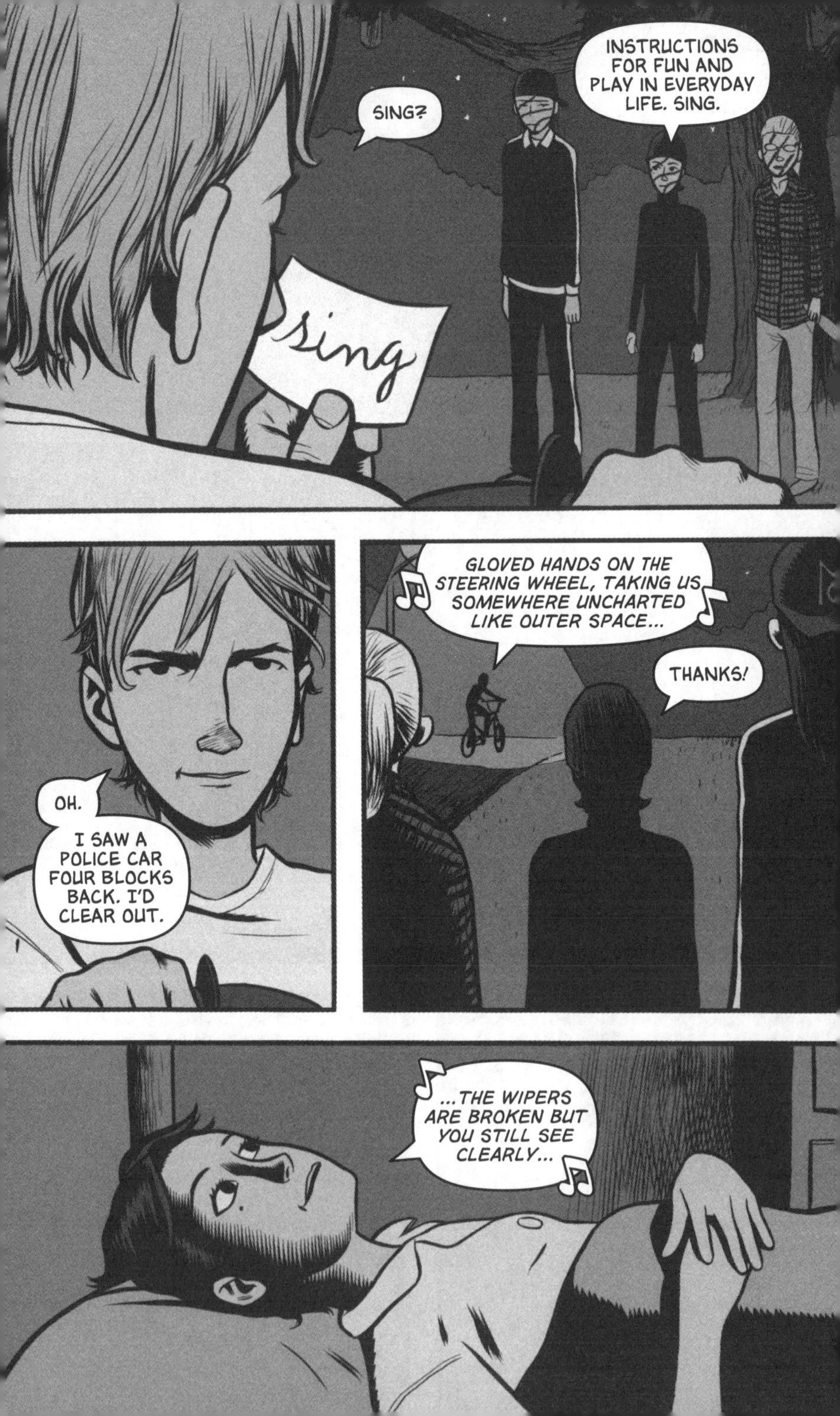
INSTRUCTIONS FOR FUN AND PLAY IN EVERYDAY LIFE. SING.
SING?
sing
OH.
I SAW A POLICE CAR FOUR BLOCKS BACK. I'D CLEAR OUT.
GLOVED HANDS ON THE STEERING WHEEL, TAKING US SOMEWHERE UNCHARTED LIKE OUTER SPACE...
THANKS!
...THE WIPERS ARE BROKEN BUT YOU STILL SEE CLEARLY...

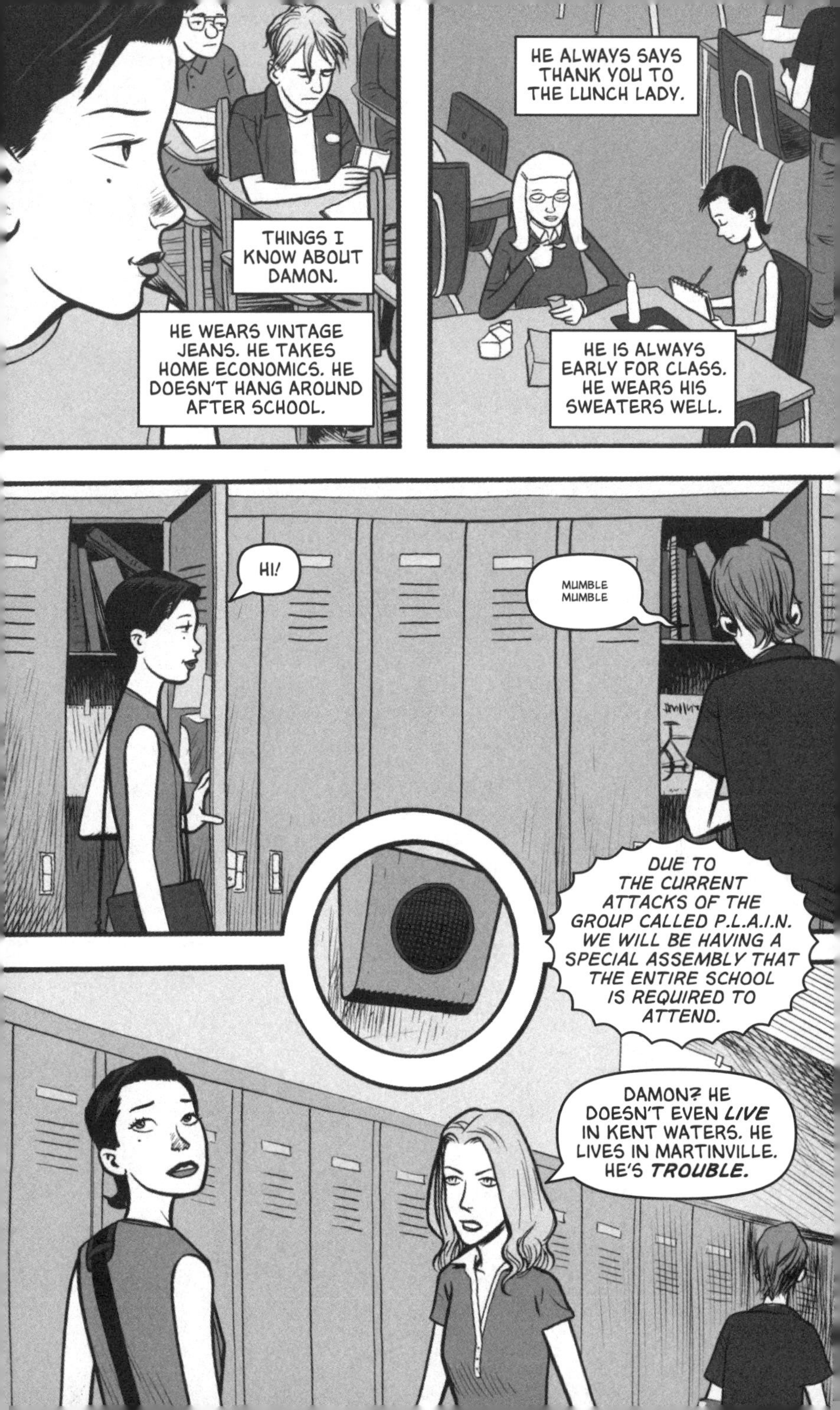
THINGS I KNOW ABOUT DAMON.
HE WEARS VINTAGE JEANS. HE TAKES HOME ECONOMICS. HE DOESN'T HANG AROUND AFTER SCHOOL.
HE ALWAYS SAYS THANK YOU TO THE LUNCH LADY.
HE IS ALWAYS EARLY FOR CLASS. HE WEARS HIS SWEATERS WELL.
HI!
MUMBLE MUMBLE
DUE TO THE CURRENT ATTACKS OF THE GROUP CALLED P.L.A.I.N. WE WILL BE HAVING A SPECIAL ASSEMBLY THAT THE ENTIRE SCHOOL IS REQUIRED TO ATTEND.
DAMON? HE DOESN'T EVEN LIVE IN KENT WATERS. HE LIVES IN MARTINVILLE. HE'S TROUBLE.

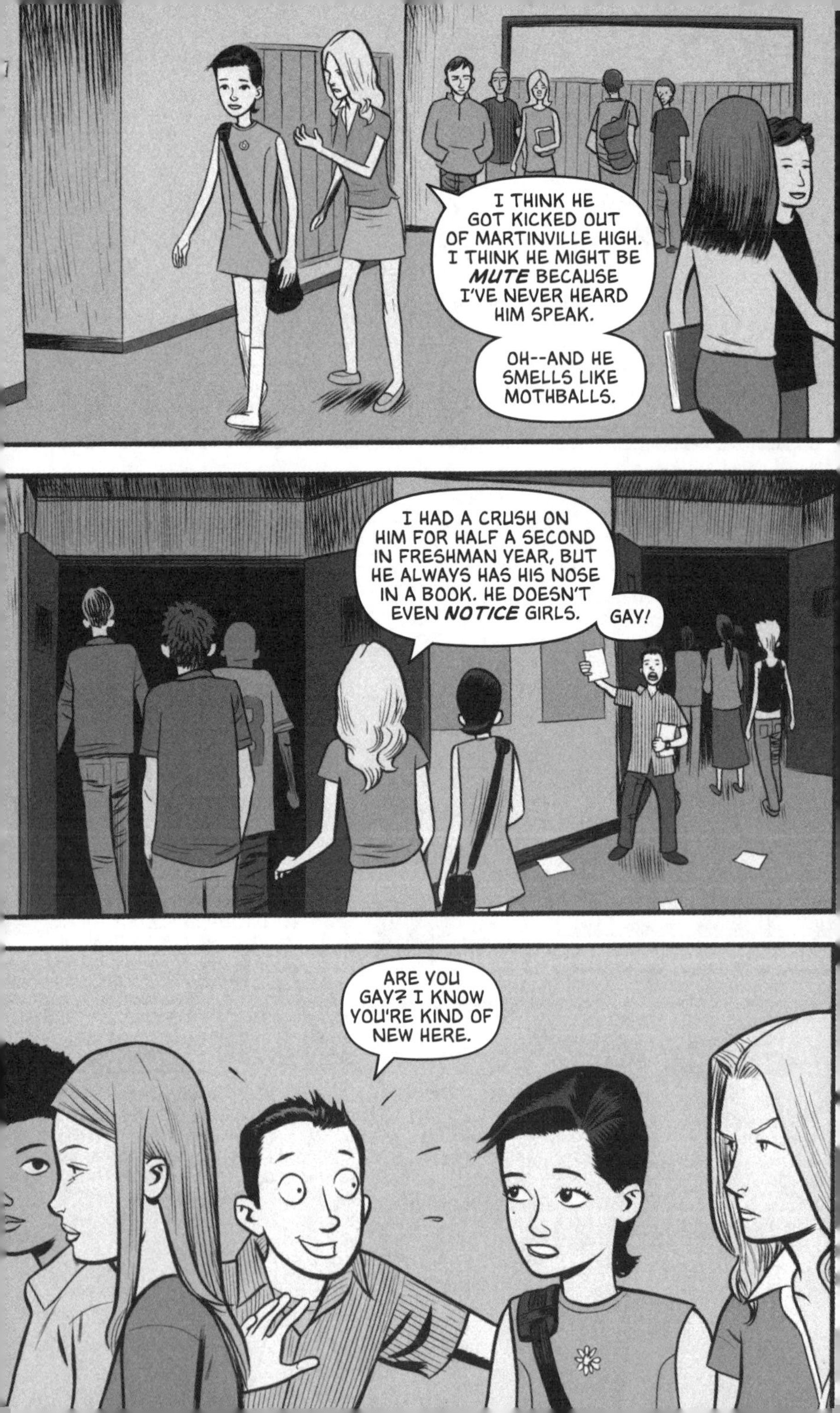
I THINK HE GOT KICKED OUT OF MARTINVILLE HIGH. I THINK HE MIGHT BE *MUTE* BECAUSE I'VE NEVER HEARD HIM SPEAK.
OH--AND HE SMELLS LIKE MOTHBALLS.
I HAD A CRUSH ON HIM FOR HALF A SECOND IN FRESHMAN YEAR, BUT HE ALWAYS HAS HIS NOSE IN A BOOK. HE DOESN'T EVEN *NOTICE* GIRLS.
GAY!
ARE YOU GAY? I KNOW YOU'RE KIND OF NEW HERE.

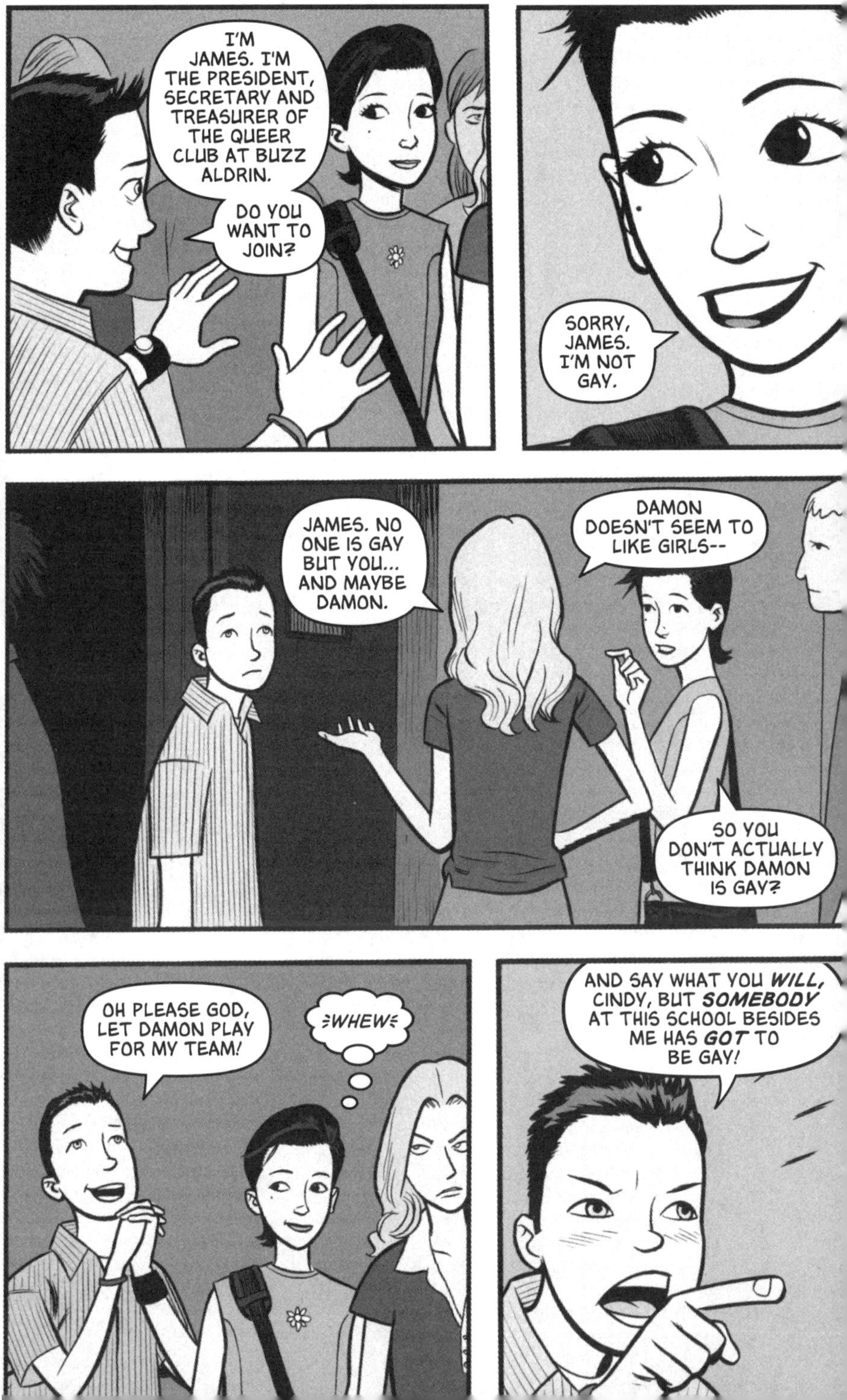
I'M JAMES. I'M THE PRESIDENT, SECRETARY AND TREASURER OF THE QUEER CLUB AT BUZZ ALDRIN.
DO YOU WANT TO JOIN?
SORRY, JAMES. I'M NOT GAY.
JAMES. NO ONE IS GAY BUT YOU... AND MAYBE DAMON.
DAMON DOESN'T SEEM TO LIKE GIRLS--
SO YOU DON'T ACTUALLY THINK DAMON IS GAY?
OH PLEASE GOD, LET DAMON PLAY FOR MY TEAM!
WHEW
AND SAY WHAT YOU WILL, CINDY, BUT SOMEBODY AT THIS SCHOOL BESIDES ME HAS GOT TO BE GAY!

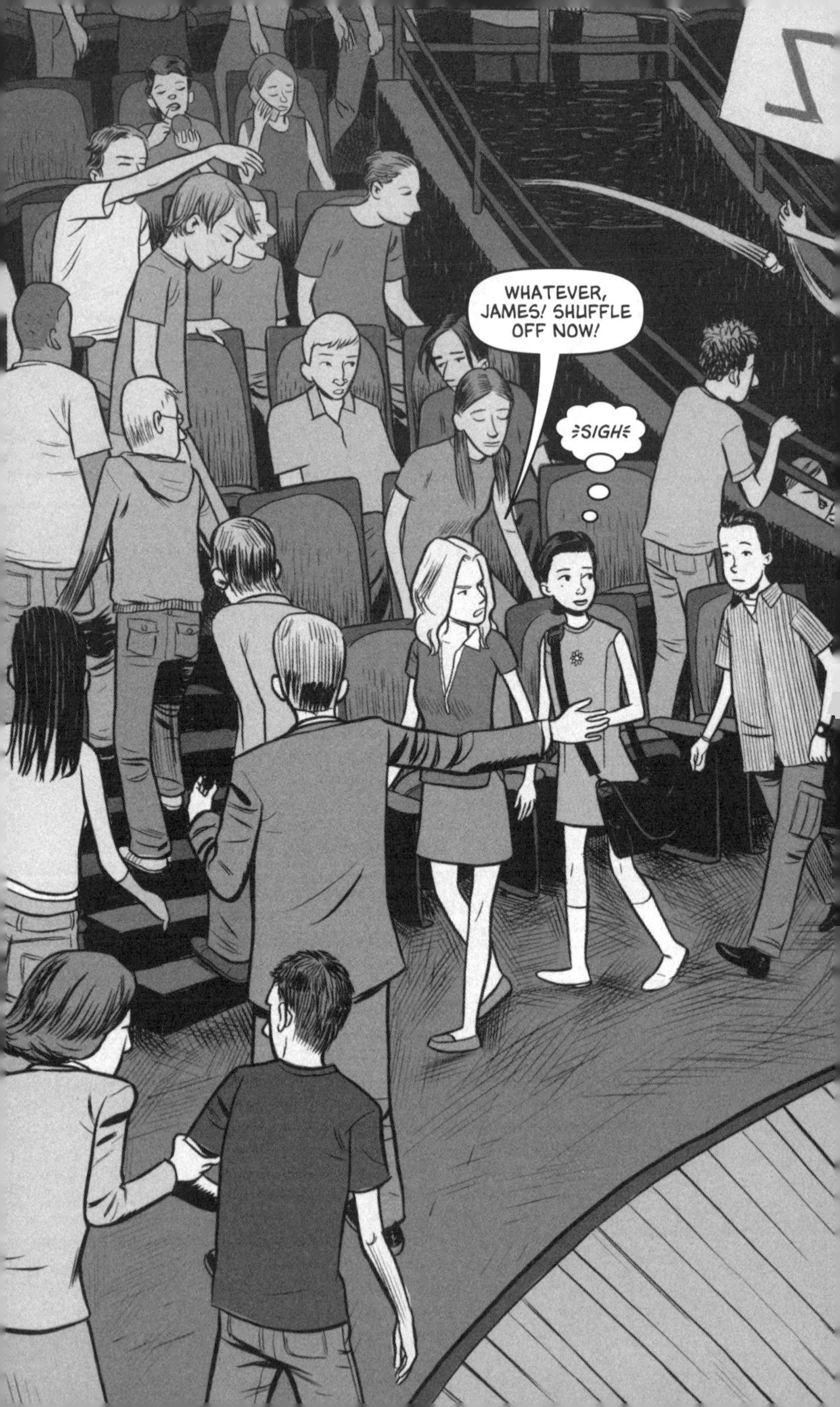
WHATEVER, JAMES! SHUFFLE OFF NOW!
SIGH

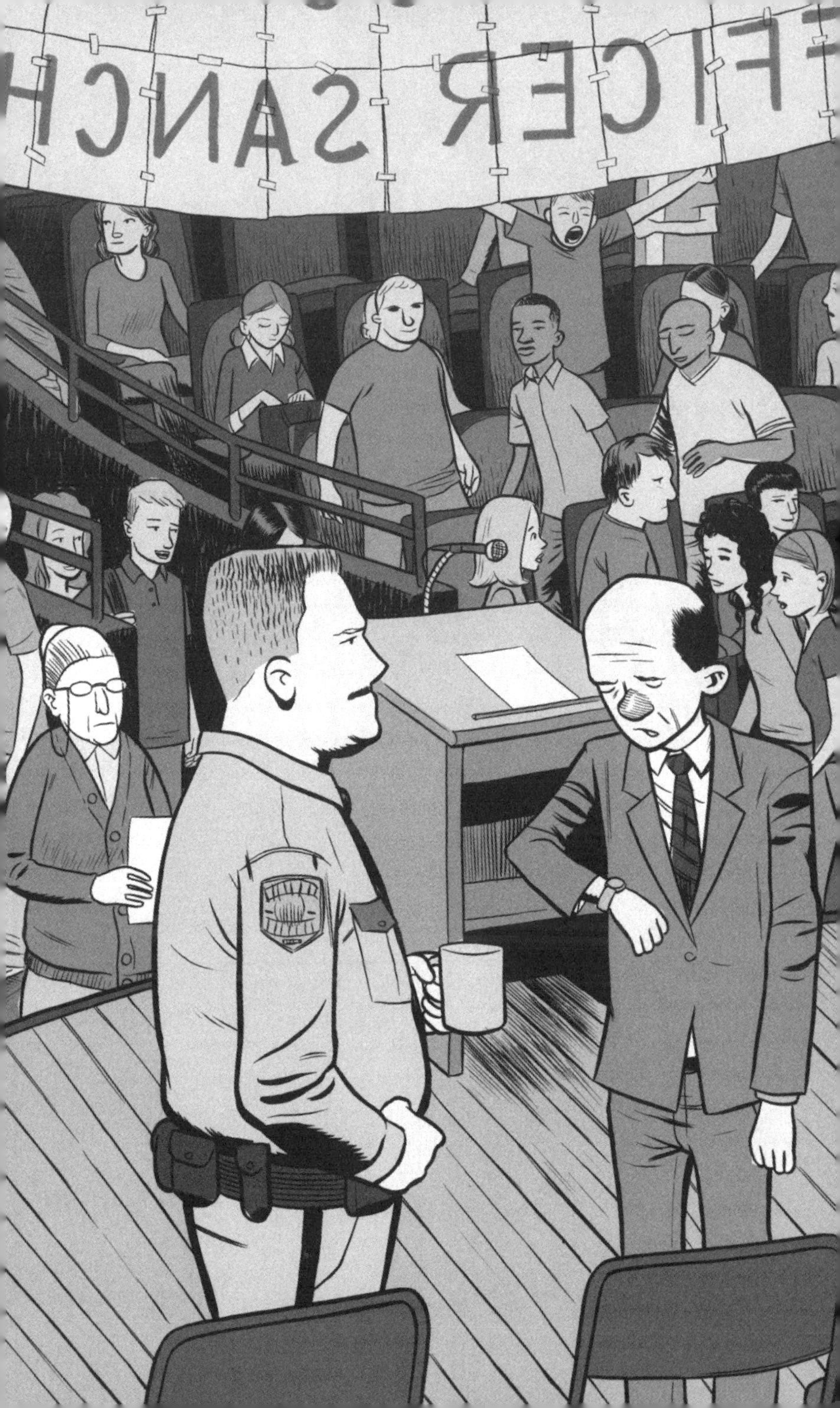
FICER SANCH

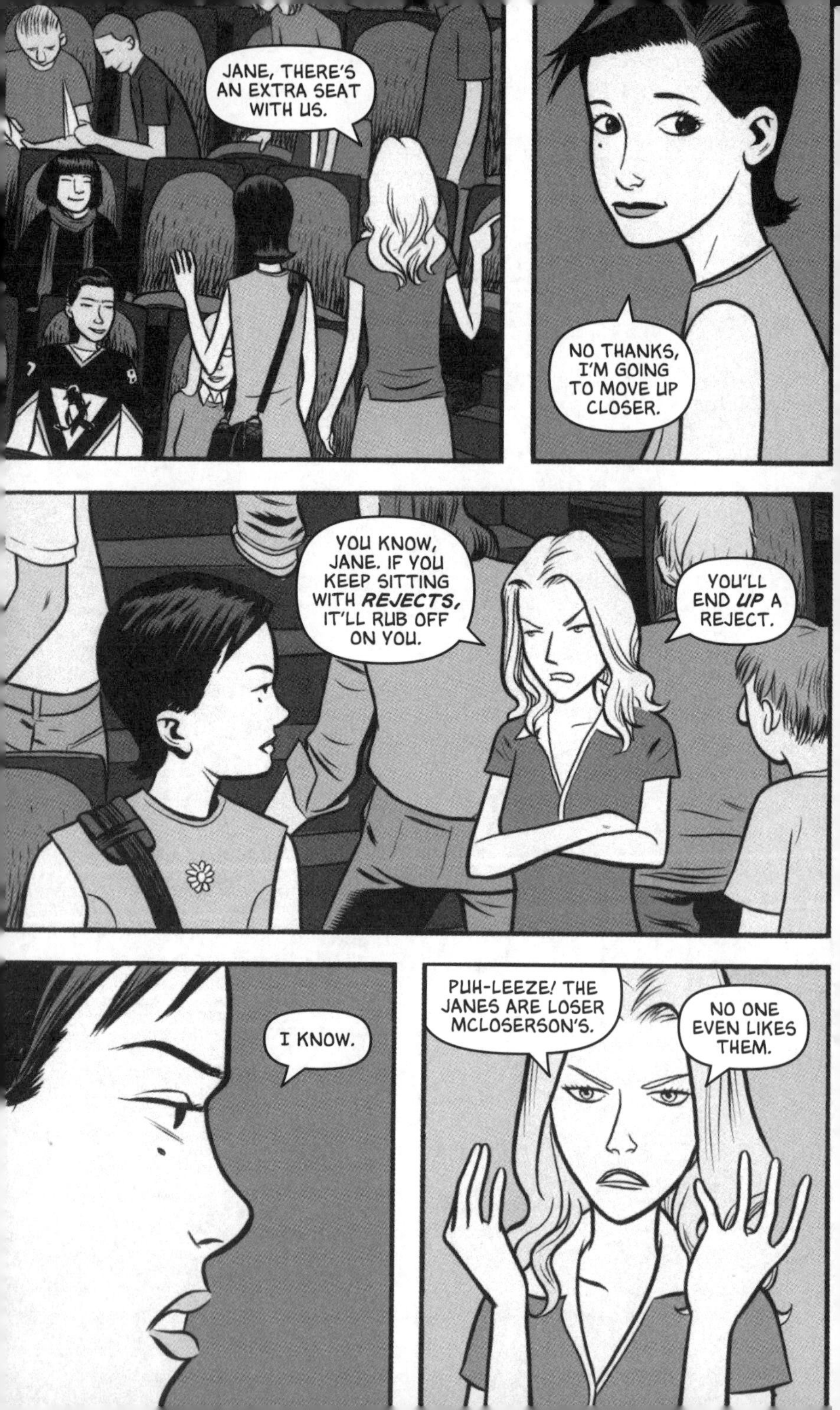
JANE, THERE'S AN EXTRA SEAT WITH US.
NO THANKS, I'M GOING TO MOVE UP CLOSER.
YOU KNOW, JANE. IF YOU KEEP SITTING WITH *REJECTS,* IT'LL RUB OFF ON YOU.
YOU'LL END *UP* A REJECT.
I KNOW.
PUH-LEEZE! THE JANES ARE LOSER MCLOSERSON'S.
NO ONE EVEN LIKES THEM.

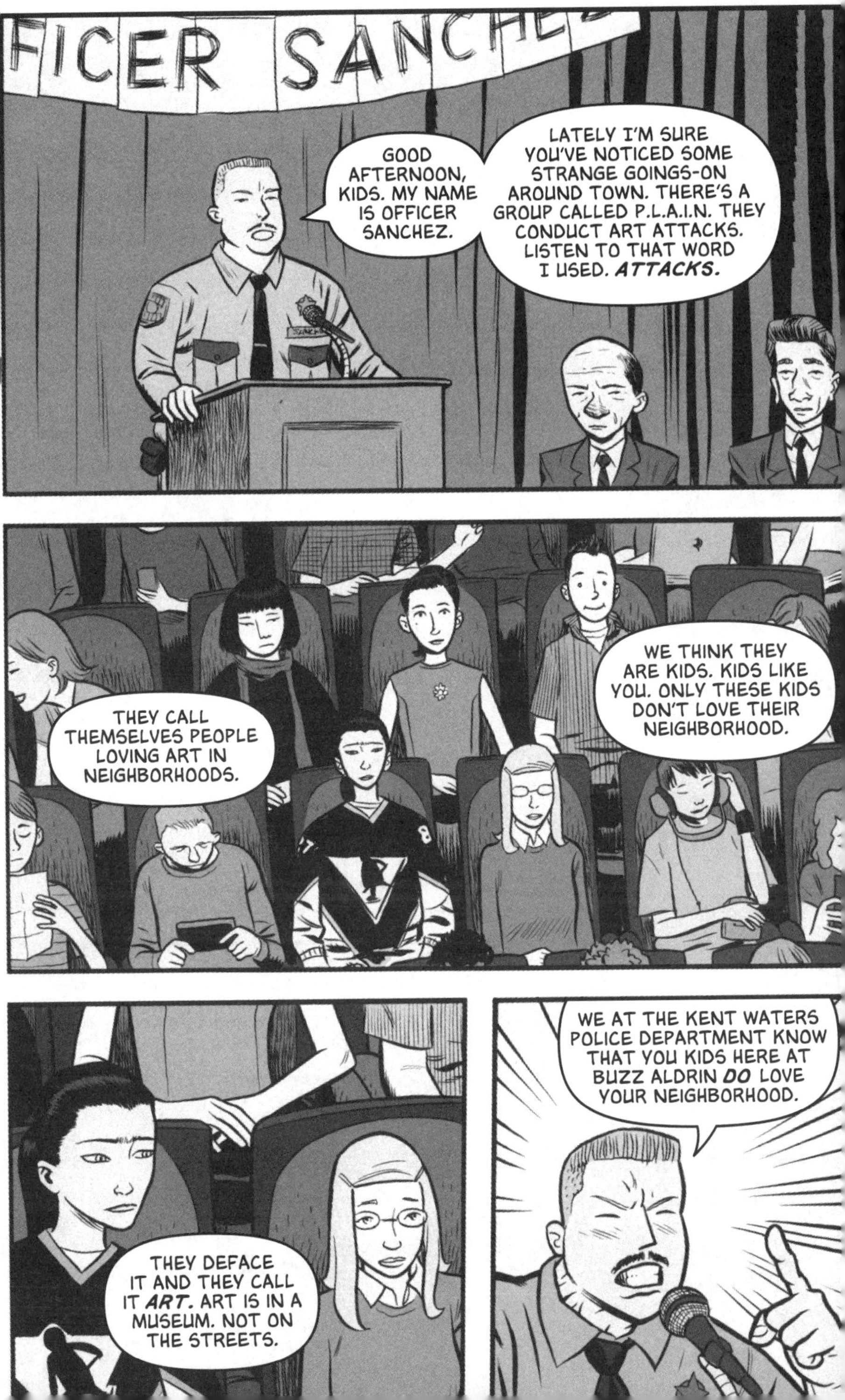
FICER SANCHEZ
GOOD AFTERNOON, KIDS. MY NAME IS OFFICER SANCHEZ.
LATELY I'M SURE YOU'VE NOTICED SOME STRANGE GOINGS-ON AROUND TOWN. THERE'S A GROUP CALLED P.L.A.I.N. THEY CONDUCT ART ATTACKS. LISTEN TO THAT WORD I USED. ***ATTACKS.***
THEY CALL THEMSELVES PEOPLE LOVING ART IN NEIGHBORHOODS.
WE THINK THEY ARE KIDS. KIDS LIKE YOU. ONLY THESE KIDS DON'T LOVE THEIR NEIGHBORHOOD.
THEY DEFACE IT AND THEY CALL IT ***ART.*** ART IS IN A MUSEUM. NOT ON THE STREETS.
WE AT THE KENT WATERS POLICE DEPARTMENT KNOW THAT YOU KIDS HERE AT BUZZ ALDRIN ***DO*** LOVE YOUR NEIGHBORHOOD.

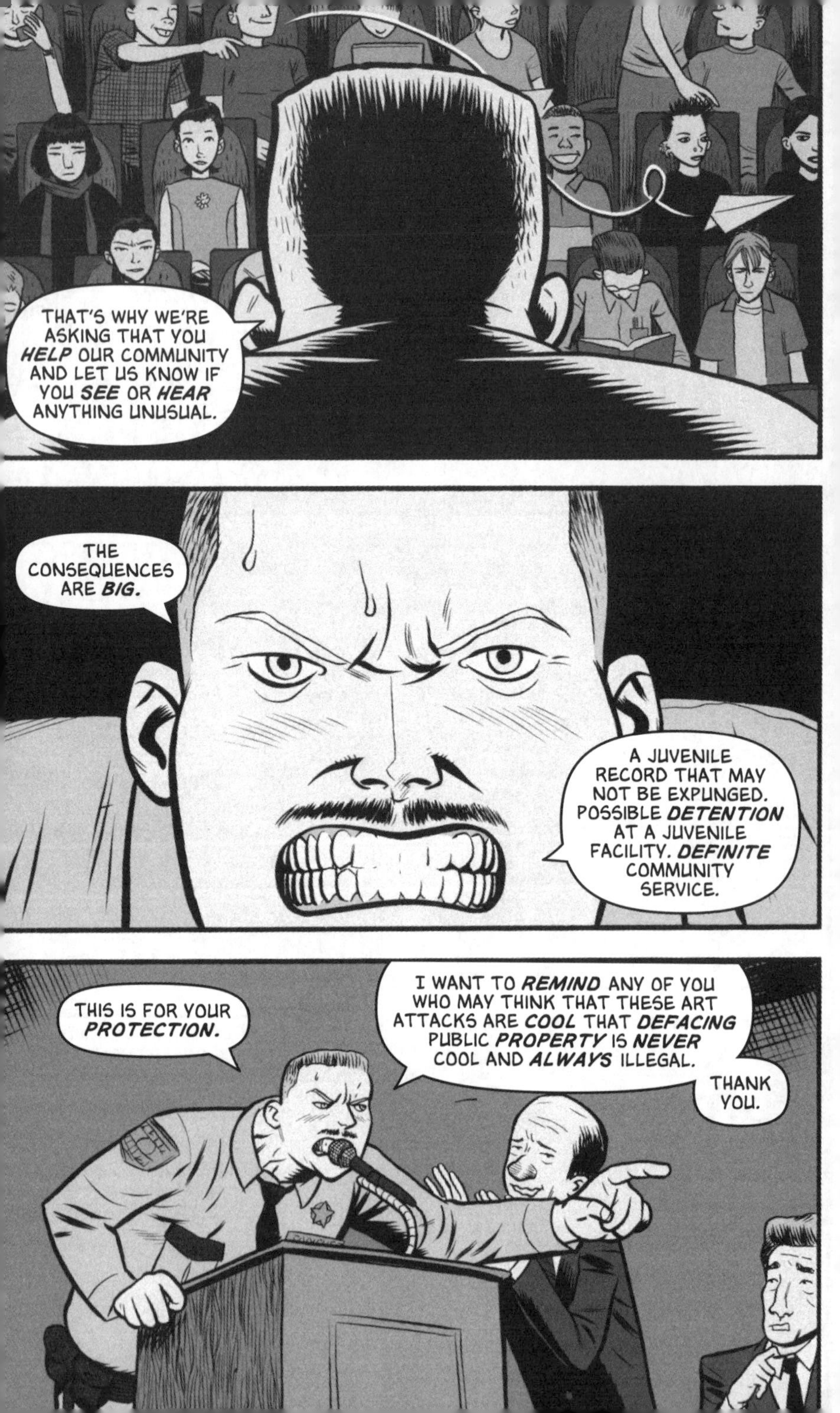
THAT'S WHY WE'RE ASKING THAT YOU HELP OUR COMMUNITY AND LET US KNOW IF YOU SEE OR HEAR ANYTHING UNUSUAL.
THE CONSEQUENCES ARE BIG.
A JUVENILE RECORD THAT MAY NOT BE EXPUNGED. POSSIBLE DETENTION AT A JUVENILE FACILITY. DEFINITE COMMUNITY SERVICE.
THIS IS FOR YOUR PROTECTION.
I WANT TO REMIND ANY OF YOU WHO MAY THINK THAT THESE ART ATTACKS ARE COOL THAT DEFACING PUBLIC PROPERTY IS NEVER COOL AND ALWAYS ILLEGAL.
THANK YOU.

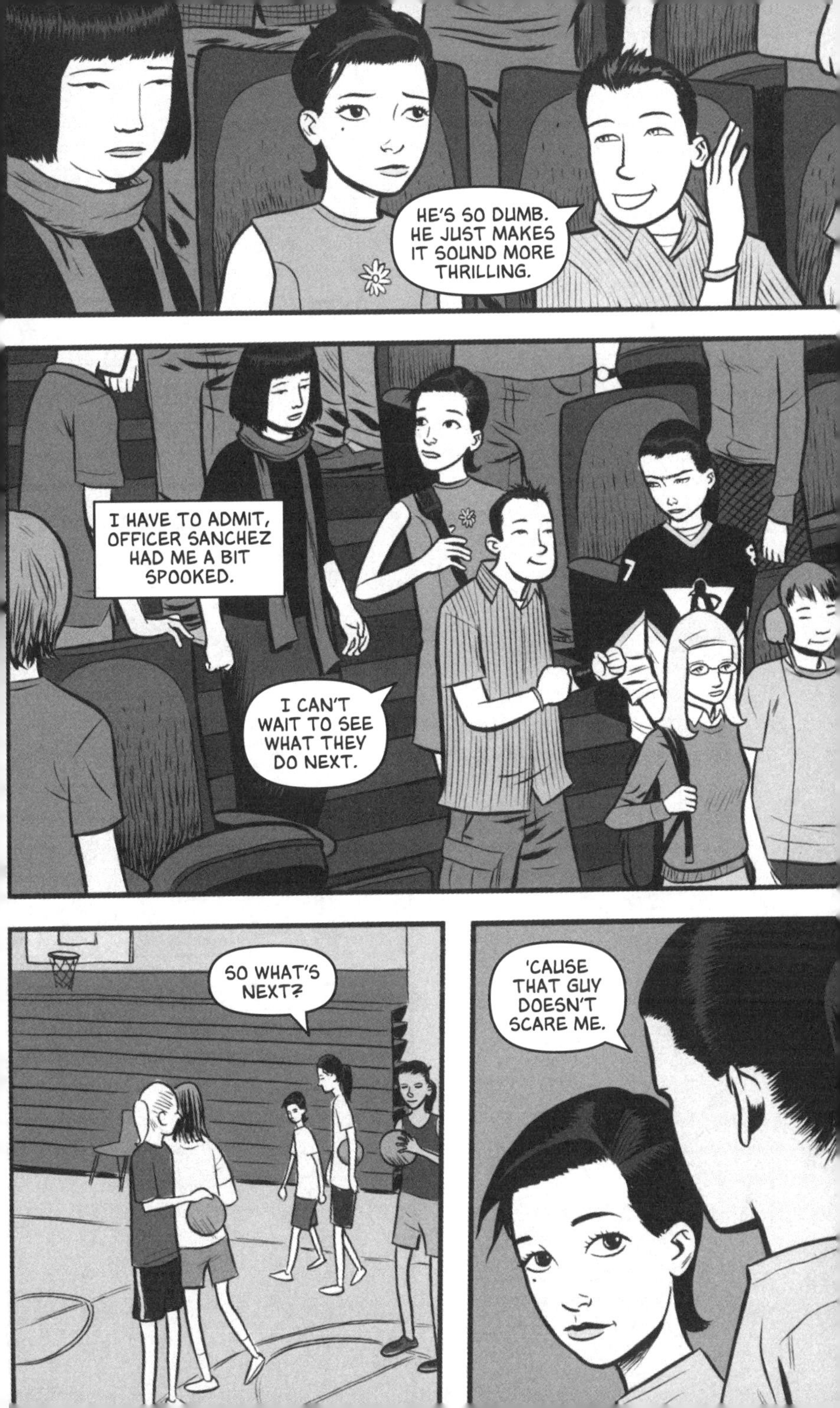
HE'S SO DUMB. HE JUST MAKES IT SOUND MORE THRILLING.
I HAVE TO ADMIT, OFFICER SANCHEZ HAD ME A BIT SPOOKED.
I CAN'T WAIT TO SEE WHAT THEY DO NEXT.
SO WHAT'S NEXT?
'CAUSE THAT GUY DOESN'T SCARE ME.

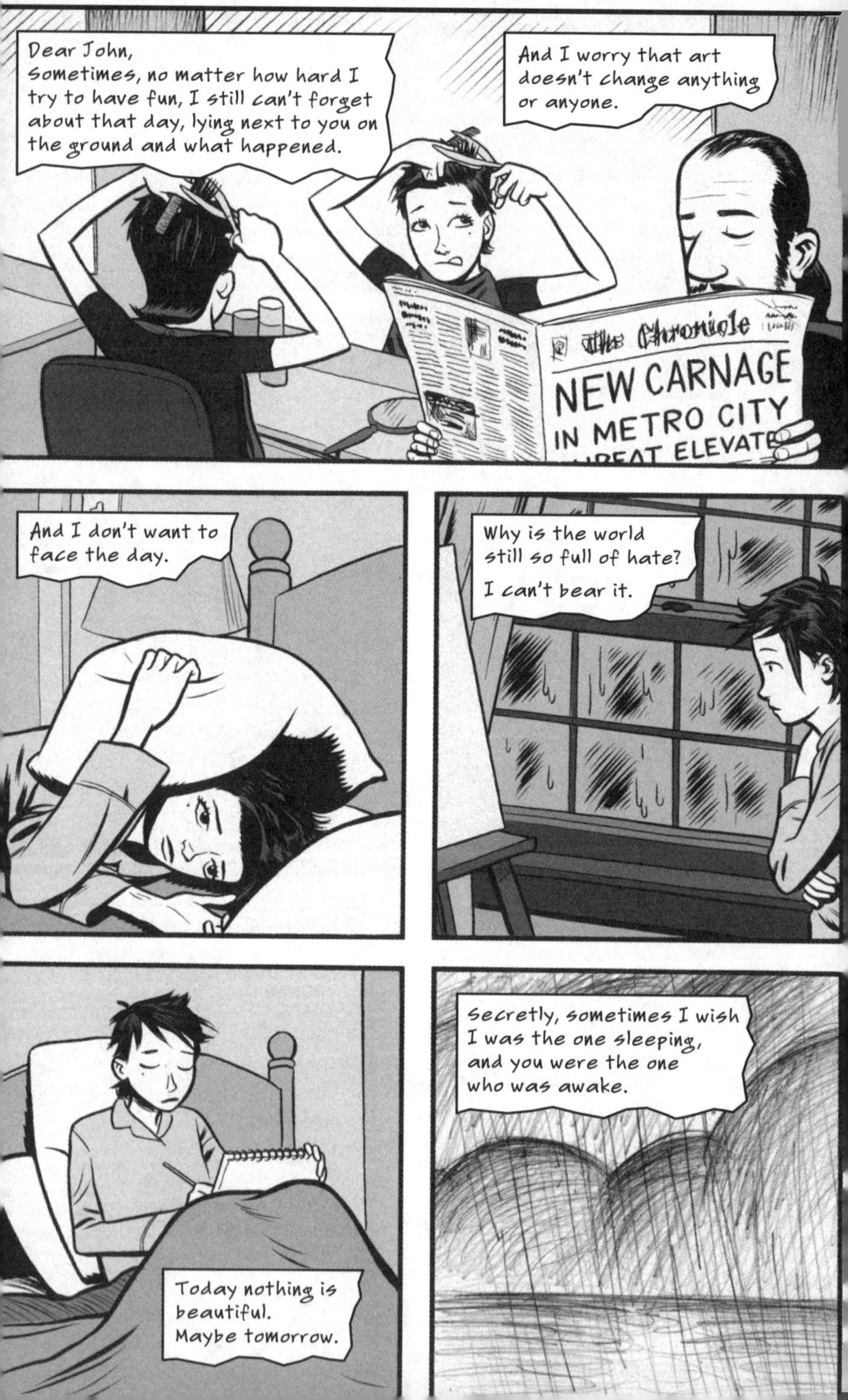
Dear John,
Sometimes, no matter how hard I try to have fun, I still can't forget about that day, lying next to you on the ground and what happened.
And I worry that art doesn't change anything or anyone.
The Chronicle
NEW CARNAGE IN METRO CITY
And I don't want to face the day.
Why is the world still so full of hate?
I can't bear it.
Today nothing is beautiful.
Maybe tomorrow.
Secretly, sometimes I wish I was the one sleeping, and you were the one who was awake.

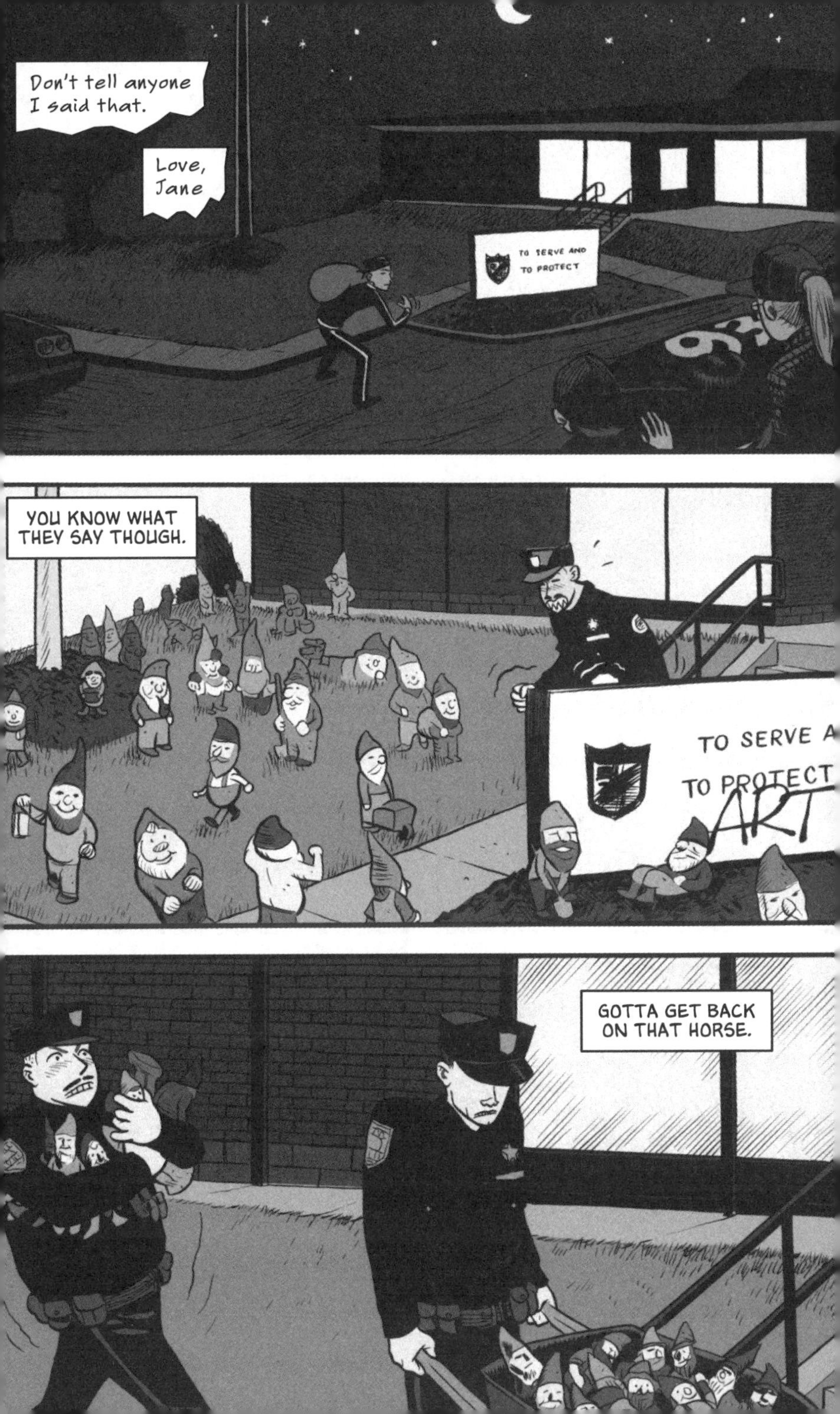

Don't tell anyone I said that.
Love, Jane
TO SERVE AND TO PROTECT
YOU KNOW WHAT THEY SAY THOUGH.
TO SERVE A
TO PROTECT
ART
GOTTA GET BACK ON THAT HORSE.

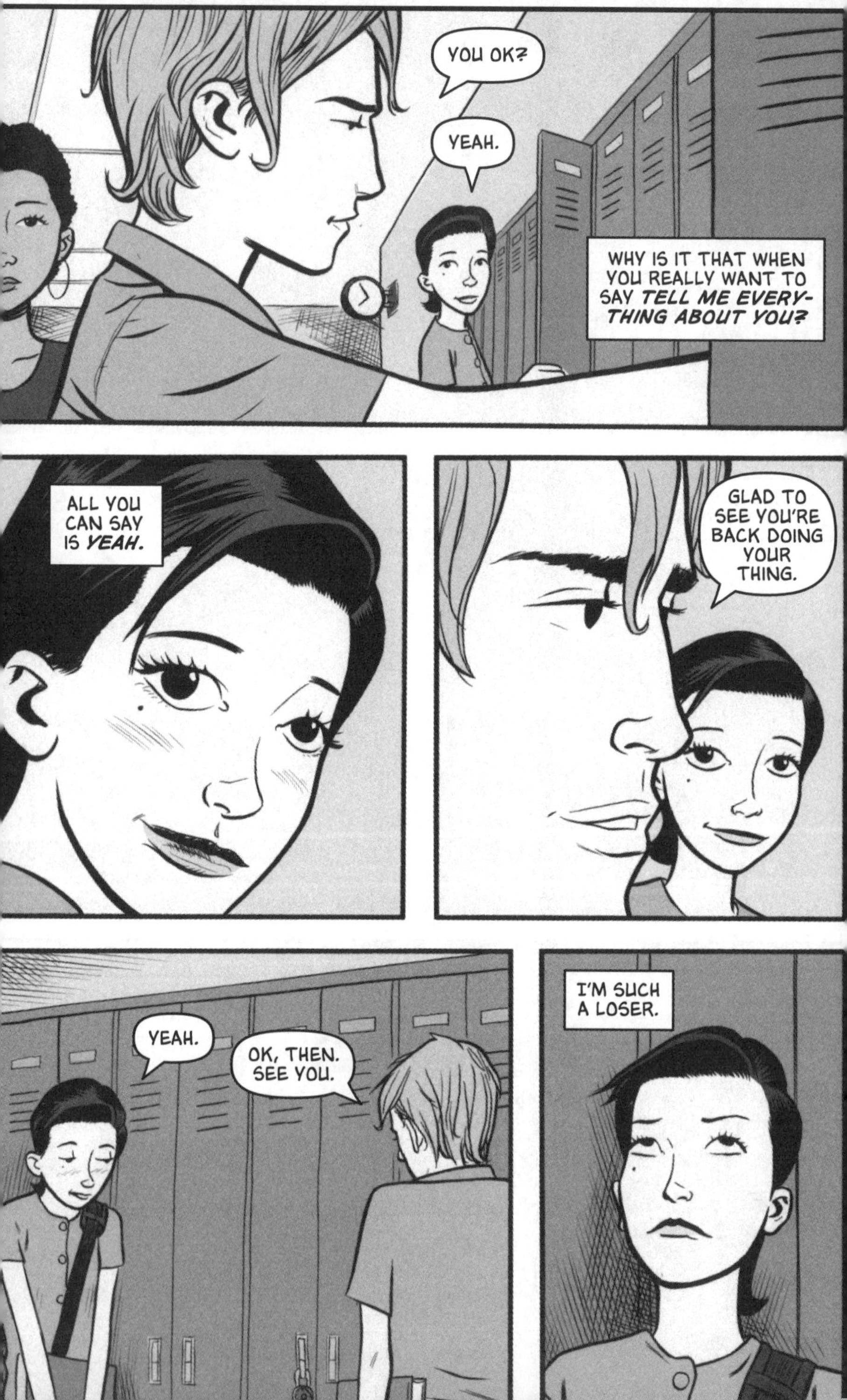
YOU OK?
YEAH.
WHY IS IT THAT WHEN YOU REALLY WANT TO SAY *TELL ME EVERY-THING ABOUT YOU?*
ALL YOU CAN SAY IS *YEAH.*
GLAD TO SEE YOU'RE BACK DOING YOUR THING.
YEAH.
OK, THEN. SEE YOU.
I'M SUCH A LOSER.

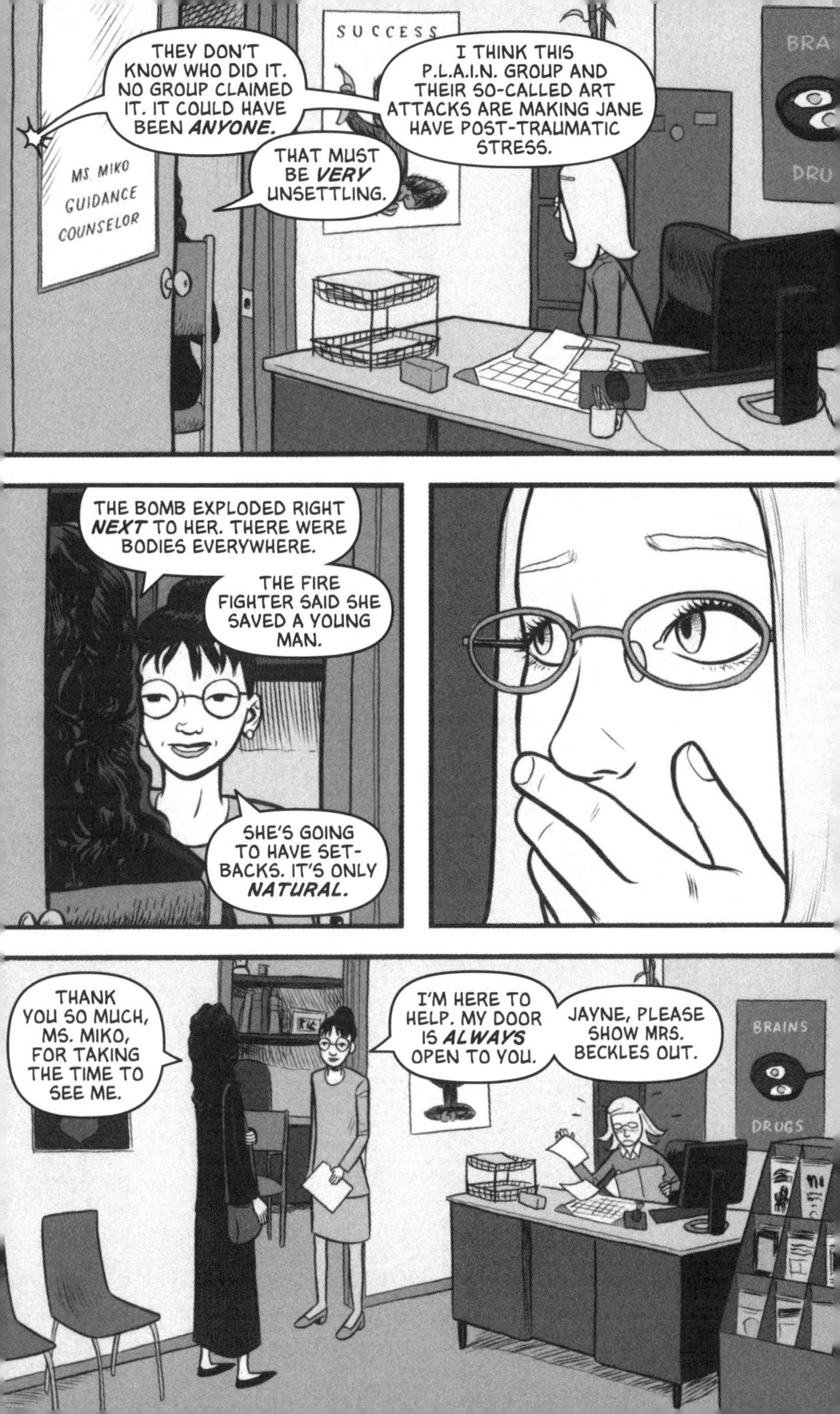
SUCCESS
MS. MIKO
GUIDANCE
COUNSELOR
THEY DON'T KNOW WHO DID IT. NO GROUP CLAIMED IT. IT COULD HAVE BEEN ANYONE.
I THINK THIS P.L.A.I.N. GROUP AND THEIR SO-CALLED ART ATTACKS ARE MAKING JANE HAVE POST-TRAUMATIC STRESS.
THAT MUST BE VERY UNSETTLING.
THE BOMB EXPLODED RIGHT NEXT TO HER. THERE WERE BODIES EVERYWHERE.
THE FIRE FIGHTER SAID SHE SAVED A YOUNG MAN.
SHE'S GOING TO HAVE SET-BACKS. IT'S ONLY NATURAL.
THANK YOU SO MUCH, MS. MIKO, FOR TAKING THE TIME TO SEE ME.
I'M HERE TO HELP. MY DOOR IS ALWAYS OPEN TO YOU.
JAYNE, PLEASE SHOW MRS. BECKLES OUT.
BRAINS
DRUGS

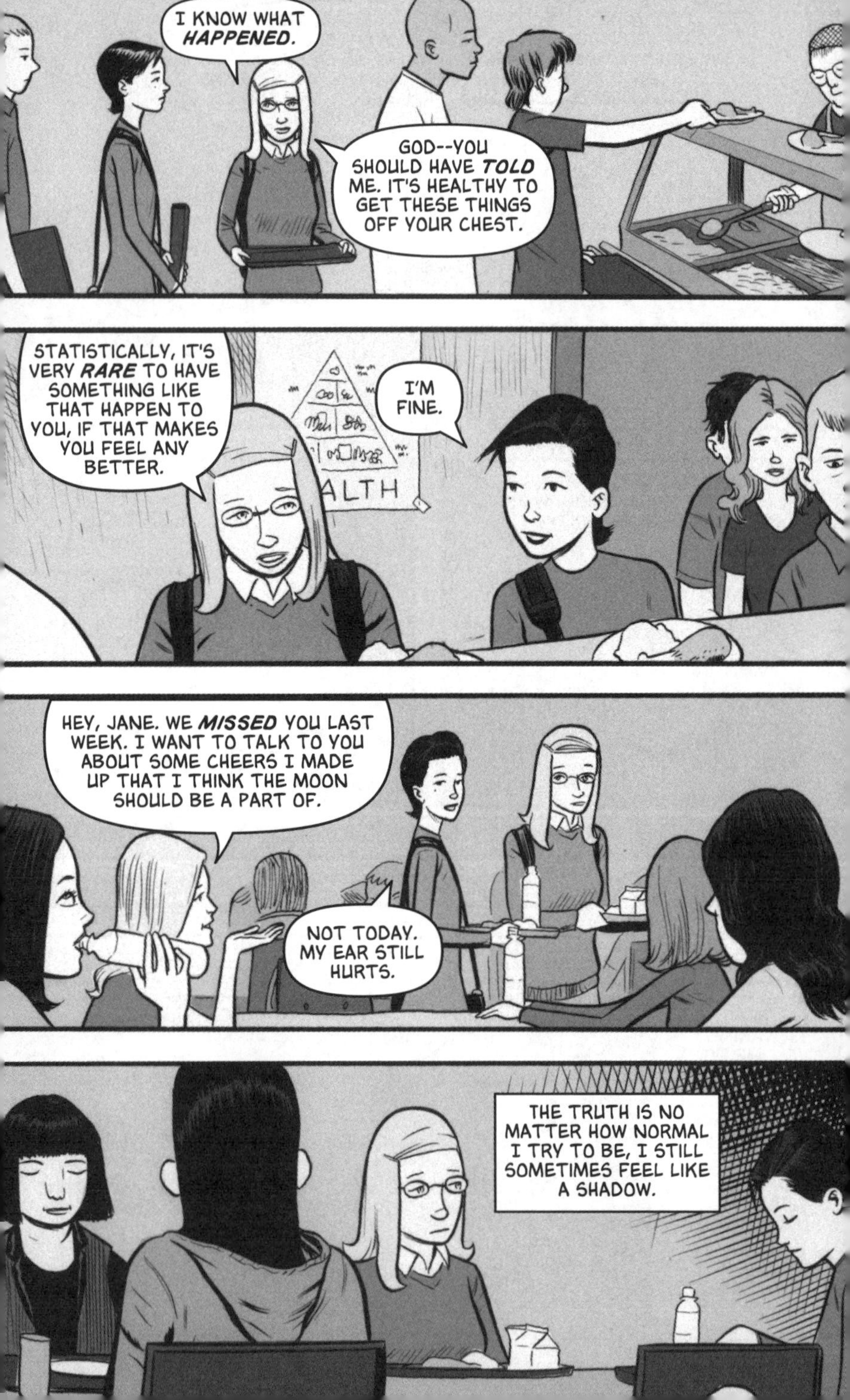
I KNOW WHAT *HAPPENED.*
GOD--YOU SHOULD HAVE *TOLD* ME. IT'S HEALTHY TO GET THESE THINGS OFF YOUR CHEST.
STATISTICALLY, IT'S VERY *RARE* TO HAVE SOMETHING LIKE THAT HAPPEN TO YOU, IF THAT MAKES YOU FEEL ANY BETTER.
I'M FINE.
ALTH
HEY, JANE. WE *MISSED* YOU LAST WEEK. I WANT TO TALK TO YOU ABOUT SOME CHEERS I MADE UP THAT I THINK THE MOON SHOULD BE A PART OF.
NOT TODAY. MY EAR STILL HURTS.
THE TRUTH IS NO MATTER HOW NORMAL I TRY TO BE, I STILL SOMETIMES FEEL LIKE A SHADOW.

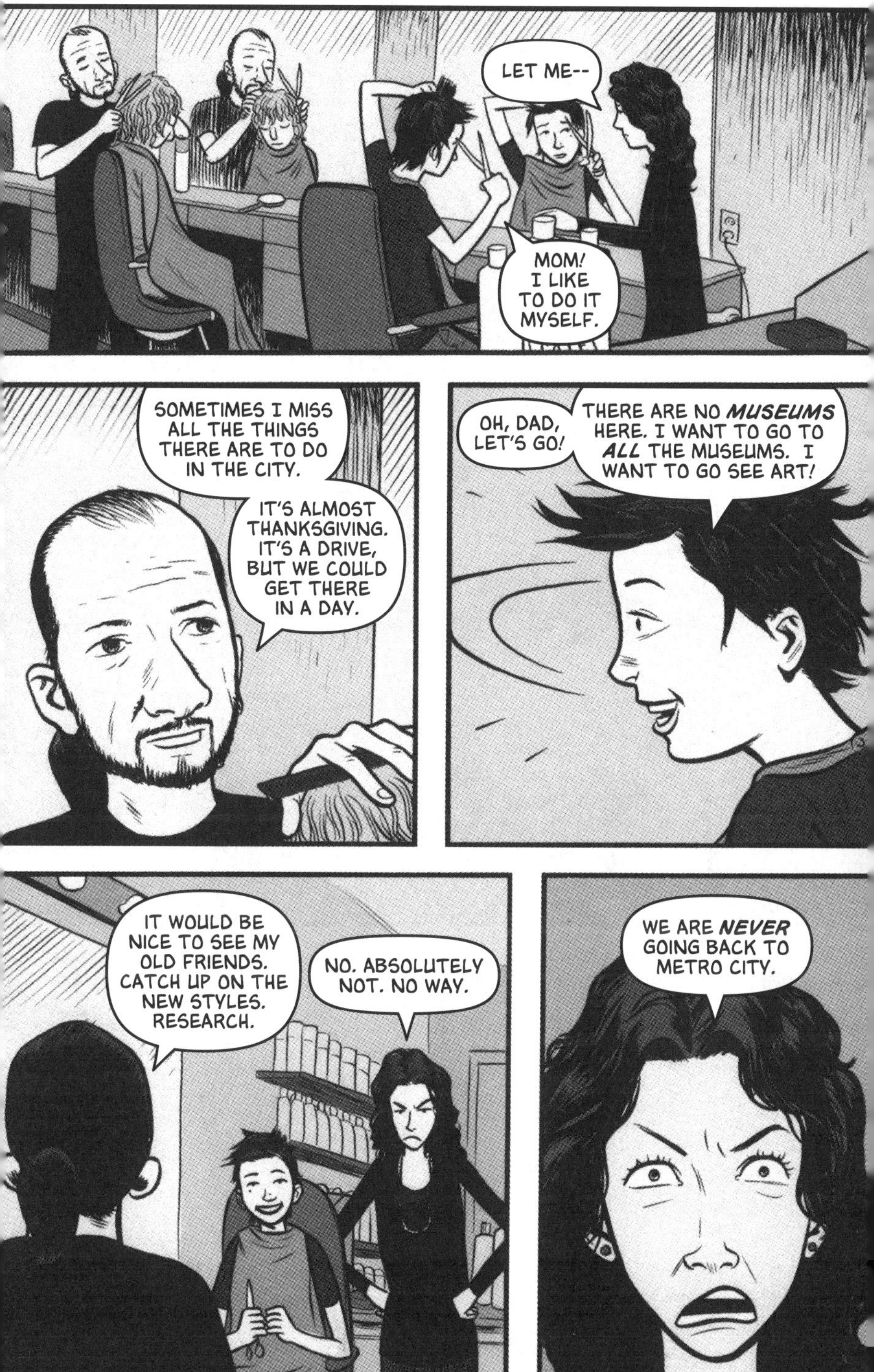
LET ME--
MOM! I LIKE TO DO IT MYSELF.
SOMETIMES I MISS ALL THE THINGS THERE ARE TO DO IN THE CITY.
IT'S ALMOST THANKSGIVING. IT'S A DRIVE, BUT WE COULD GET THERE IN A DAY.
OH, DAD, LET'S GO!
THERE ARE NO *MUSEUMS* HERE. I WANT TO GO TO *ALL* THE MUSEUMS. I WANT TO GO SEE ART!
IT WOULD BE NICE TO SEE MY OLD FRIENDS. CATCH UP ON THE NEW STYLES. RESEARCH.
NO. ABSOLUTELY NOT. NO WAY.
WE ARE *NEVER* GOING BACK TO METRO CITY.

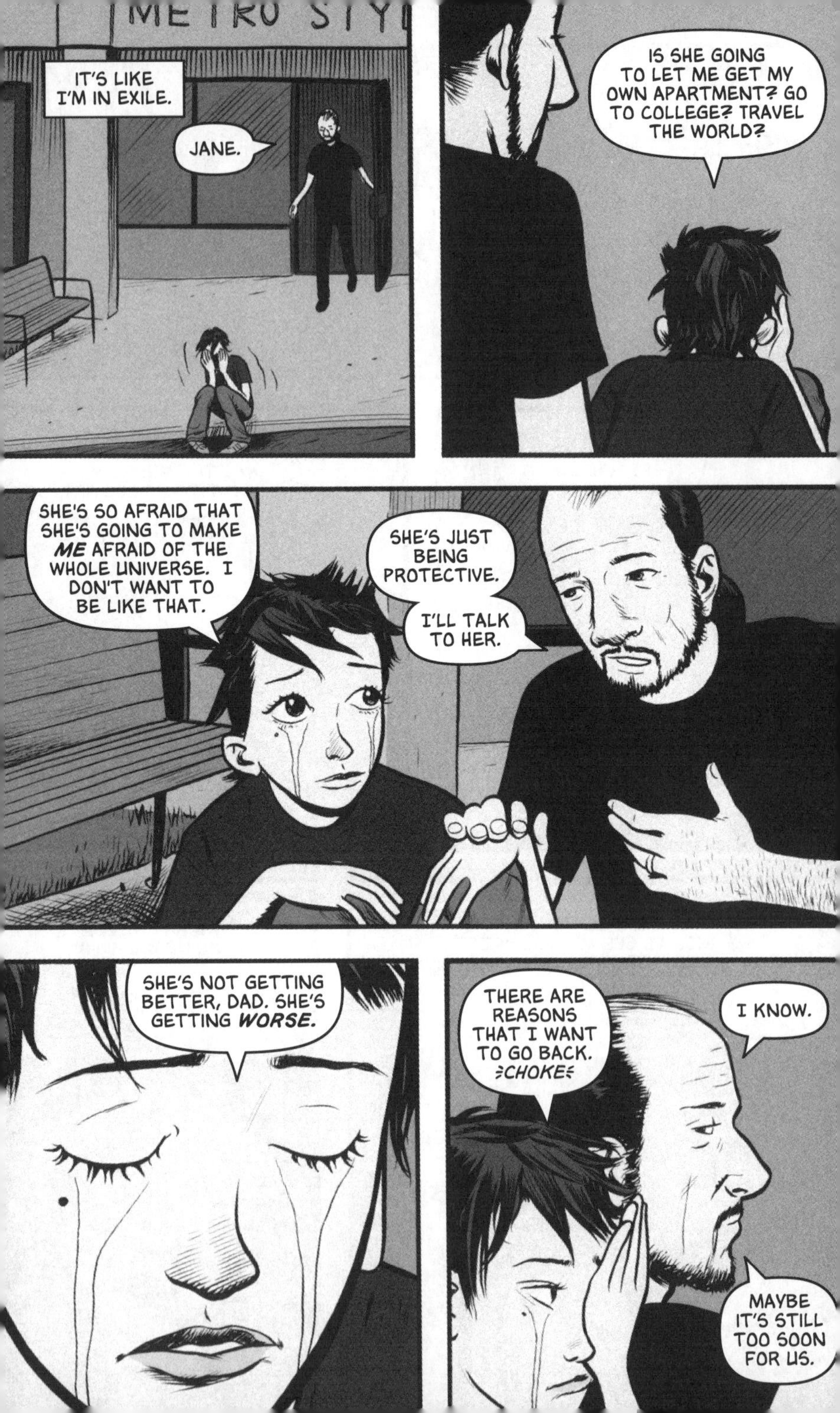

METRO STY
IT'S LIKE I'M IN EXILE.
JANE.
IS SHE GOING TO LET ME GET MY OWN APARTMENT? GO TO COLLEGE? TRAVEL THE WORLD?
SHE'S SO AFRAID THAT SHE'S GOING TO MAKE *ME* AFRAID OF THE WHOLE UNIVERSE. I DON'T WANT TO BE LIKE THAT.
SHE'S JUST BEING PROTECTIVE.
I'LL TALK TO HER.
SHE'S NOT GETTING BETTER, DAD. SHE'S GETTING *WORSE.*
THERE ARE REASONS THAT I WANT TO GO BACK. *CHOKE*
I KNOW.
MAYBE IT'S STILL TOO SOON FOR US.

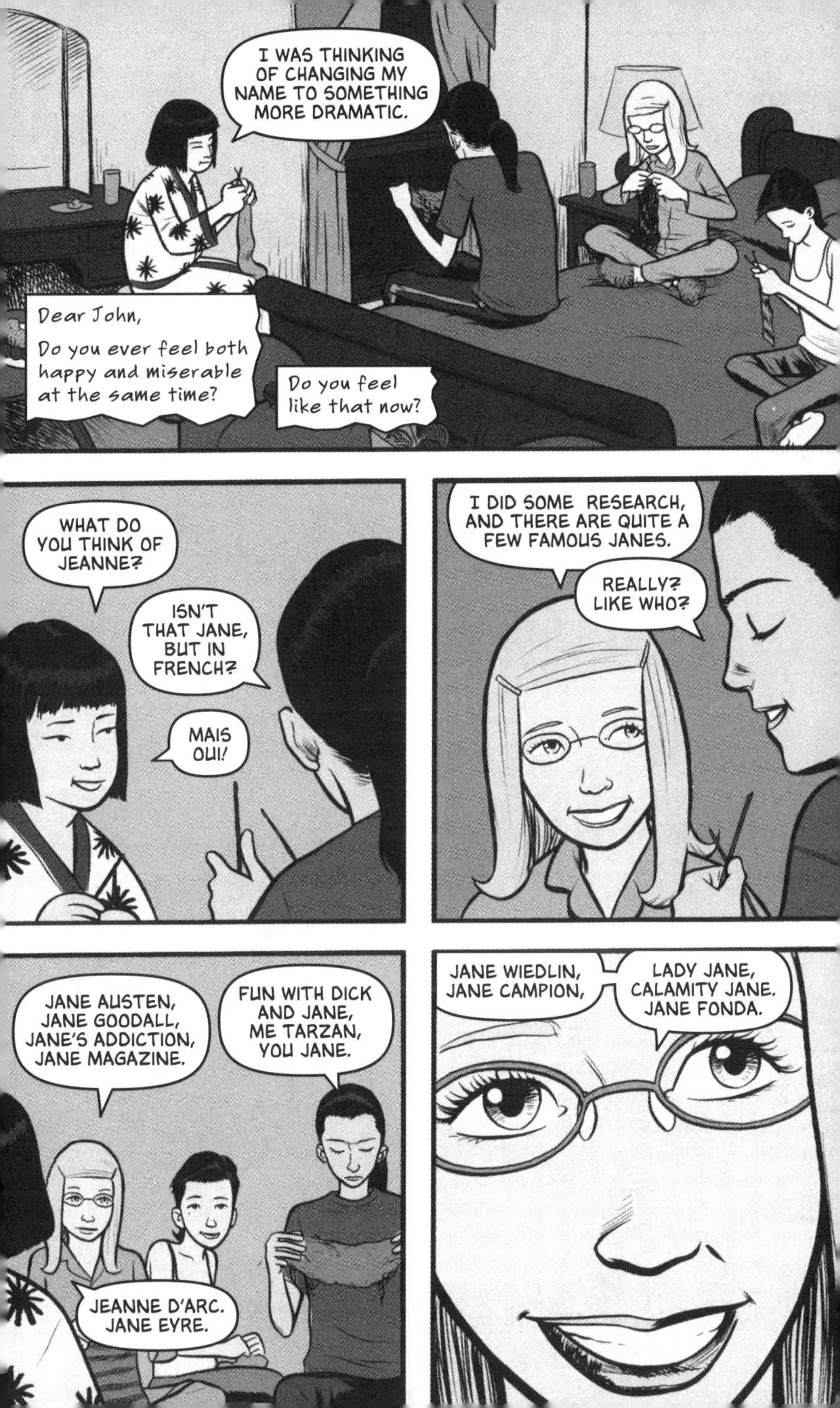
I WAS THINKING OF CHANGING MY NAME TO SOMETHING MORE DRAMATIC.
Dear John,
Do you ever feel both happy and miserable at the same time?
Do you feel like that now?
WHAT DO YOU THINK OF JEANNE?
ISN'T THAT JANE, BUT IN FRENCH?
MAIS OUI!
I DID SOME RESEARCH, AND THERE ARE QUITE A FEW FAMOUS JANES.
REALLY? LIKE WHO?
JANE AUSTEN, JANE GOODALL, JANE'S ADDICTION, JANE MAGAZINE.
FUN WITH DICK AND JANE, ME TARZAN, YOU JANE.
JEANNE D'ARC. JANE EYRE.
JANE WIEDLIN, JANE CAMPION,
LADY JANE, CALAMITY JANE. JANE FONDA.

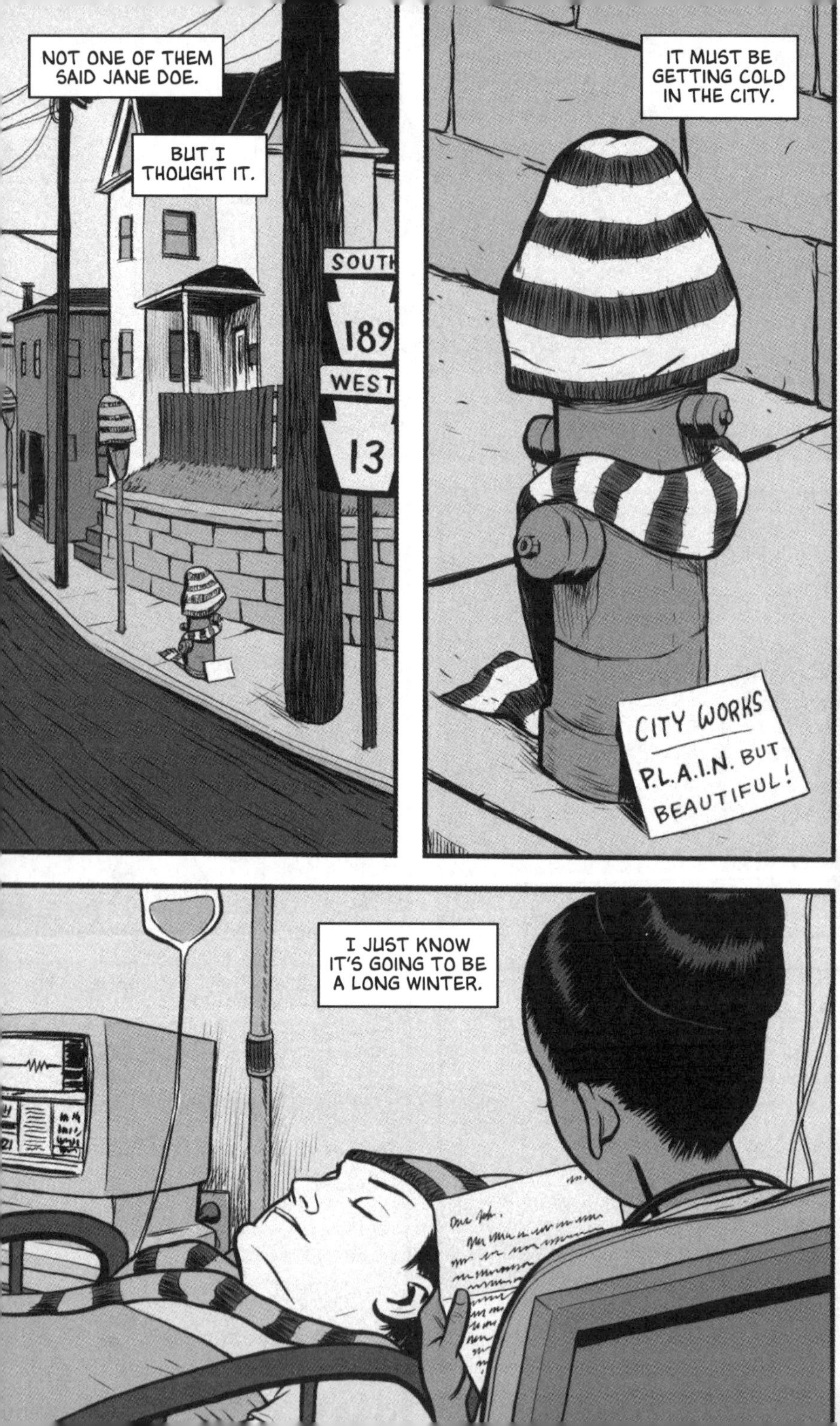
NOT ONE OF THEM SAID JANE DOE.
BUT I THOUGHT IT.
SOUTH
189
WEST
13
IT MUST BE GETTING COLD IN THE CITY.
CITY WORKS
P.L.A.I.N. BUT BEAUTIFUL!
I JUST KNOW IT'S GOING TO BE A LONG WINTER.

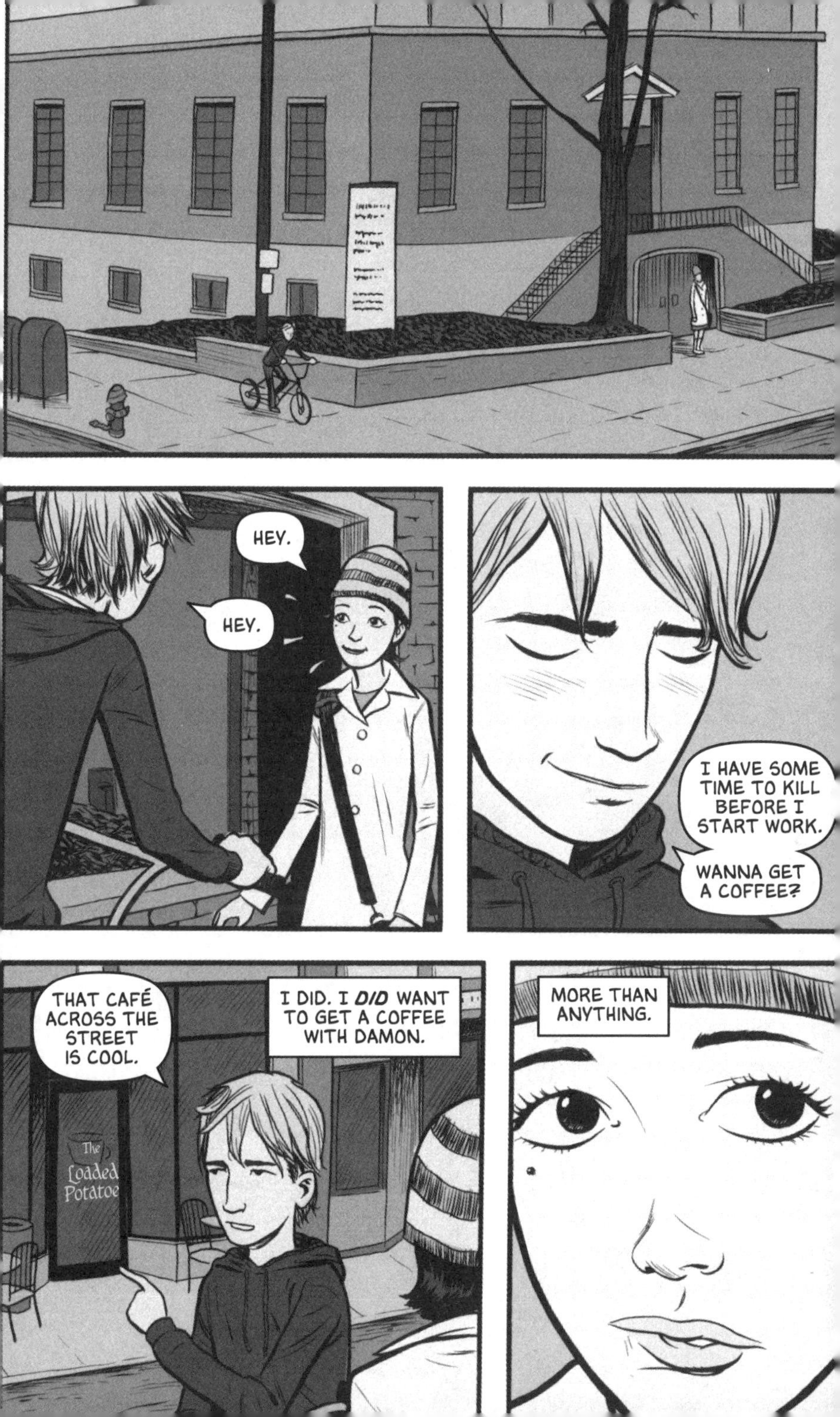
HEY.
HEY.
I HAVE SOME TIME TO KILL BEFORE I START WORK.
WANNA GET A COFFEE?
THAT CAFÉ ACROSS THE STREET IS COOL.
I DID. I *DID* WANT TO GET A COFFEE WITH DAMON.
The Loaded Potatoe
MORE THAN ANYTHING.

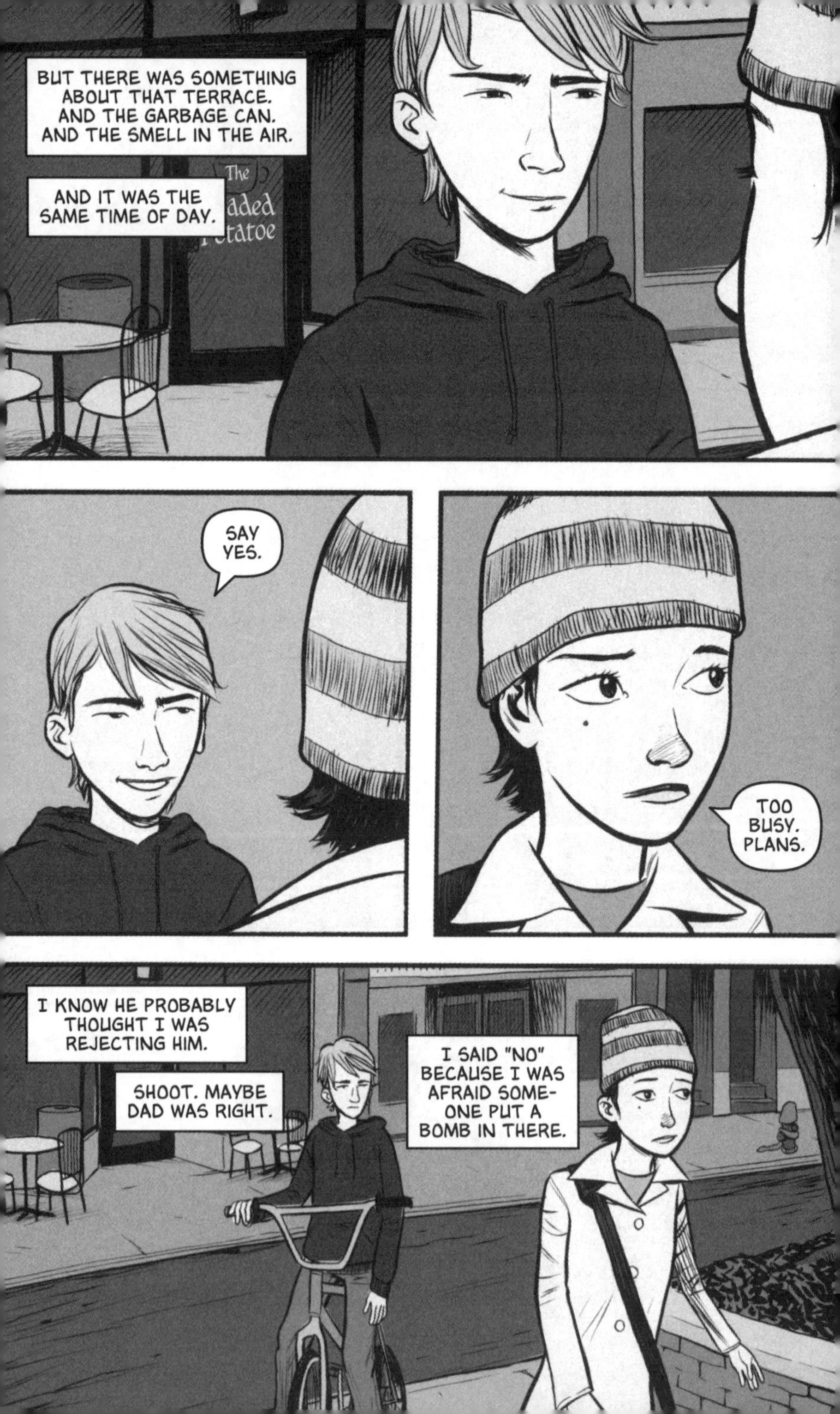
BUT THERE WAS SOMETHING ABOUT THAT TERRACE. AND THE GARBAGE CAN. AND THE SMELL IN THE AIR.
AND IT WAS THE SAME TIME OF DAY.
SAY YES.
TOO BUSY. PLANS.
I KNOW HE PROBABLY THOUGHT I WAS REJECTING HIM.
SHOOT. MAYBE DAD WAS RIGHT.
I SAID "NO" BECAUSE I WAS AFRAID SOME-ONE PUT A BOMB IN THERE.

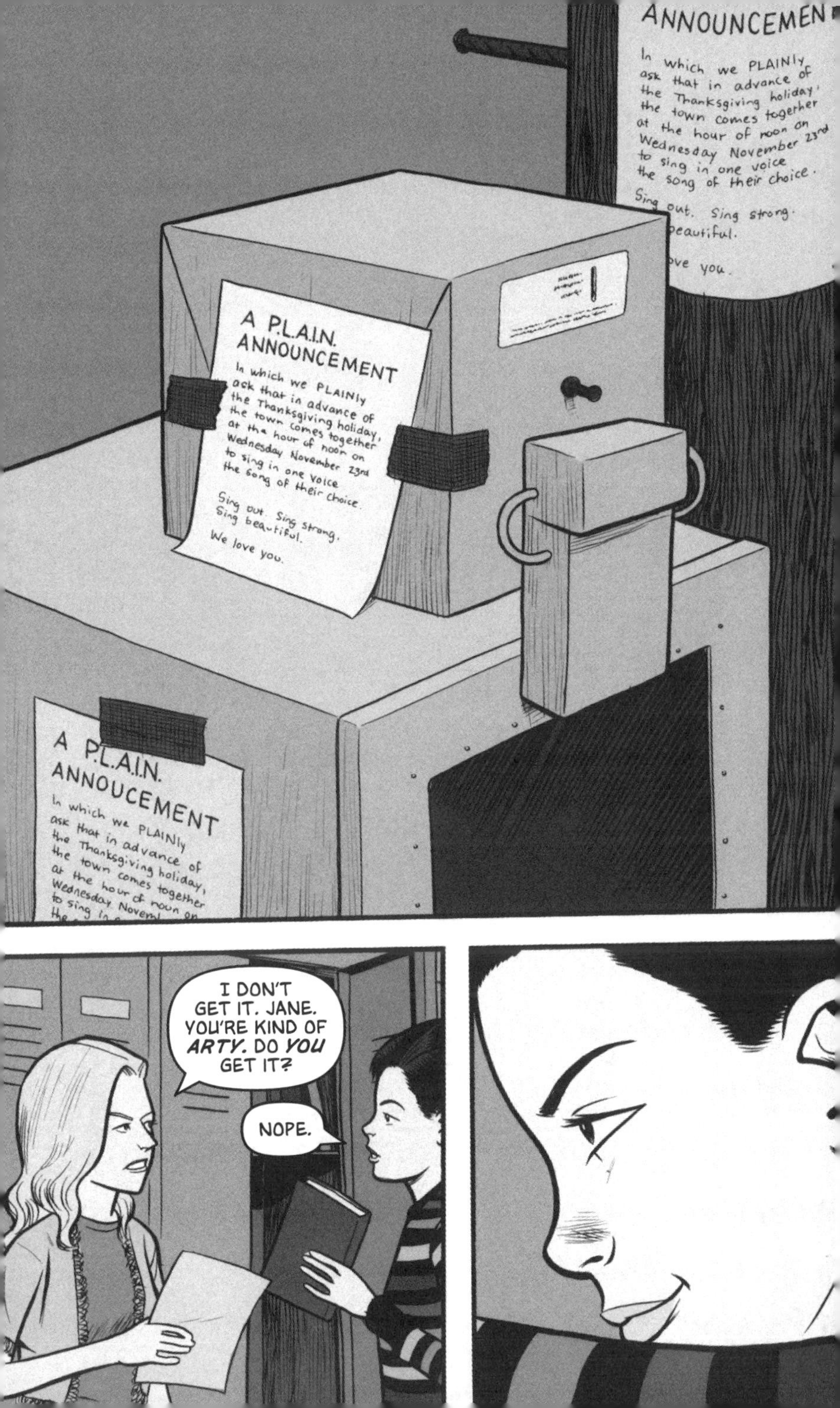

ANNOUNCEMEN
In which we PLAINly ask that in advance of the Thanksgiving holiday, the town comes together at the hour of noon on Wednesday November 23rd to sing in one voice the song of their choice.
Sing out. Sing strong.
beautiful.
ove you.
A P.L.A.I.N. ANNOUNCEMENT
In which we PLAINly ask that in advance of the Thanksgiving holiday, the town comes together at the hour of noon on Wednesday November 23rd to sing in one voice the song of their choice.
Sing out. Sing strong. Sing beautiful.
We love you.
A P.L.A.I.N. ANNOUCEMENT
In which we PLAINly ask that in advance of the Thanksgiving holiday, the town comes together at the hour of noon on Wednesday Novem
I DON'T GET IT. JANE. YOU'RE KIND OF ARTY. DO YOU GET IT?
NOPE.

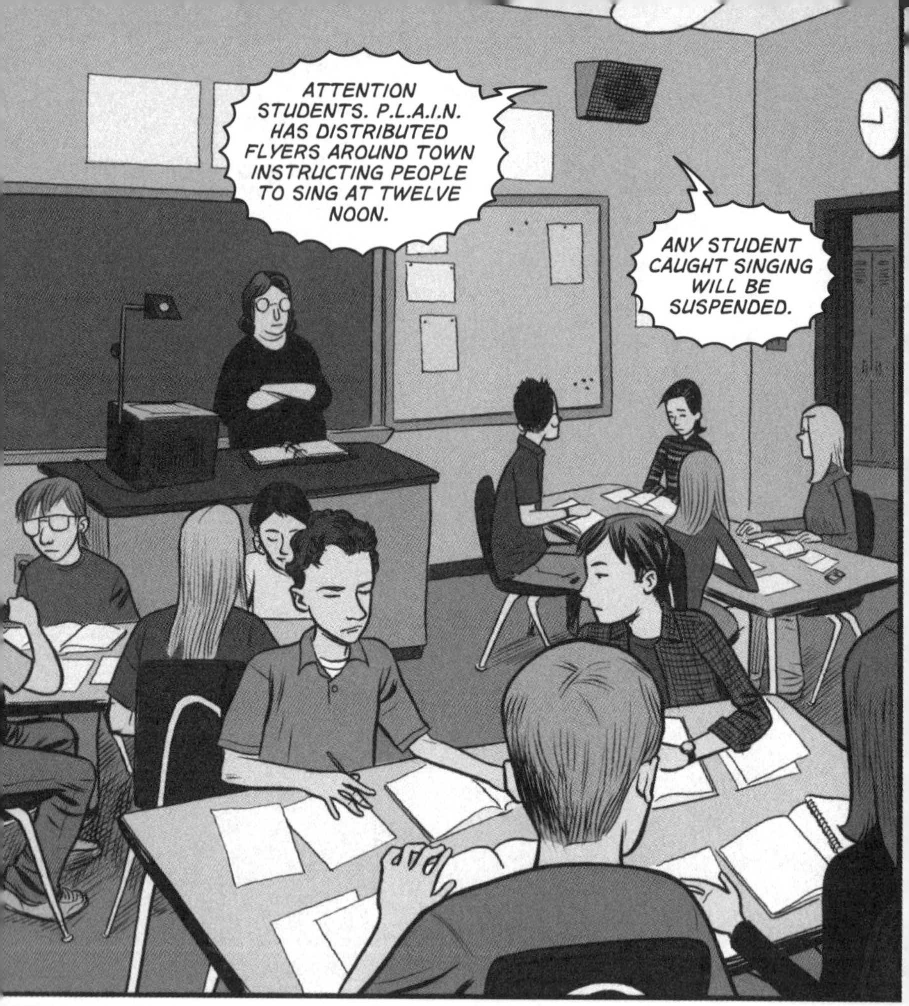
ATTENTION STUDENTS. P.L.A.I.N. HAS DISTRIBUTED FLYERS AROUND TOWN INSTRUCTING PEOPLE TO SING AT TWELVE NOON.
ANY STUDENT CAUGHT SINGING WILL BE SUSPENDED.

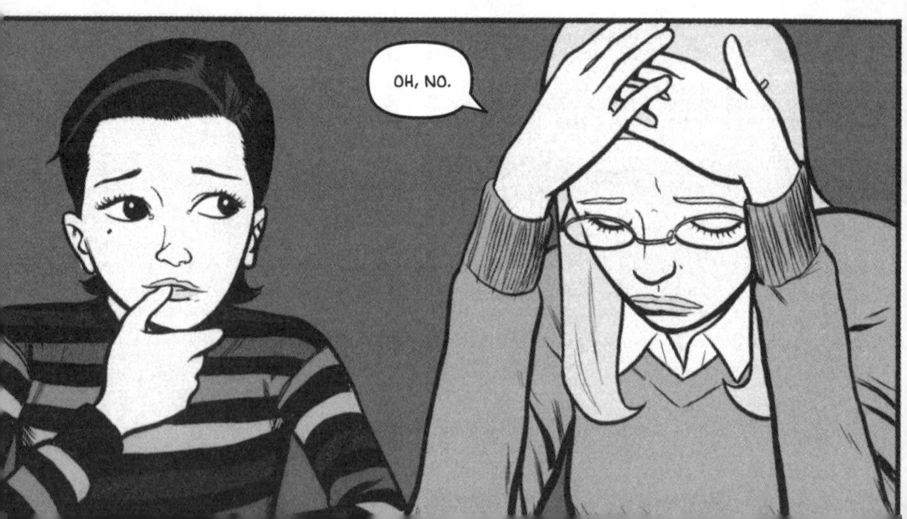
OH, NO.

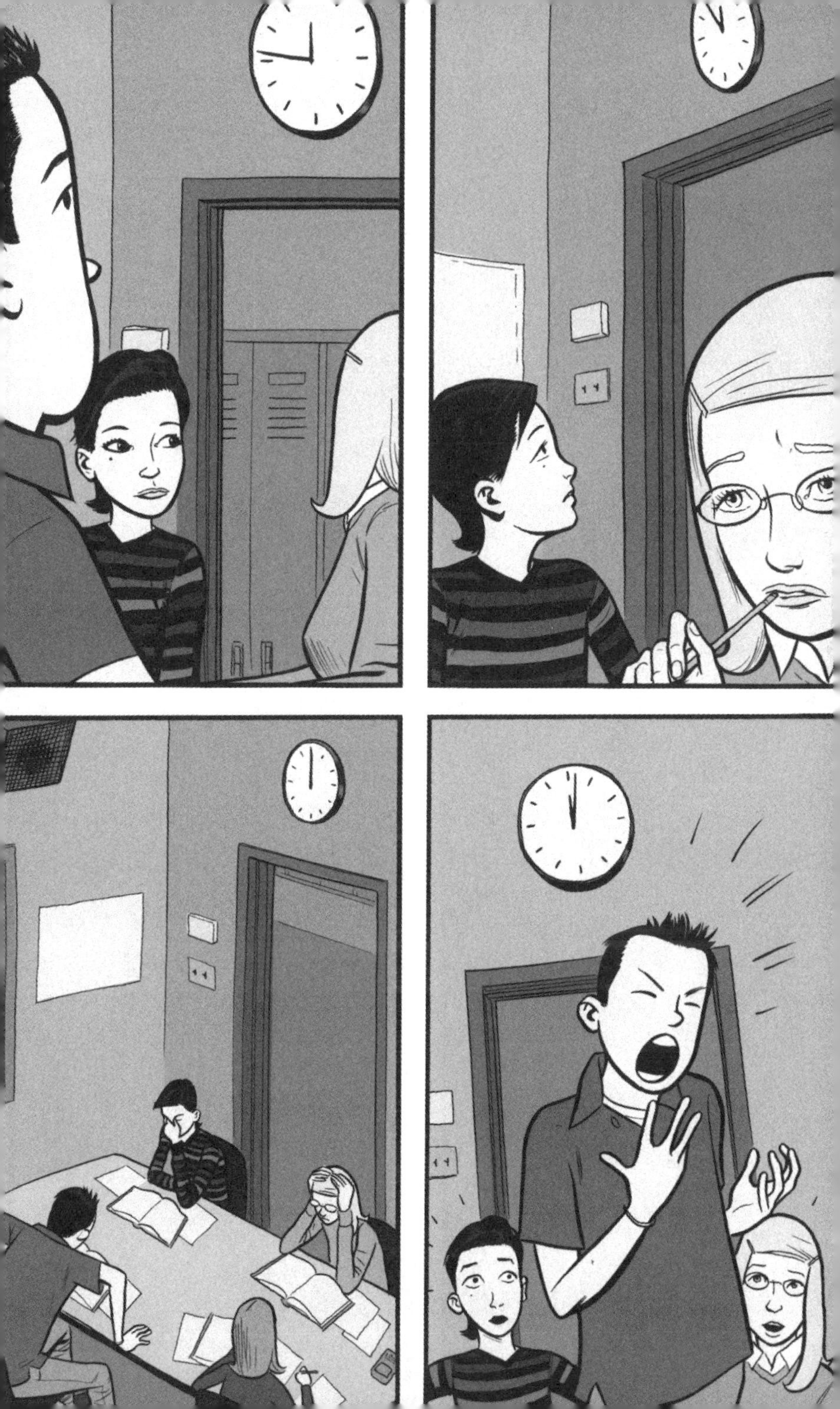

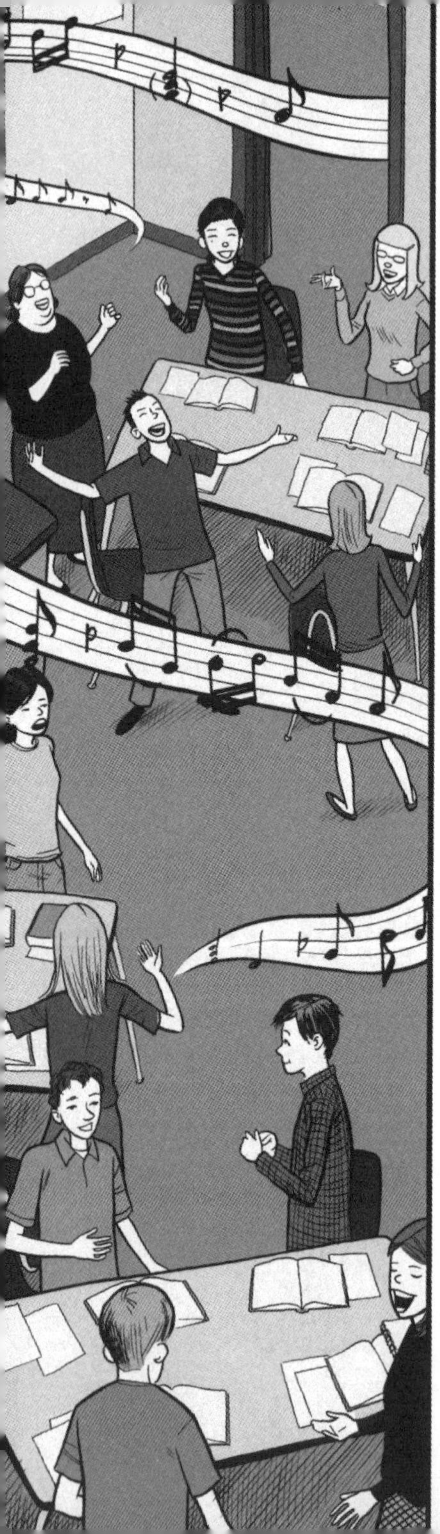

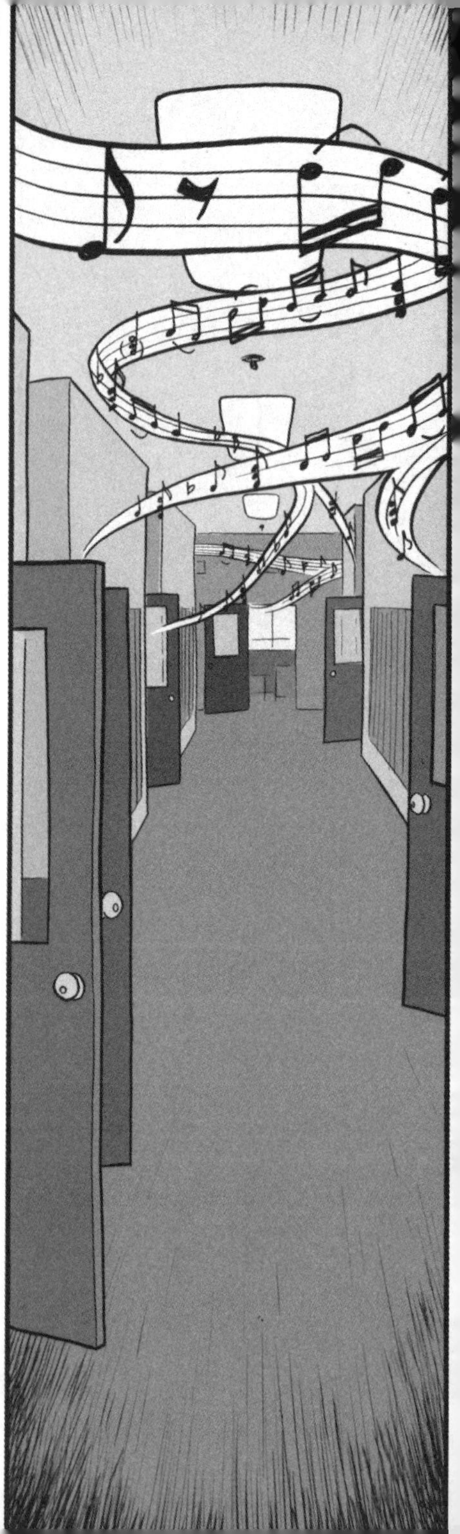

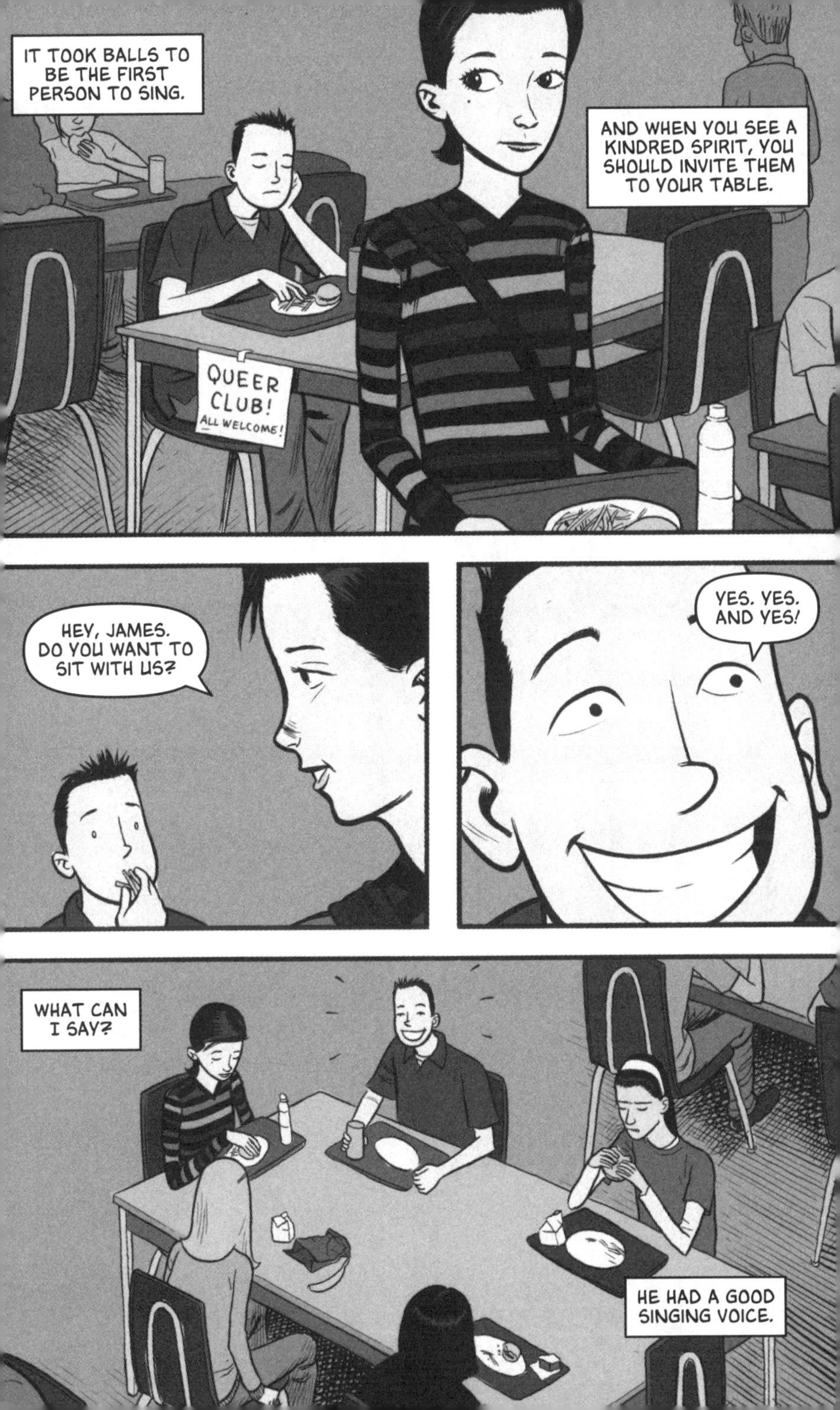
IT TOOK BALLS TO BE THE FIRST PERSON TO SING.
AND WHEN YOU SEE A KINDRED SPIRIT, YOU SHOULD INVITE THEM TO YOUR TABLE.
QUEER CLUB! ALL WELCOME!
HEY, JAMES. DO YOU WANT TO SIT WITH US?
YES. YES. AND YES!
WHAT CAN I SAY?
HE HAD A GOOD SINGING VOICE.

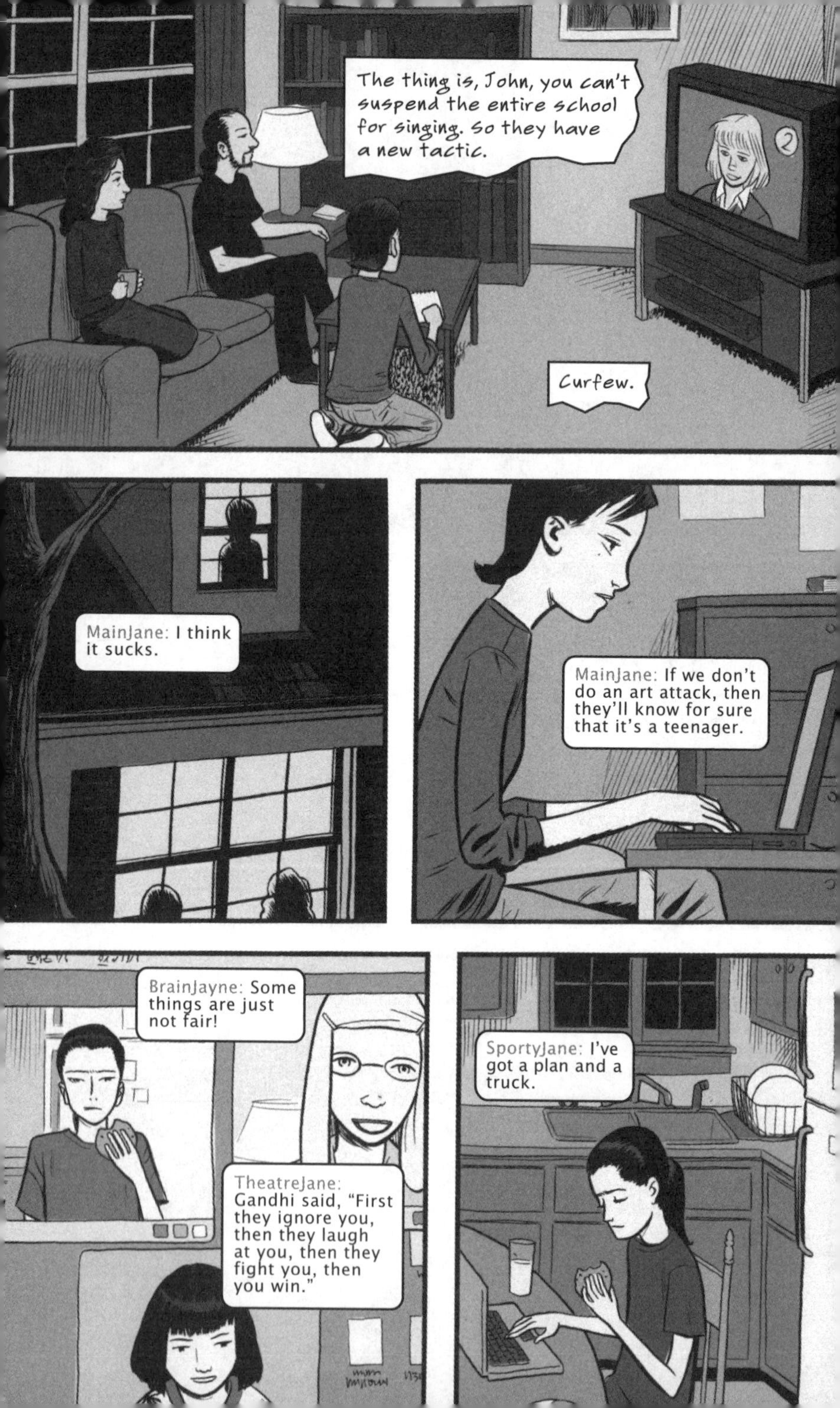

The thing is, John, you can't suspend the entire school for singing. So they have a new tactic.
Curfew.
MainJane: I think it sucks.
MainJane: If we don't do an art attack, then they'll know for sure that it's a teenager.
BrainJayne: Some things are just not fair!
TheatreJane: Gandhi said, "First they ignore you, then they laugh at you, then they fight you, then you win."
SportyJane: I've got a plan and a truck.

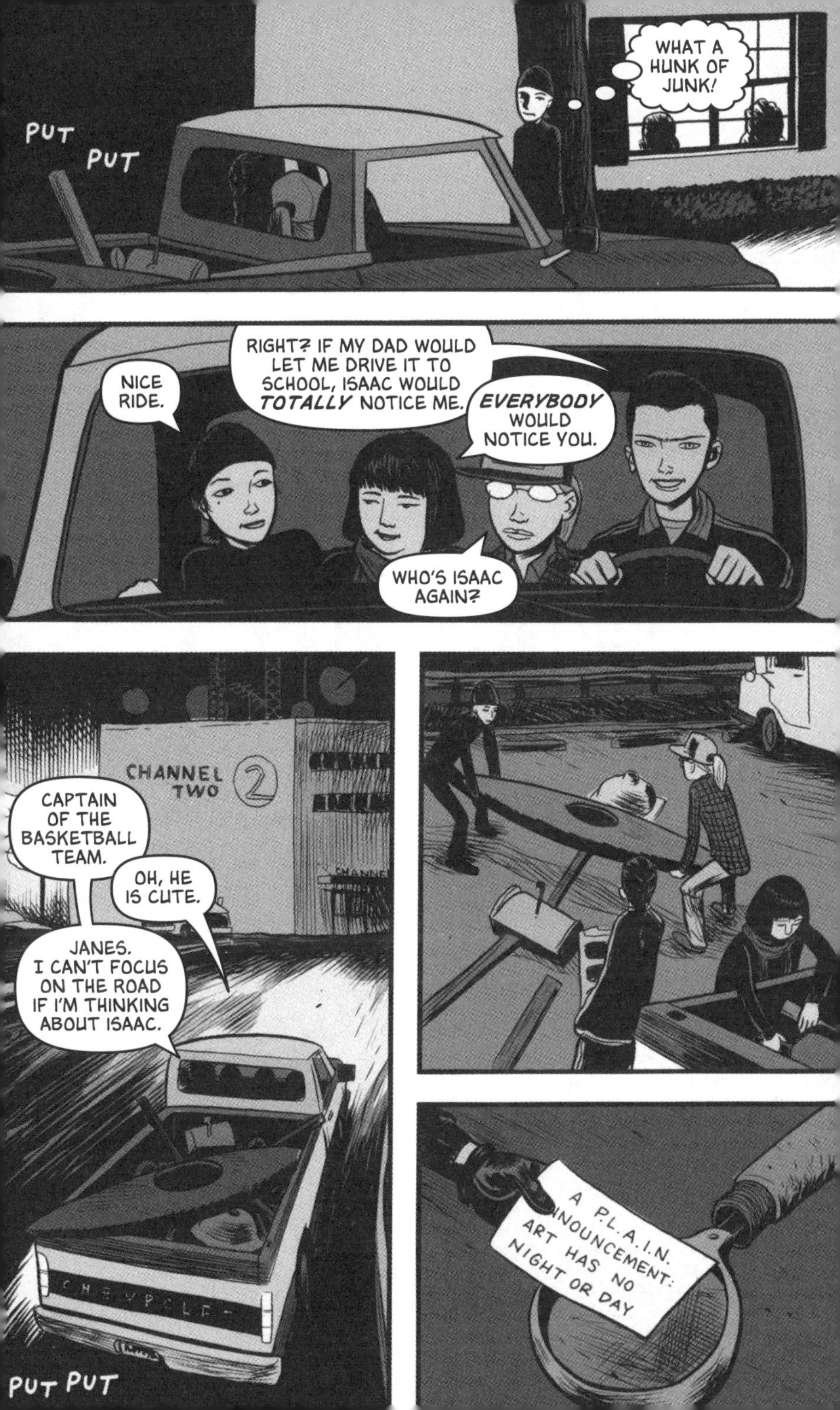
PUT PUT
WHAT A HUNK OF JUNK!
NICE RIDE.
RIGHT? IF MY DAD WOULD LET ME DRIVE IT TO SCHOOL, ISAAC WOULD TOTALLY NOTICE ME.
EVERYBODY WOULD NOTICE YOU.
WHO'S ISAAC AGAIN?
CHANNEL TWO 2
CAPTAIN OF THE BASKETBALL TEAM.
OH, HE IS CUTE.
JANES. I CAN'T FOCUS ON THE ROAD IF I'M THINKING ABOUT ISAAC.
PUT PUT
A P.L.A.I.N. ANNOUNCEMENT: ART HAS NO NIGHT OR DAY

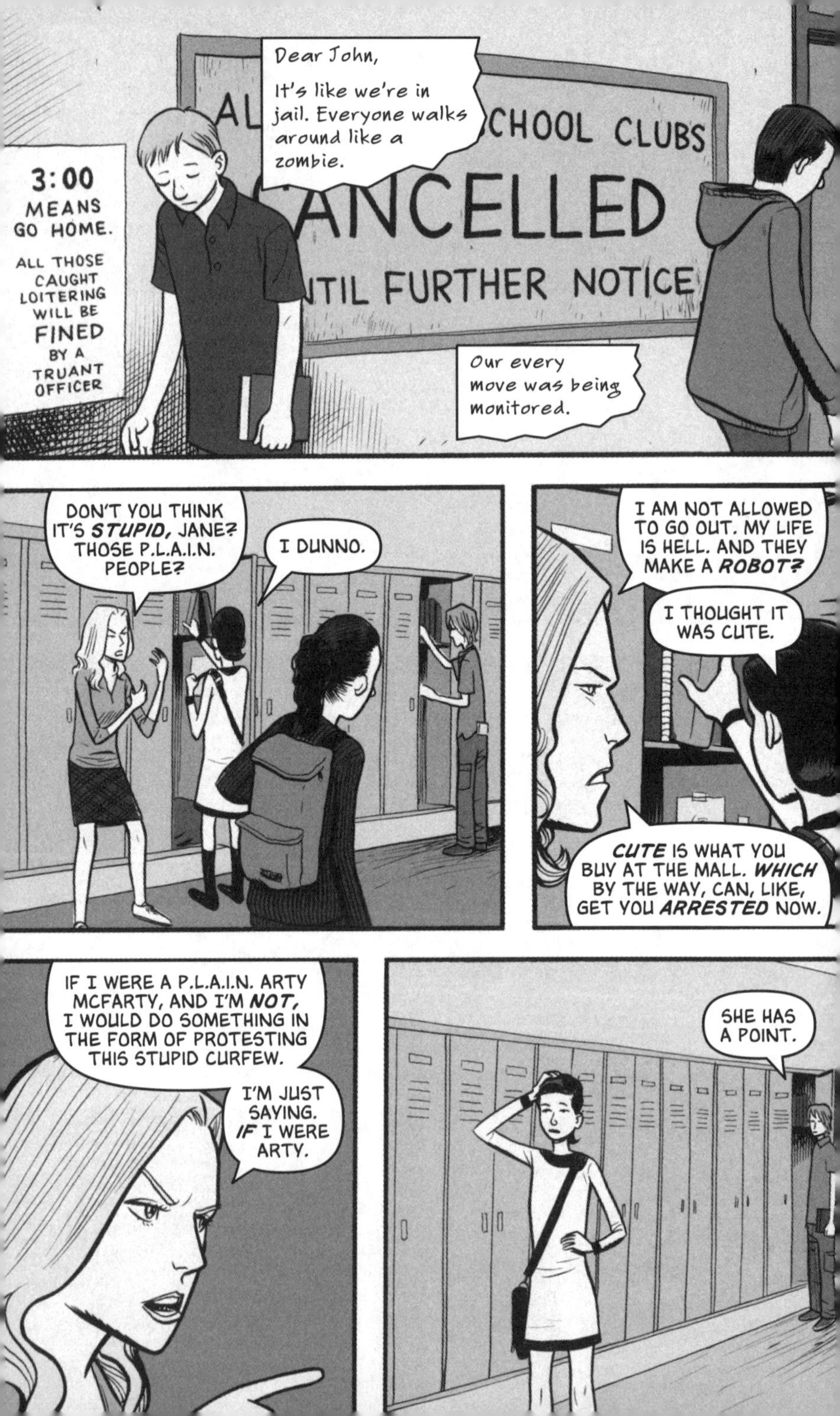

3:00 MEANS GO HOME. ALL THOSE CAUGHT LOITERING WILL BE FINED BY A TRUANT OFFICER
Dear John,
It's like we're in jail. Everyone walks around like a zombie.
CHOOL CLUBS ANCELLED NTIL FURTHER NOTICE
Our every move was being monitored.
DON'T YOU THINK IT'S STUPID, JANE? THOSE P.L.A.I.N. PEOPLE?
I DUNNO.
I AM NOT ALLOWED TO GO OUT. MY LIFE IS HELL. AND THEY MAKE A ROBOT?
I THOUGHT IT WAS CUTE.
CUTE IS WHAT YOU BUY AT THE MALL. WHICH BY THE WAY, CAN, LIKE, GET YOU ARRESTED NOW.
IF I WERE A P.L.A.I.N. ARTY MCFARTY, AND I'M NOT, I WOULD DO SOMETHING IN THE FORM OF PROTESTING THIS STUPID CURFEW.
I'M JUST SAYING. IF I WERE ARTY.
SHE HAS A POINT.

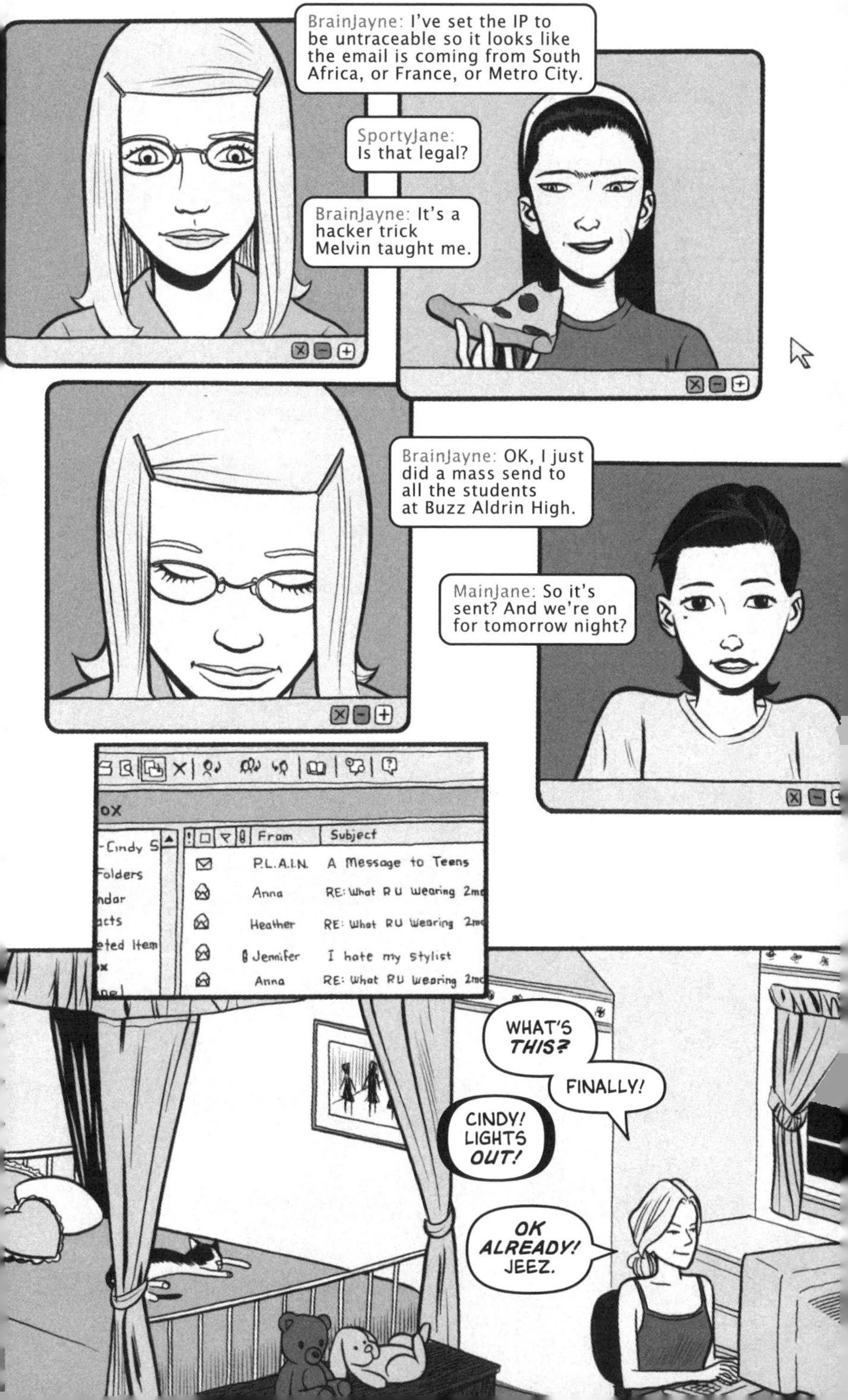
BrainJayne: I've set the IP to be untraceable so it looks like the email is coming from South Africa, or France, or Metro City.
SportyJane: Is that legal?
BrainJayne: It's a hacker trick Melvin taught me.
BrainJayne: OK, I just did a mass send to all the students at Buzz Aldrin High.
MainJane: So it's sent? And we're on for tomorrow night?
From
Subject
P.L.A.I.N. A Message to Teens
Anna RE: What R U Wearing
Heather RE: What RU Wearing
Jennifer I hate my stylist
Anna RE: What RU Wearing
WHAT'S *THIS?*
FINALLY!
CINDY! LIGHTS *OUT!*
OK ALREADY! JEEZ.

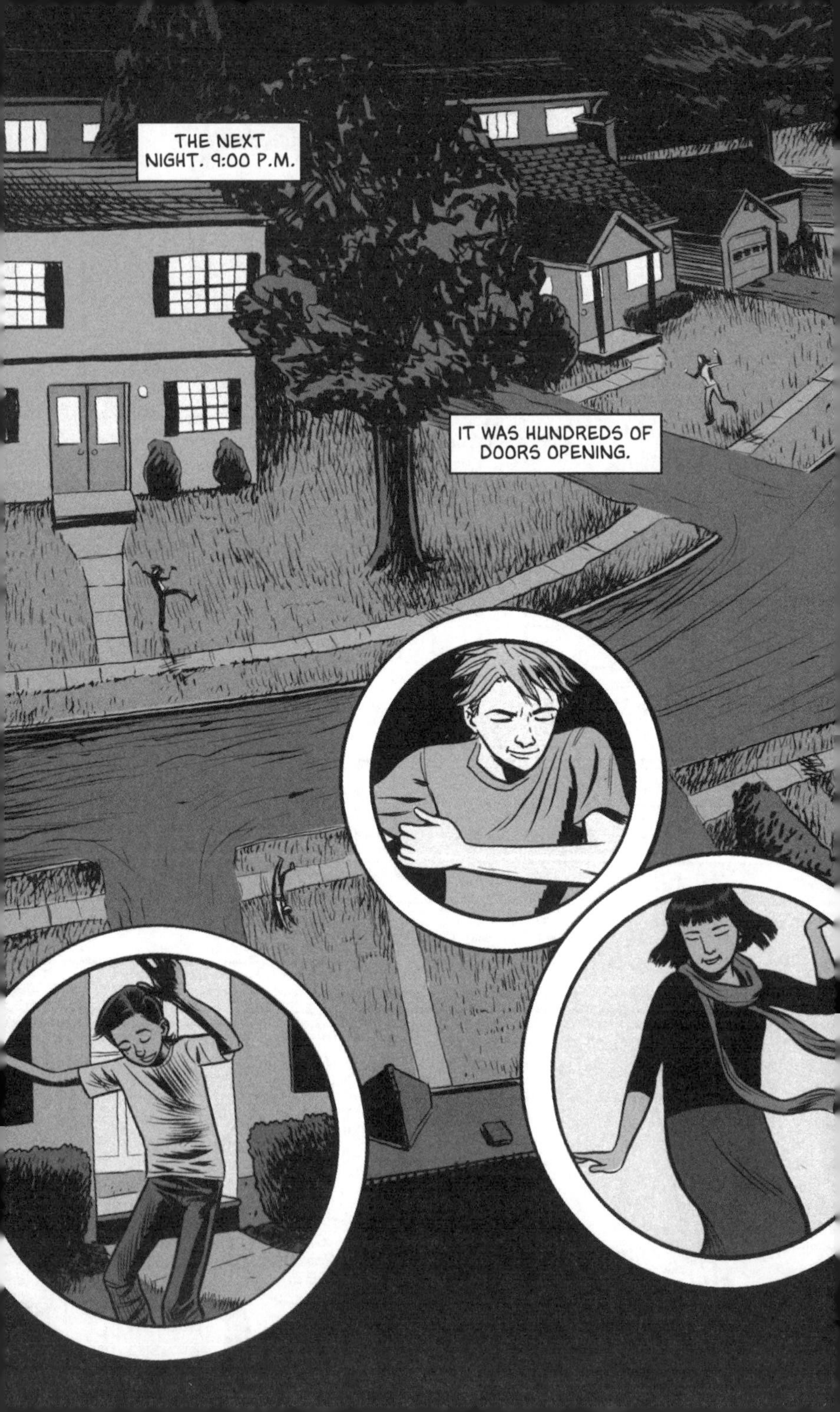
THE NEXT NIGHT. 9:00 P.M.
IT WAS HUNDREDS OF DOORS OPENING.

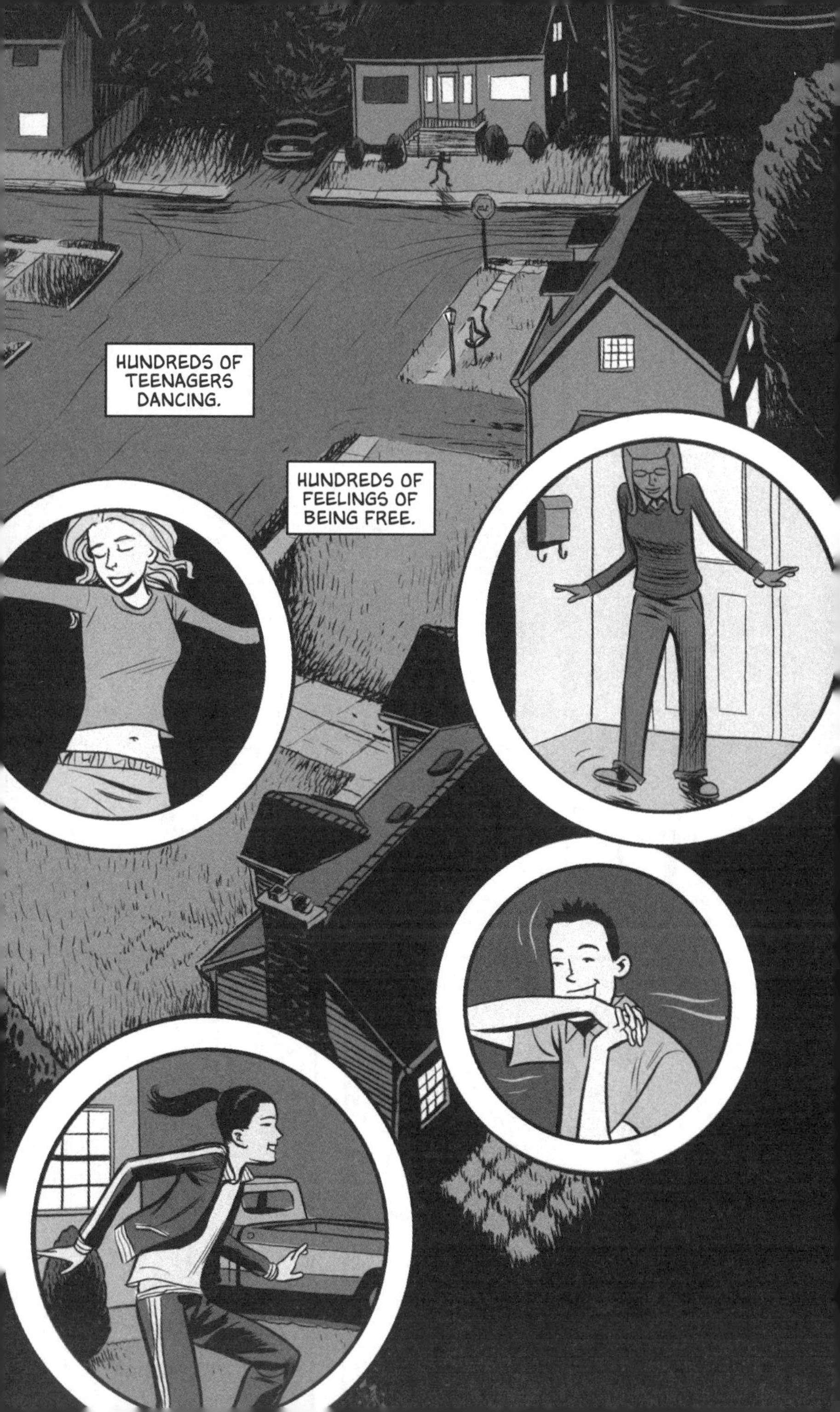
HUNDREDS OF TEENAGERS DANCING.
HUNDREDS OF FEELINGS OF BEING FREE.

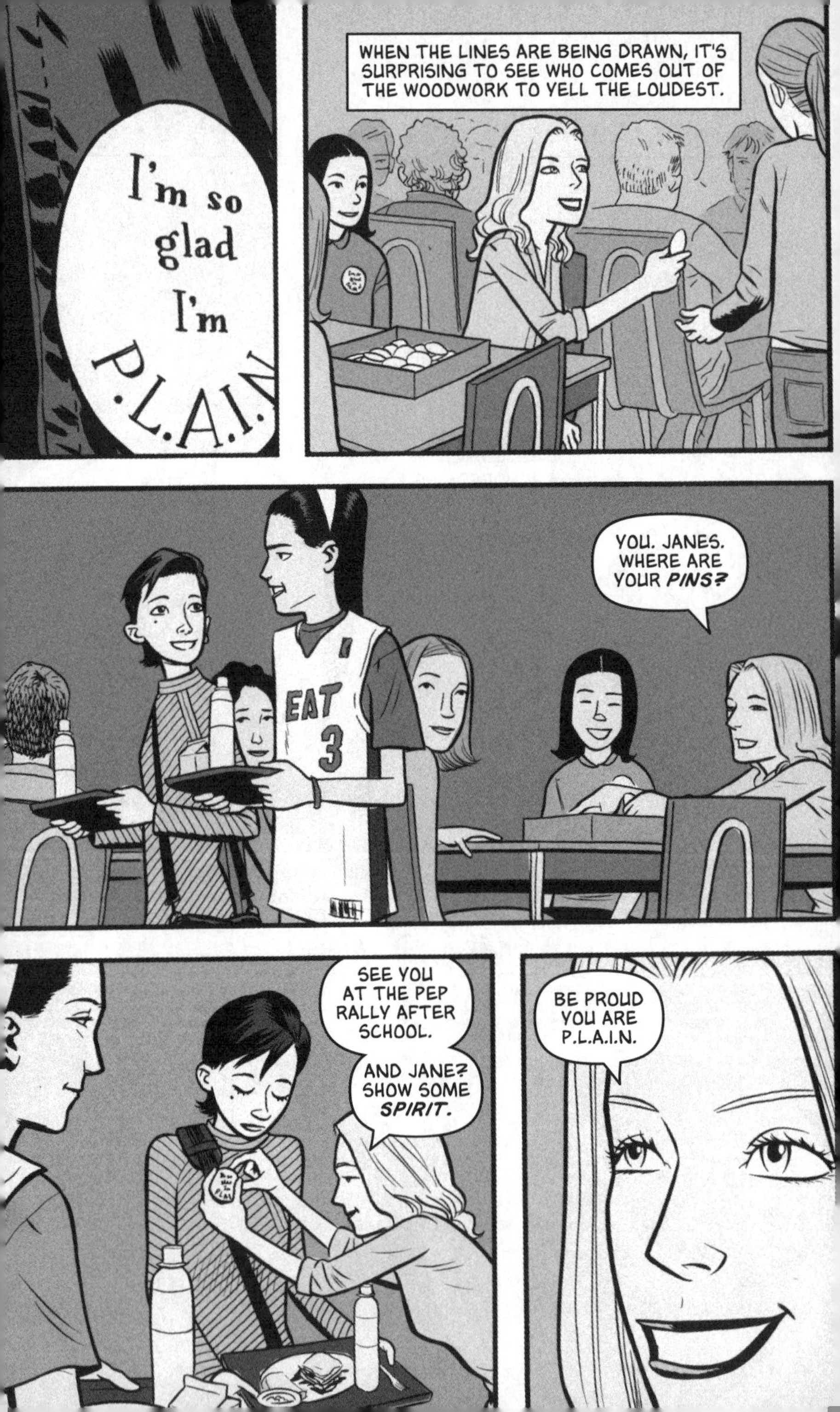
I'm so glad I'm P.L.A.I.N
WHEN THE LINES ARE BEING DRAWN, IT'S SURPRISING TO SEE WHO COMES OUT OF THE WOODWORK TO YELL THE LOUDEST.
YOU. JANES. WHERE ARE YOUR PINS?
SEE YOU AT THE PEP RALLY AFTER SCHOOL.
AND JANE? SHOW SOME SPIRIT.
BE PROUD YOU ARE P.L.A.I.N.

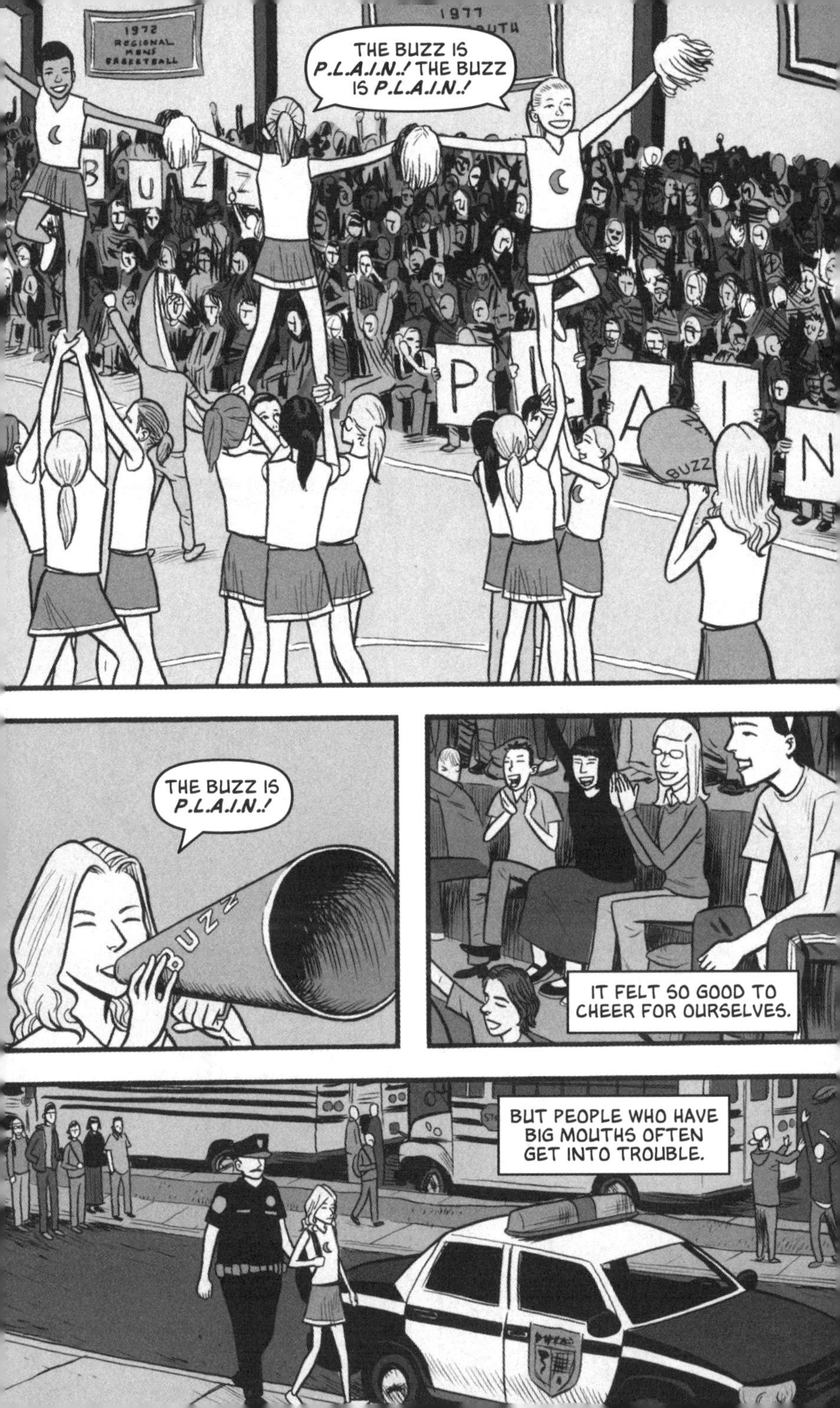
1972 REGIONAL MENS BASKETBALL
THE BUZZ IS *P.L.A.I.N.!* THE BUZZ IS *P.L.A.I.N.!*
THE BUZZ IS *P.L.A.I.N.!*
BUZZ
IT FELT SO GOOD TO CHEER FOR OURSELVES.
BUT PEOPLE WHO HAVE BIG MOUTHS OFTEN GET INTO TROUBLE.

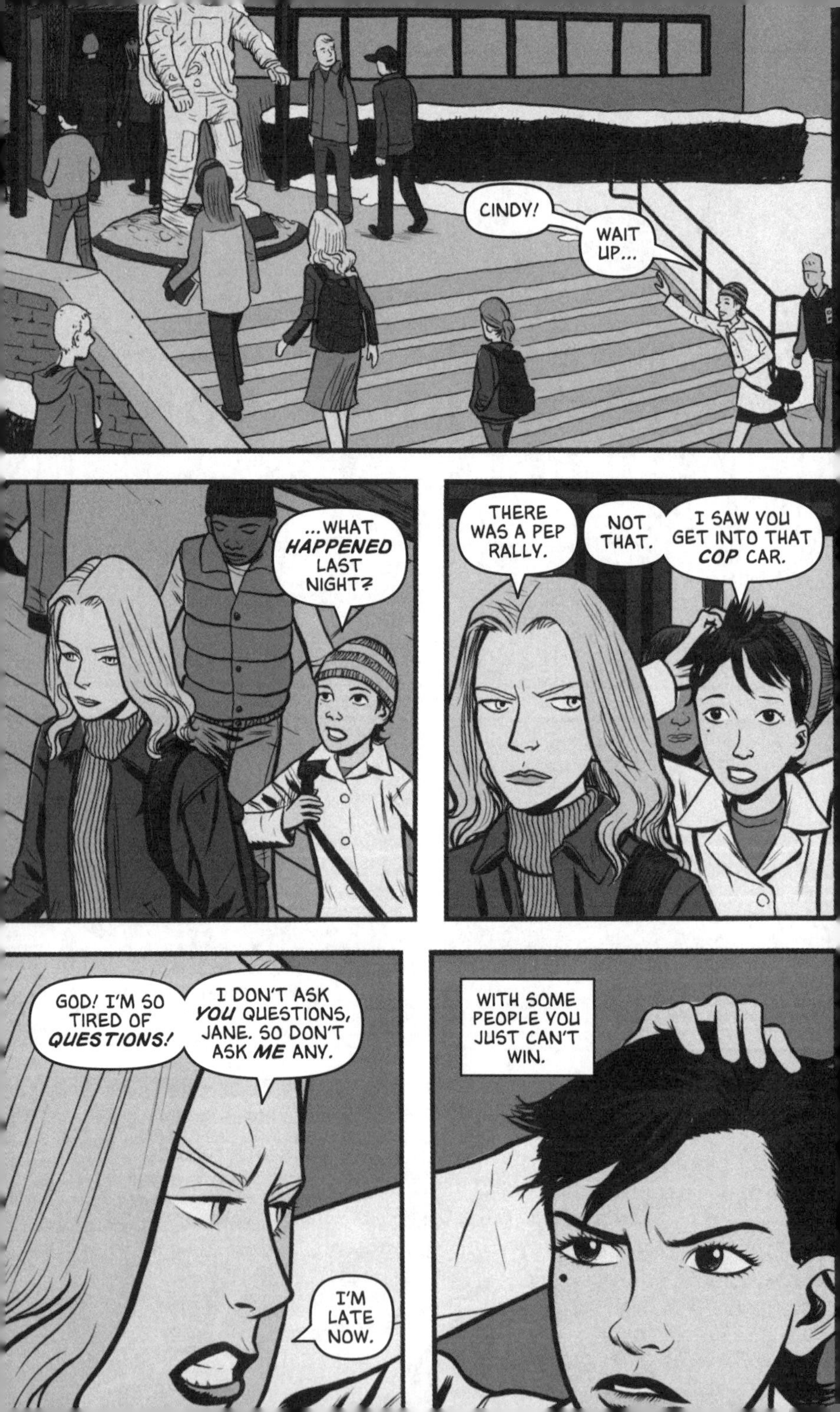
CINDY!
WAIT UP...
...WHAT HAPPENED LAST NIGHT?
THERE WAS A PEP RALLY.
NOT THAT.
I SAW YOU GET INTO THAT COP CAR.
GOD! I'M SO TIRED OF QUESTIONS!
I DON'T ASK YOU QUESTIONS, JANE. SO DON'T ASK ME ANY.
I'M LATE NOW.
WITH SOME PEOPLE YOU JUST CAN'T WIN.

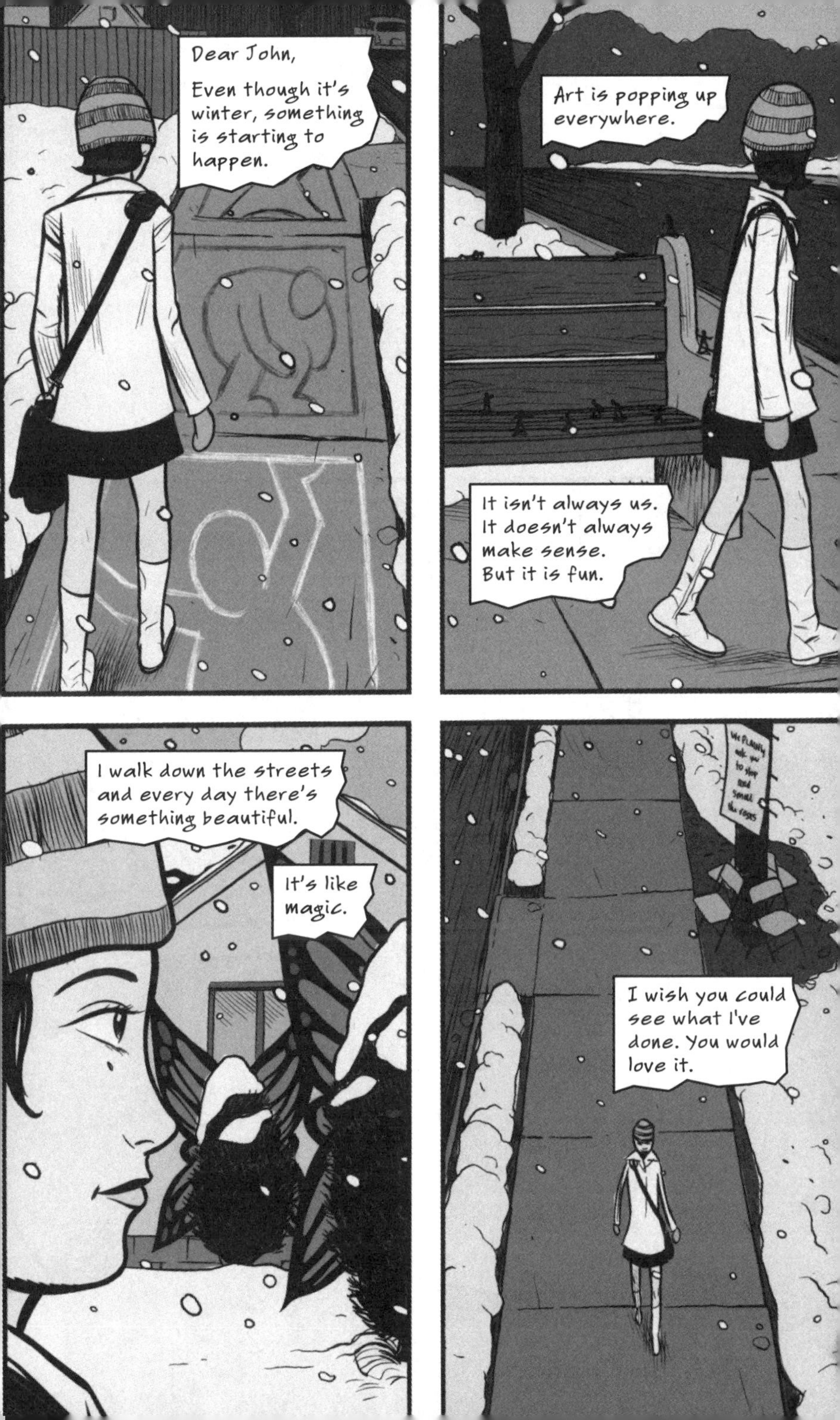
Dear John,
Even though it's winter, something is starting to happen.
Art is popping up everywhere.
It isn't always us. It doesn't always make sense. But it is fun.
I walk down the streets and every day there's something beautiful.
It's like magic.
I wish you could see what I've done. You would love it.

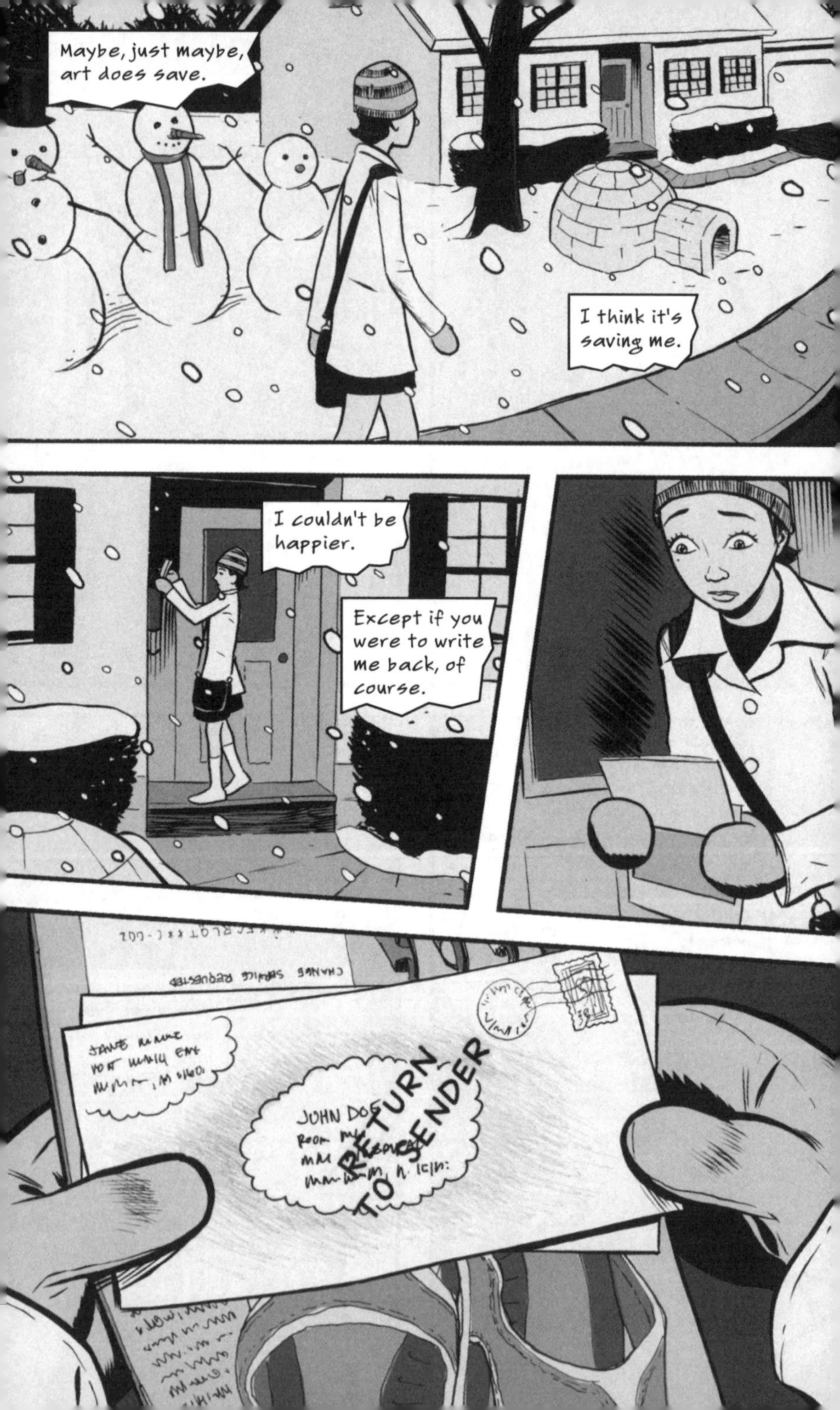

Maybe, just maybe, art does save.
I think it's saving me.
I couldn't be happier.
Except if you were to write me back, of course.
CHANGE SERVICE REQUESTED
JOHN DOE
RETURN TO SENDER

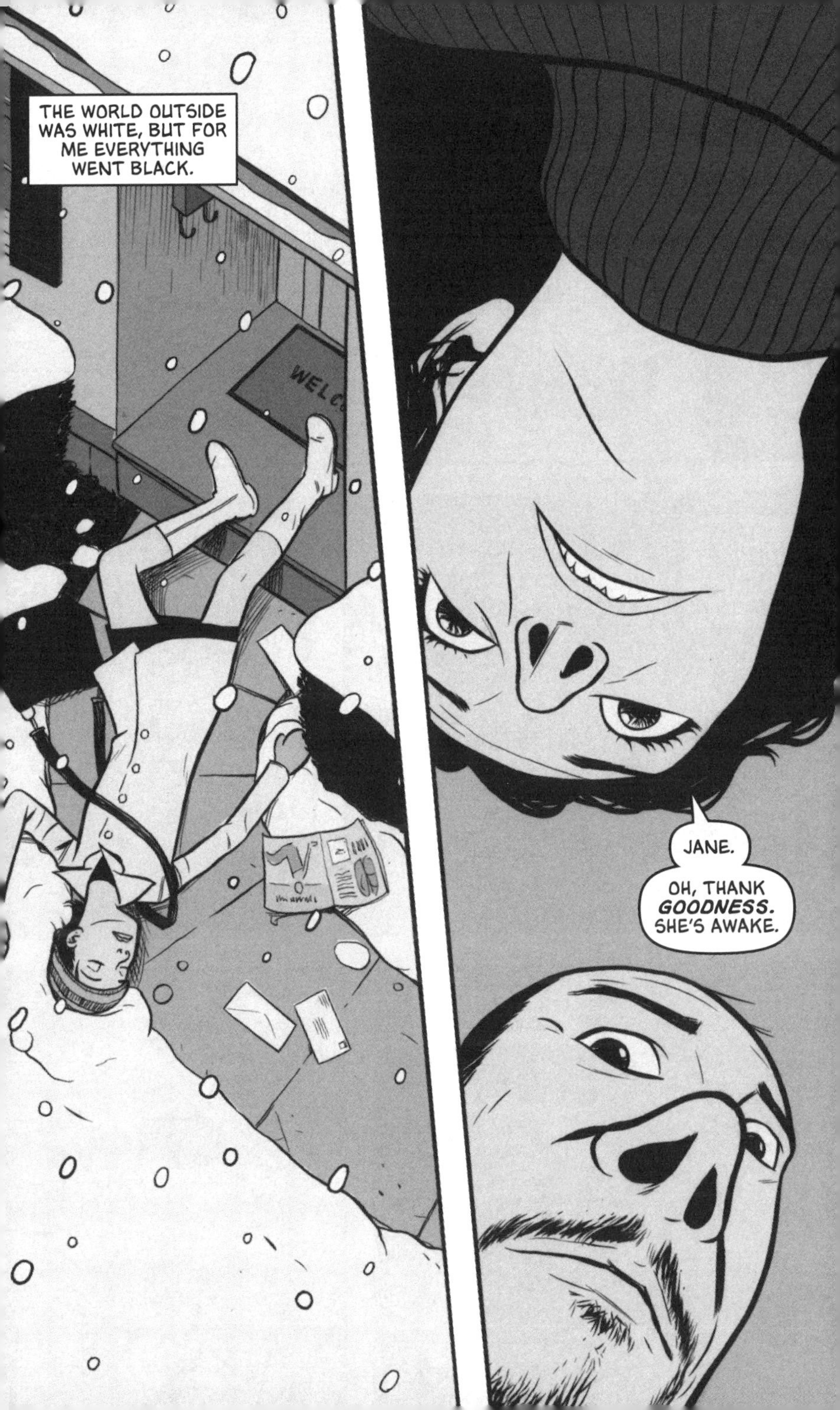
THE WORLD OUTSIDE WAS WHITE, BUT FOR ME EVERYTHING WENT BLACK.
WELC
JANE.
OH, THANK *GOODNESS.* SHE'S AWAKE.

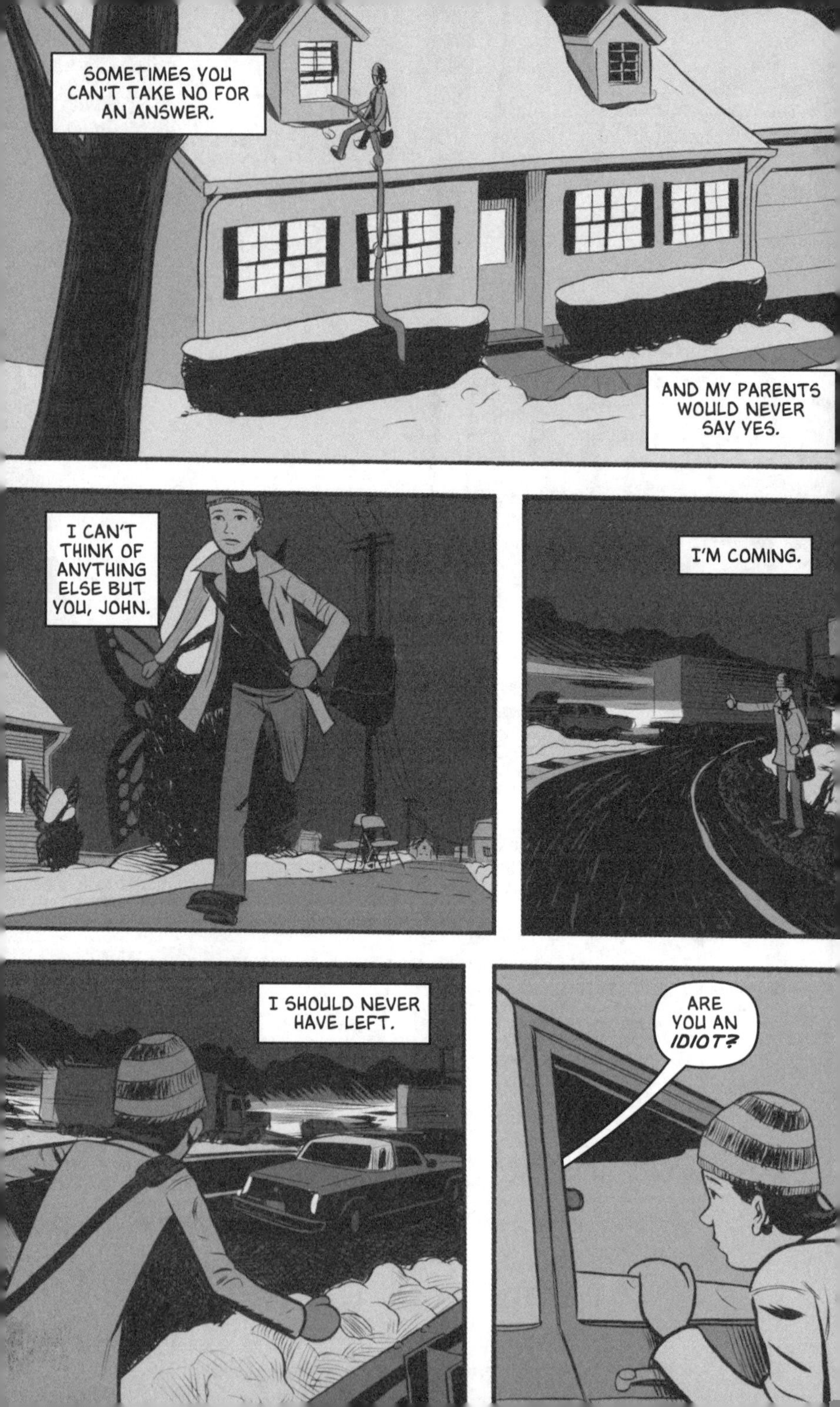
SOMETIMES YOU CAN'T TAKE NO FOR AN ANSWER.
AND MY PARENTS WOULD NEVER SAY YES.
I CAN'T THINK OF ANYTHING ELSE BUT YOU, JOHN.
I'M COMING.
I SHOULD NEVER HAVE LEFT.
ARE YOU AN *IDIOT?*

DO YOU KNOW HOW *DANGEROUS* HITCHHIKING IS?

HEY, ARE YOU OK?

WILL YOU GIVE ME A LIFT?

OF *COURSE.*

WHERE DO YOU WANT TO GO?

METRO CITY.

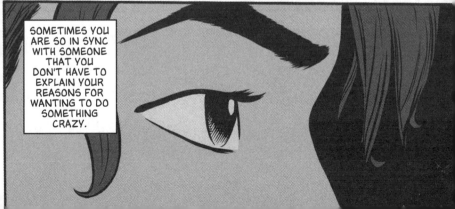

SOMETIMES YOU ARE SO IN SYNC WITH SOMEONE THAT YOU DON'T HAVE TO EXPLAIN YOUR REASONS FOR WANTING TO DO SOMETHING CRAZY.

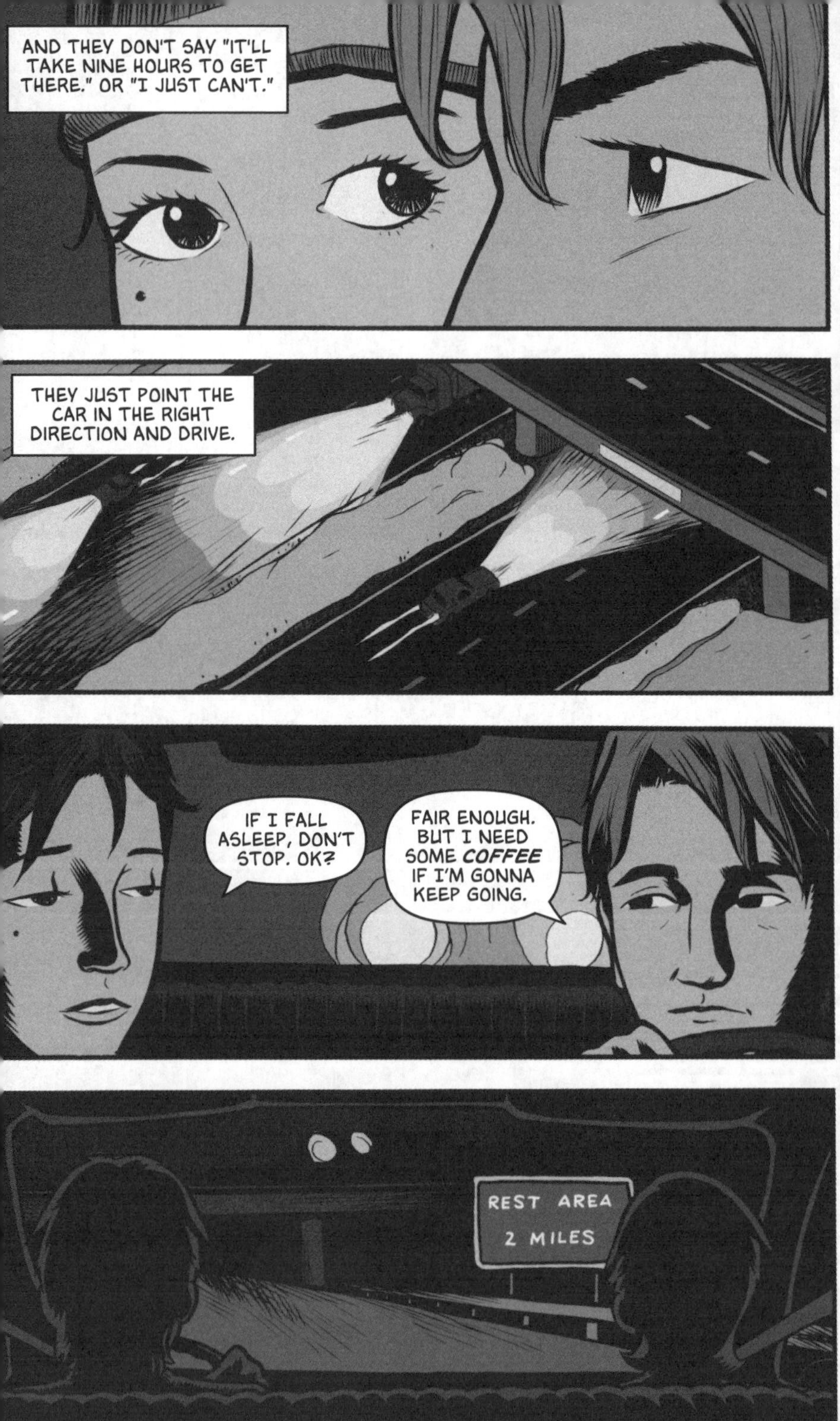
AND THEY DON'T SAY "IT'LL TAKE NINE HOURS TO GET THERE." OR "I JUST CAN'T."
THEY JUST POINT THE CAR IN THE RIGHT DIRECTION AND DRIVE.
IF I FALL ASLEEP, DON'T STOP. OK?
FAIR ENOUGH. BUT I NEED SOME *COFFEE* IF I'M GONNA KEEP GOING.
REST AREA 2 MILES

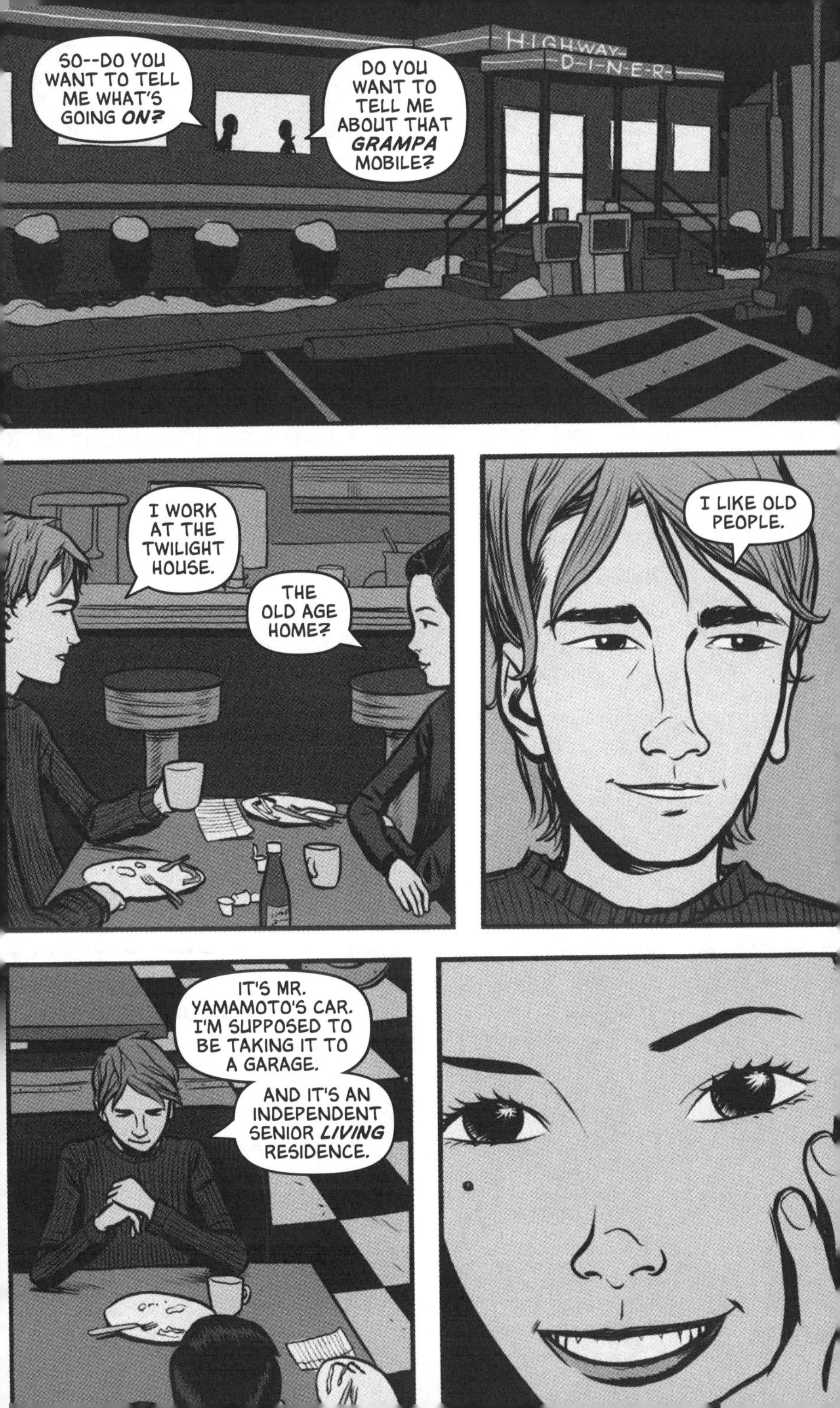
HIGHWAY DINER
SO--DO YOU WANT TO TELL ME WHAT'S GOING ON?
DO YOU WANT TO TELL ME ABOUT THAT GRAMPA MOBILE?
I WORK AT THE TWILIGHT HOUSE.
THE OLD AGE HOME?
I LIKE OLD PEOPLE.
IT'S MR. YAMAMOTO'S CAR. I'M SUPPOSED TO BE TAKING IT TO A GARAGE.
AND IT'S AN INDEPENDENT SENIOR LIVING RESIDENCE.

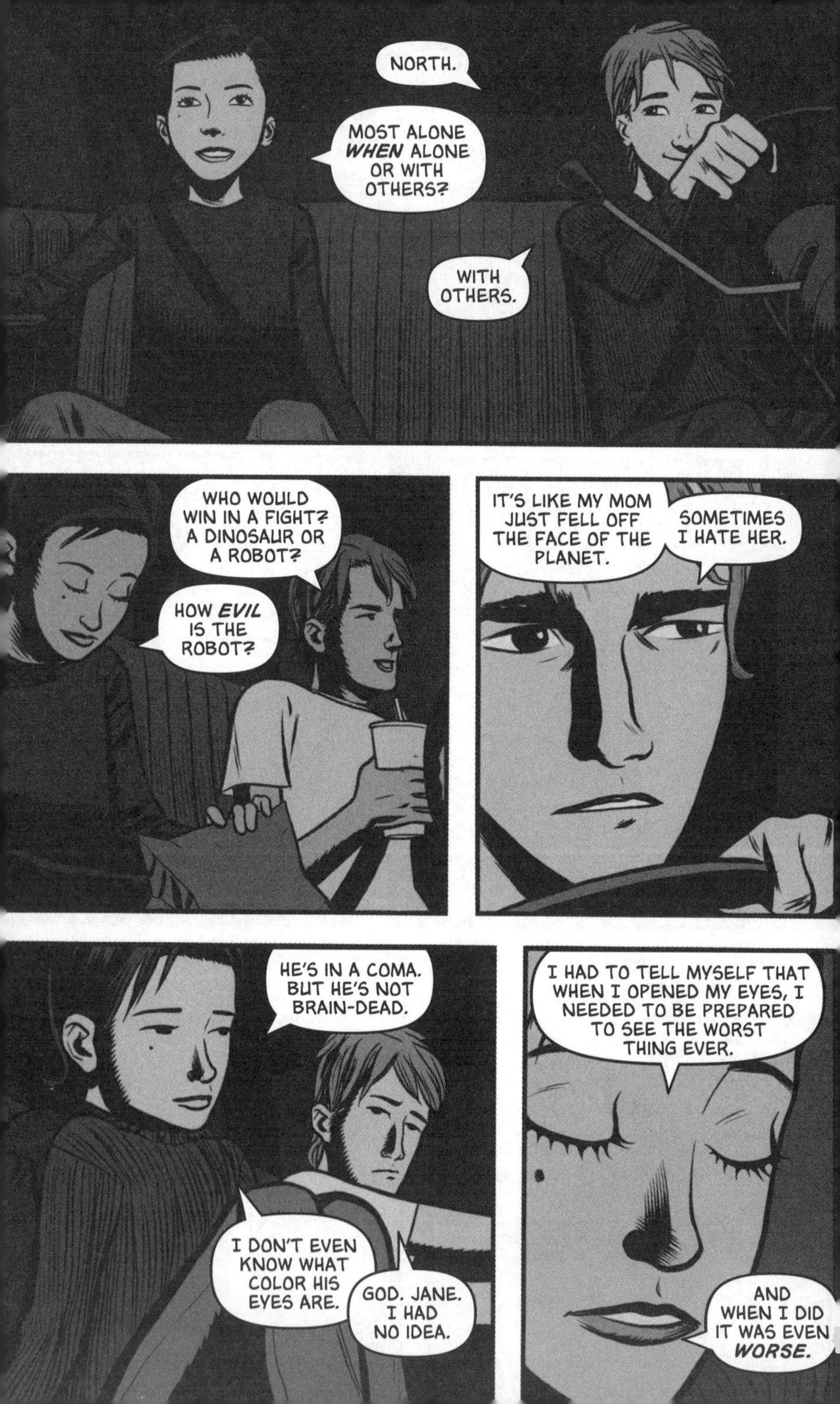
NORTH.
MOST ALONE *WHEN* ALONE OR WITH OTHERS?
WITH OTHERS.
WHO WOULD WIN IN A FIGHT? A DINOSAUR OR A ROBOT?
HOW *EVIL* IS THE ROBOT?
IT'S LIKE MY MOM JUST FELL OFF THE FACE OF THE PLANET.
SOMETIMES I HATE HER.
HE'S IN A COMA. BUT HE'S NOT BRAIN-DEAD.
I DON'T EVEN KNOW WHAT COLOR HIS EYES ARE.
GOD. JANE. I HAD NO IDEA.
I HAD TO TELL MYSELF THAT WHEN I OPENED MY EYES, I NEEDED TO BE PREPARED TO SEE THE WORST THING EVER.
AND WHEN I DID IT WAS EVEN *WORSE*.

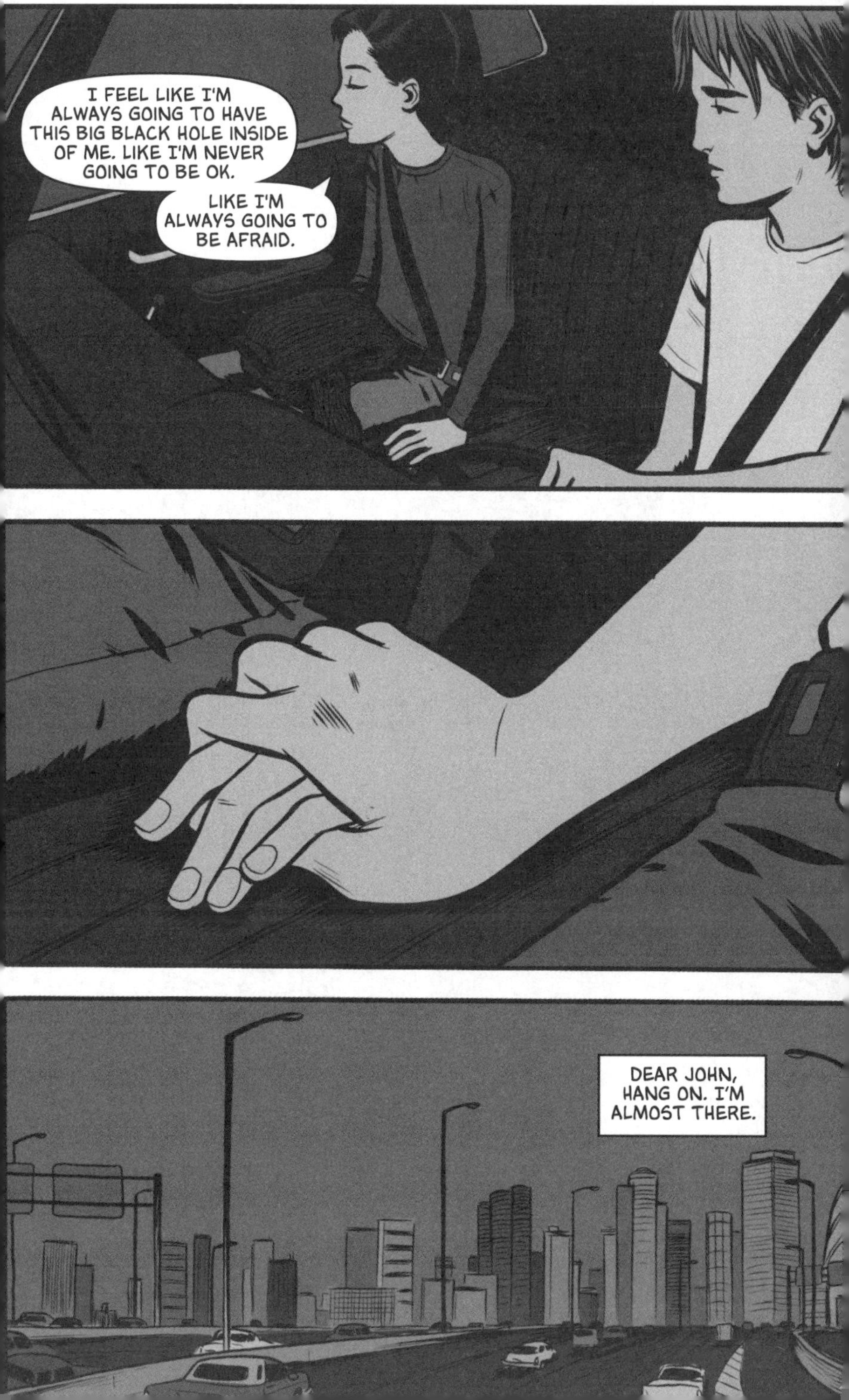
I FEEL LIKE I'M ALWAYS GOING TO HAVE THIS BIG BLACK HOLE INSIDE OF ME. LIKE I'M NEVER GOING TO BE OK.
LIKE I'M ALWAYS GOING TO BE AFRAID.
DEAR JOHN, HANG ON. I'M ALMOST THERE.

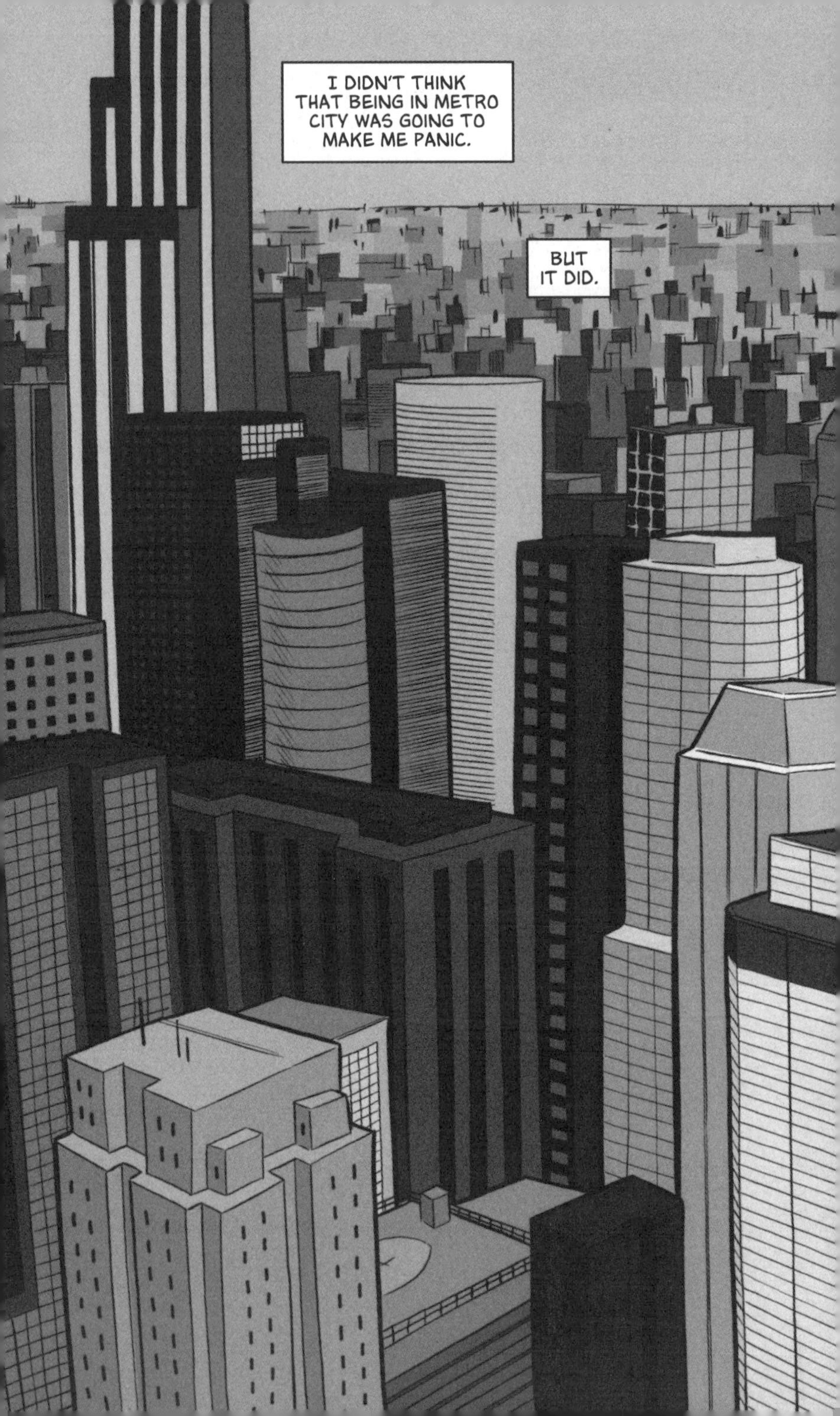
I DIDN'T THINK THAT BEING IN METRO CITY WAS GOING TO MAKE ME PANIC.
BUT IT DID.

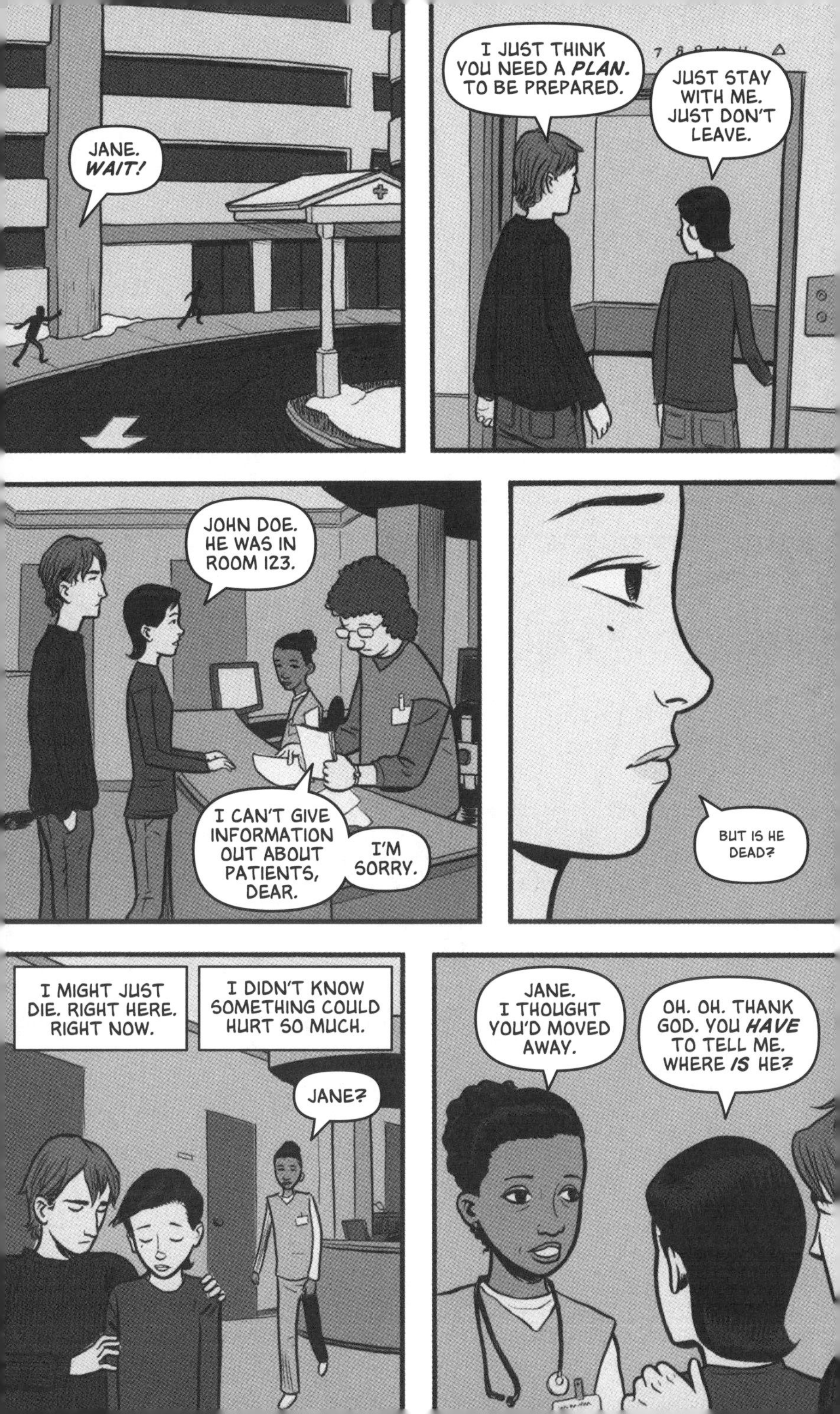
JANE. WAIT!
I JUST THINK YOU NEED A PLAN. TO BE PREPARED.
JUST STAY WITH ME. JUST DON'T LEAVE.
JOHN DOE. HE WAS IN ROOM 123.
I CAN'T GIVE INFORMATION OUT ABOUT PATIENTS, DEAR.
I'M SORRY.
BUT IS HE DEAD?
I MIGHT JUST DIE. RIGHT HERE. RIGHT NOW.
I DIDN'T KNOW SOMETHING COULD HURT SO MUCH.
JANE?
JANE. I THOUGHT YOU'D MOVED AWAY.
OH. OH. THANK GOD. YOU HAVE TO TELL ME. WHERE IS HE?

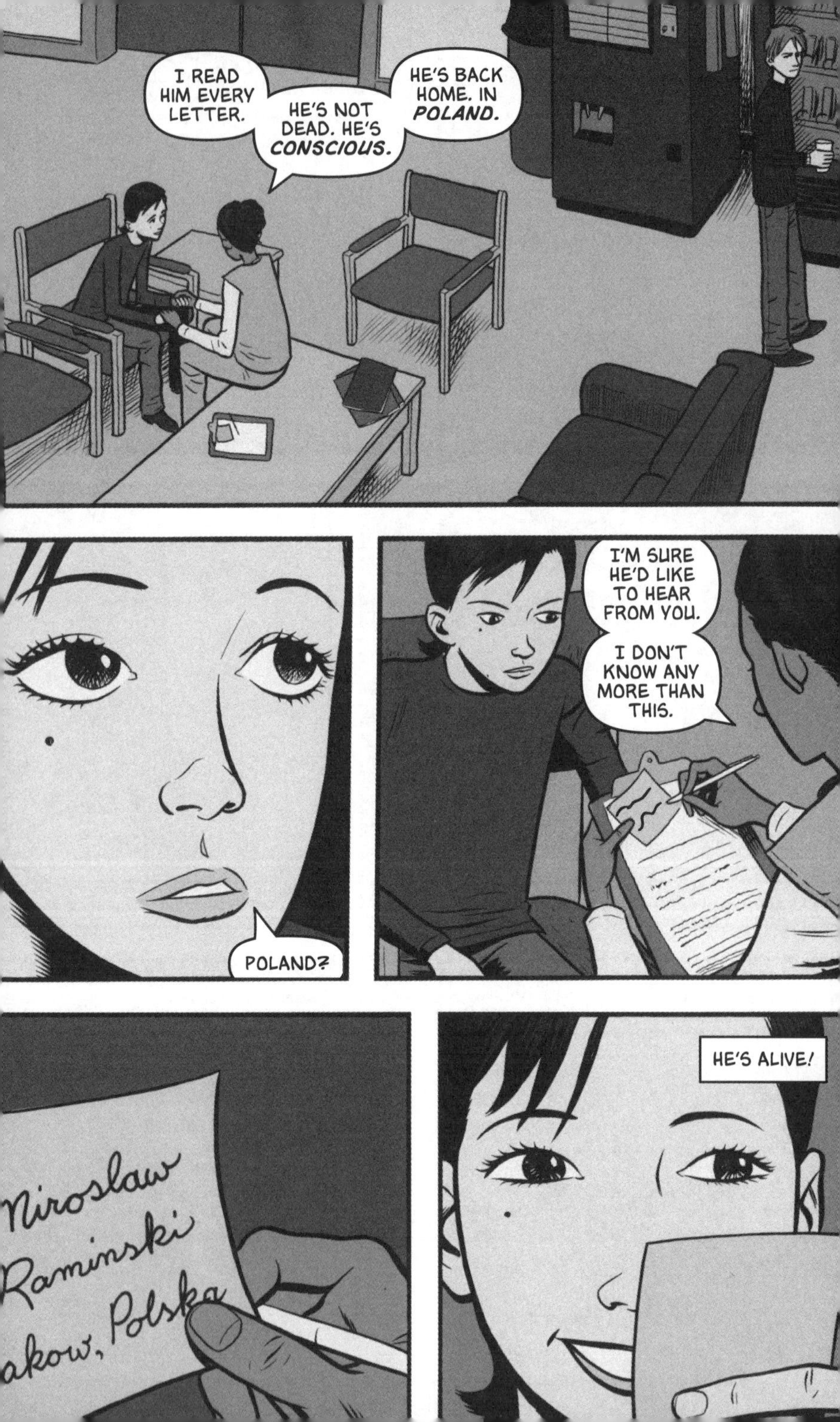
I READ HIM EVERY LETTER.
HE'S NOT DEAD. HE'S CONSCIOUS.
HE'S BACK HOME. IN POLAND.
POLAND?
I'M SURE HE'D LIKE TO HEAR FROM YOU.
I DON'T KNOW ANY MORE THAN THIS.
Miroslaw
Raminski
akow, Polska
HE'S ALIVE!

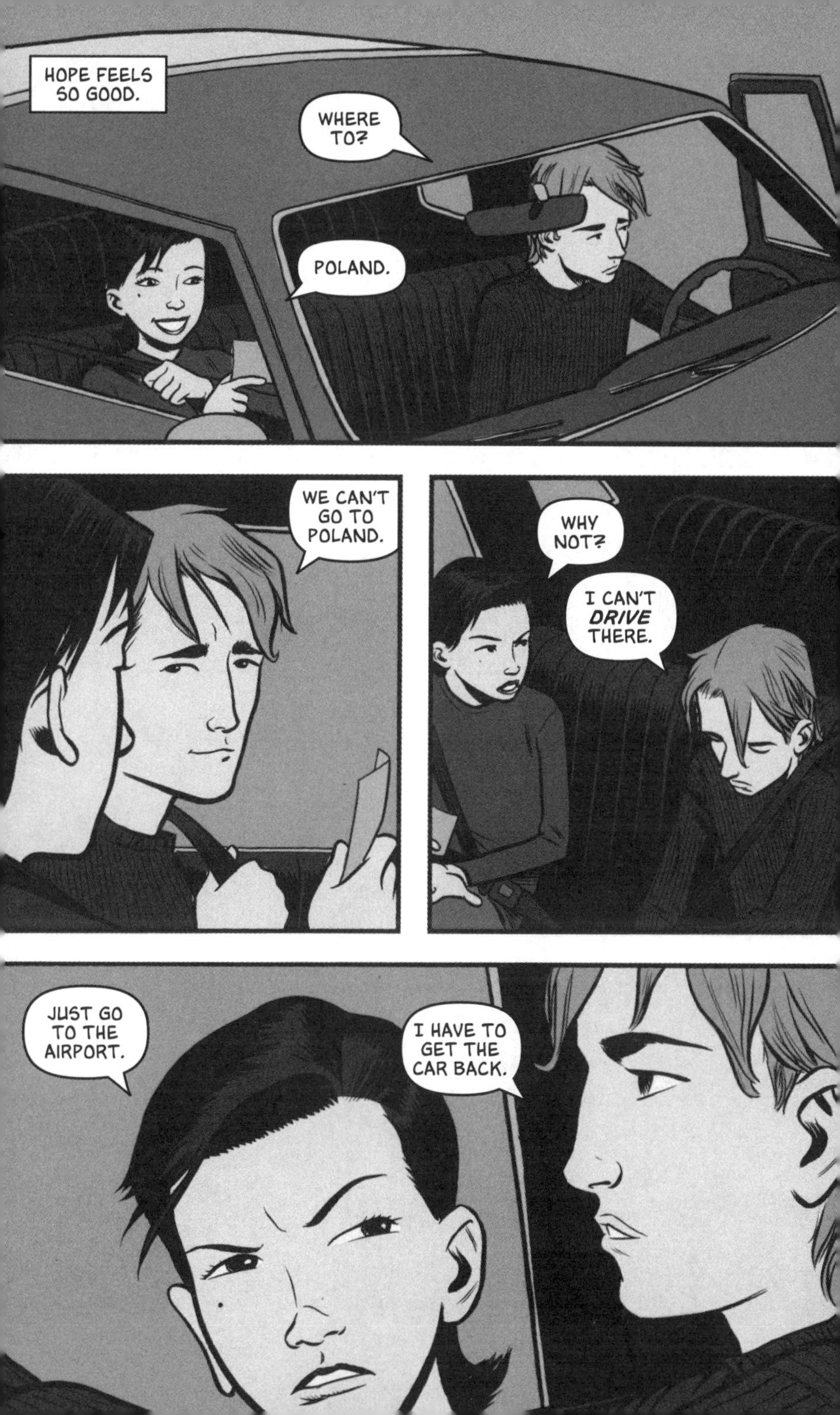

HOPE FEELS SO GOOD.
WHERE TO?
POLAND.
WE CAN'T GO TO POLAND.
WHY NOT?
I CAN'T *DRIVE* THERE.
JUST GO TO THE AIRPORT.
I HAVE TO GET THE CAR BACK.

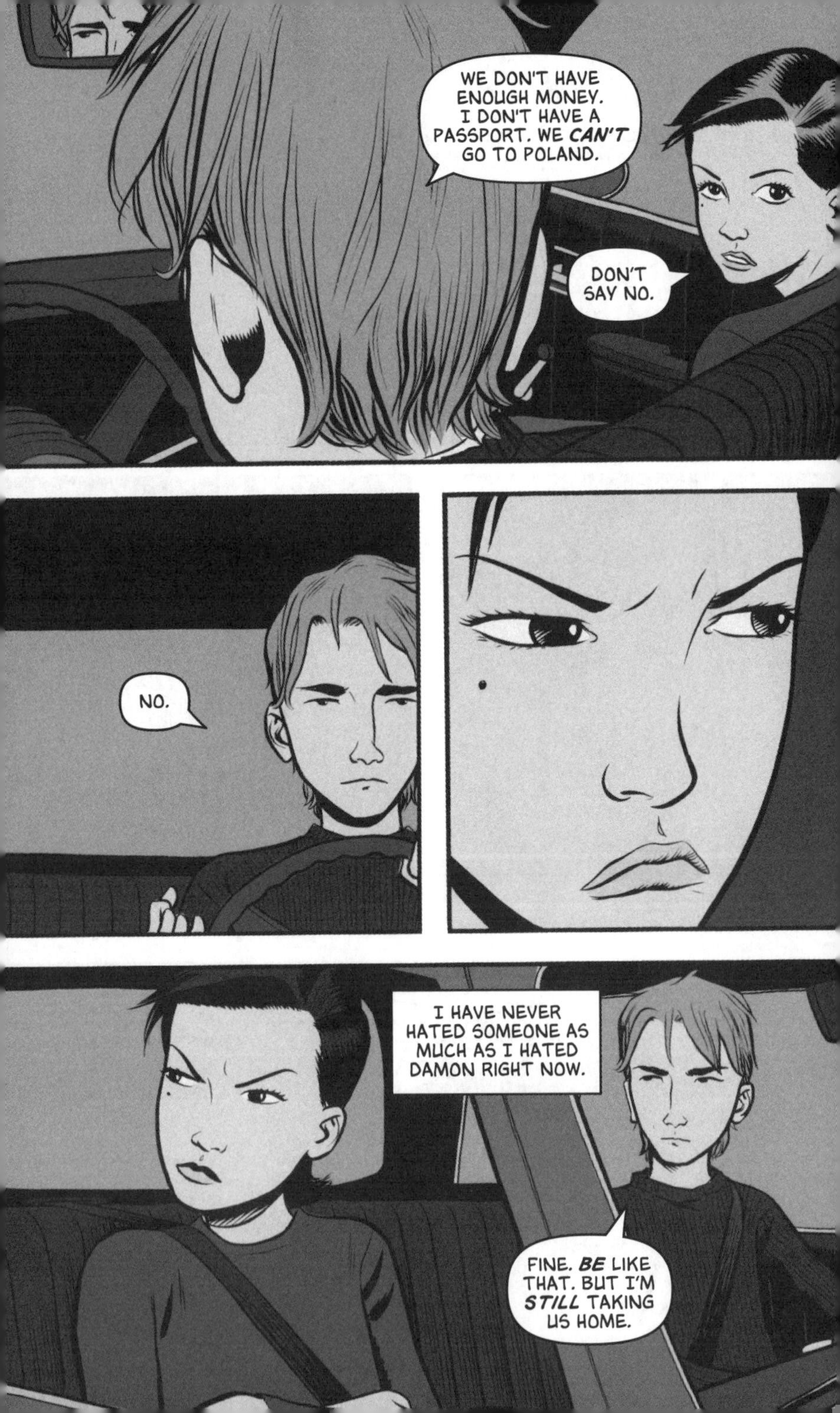

WE DON'T HAVE ENOUGH MONEY. I DON'T HAVE A PASSPORT. WE *CAN'T* GO TO POLAND.
DON'T SAY NO.
NO.
I HAVE NEVER HATED SOMEONE AS MUCH AS I HATED DAMON RIGHT NOW.
FINE. *BE* LIKE THAT. BUT I'M *STILL* TAKING US HOME.

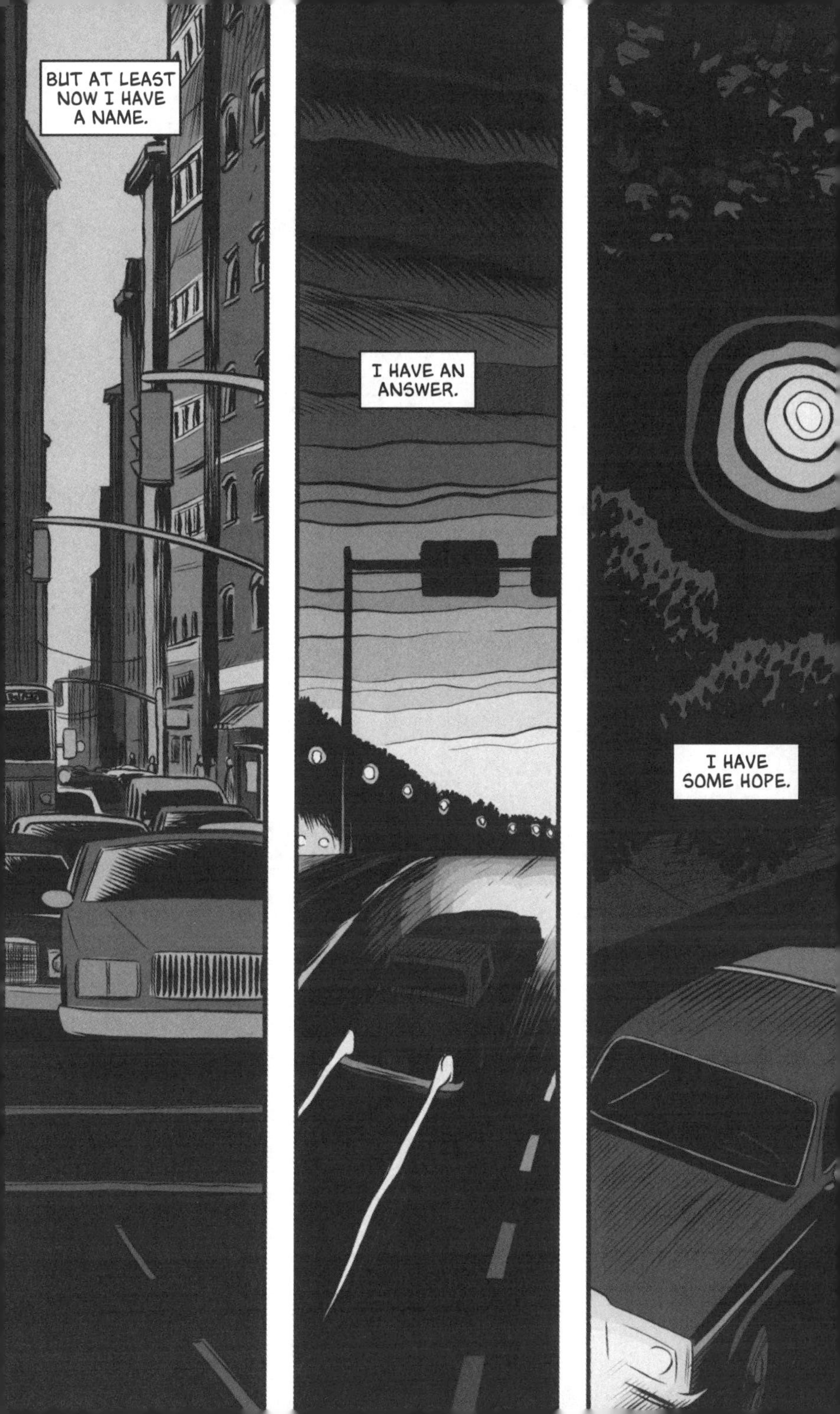
BUT AT LEAST NOW I HAVE A NAME.
I HAVE AN ANSWER.
I HAVE SOME HOPE.

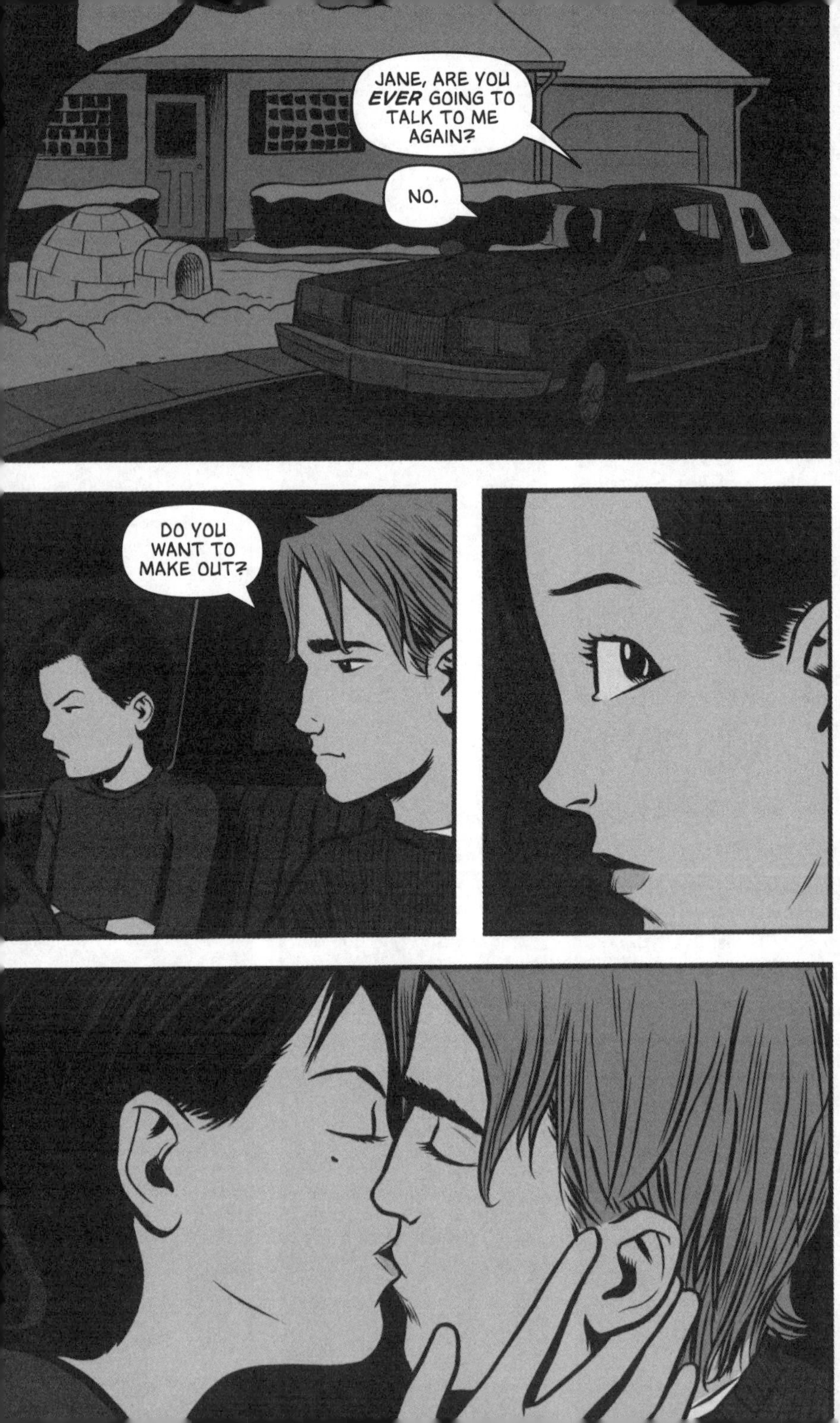
JANE, ARE YOU *EVER* GOING TO TALK TO ME AGAIN?
NO.
DO YOU WANT TO MAKE OUT?

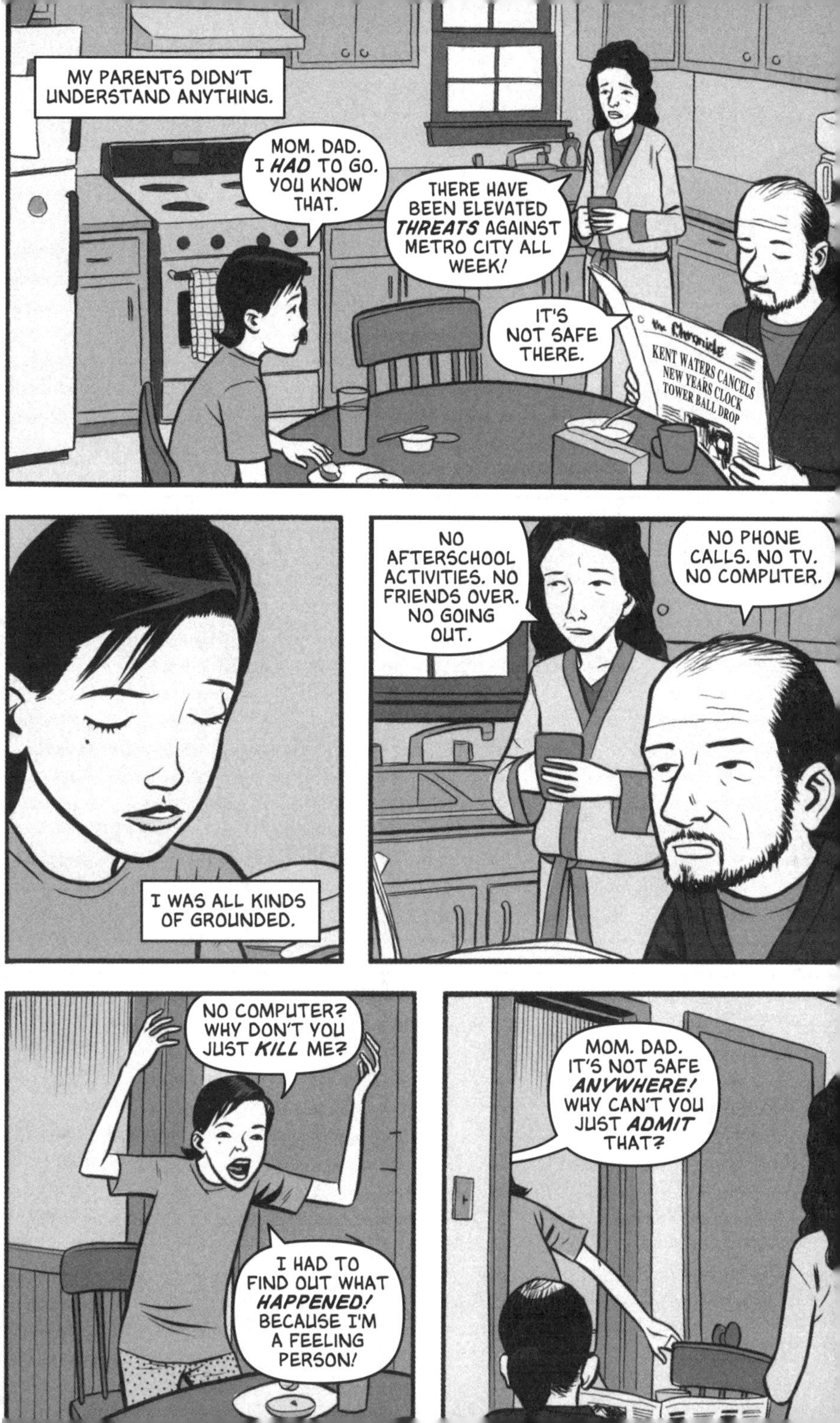
MY PARENTS DIDN'T UNDERSTAND ANYTHING.
MOM. DAD. I HAD TO GO. YOU KNOW THAT.
THERE HAVE BEEN ELEVATED THREATS AGAINST METRO CITY ALL WEEK!
IT'S NOT SAFE THERE.
the Chronicle
KENT WATERS CANCELS NEW YEARS CLOCK TOWER BALL DROP
I WAS ALL KINDS OF GROUNDED.
NO AFTERSCHOOL ACTIVITIES. NO FRIENDS OVER. NO GOING OUT.
NO PHONE CALLS. NO TV. NO COMPUTER.
NO COMPUTER? WHY DON'T YOU JUST KILL ME?
I HAD TO FIND OUT WHAT HAPPENED! BECAUSE I'M A FEELING PERSON!
MOM. DAD. IT'S NOT SAFE ANYWHERE! WHY CAN'T YOU JUST ADMIT THAT?

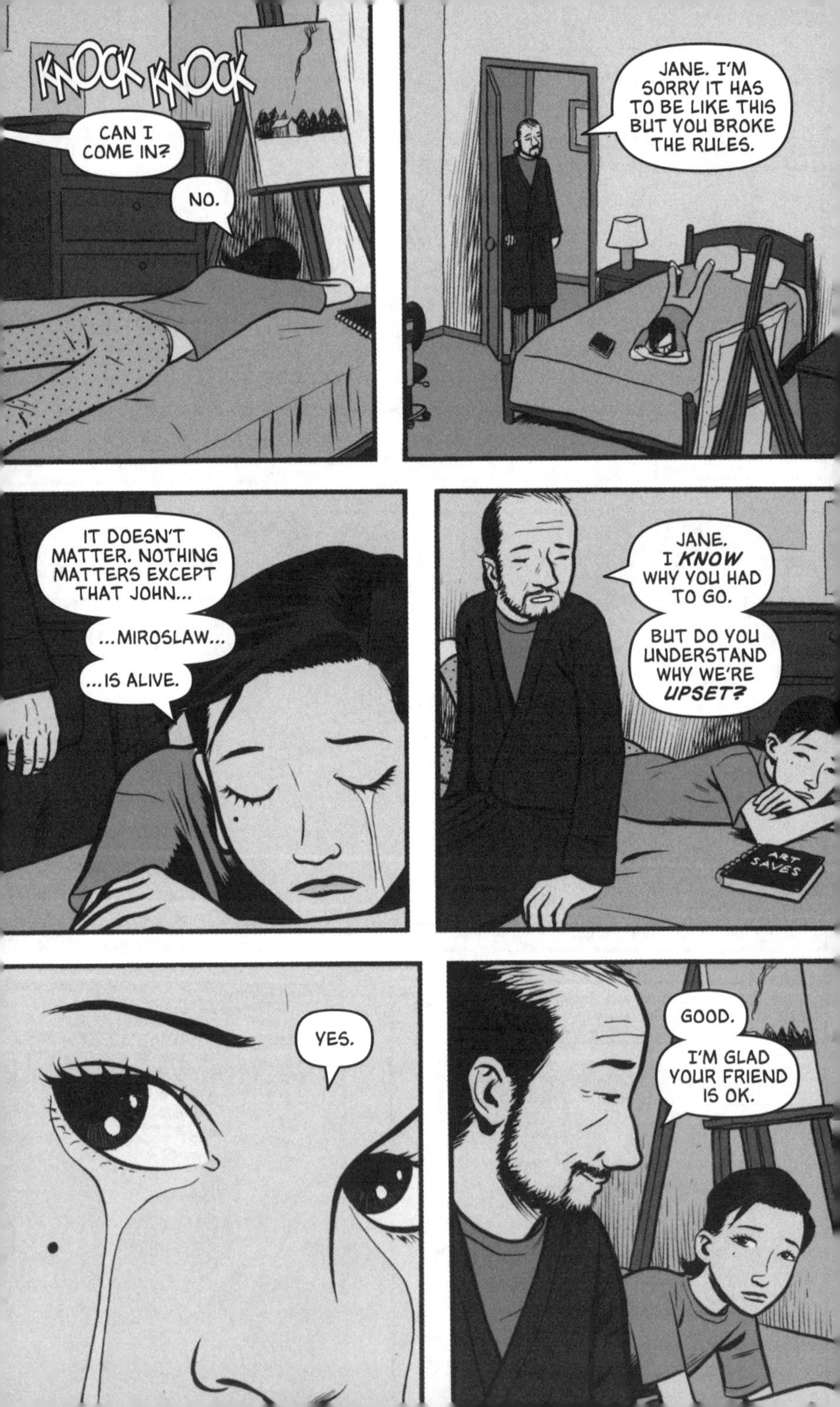
KNOCK KNOCK
CAN I COME IN?
NO.
JANE. I'M SORRY IT HAS TO BE LIKE THIS BUT YOU BROKE THE RULES.
IT DOESN'T MATTER. NOTHING MATTERS EXCEPT THAT JOHN...
...MIROSLAW...
...IS ALIVE.
JANE. I KNOW WHY YOU HAD TO GO.
BUT DO YOU UNDERSTAND WHY WE'RE UPSET?
ART SAVES
YES.
GOOD.
I'M GLAD YOUR FRIEND IS OK.

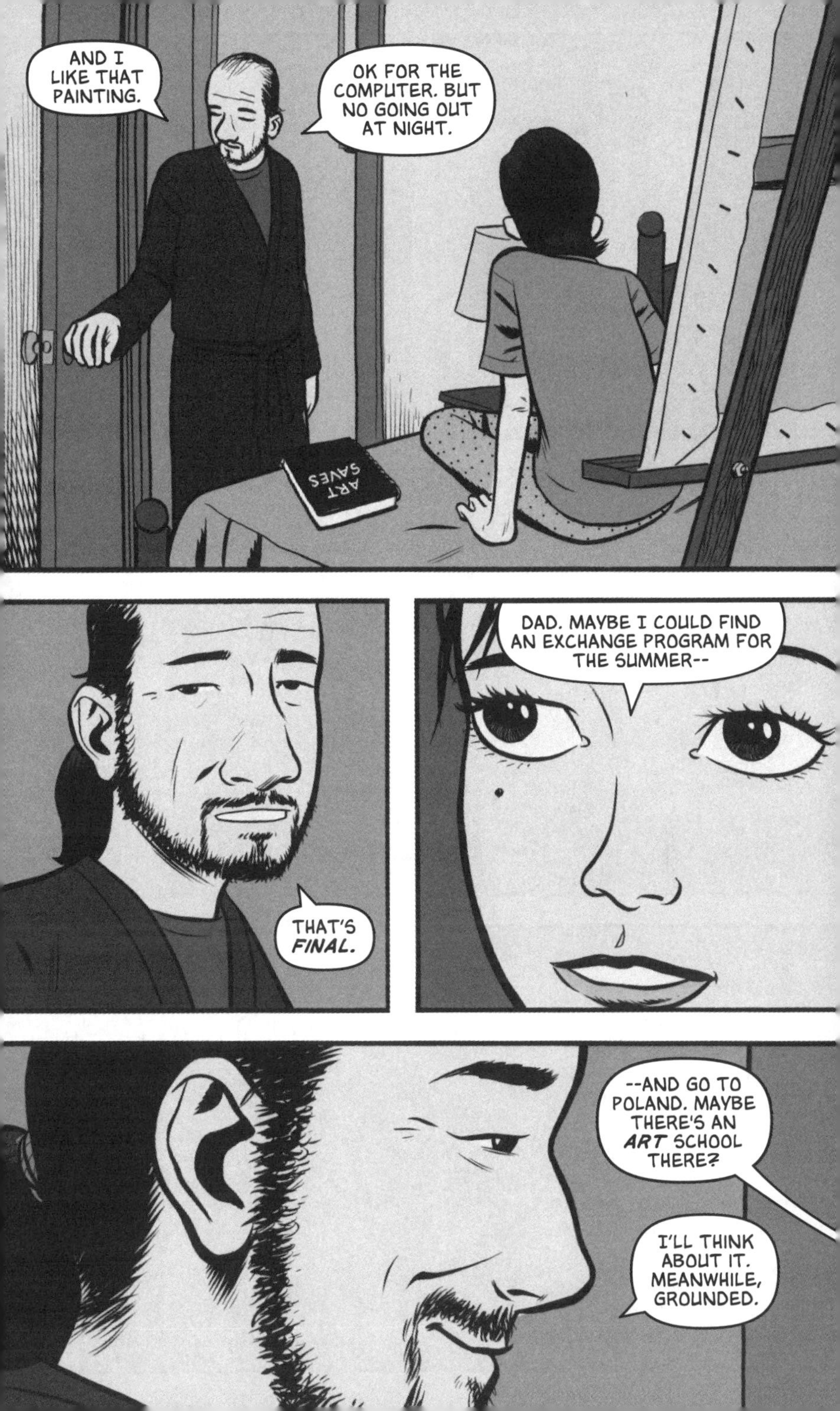
AND I LIKE THAT PAINTING.
OK FOR THE COMPUTER. BUT NO GOING OUT AT NIGHT.
ART SAVES
THAT'S *FINAL.*
DAD. MAYBE I COULD FIND AN EXCHANGE PROGRAM FOR THE SUMMER--
--AND GO TO POLAND. MAYBE THERE'S AN *ART* SCHOOL THERE?
I'LL THINK ABOUT IT. MEANWHILE, GROUNDED.

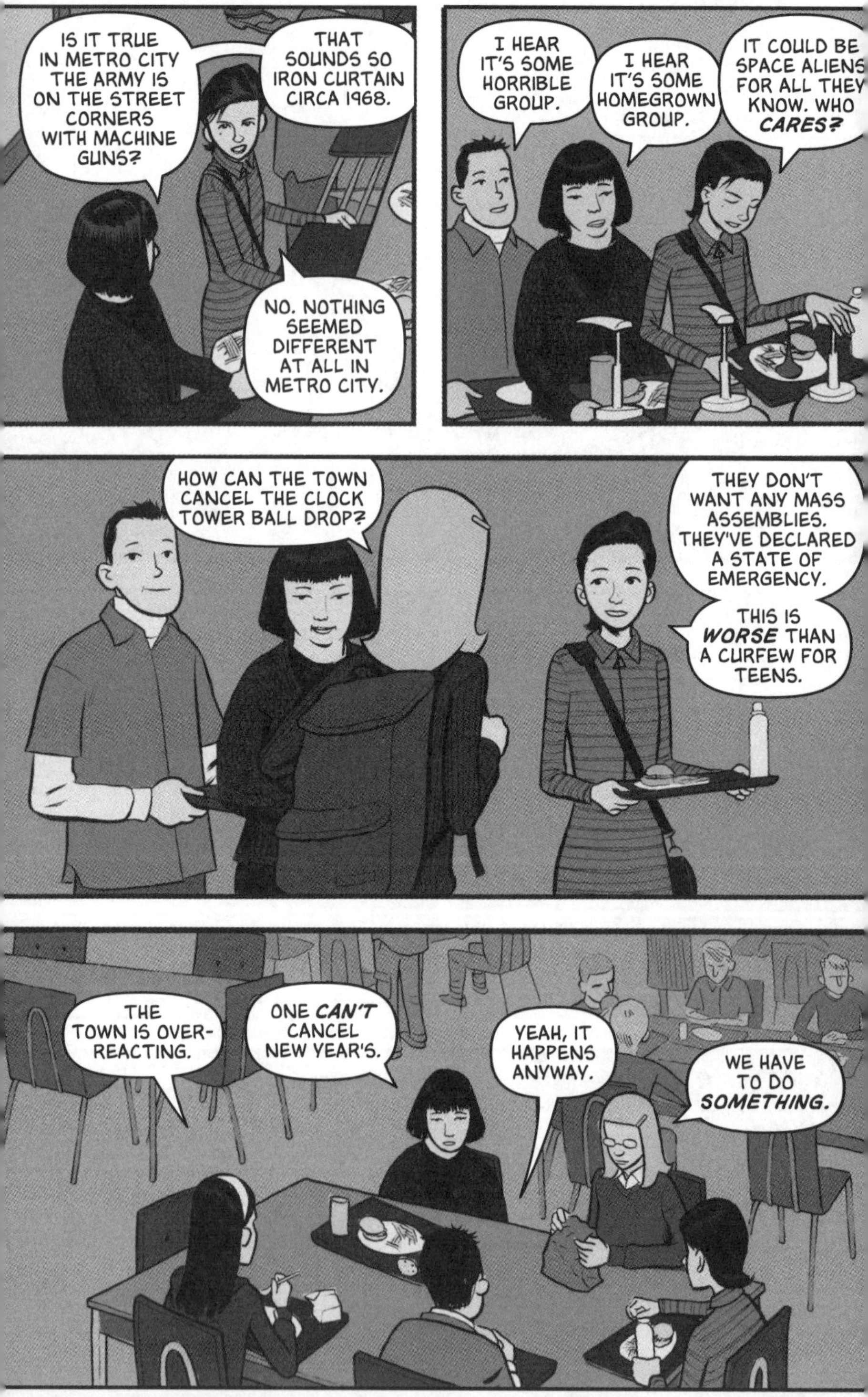
IS IT TRUE IN METRO CITY THE ARMY IS ON THE STREET CORNERS WITH MACHINE GUNS?
THAT SOUNDS SO IRON CURTAIN CIRCA 1968.
NO. NOTHING SEEMED DIFFERENT AT ALL IN METRO CITY.
I HEAR IT'S SOME HORRIBLE GROUP.
I HEAR IT'S SOME HOMEGROWN GROUP.
IT COULD BE SPACE ALIENS FOR ALL THEY KNOW. WHO CARES?
HOW CAN THE TOWN CANCEL THE CLOCK TOWER BALL DROP?
THEY DON'T WANT ANY MASS ASSEMBLIES. THEY'VE DECLARED A STATE OF EMERGENCY.
THIS IS WORSE THAN A CURFEW FOR TEENS.
THE TOWN IS OVER-REACTING.
ONE CAN'T CANCEL NEW YEAR'S.
YEAH, IT HAPPENS ANYWAY.
WE HAVE TO DO SOMETHING.

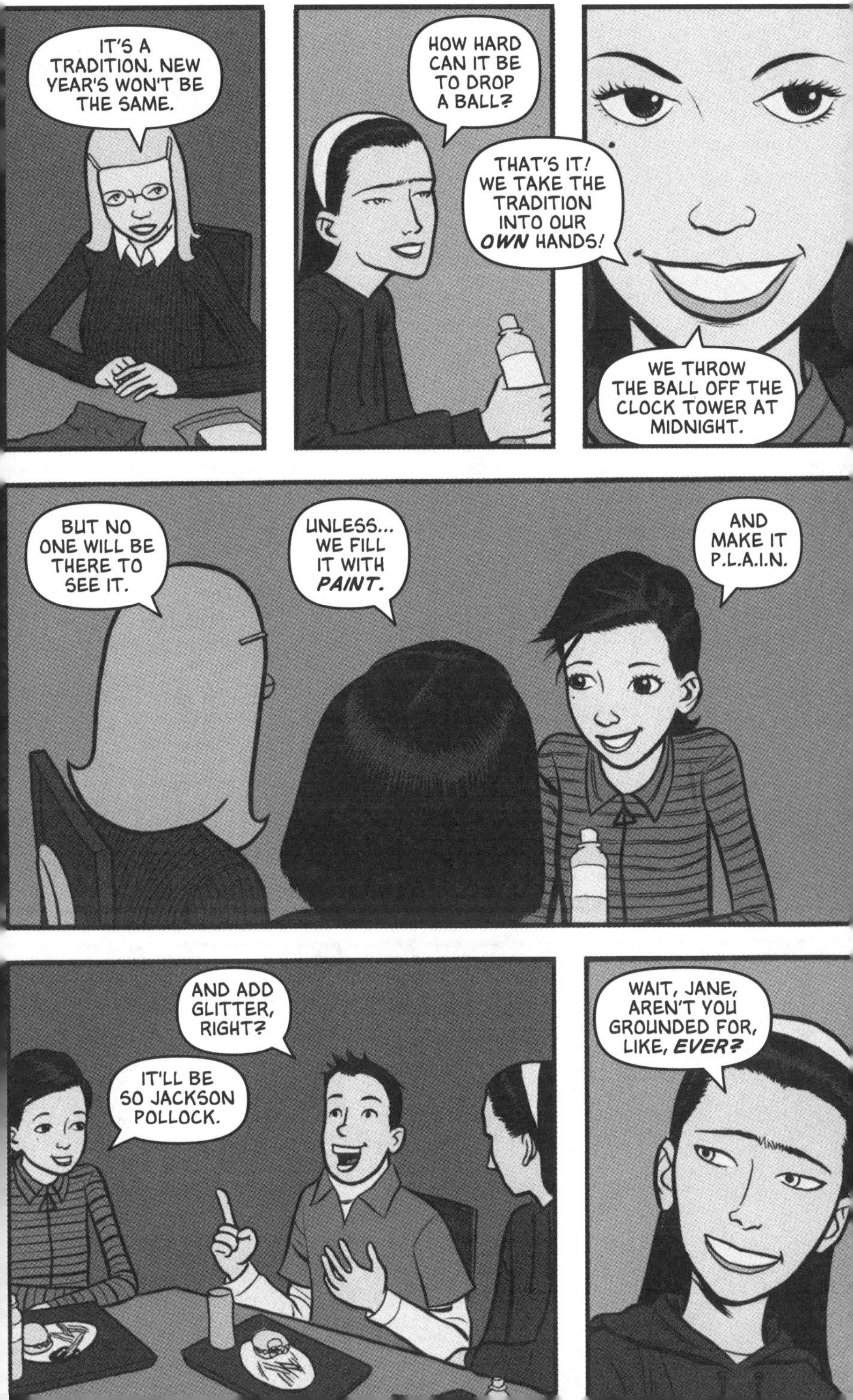
IT'S A TRADITION. NEW YEAR'S WON'T BE THE SAME.
HOW HARD CAN IT BE TO DROP A BALL?
THAT'S IT! WE TAKE THE TRADITION INTO OUR *OWN* HANDS!
WE THROW THE BALL OFF THE CLOCK TOWER AT MIDNIGHT.
BUT NO ONE WILL BE THERE TO SEE IT.
UNLESS... WE FILL IT WITH *PAINT*.
AND MAKE IT P.L.A.I.N.
AND ADD GLITTER, RIGHT?
IT'LL BE SO JACKSON POLLOCK.
WAIT, JANE, AREN'T YOU GROUNDED FOR, LIKE, *EVER*?

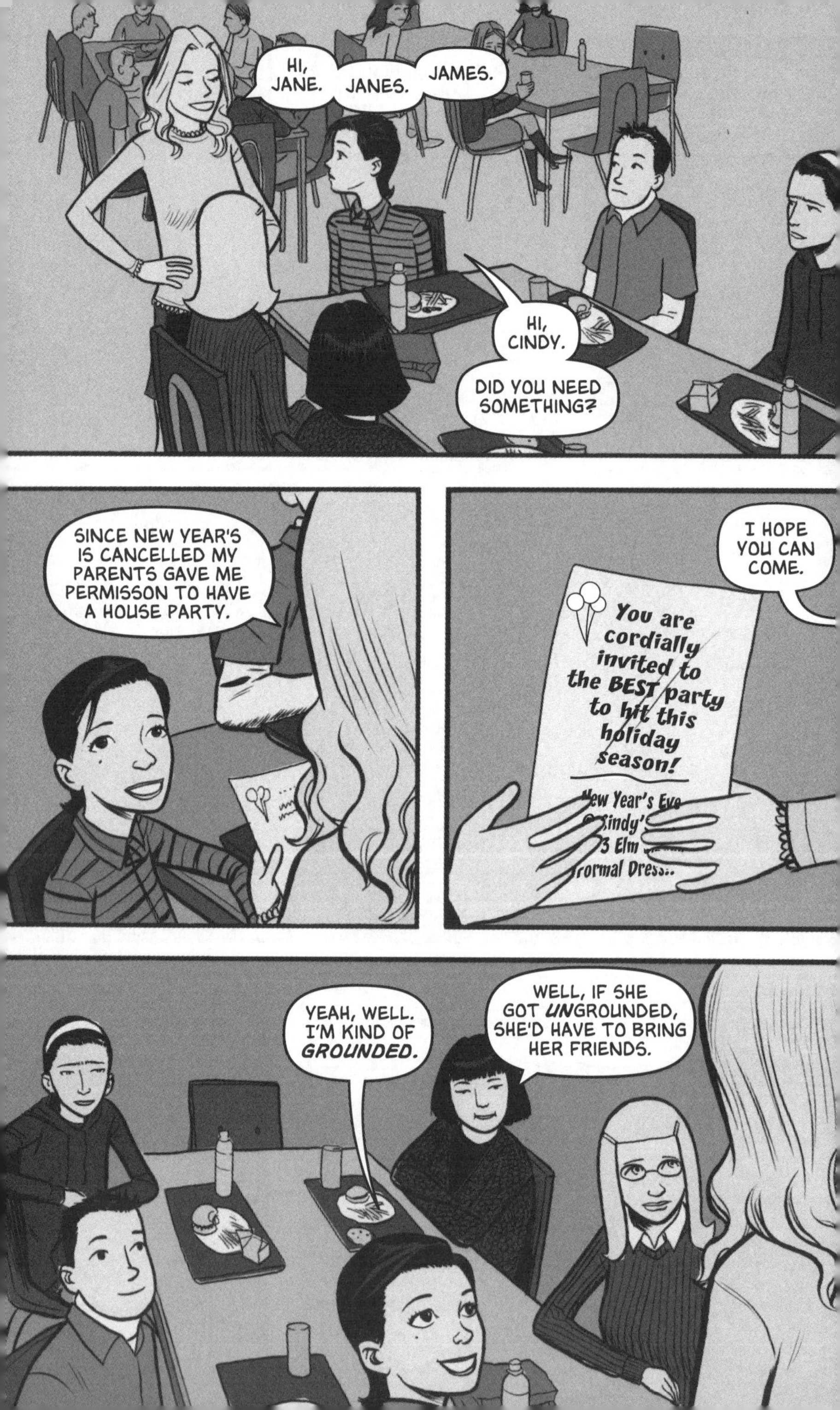
HI, JANE.
JANES.
JAMES.
HI, CINDY.
DID YOU NEED SOMETHING?
SINCE NEW YEAR'S IS CANCELLED MY PARENTS GAVE ME PERMISSON TO HAVE A HOUSE PARTY.
You are cordially invited to the BEST party to hit this holiday season!
New Year's Eve
I HOPE YOU CAN COME.
YEAH, WELL. I'M KIND OF GROUNDED.
WELL, IF SHE GOT UNGROUNDED, SHE'D HAVE TO BRING HER FRIENDS.

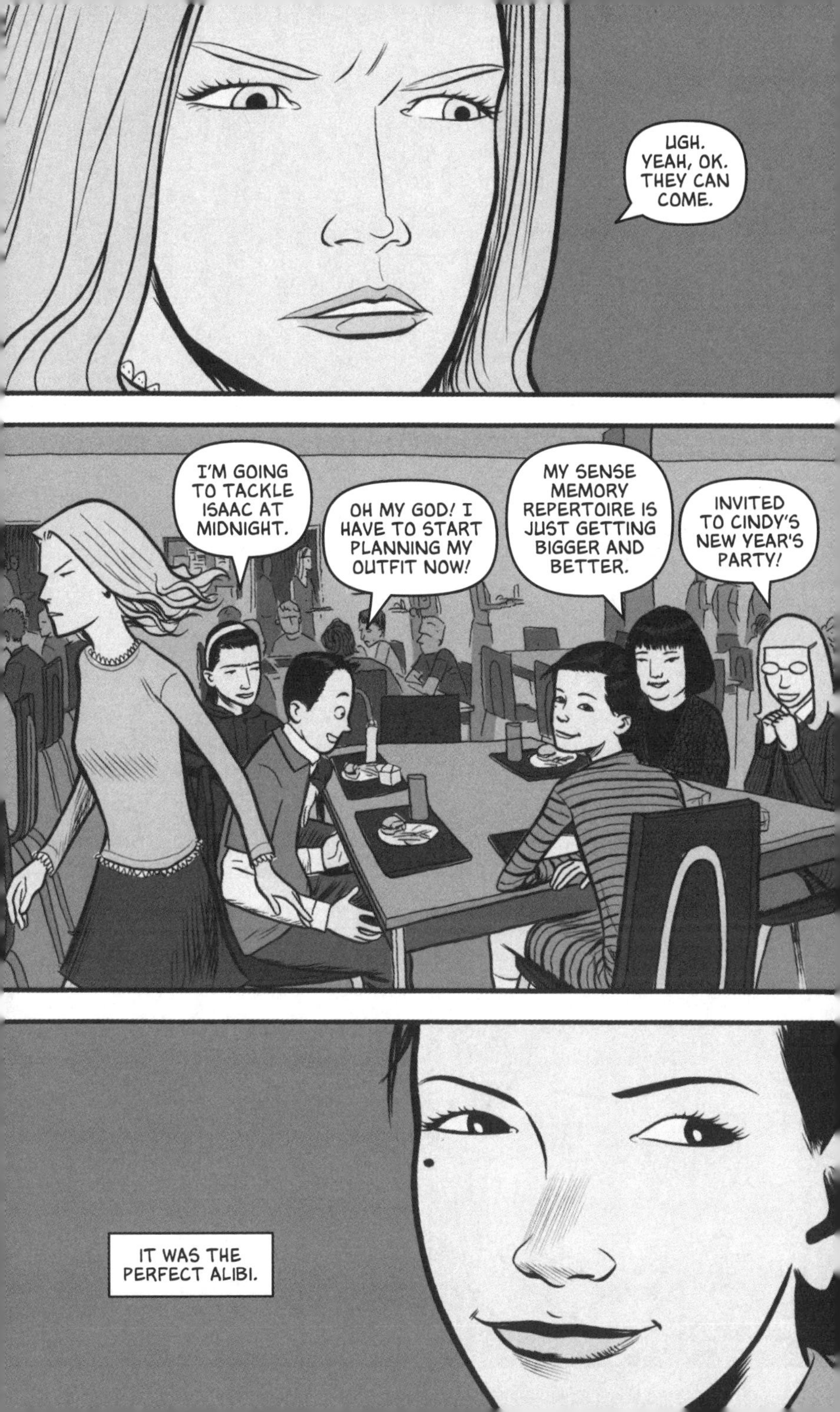
UGH. YEAH, OK. THEY CAN COME.
I'M GOING TO TACKLE ISAAC AT MIDNIGHT.
OH MY GOD! I HAVE TO START PLANNING MY OUTFIT NOW!
MY SENSE MEMORY REPERTOIRE IS JUST GETTING BIGGER AND BETTER.
INVITED TO CINDY'S NEW YEAR'S PARTY!
IT WAS THE PERFECT ALIBI.

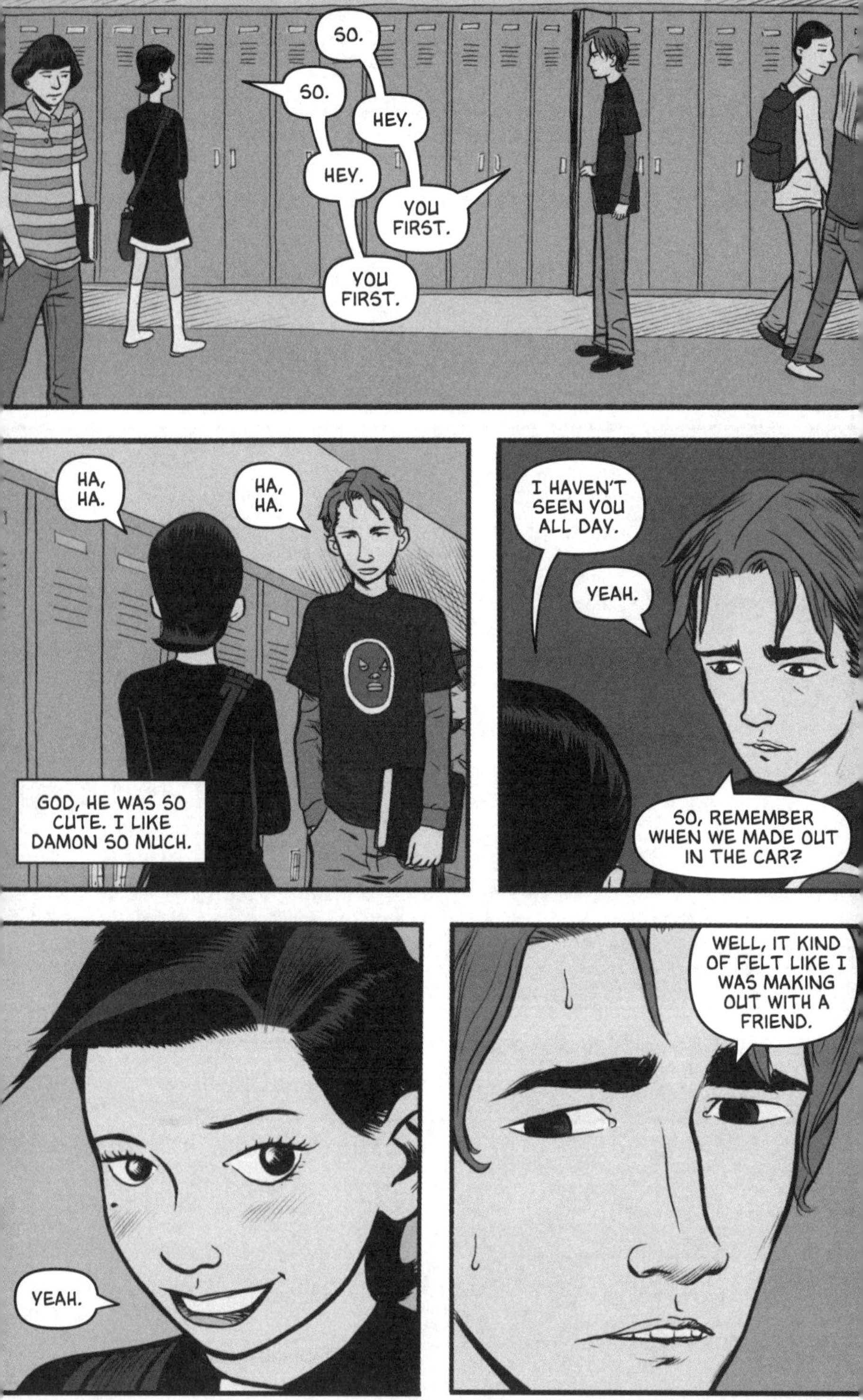

SO.
SO.
HEY.
HEY.
YOU FIRST.
YOU FIRST.
HA, HA.
HA, HA.
GOD, HE WAS SO CUTE. I LIKE DAMON SO MUCH.
I HAVEN'T SEEN YOU ALL DAY.
YEAH.
SO, REMEMBER WHEN WE MADE OUT IN THE CAR?
YEAH.
WELL, IT KIND OF FELT LIKE I WAS MAKING OUT WITH A FRIEND.

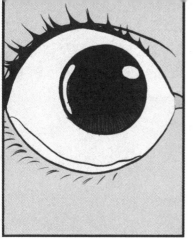

I JUST THINK WE'RE SUPPOSED TO BE *FRIENDS.*

NO HARD FEELINGS, RIGHT?

BRIIING

COOL.

BOYS SUCK.

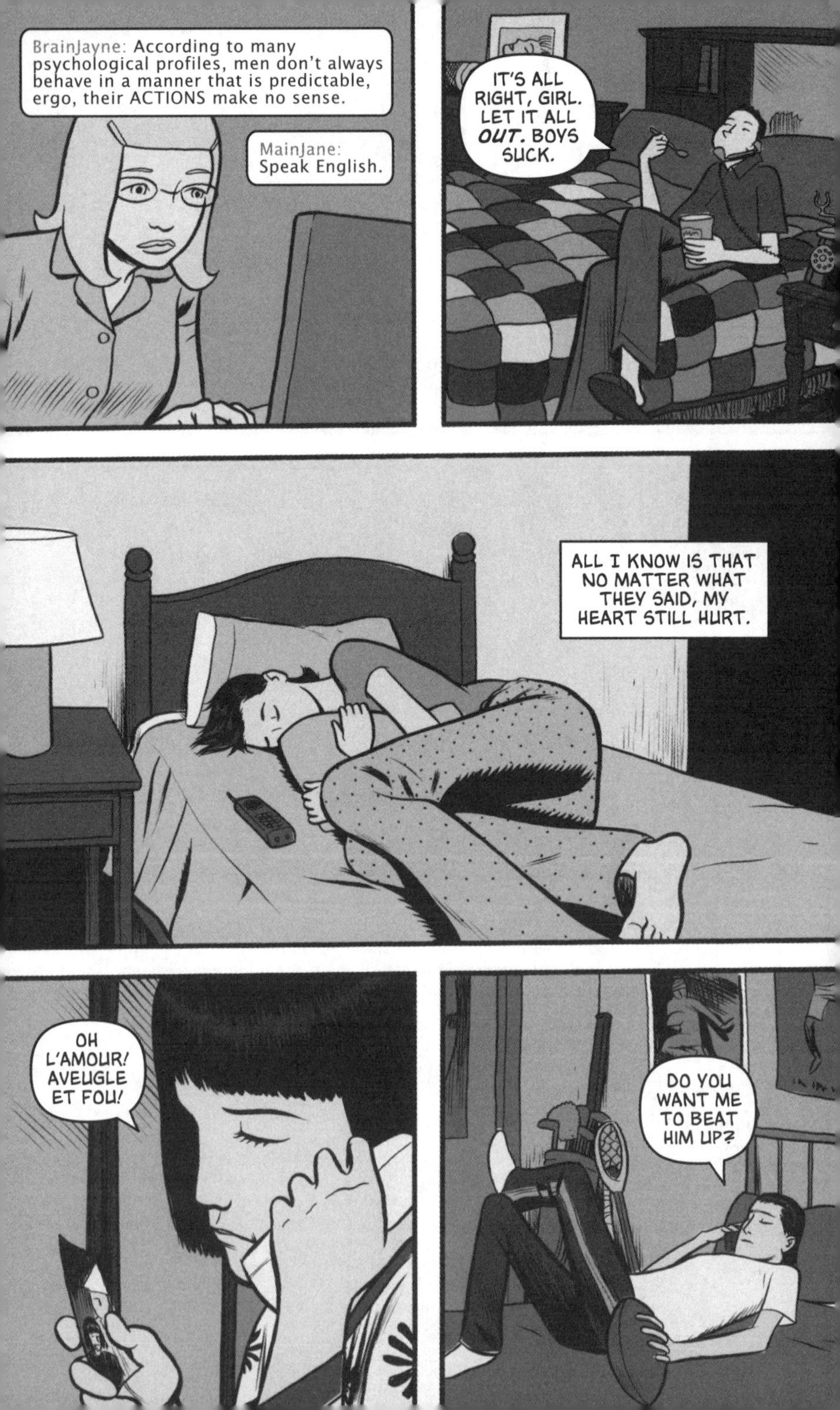
BrainJayne: According to many psychological profiles, men don't always behave in a manner that is predictable, ergo, their ACTIONS make no sense.
MainJane: Speak English.
IT'S ALL RIGHT, GIRL. LET IT ALL OUT. BOYS SUCK.
ALL I KNOW IS THAT NO MATTER WHAT THEY SAID, MY HEART STILL HURT.
OH L'AMOUR! AVEUGLE ET FOU!
DO YOU WANT ME TO BEAT HIM UP?

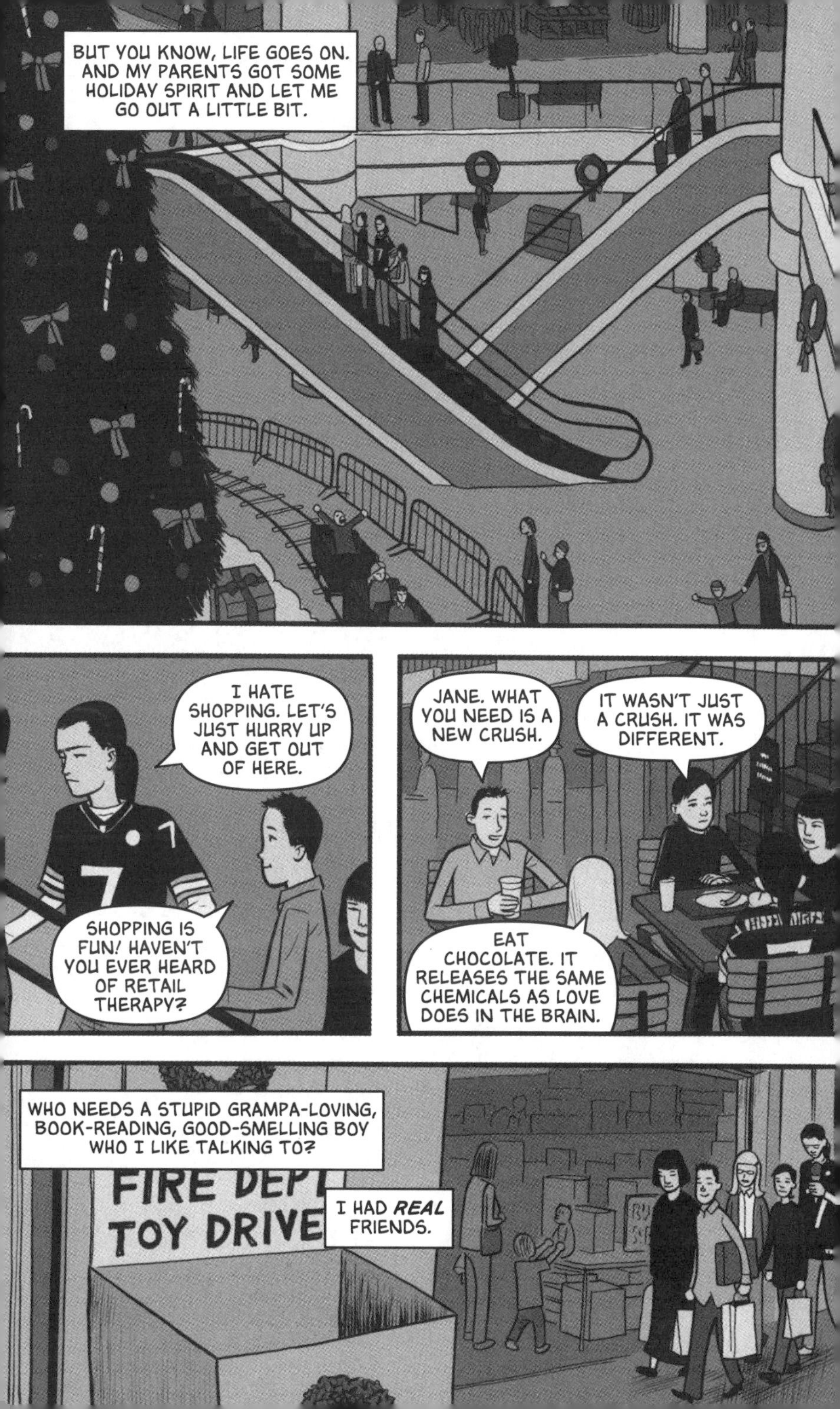
BUT YOU KNOW, LIFE GOES ON. AND MY PARENTS GOT SOME HOLIDAY SPIRIT AND LET ME GO OUT A LITTLE BIT.
I HATE SHOPPING. LET'S JUST HURRY UP AND GET OUT OF HERE.
SHOPPING IS FUN! HAVEN'T YOU EVER HEARD OF RETAIL THERAPY?
JANE. WHAT YOU NEED IS A NEW CRUSH.
IT WASN'T JUST A CRUSH. IT WAS DIFFERENT.
EAT CHOCOLATE. IT RELEASES THE SAME CHEMICALS AS LOVE DOES IN THE BRAIN.
WHO NEEDS A STUPID GRAMPA-LOVING, BOOK-READING, GOOD-SMELLING BOY WHO I LIKE TALKING TO?
FIRE DEPT
TOY DRIVE
I HAD *REAL* FRIENDS.

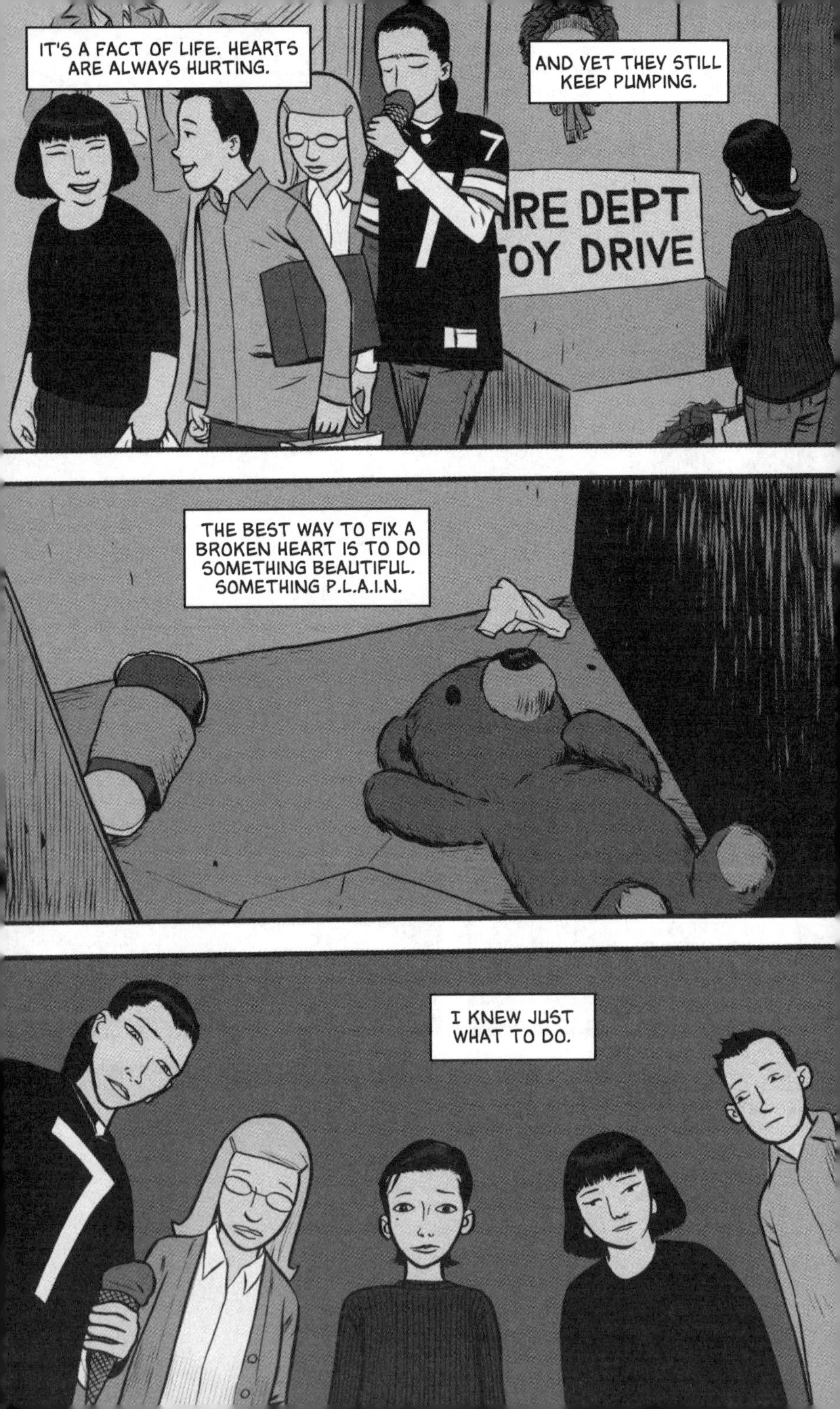
IT'S A FACT OF LIFE. HEARTS ARE ALWAYS HURTING.
AND YET THEY STILL KEEP PUMPING.
RE DEPT
OY DRIVE
THE BEST WAY TO FIX A BROKEN HEART IS TO DO SOMETHING BEAUTIFUL. SOMETHING P.L.A.I.N.
I KNEW JUST WHAT TO DO.

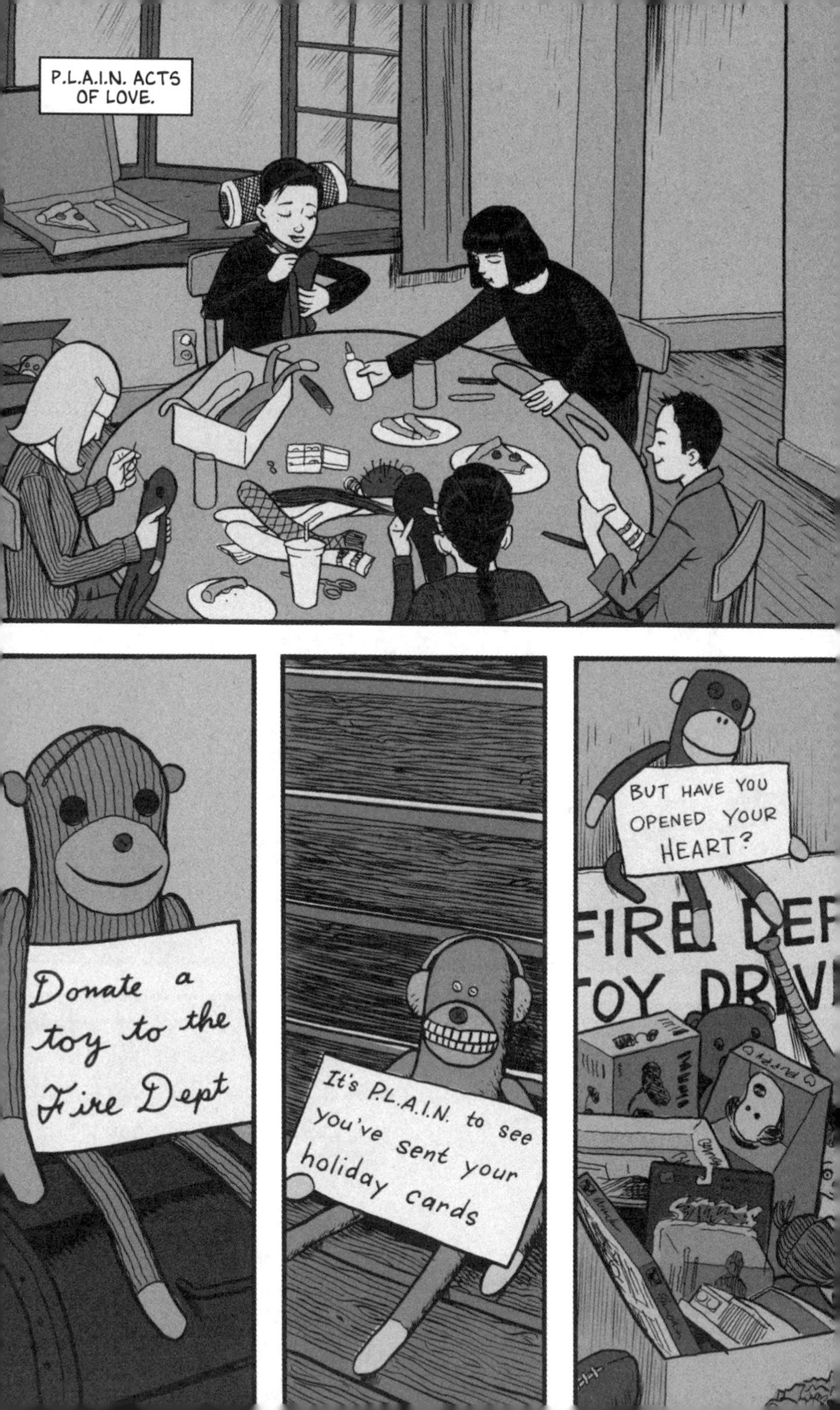
P.L.A.I.N. ACTS OF LOVE.
Donate a toy to the Fire Dept
It's P.L.A.I.N. to see you've sent your holiday cards
BUT HAVE YOU OPENED YOUR HEART?
FIRE DEP
TOY DRIV

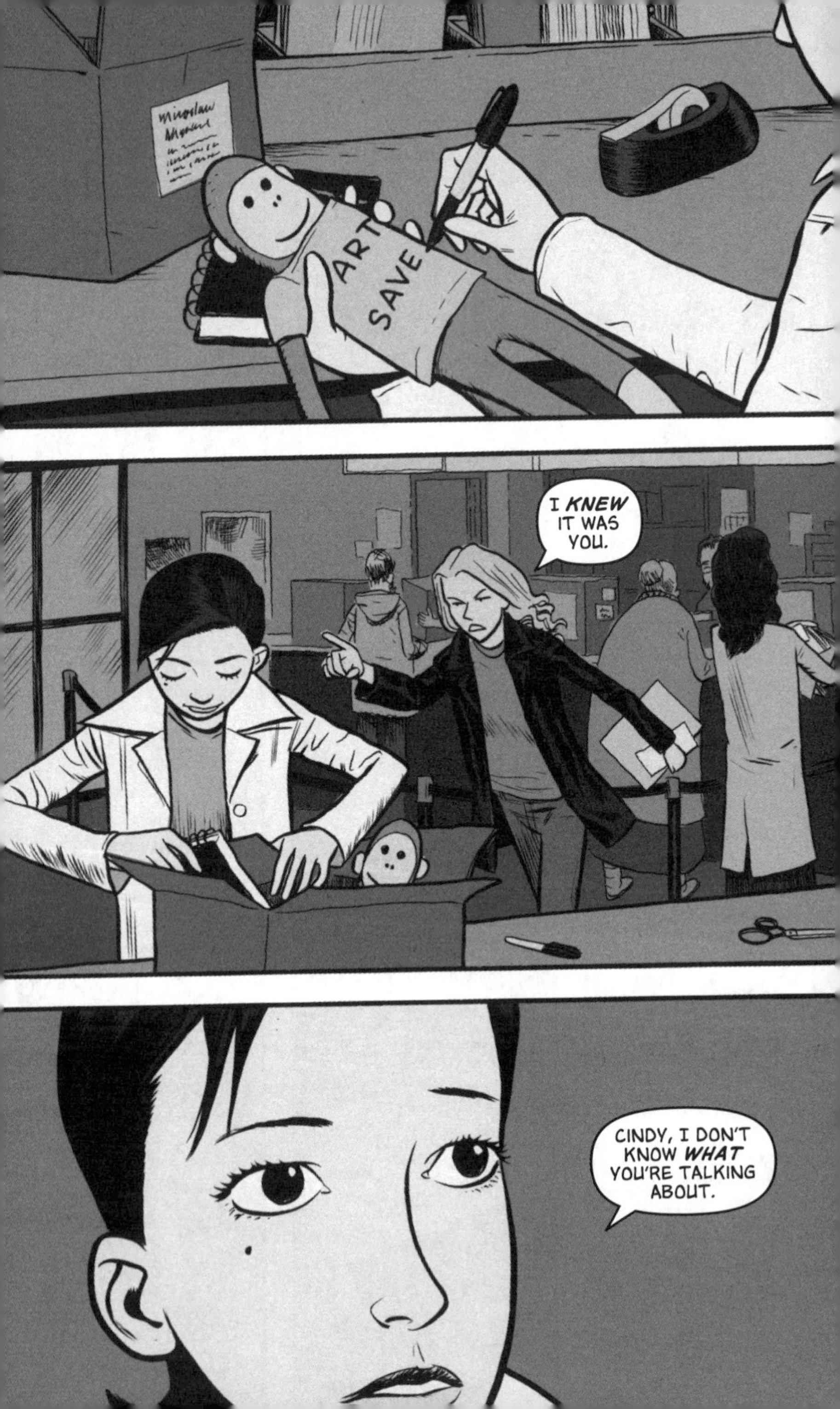

ART SAVE
I KNEW IT WAS YOU.
CINDY, I DON'T KNOW WHAT YOU'RE TALKING ABOUT.

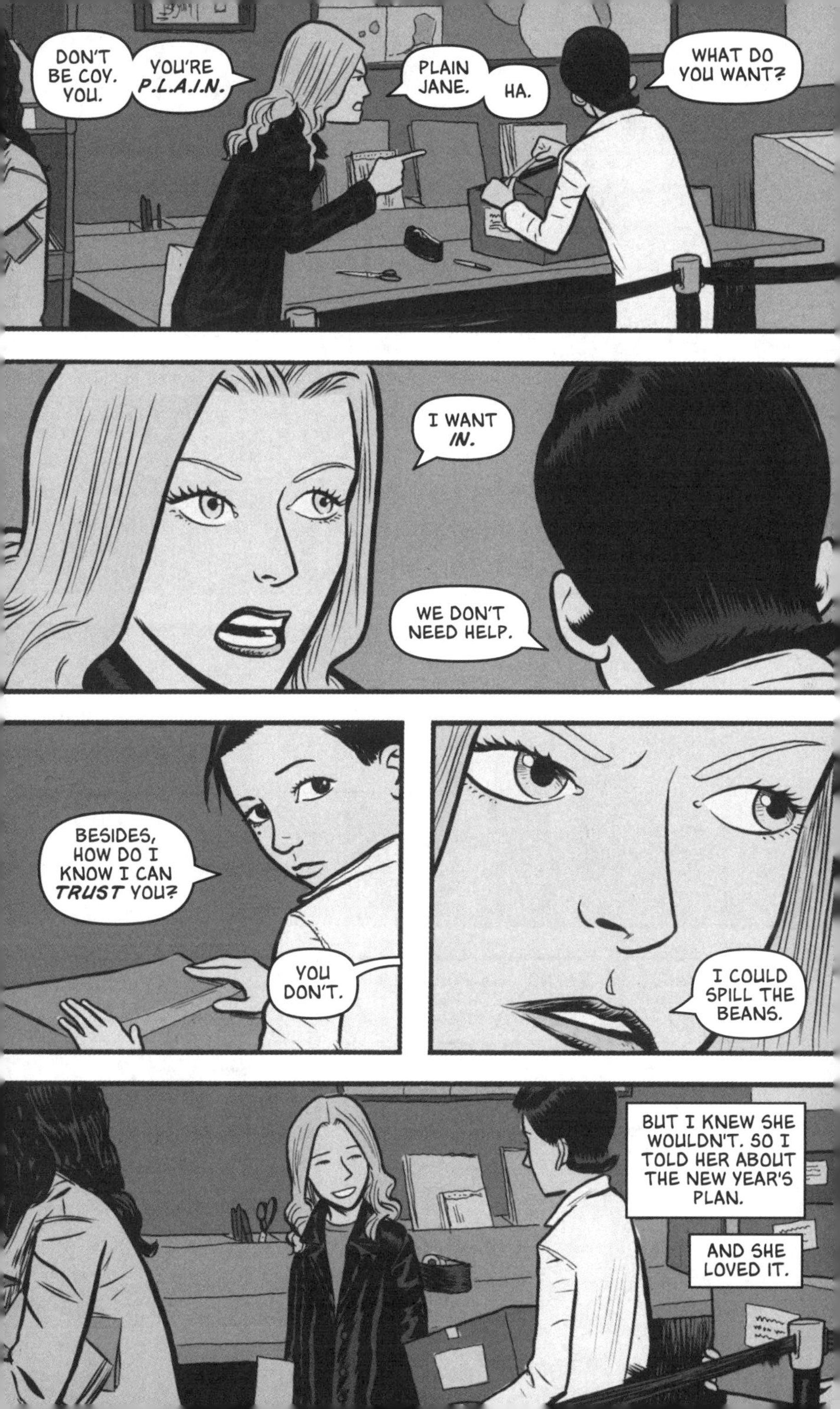
DON'T BE COY. YOU.
YOU'RE *P.L.A.I.N.*
PLAIN JANE.
HA.
WHAT DO YOU WANT?
I WANT *IN.*
WE DON'T NEED HELP.
BESIDES, HOW DO I KNOW I CAN *TRUST* YOU?
YOU DON'T.
I COULD SPILL THE BEANS.
BUT I KNEW SHE WOULDN'T. SO I TOLD HER ABOUT THE NEW YEAR'S PLAN.
AND SHE LOVED IT.

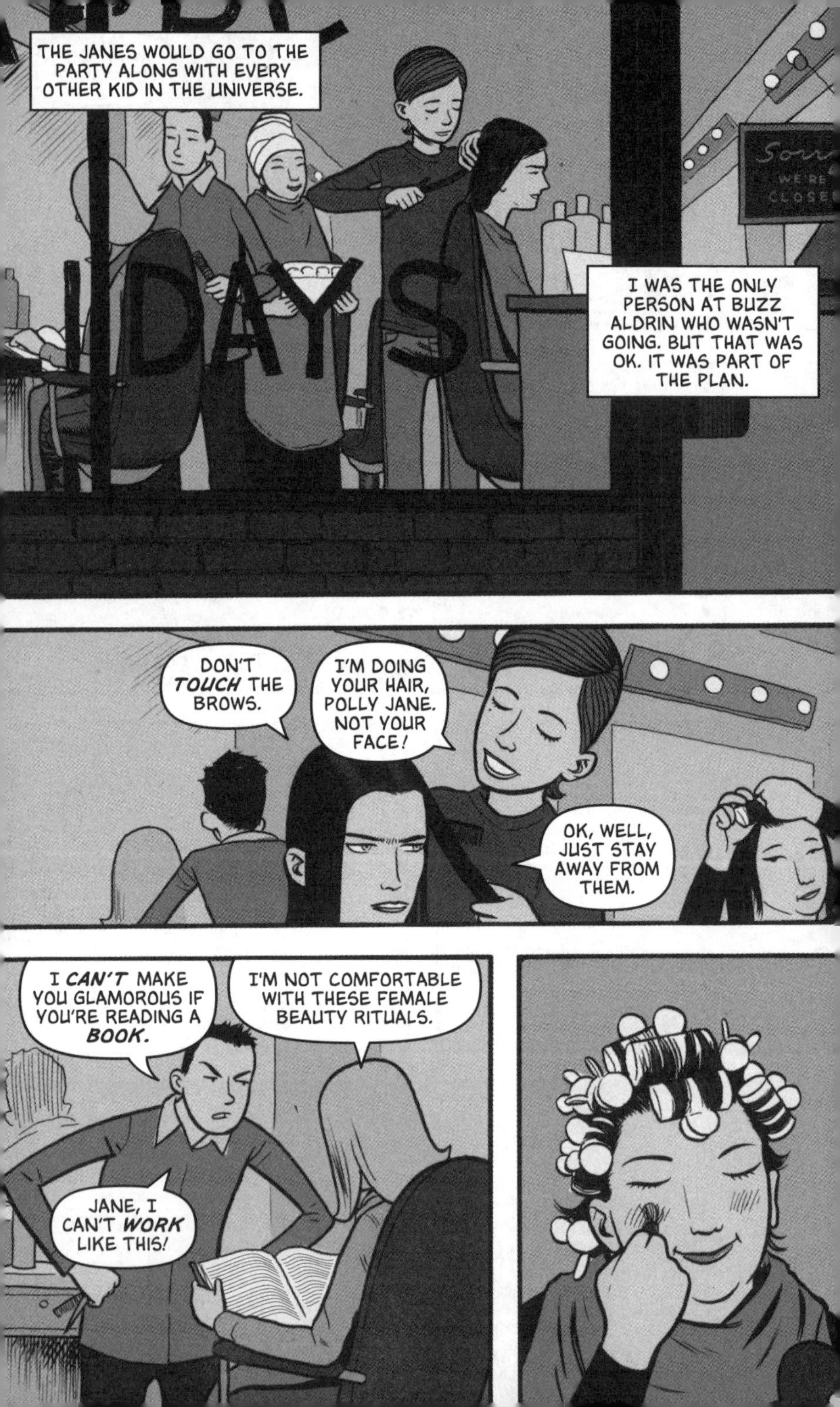
THE JANES WOULD GO TO THE PARTY ALONG WITH EVERY OTHER KID IN THE UNIVERSE.
DAYS
I WAS THE ONLY PERSON AT BUZZ ALDRIN WHO WASN'T GOING. BUT THAT WAS OK. IT WAS PART OF THE PLAN.
DON'T *TOUCH* THE BROWS.
I'M DOING YOUR HAIR, POLLY JANE. NOT YOUR FACE!
OK, WELL, JUST STAY AWAY FROM THEM.
I *CAN'T* MAKE YOU GLAMOROUS IF YOU'RE READING A ***BOOK.***
I'M NOT COMFORTABLE WITH THESE FEMALE BEAUTY RITUALS.
JANE, I CAN'T ***WORK*** LIKE THIS!

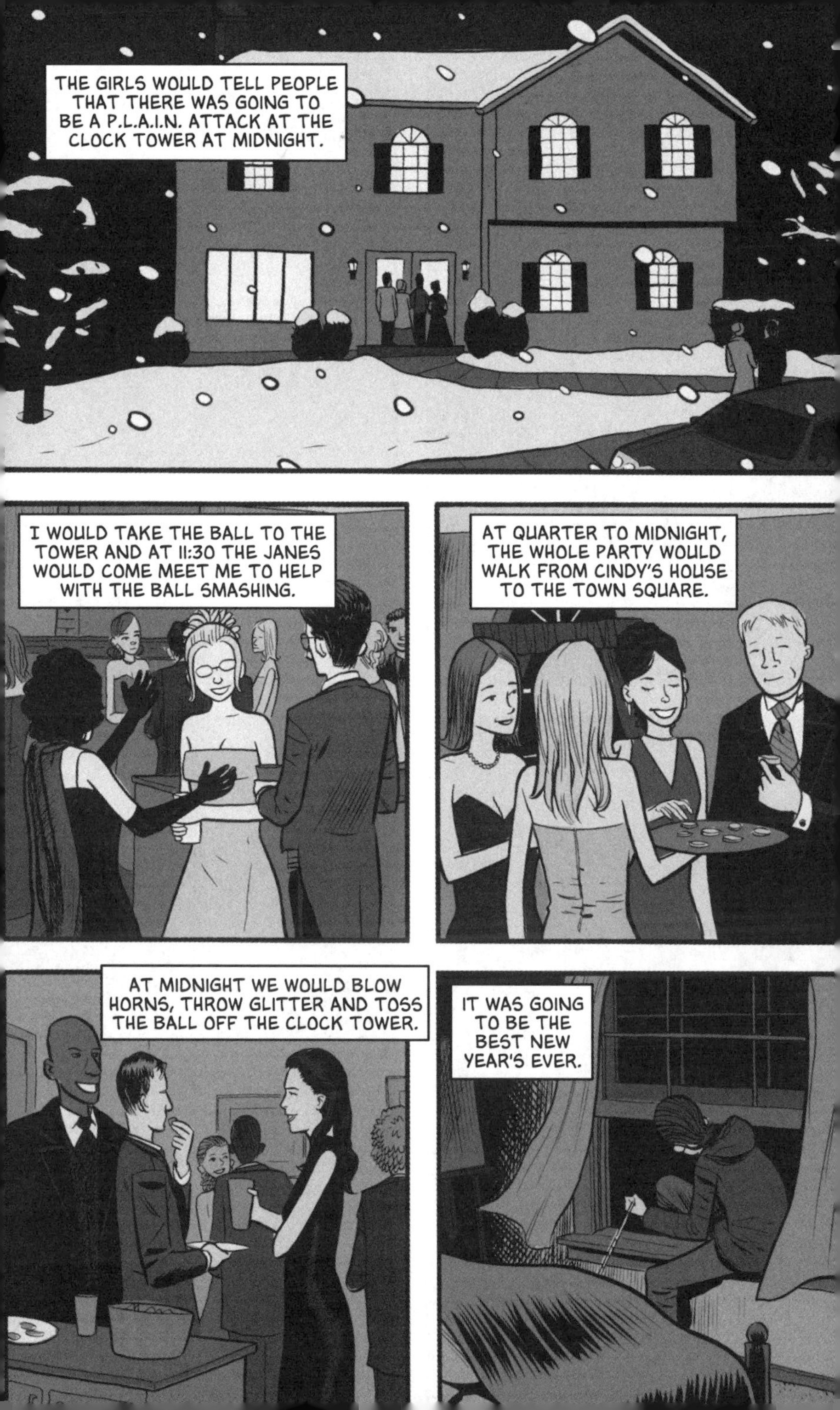
THE GIRLS WOULD TELL PEOPLE THAT THERE WAS GOING TO BE A P.L.A.I.N. ATTACK AT THE CLOCK TOWER AT MIDNIGHT.
I WOULD TAKE THE BALL TO THE TOWER AND AT 11:30 THE JANES WOULD COME MEET ME TO HELP WITH THE BALL SMASHING.
AT QUARTER TO MIDNIGHT, THE WHOLE PARTY WOULD WALK FROM CINDY'S HOUSE TO THE TOWN SQUARE.
AT MIDNIGHT WE WOULD BLOW HORNS, THROW GLITTER AND TOSS THE BALL OFF THE CLOCK TOWER.
IT WAS GOING TO BE THE BEST NEW YEAR'S EVER.

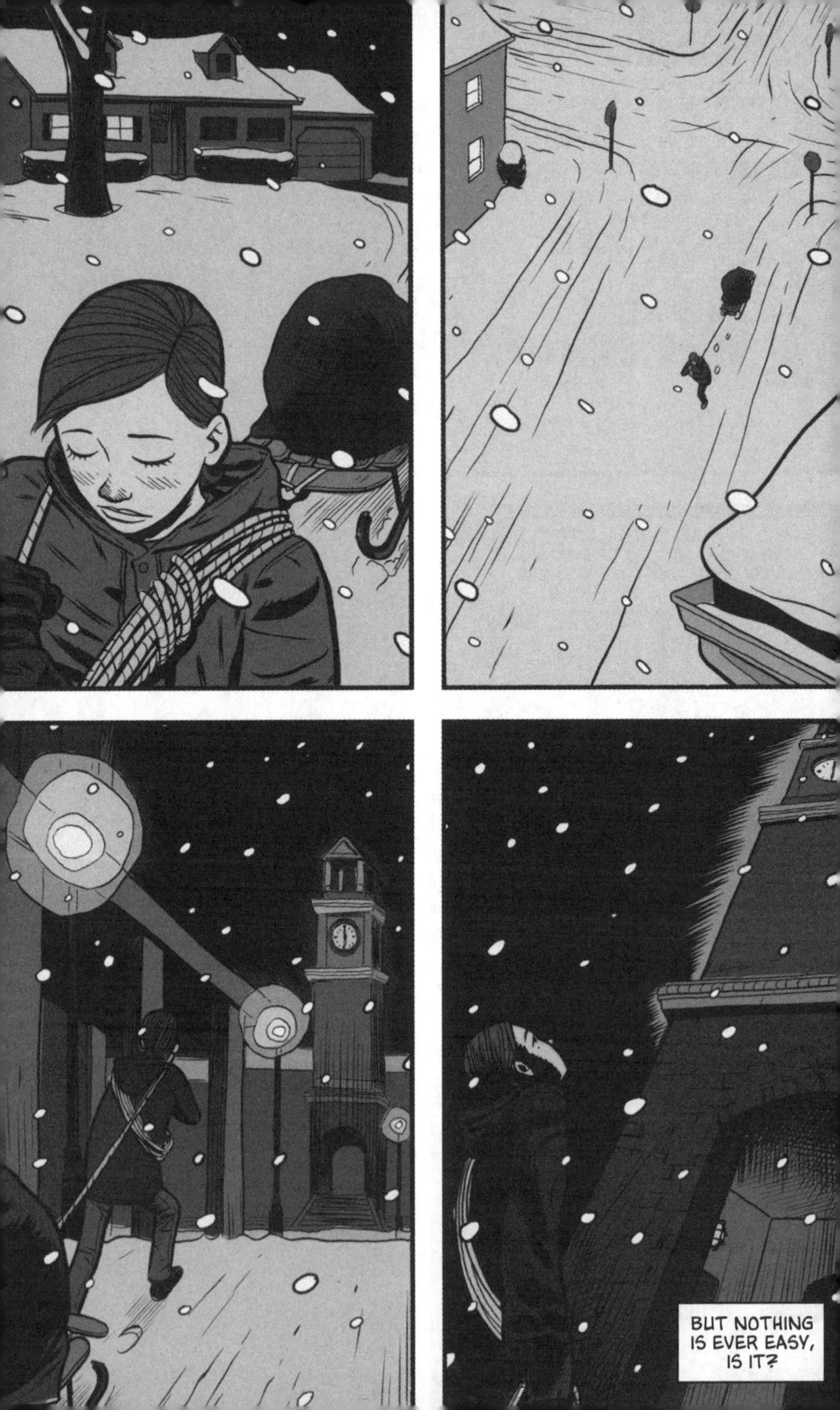

BUT NOTHING
IS EVER EASY,
IS IT?

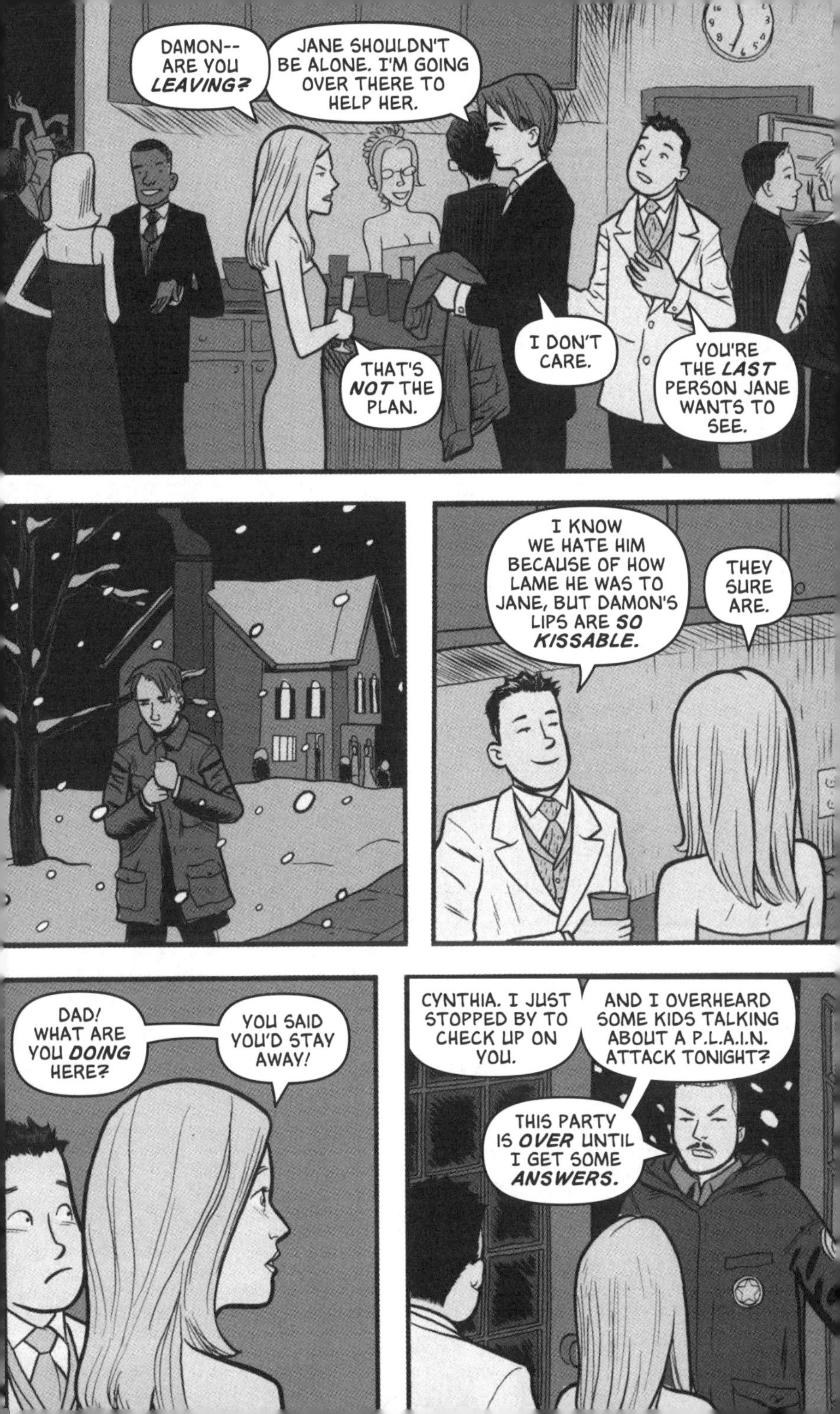
DAMON-- ARE YOU *LEAVING?*
JANE SHOULDN'T BE ALONE. I'M GOING OVER THERE TO HELP HER.
THAT'S *NOT* THE PLAN.
I DON'T CARE.
YOU'RE THE *LAST* PERSON JANE WANTS TO SEE.
I KNOW WE HATE HIM BECAUSE OF HOW LAME HE WAS TO JANE, BUT DAMON'S LIPS ARE *SO KISSABLE.*
THEY SURE ARE.
DAD! WHAT ARE YOU *DOING* HERE?
YOU SAID YOU'D STAY AWAY!
CYNTHIA. I JUST STOPPED BY TO CHECK UP ON YOU.
AND I OVERHEARD SOME KIDS TALKING ABOUT A P.L.A.I.N. ATTACK TONIGHT?
THIS PARTY IS *OVER* UNTIL I GET SOME *ANSWERS.*

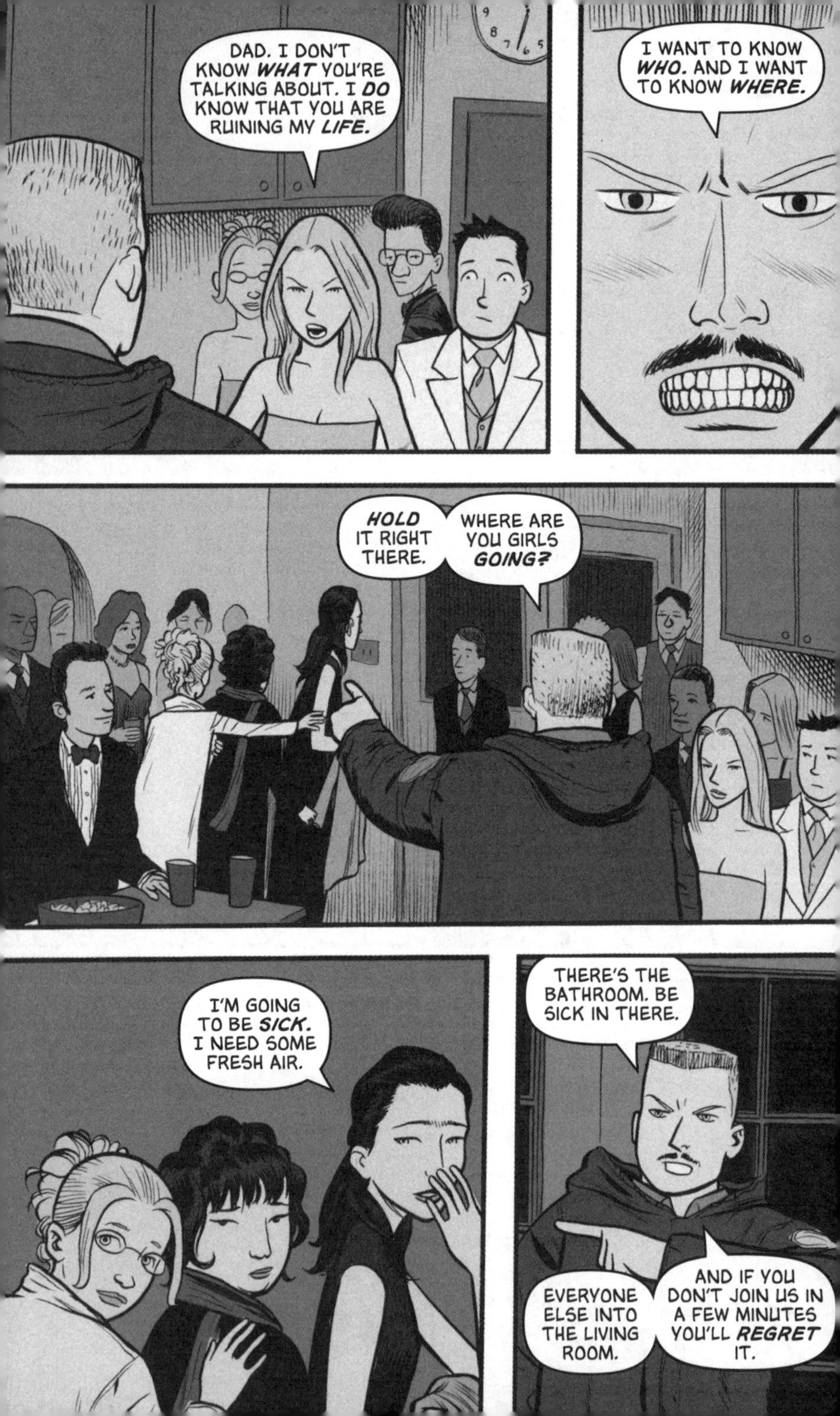
DAD. I DON'T KNOW WHAT YOU'RE TALKING ABOUT. I DO KNOW THAT YOU ARE RUINING MY LIFE.
I WANT TO KNOW WHO. AND I WANT TO KNOW WHERE.
HOLD IT RIGHT THERE.
WHERE ARE YOU GIRLS GOING?
I'M GOING TO BE SICK. I NEED SOME FRESH AIR.
THERE'S THE BATHROOM. BE SICK IN THERE.
EVERYONE ELSE INTO THE LIVING ROOM.
AND IF YOU DON'T JOIN US IN A FEW MINUTES YOU'LL REGRET IT.

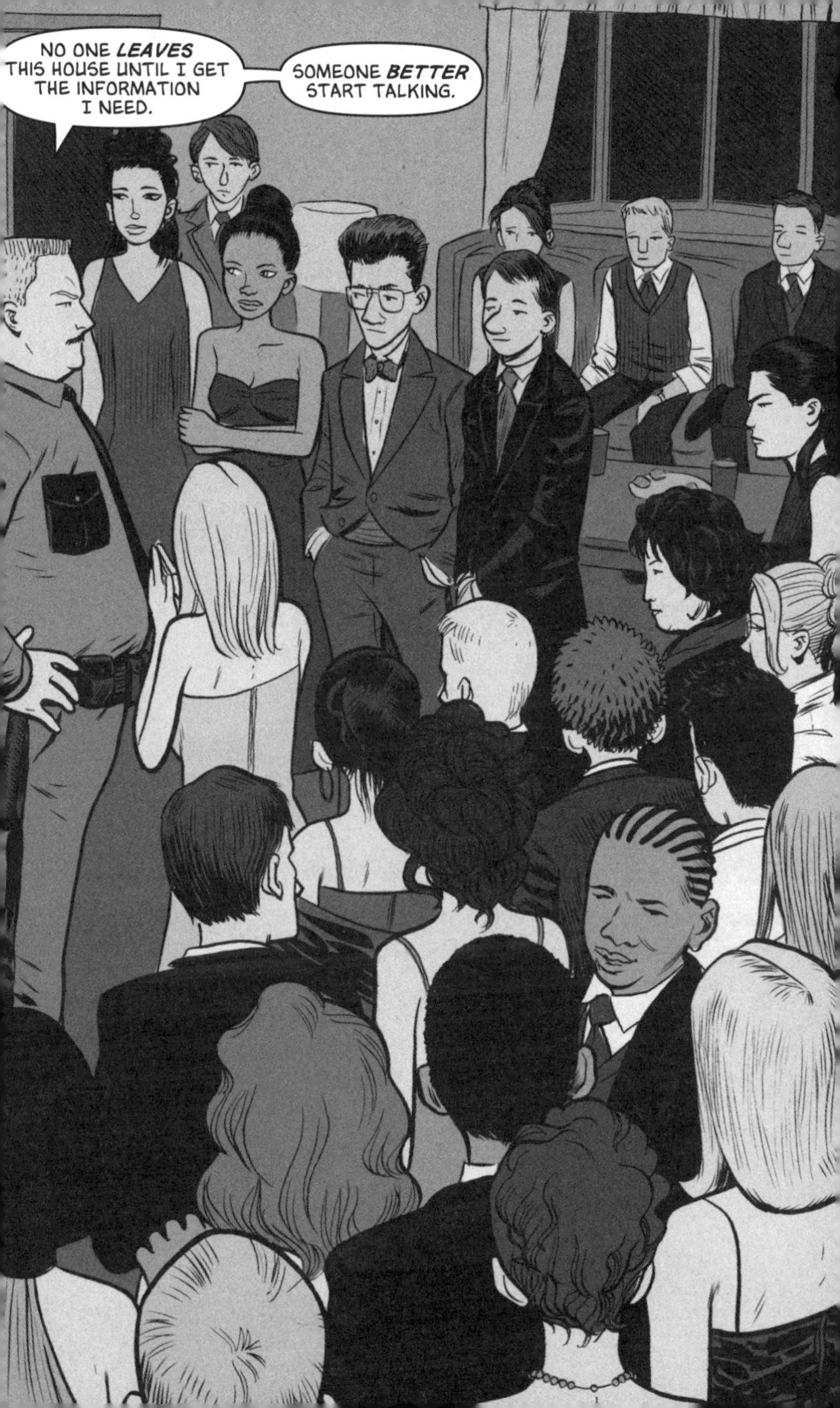
NO ONE *LEAVES* THIS HOUSE UNTIL I GET THE INFORMATION I NEED.
SOMEONE *BETTER* START TALKING.

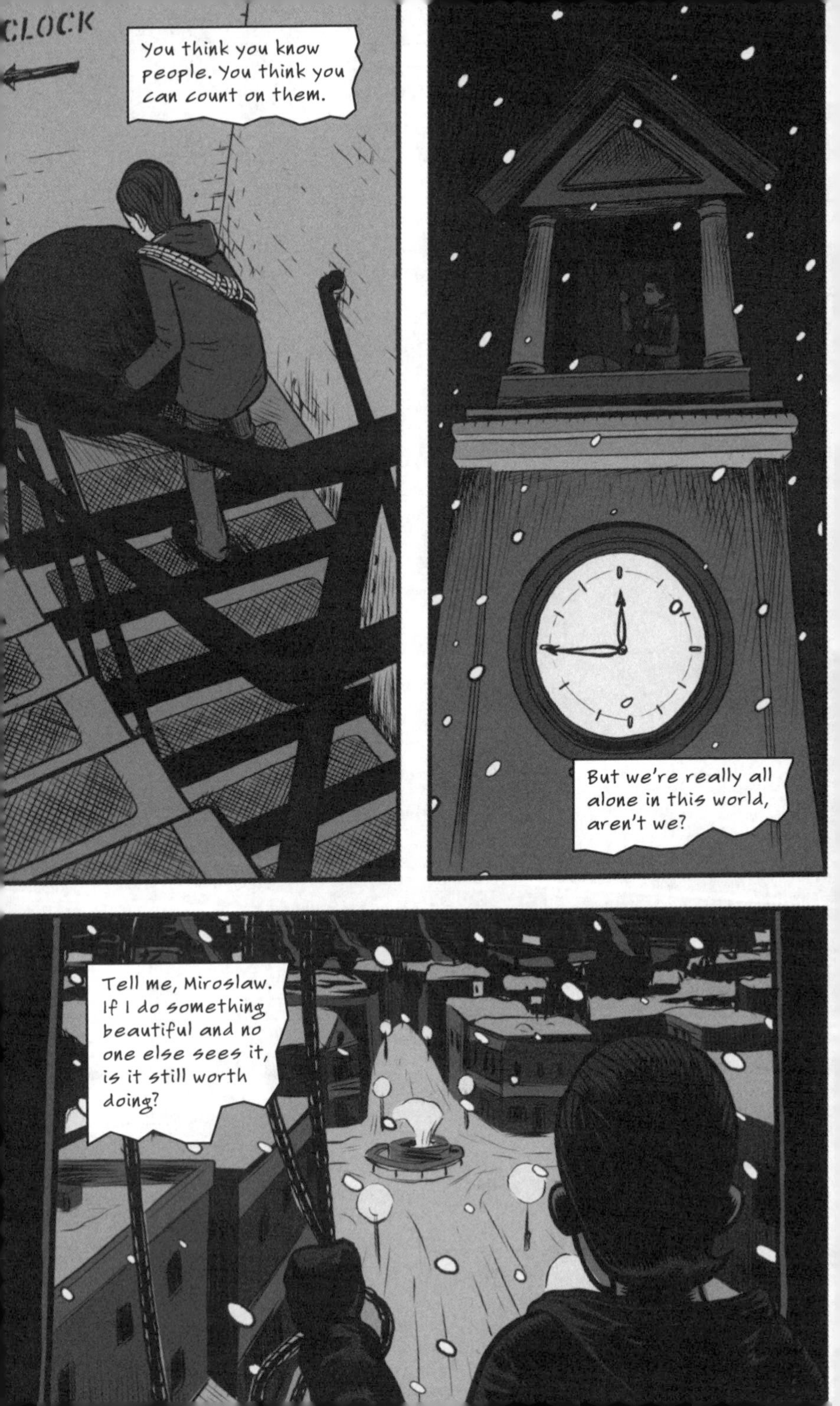
CLOCK
You think you know people. You think you can count on them.
But we're really all alone in this world, aren't we?
Tell me, Miroslaw. If I do something beautiful and no one else sees it, is it still worth doing?

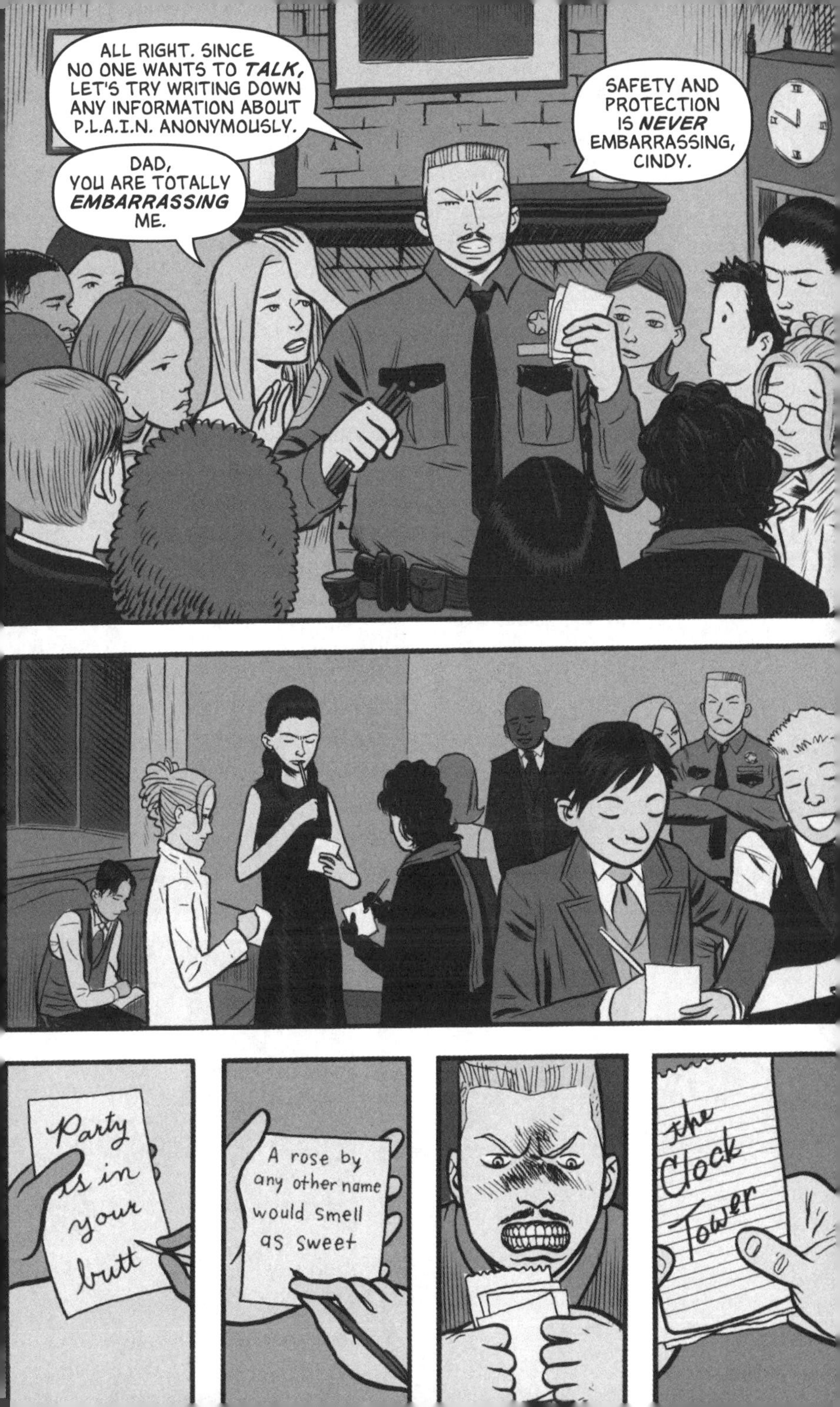
ALL RIGHT. SINCE NO ONE WANTS TO *TALK,* LET'S TRY WRITING DOWN ANY INFORMATION ABOUT P.L.A.I.N. ANONYMOUSLY.
DAD, YOU ARE TOTALLY *EMBARRASSING* ME.
SAFETY AND PROTECTION IS *NEVER* EMBARRASSING, CINDY.
Party is in your butt
A rose by any other name would smell as sweet
the Clock Tower

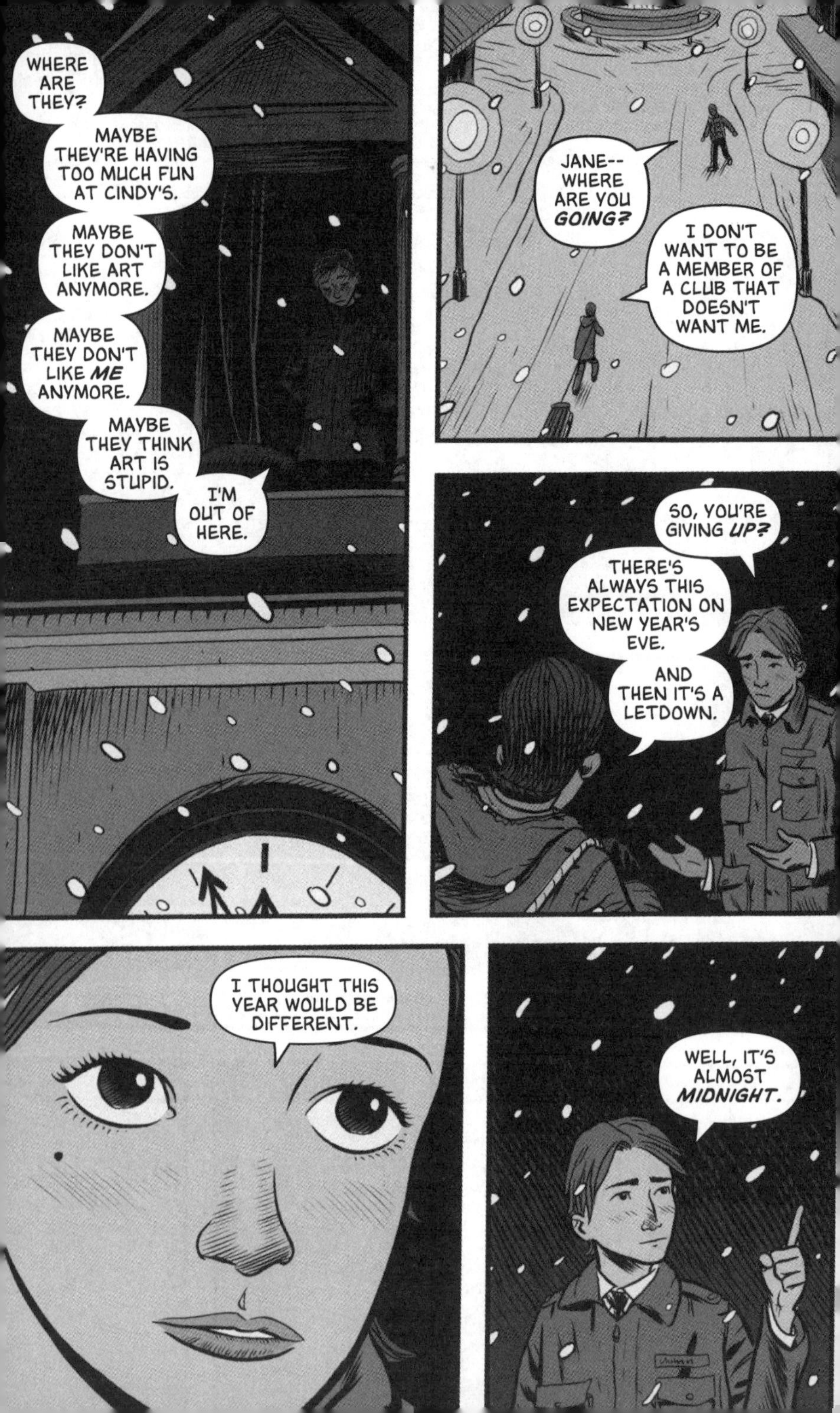
WHERE ARE THEY?
MAYBE THEY'RE HAVING TOO MUCH FUN AT CINDY'S.
MAYBE THEY DON'T LIKE ART ANYMORE.
MAYBE THEY DON'T LIKE *ME* ANYMORE.
MAYBE THEY THINK ART IS STUPID.
I'M OUT OF HERE.
JANE-- WHERE ARE YOU *GOING?*
I DON'T WANT TO BE A MEMBER OF A CLUB THAT DOESN'T WANT ME.
SO, YOU'RE GIVING *UP?*
THERE'S ALWAYS THIS EXPECTATION ON NEW YEAR'S EVE.
AND THEN IT'S A LETDOWN.
I THOUGHT THIS YEAR WOULD BE DIFFERENT.
WELL, IT'S ALMOST *MIDNIGHT*.

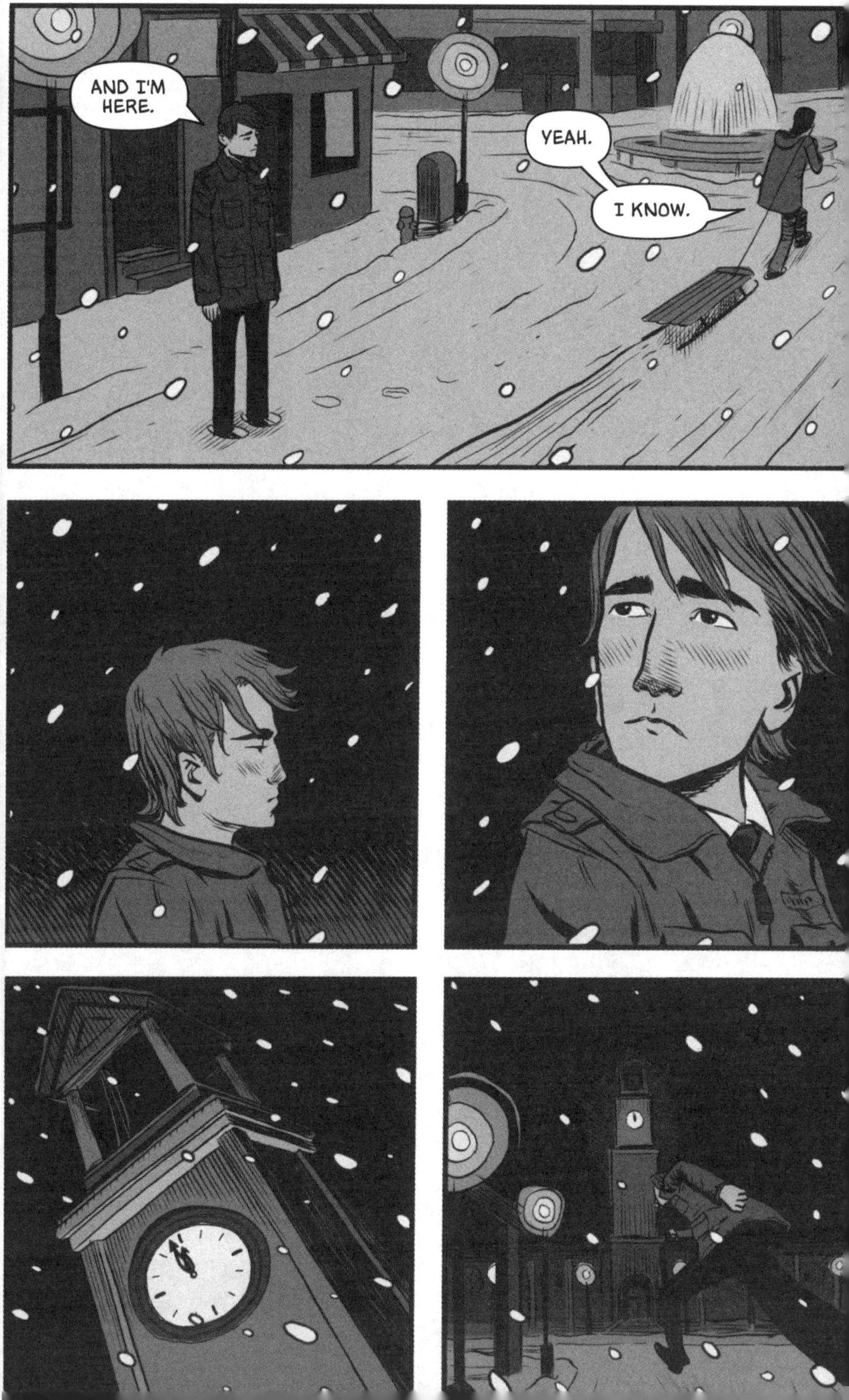
AND I'M HERE.
YEAH.
I KNOW.

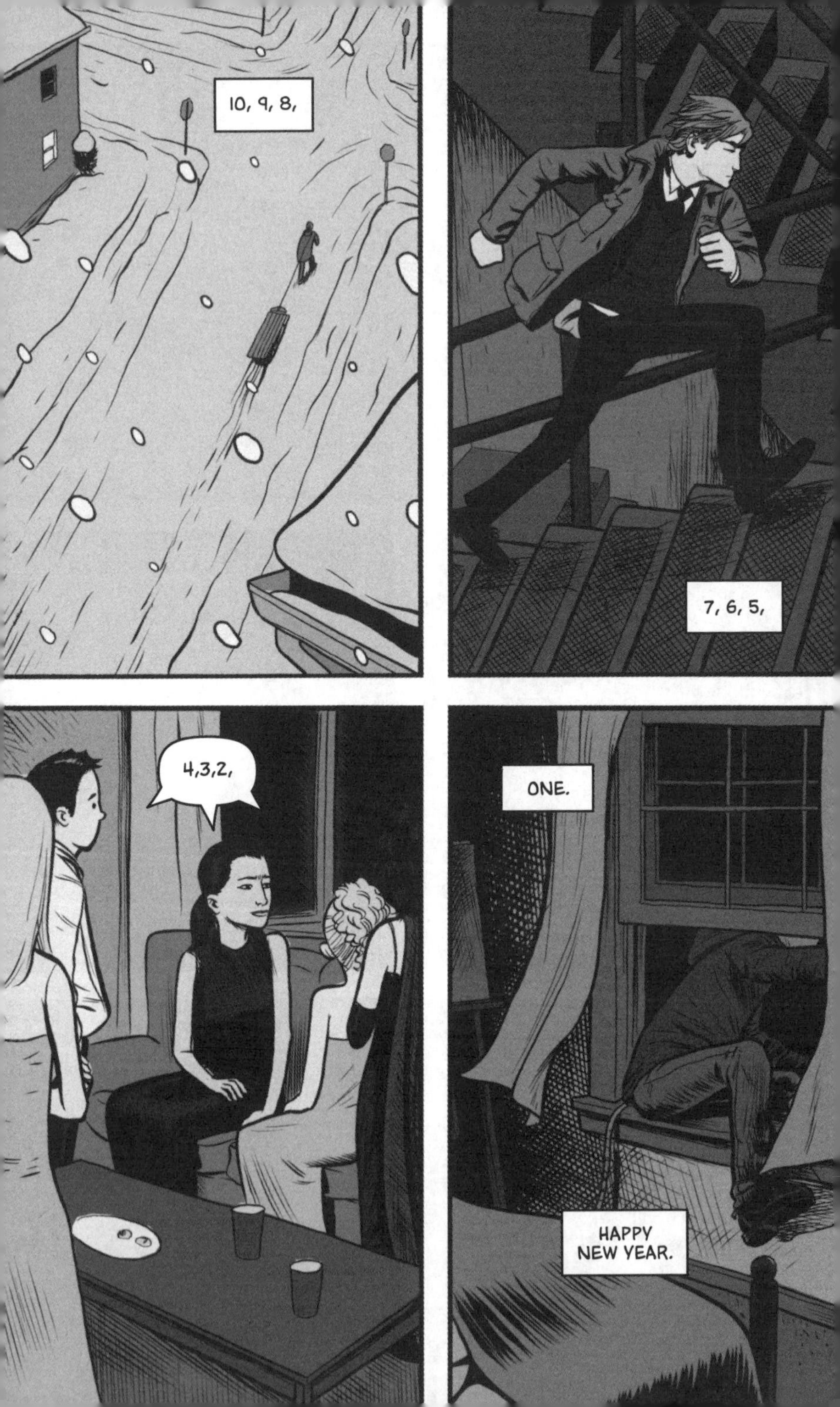
10, 9, 8,
7, 6, 5,
4,3,2,
ONE.
HAPPY NEW YEAR.

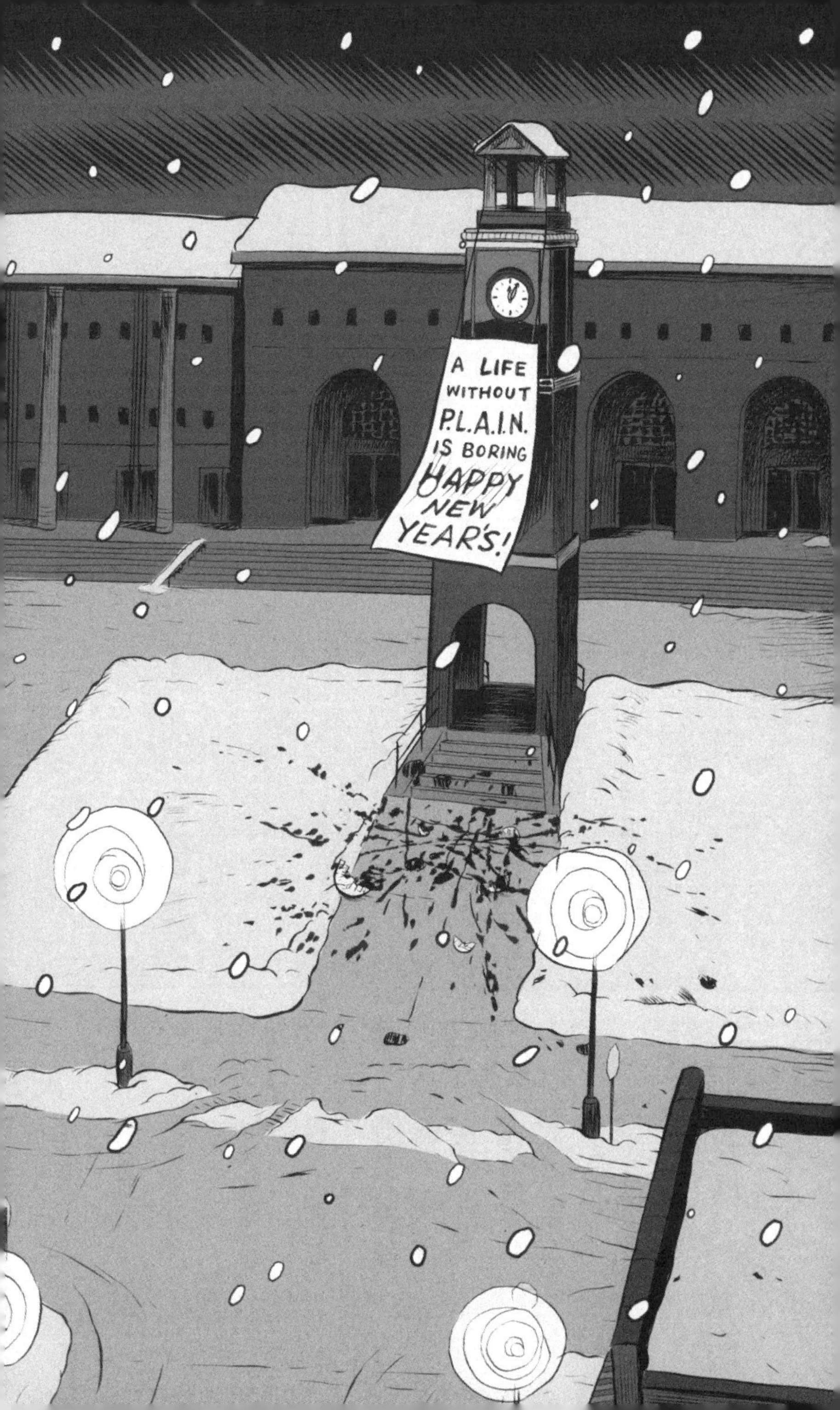
A LIFE WITHOUT P.L.A.I.N. IS BORING
HAPPY NEW YEARS!

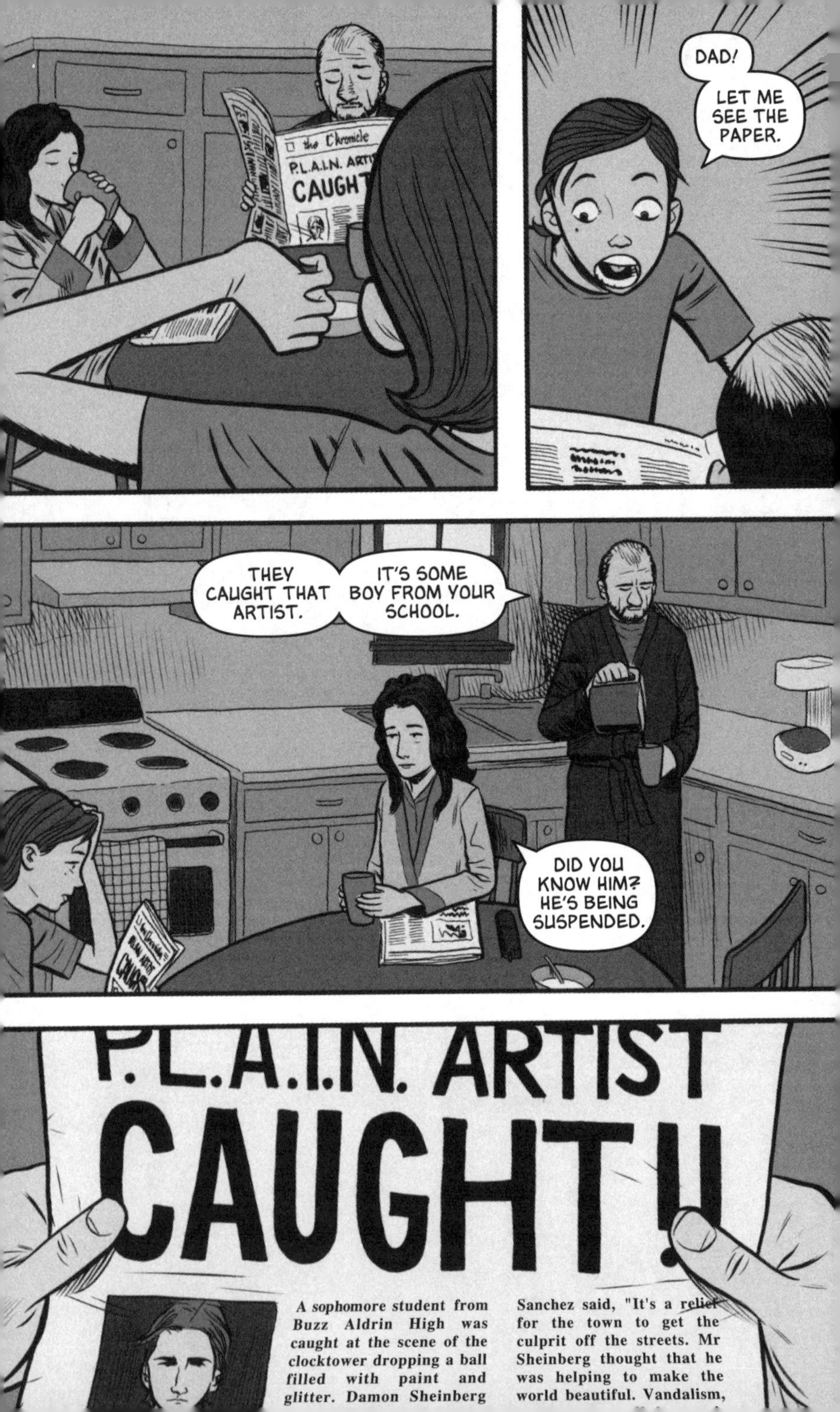
the Chronicle
DAD!
LET ME SEE THE PAPER.
THEY CAUGHT THAT ARTIST.
IT'S SOME BOY FROM YOUR SCHOOL.
DID YOU KNOW HIM? HE'S BEING SUSPENDED.
P.L.A.I.N. ARTIST
CAUGHT!!
A sophomore student from Buzz Aldrin High was caught at the scene of the clocktower dropping a ball filled with paint and glitter. Damon Sheinberg
Sanchez said, "It's a relief for the town to get the culprit off the streets. Mr Sheinberg thought that he was helping to make the world beautiful. Vandalism,

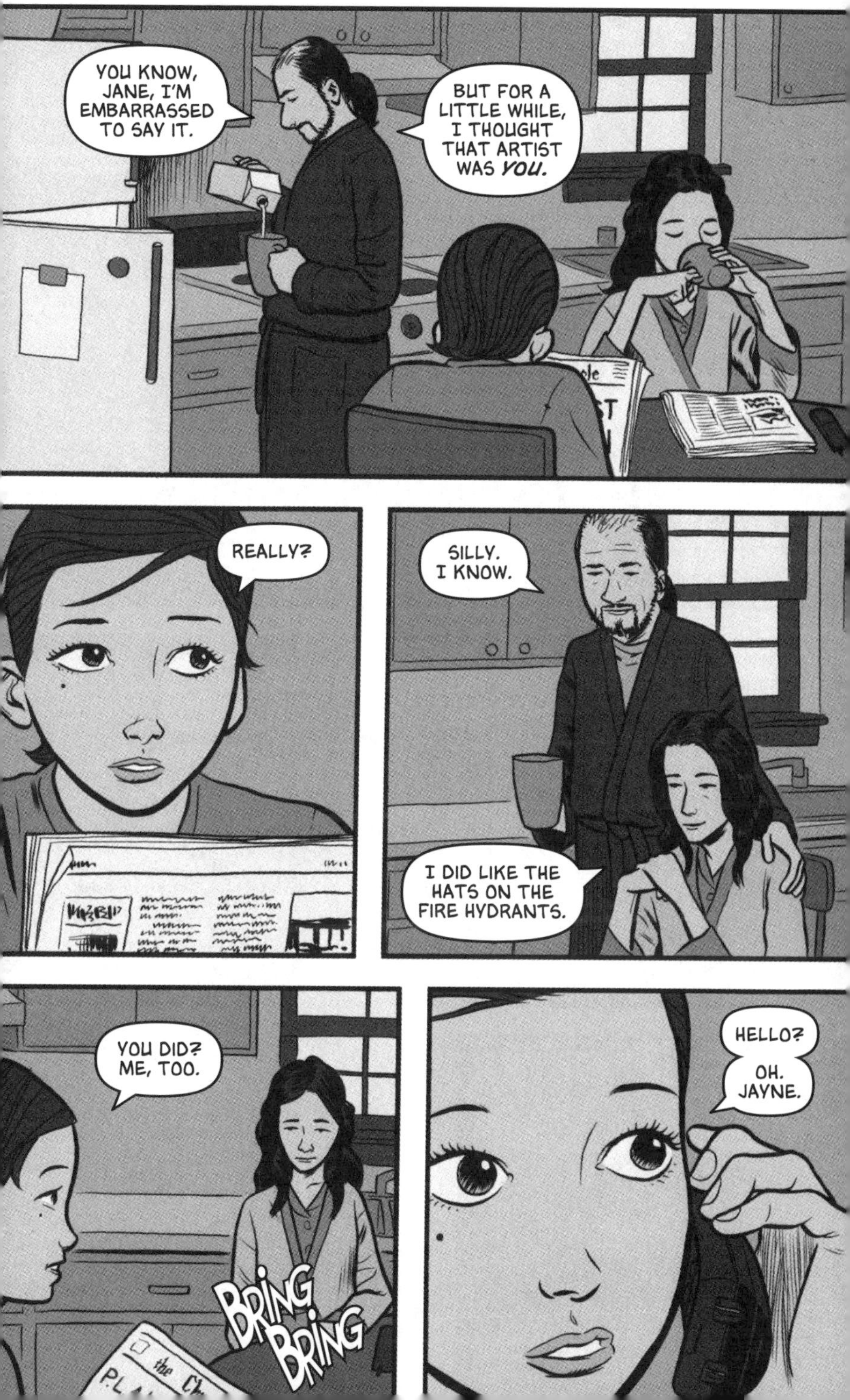
YOU KNOW, JANE, I'M EMBARRASSED TO SAY IT.
BUT FOR A LITTLE WHILE, I THOUGHT THAT ARTIST WAS *YOU.*
REALLY?
SILLY. I KNOW.
I DID LIKE THE HATS ON THE FIRE HYDRANTS.
YOU DID? ME, TOO.
BRING BRING
HELLO?
OH. JAYNE.

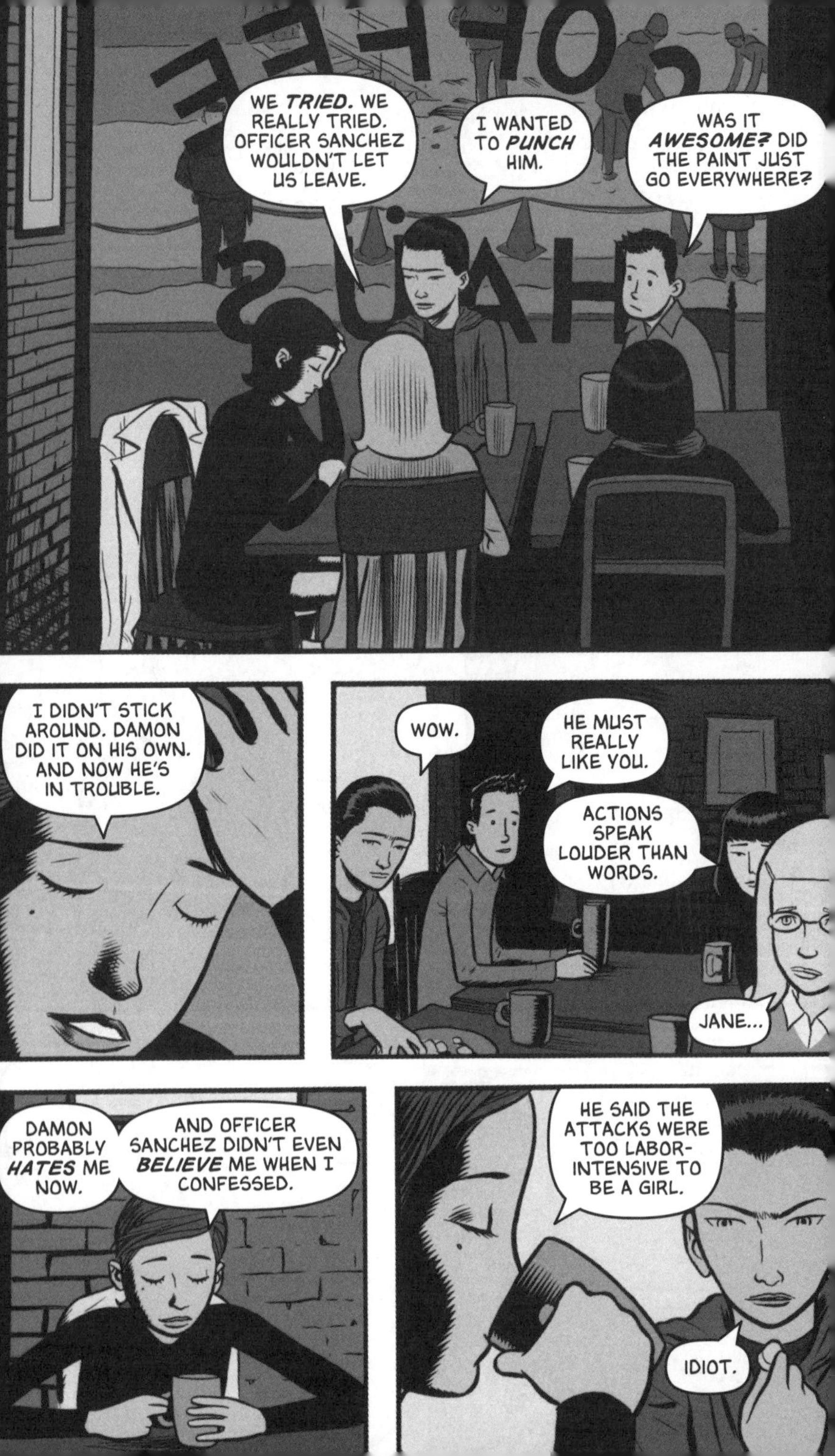
WE TRIED. WE REALLY TRIED. OFFICER SANCHEZ WOULDN'T LET US LEAVE.
I WANTED TO PUNCH HIM.
WAS IT AWESOME? DID THE PAINT JUST GO EVERYWHERE?
I DIDN'T STICK AROUND. DAMON DID IT ON HIS OWN. AND NOW HE'S IN TROUBLE.
WOW.
HE MUST REALLY LIKE YOU.
ACTIONS SPEAK LOUDER THAN WORDS.
JANE...
DAMON PROBABLY HATES ME NOW.
AND OFFICER SANCHEZ DIDN'T EVEN BELIEVE ME WHEN I CONFESSED.
HE SAID THE ATTACKS WERE TOO LABOR-INTENSIVE TO BE A GIRL.
IDIOT.

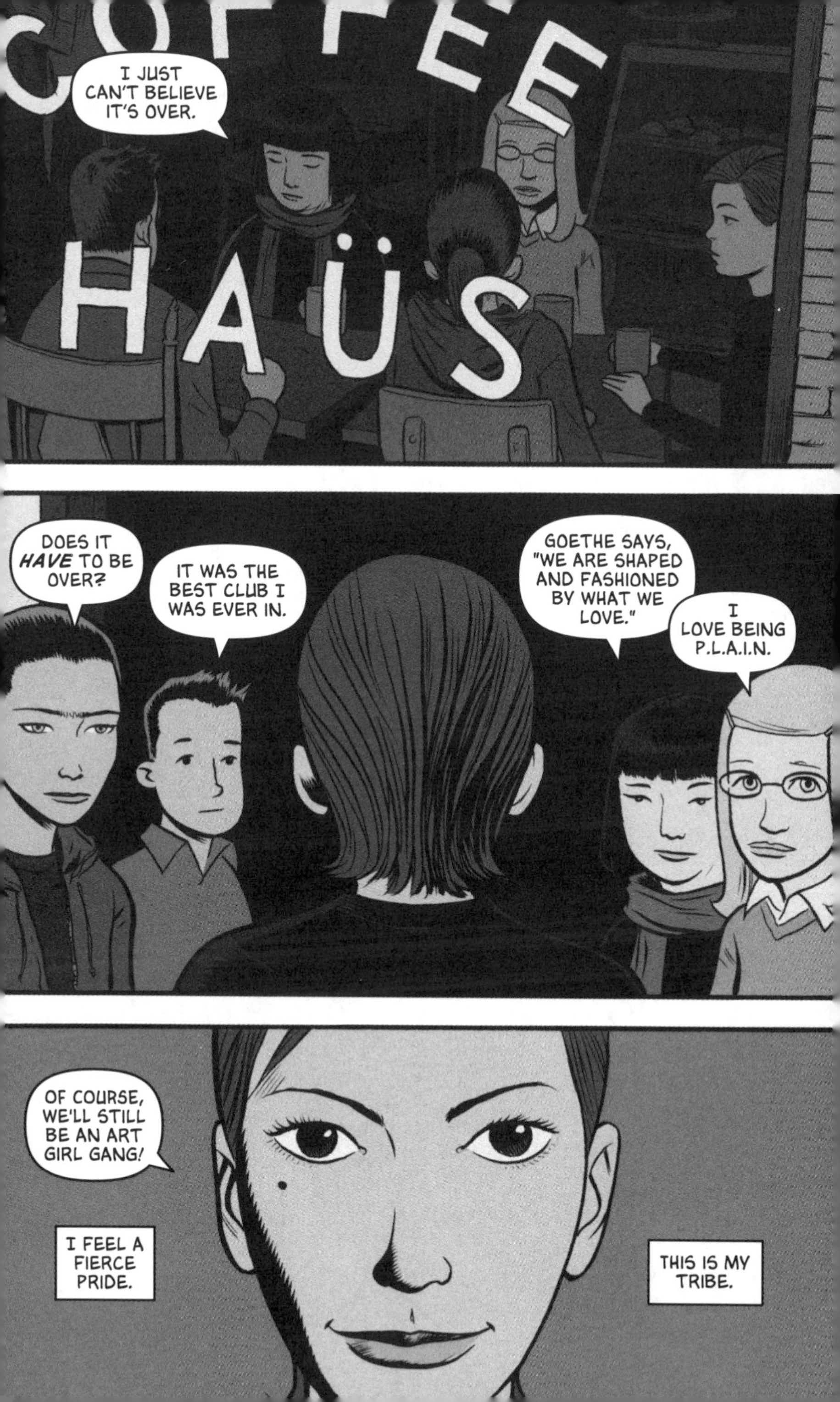
COFFEE HAÜS
I JUST CAN'T BELIEVE IT'S OVER.
DOES IT *HAVE* TO BE OVER?
IT WAS THE BEST CLUB I WAS EVER IN.
GOETHE SAYS, "WE ARE SHAPED AND FASHIONED BY WHAT WE LOVE."
I LOVE BEING P.L.A.I.N.
OF COURSE, WE'LL STILL BE AN ART GIRL GANG!
I FEEL A FIERCE PRIDE.
THIS IS MY TRIBE.

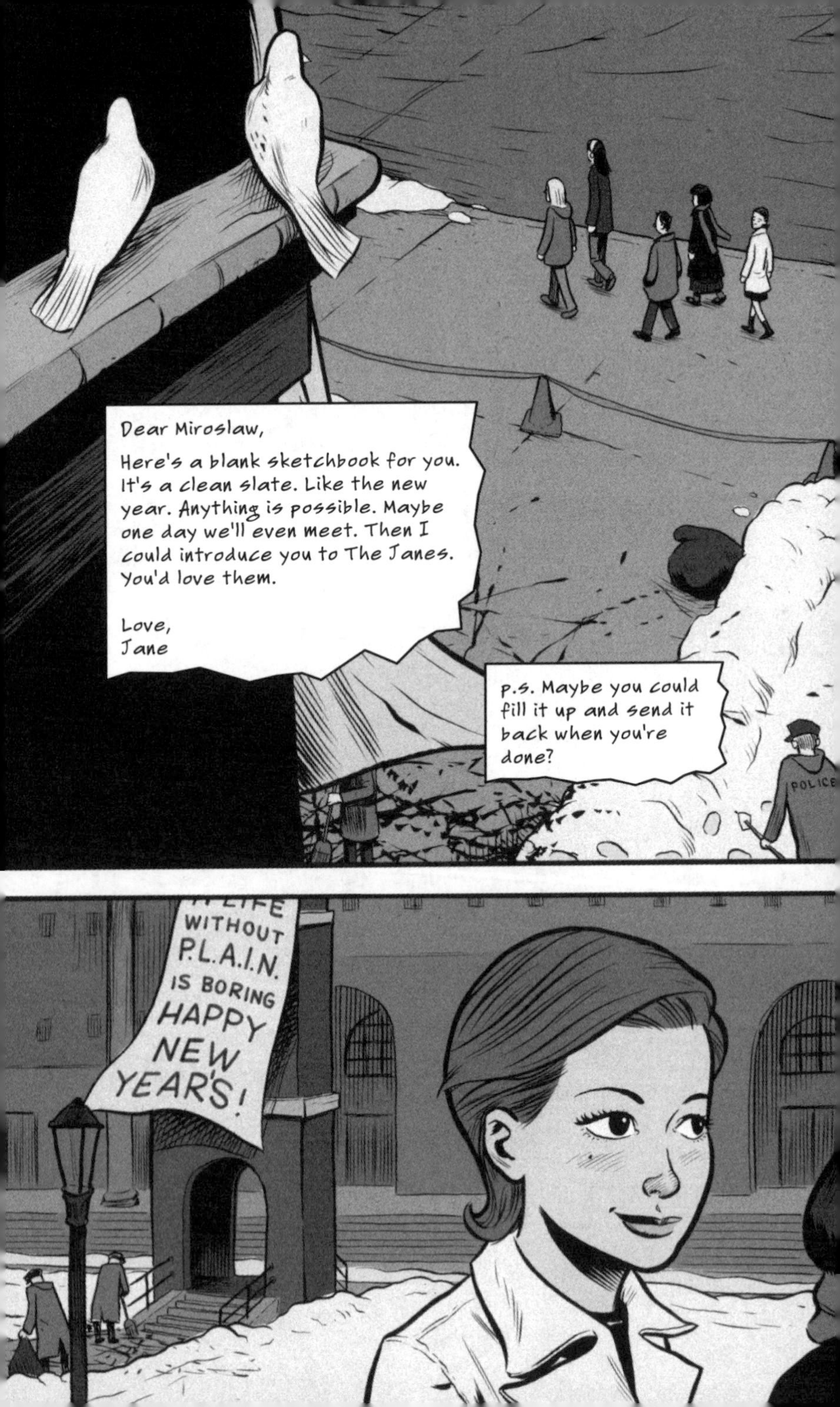
Dear Miroslaw,
Here's a blank sketchbook for you. It's a clean slate. Like the new year. Anything is possible. Maybe one day we'll even meet. Then I could introduce you to The Janes. You'd love them.
Love,
Jane
p.s. Maybe you could fill it up and send it back when you're done?
POLICE
WITHOUT P.L.A.I.N. IS BORING HAPPY NEW YEAR'S!

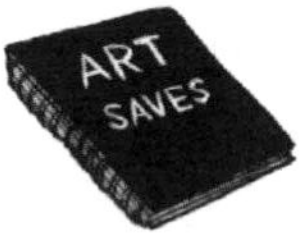
ART
SAVES

The End.

CECIL CASTELLUCCI

Cecil grew up in New York City, is French Canadian and makes her home in Los Angeles. She's the author of three young adult novels, **Boy Proof**, **The Queen of Cool**, and the upcoming **Beige**. Cecil is also an indie rock musician, an independent filmmaker and a playwright. During her years at the LaGuardia High School of Performing Arts, she'd see Keith Haring's drawings in the subways in New York. She still looks for street art whenever she's on a walk.

JIM RUGG

Jim is the artist and co-creator of **Street Angel**. His comics have also appeared in anthologies including **Project: Superior**, **SPX**, **Orchid**, and **Meathaus**. He grew up near Pittsburgh and hasn't come up with a good excuse to skip town. He's disappointed his school didn't have a girl gang like the Janes or the Dagger Debs.

SPECIAL BACKSTAGE PASS:

If you liked the story you've just read, fear not: other MINX

books will be available in the months to come. MINX is a line

of books that's designed especially for you — someone who's

a bit bored with straight fiction and ready for

stories that are visually exciting beyond words — literally.

In fact, we thought you might like to get in on a secret,

behind-the-scenes look at a few of the new MINX titles that

will aid in your escape to cool places during the long hot

summer. So hurry up and turn the page already! And be

sure to check out other exclusive material at

www.titanbooks.com

A Korean-American California girl who's into

martial arts learns that in romance and recycled gifts,

what goes around comes around.

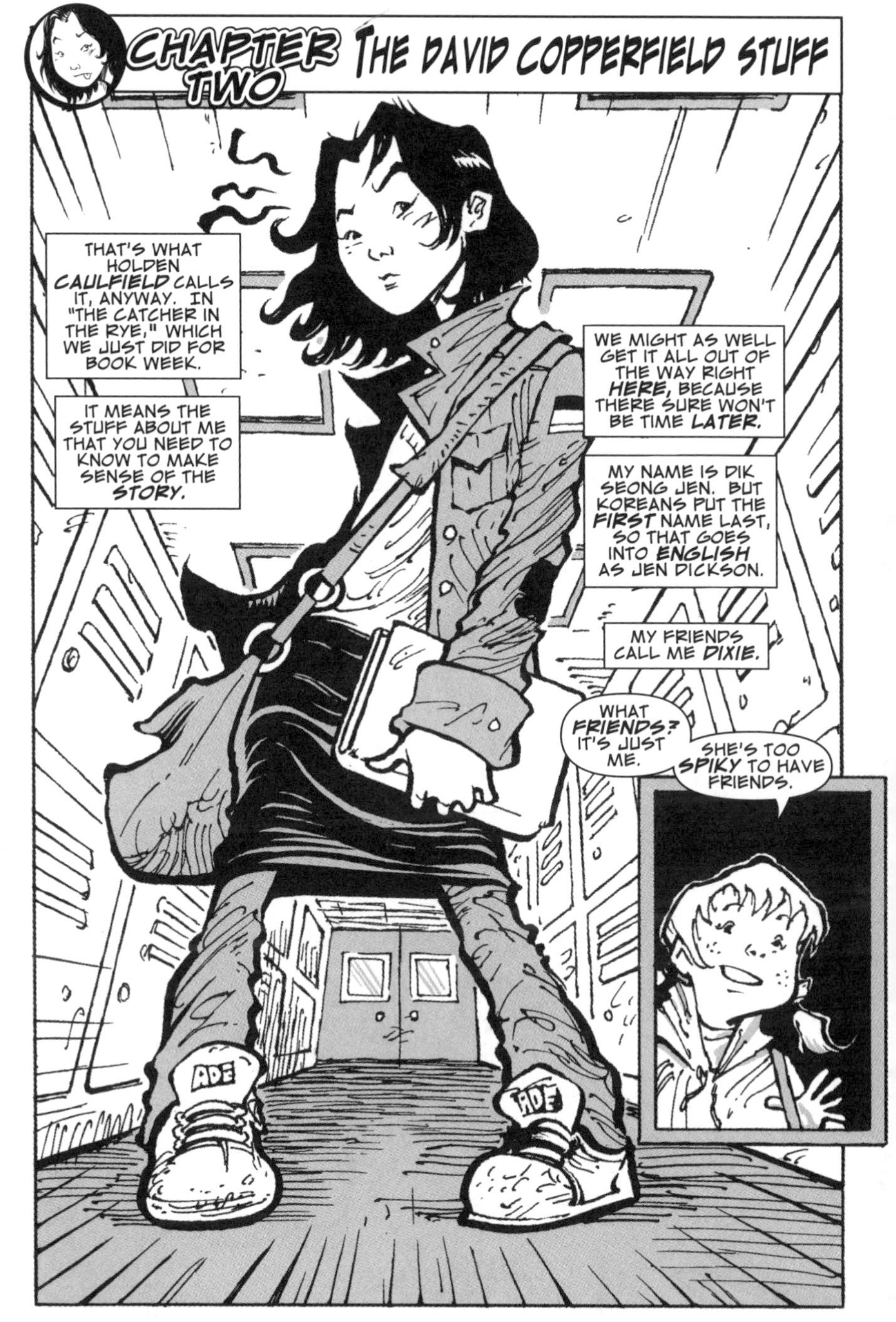
CHAPTER TWO
THE DAVID COPPERFIELD STUFF
THAT'S WHAT HOLDEN CAULFIELD CALLS IT, ANYWAY. IN "THE CATCHER IN THE RYE," WHICH WE JUST DID FOR BOOK WEEK.
IT MEANS THE STUFF ABOUT ME THAT YOU NEED TO KNOW TO MAKE SENSE OF THE STORY.
WE MIGHT AS WELL GET IT ALL OUT OF THE WAY RIGHT HERE, BECAUSE THERE SURE WON'T BE TIME LATER.
MY NAME IS DIK SEONG JEN. BUT KOREANS PUT THE FIRST NAME LAST, SO THAT GOES INTO ENGLISH AS JEN DICKSON.
MY FRIENDS CALL ME DIXIE.
WHAT FRIENDS? IT'S JUST ME.
SHE'S TOO SPIKY TO HAVE FRIENDS.
ADE
ADE

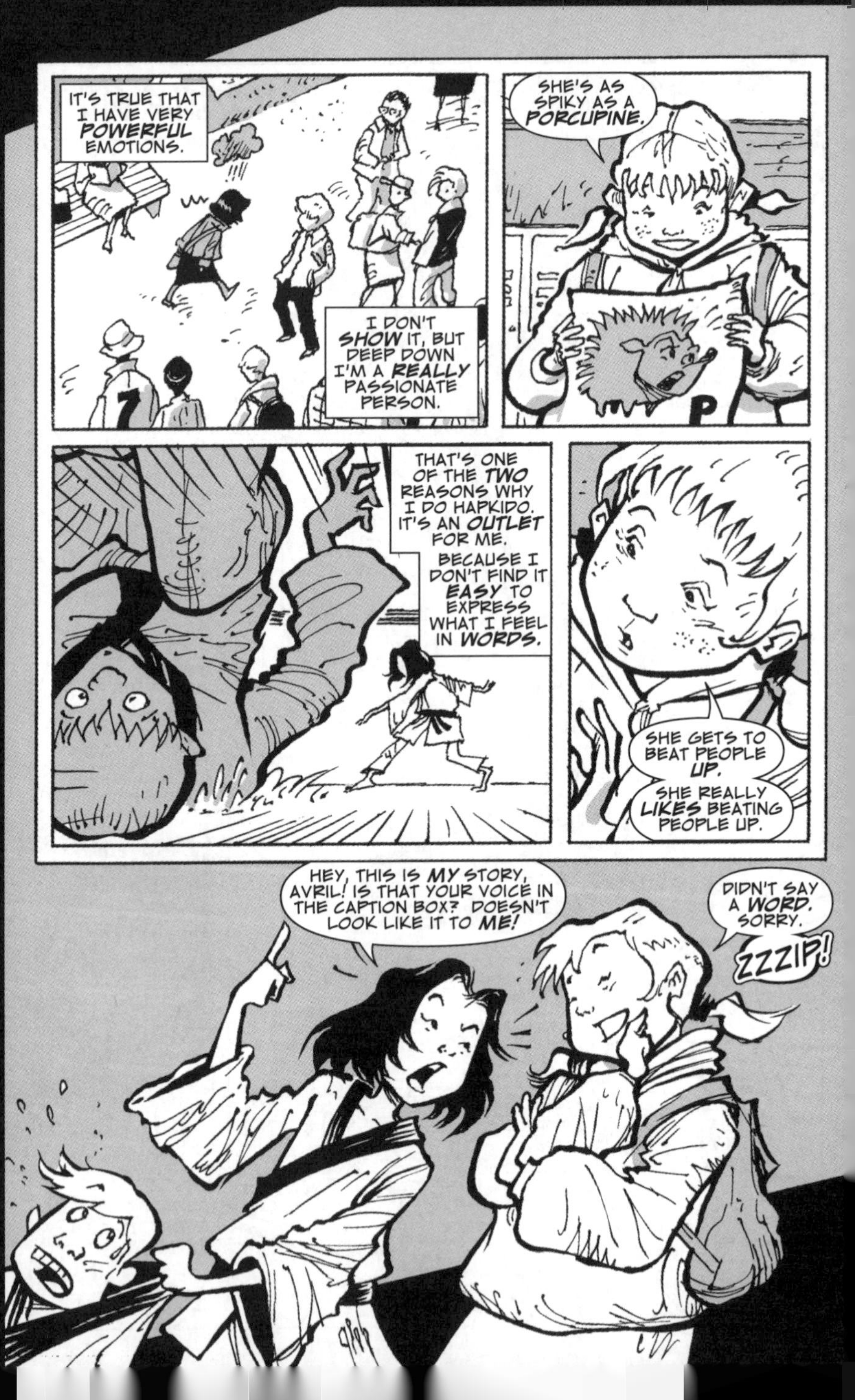
IT'S TRUE THAT I HAVE VERY POWERFUL EMOTIONS.
I DON'T SHOW IT, BUT DEEP DOWN I'M A REALLY PASSIONATE PERSON.
SHE'S AS SPIKY AS A PORCUPINE.
THAT'S ONE OF THE TWO REASONS WHY I DO HAPKIDO. IT'S AN OUTLET FOR ME.
BECAUSE I DON'T FIND IT EASY TO EXPRESS WHAT I FEEL IN WORDS.
SHE GETS TO BEAT PEOPLE UP.
SHE REALLY LIKES BEATING PEOPLE UP.
HEY, THIS IS MY STORY, AVRIL! IS THAT YOUR VOICE IN THE CAPTION BOX? DOESN'T LOOK LIKE IT TO ME!
DIDN'T SAY A WORD. SORRY.
ZZZIP!

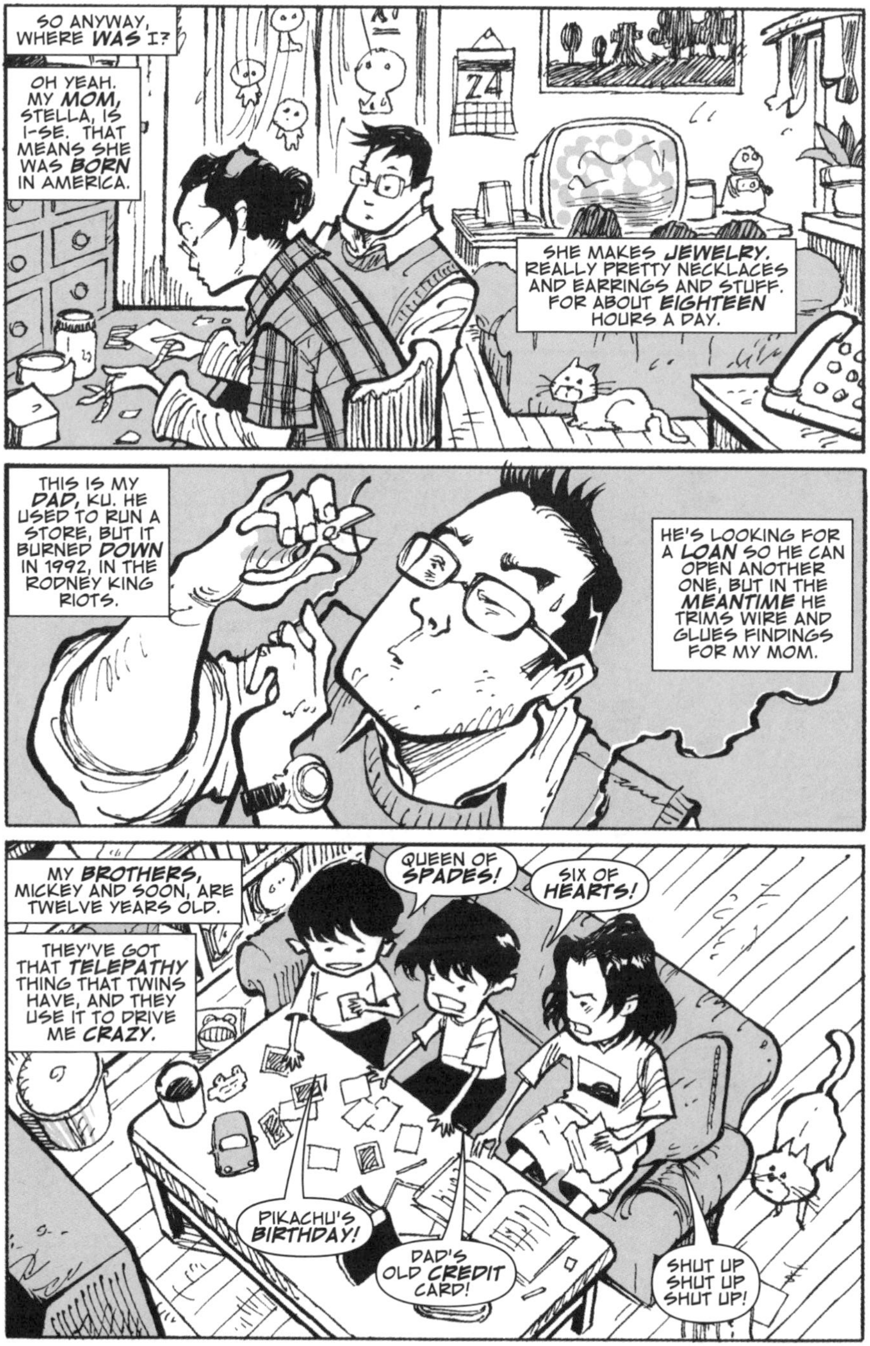
SO ANYWAY, WHERE WAS I?
OH YEAH. MY MOM, STELLA, IS I-SE. THAT MEANS SHE WAS BORN IN AMERICA.
SHE MAKES JEWELRY. REALLY PRETTY NECKLACES AND EARRINGS AND STUFF. FOR ABOUT EIGHTEEN HOURS A DAY.
THIS IS MY DAD, KU. HE USED TO RUN A STORE, BUT IT BURNED DOWN IN 1992, IN THE RODNEY KING RIOTS.
HE'S LOOKING FOR A LOAN SO HE CAN OPEN ANOTHER ONE, BUT IN THE MEANTIME HE TRIMS WIRE AND GLUES FINDINGS FOR MY MOM.
MY BROTHERS, MICKEY AND SOON, ARE TWELVE YEARS OLD.
THEY'VE GOT THAT TELEPATHY THING THAT TWINS HAVE, AND THEY USE IT TO DRIVE ME CRAZY.
QUEEN OF SPADES!
SIX OF HEARTS!
PIKACHU'S BIRTHDAY!
DAD'S OLD CREDIT CARD!
SHUT UP SHUT UP SHUT UP!

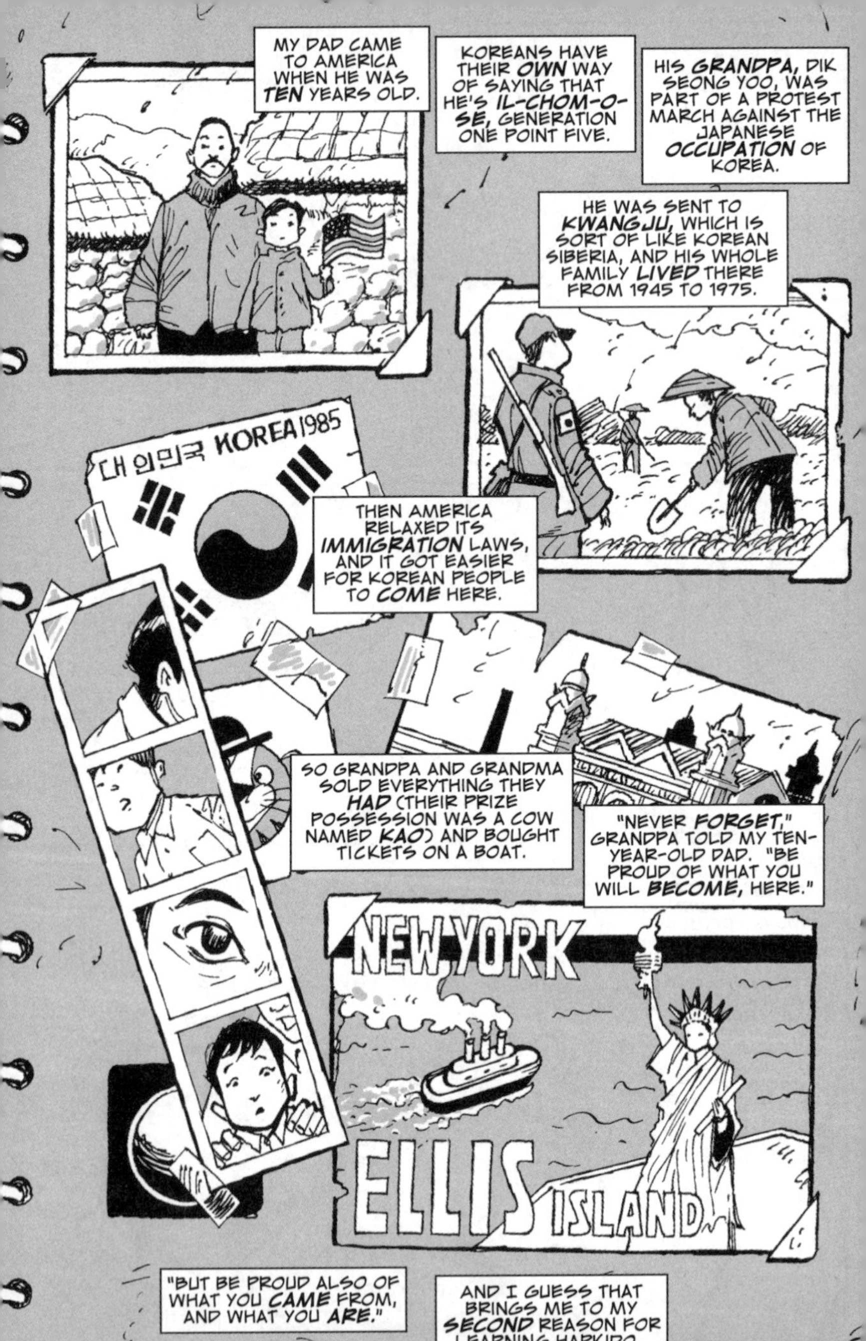

MY DAD CAME TO AMERICA WHEN HE WAS TEN YEARS OLD.
KOREANS HAVE THEIR OWN WAY OF SAYING THAT HE'S IL-CHOM-O-SE, GENERATION ONE POINT FIVE.
HIS GRANDPA, DIK SEONG YOO, WAS PART OF A PROTEST MARCH AGAINST THE JAPANESE OCCUPATION OF KOREA.
HE WAS SENT TO KWANGJU, WHICH IS SORT OF LIKE KOREAN SIBERIA, AND HIS WHOLE FAMILY LIVED THERE FROM 1945 TO 1975.
대 한민국 KOREA 1985
THEN AMERICA RELAXED ITS IMMIGRATION LAWS, AND IT GOT EASIER FOR KOREAN PEOPLE TO COME HERE.
SO GRANDPA AND GRANDMA SOLD EVERYTHING THEY HAD (THEIR PRIZE POSSESSION WAS A COW NAMED KAO) AND BOUGHT TICKETS ON A BOAT.
"NEVER FORGET," GRANDPA TOLD MY TEN-YEAR-OLD DAD. "BE PROUD OF WHAT YOU WILL BECOME, HERE."
NEW YORK
ELLIS ISLAND
"BUT BE PROUD ALSO OF WHAT YOU CAME FROM, AND WHAT YOU ARE."
AND I GUESS THAT BRINGS ME TO MY SECOND REASON FOR LEARNING HAPKIDO.

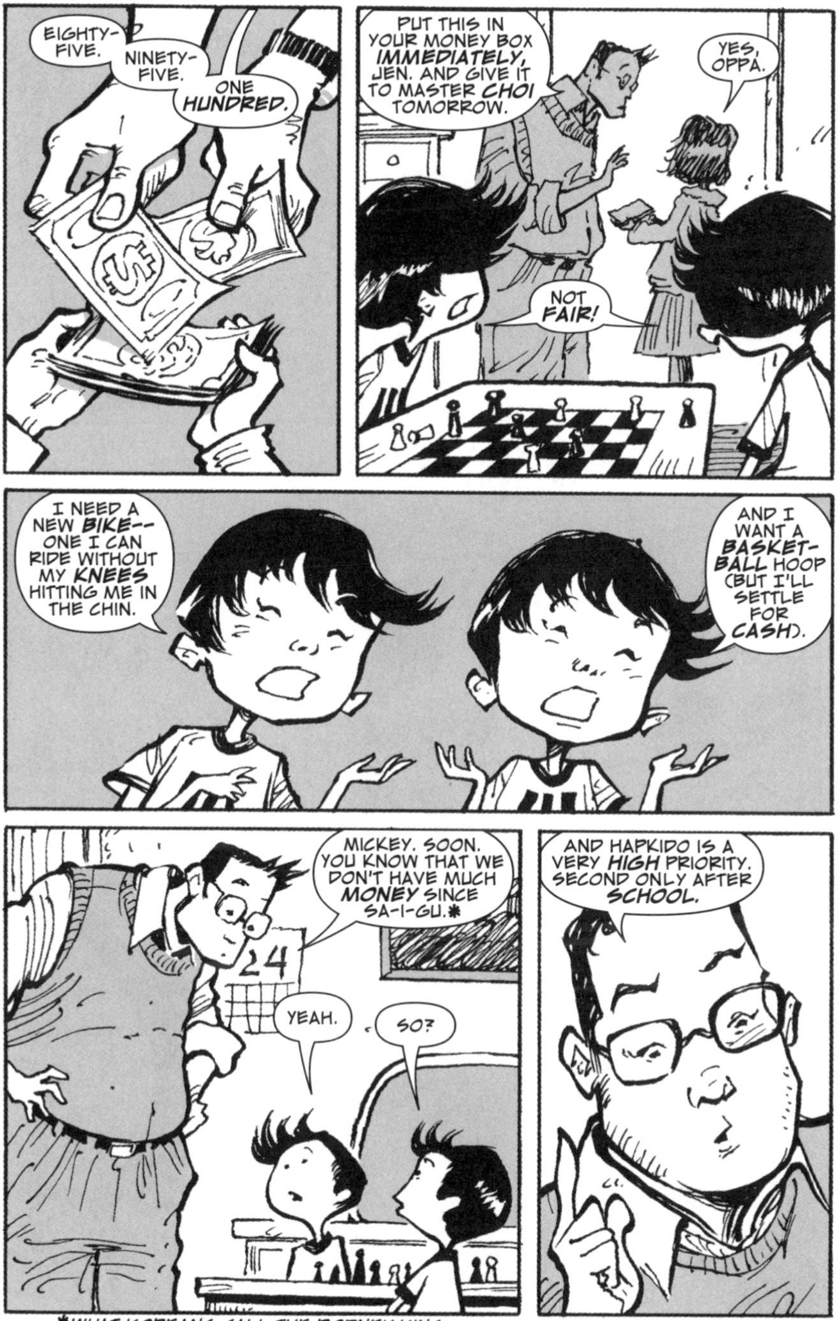
EIGHTY-FIVE.
NINETY-FIVE.
ONE HUNDRED.
PUT THIS IN YOUR MONEY BOX IMMEDIATELY, JEN. AND GIVE IT TO MASTER CHOI TOMORROW.
YES, OPPA.
NOT FAIR!
I NEED A NEW BIKE-- ONE I CAN RIDE WITHOUT MY KNEES HITTING ME IN THE CHIN.
AND I WANT A BASKET-BALL HOOP (BUT I'LL SETTLE FOR CASH).
MICKEY. SOON. YOU KNOW THAT WE DON'T HAVE MUCH MONEY SINCE SA-I-GU.*
24
YEAH.
SO?
AND HAPKIDO IS A VERY HIGH PRIORITY. SECOND ONLY AFTER SCHOOL.

*WHAT KOREANS CALL THE RODNEY KING RIOTS--LITERALLY "APRIL 29TH".

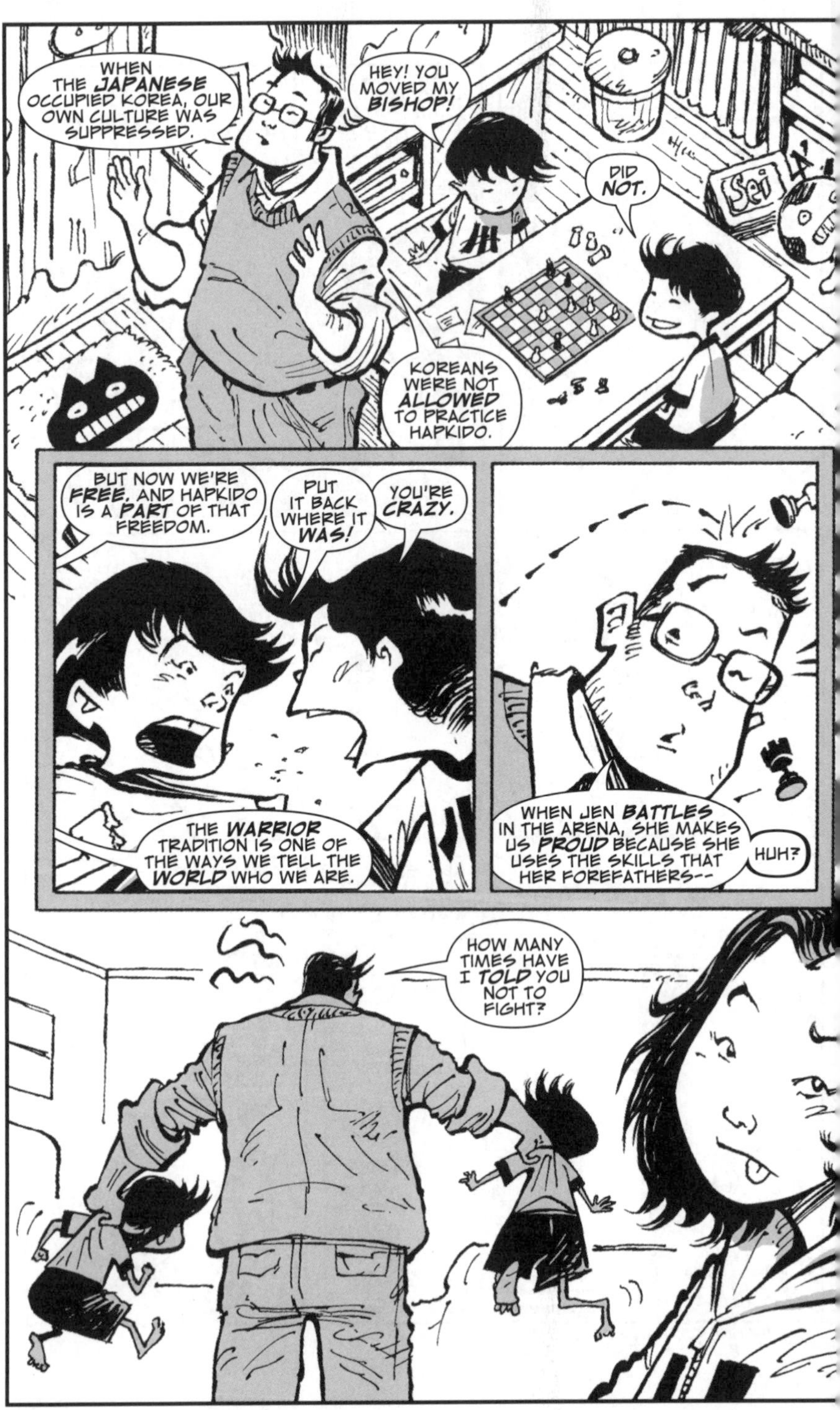
WHEN THE JAPANESE OCCUPIED KOREA, OUR OWN CULTURE WAS SUPPRESSED.
HEY! YOU MOVED MY BISHOP!
DID NOT.
KOREANS WERE NOT ALLOWED TO PRACTICE HAPKIDO.
Sei
BUT NOW WE'RE FREE, AND HAPKIDO IS A PART OF THAT FREEDOM.
PUT IT BACK WHERE IT WAS!
YOU'RE CRAZY.
THE WARRIOR TRADITION IS ONE OF THE WAYS WE TELL THE WORLD WHO WE ARE.
WHEN JEN BATTLES IN THE ARENA, SHE MAKES US PROUD BECAUSE SHE USES THE SKILLS THAT HER FOREFATHERS--
HUH?
HOW MANY TIMES HAVE I TOLD YOU NOT TO FIGHT?

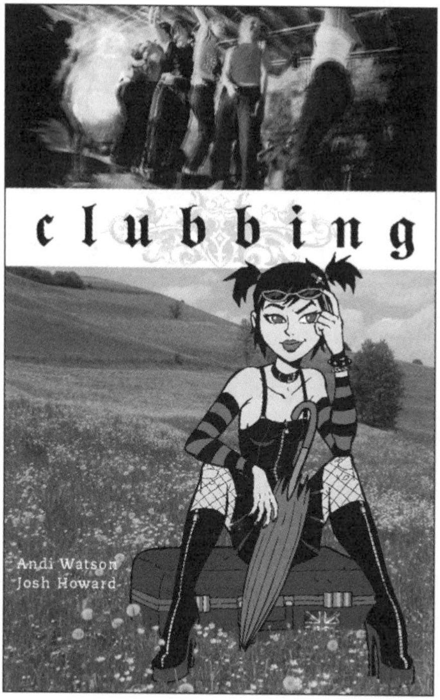
clubbing
Andi Watson
Josh Howard

A spoiled, rebellious Londoner conquers the stuffy English countryside when she solves a murder mystery on the 19th hole of her grandparents' golf course.

COMING IN AUGUST 2007 ■ Read on.

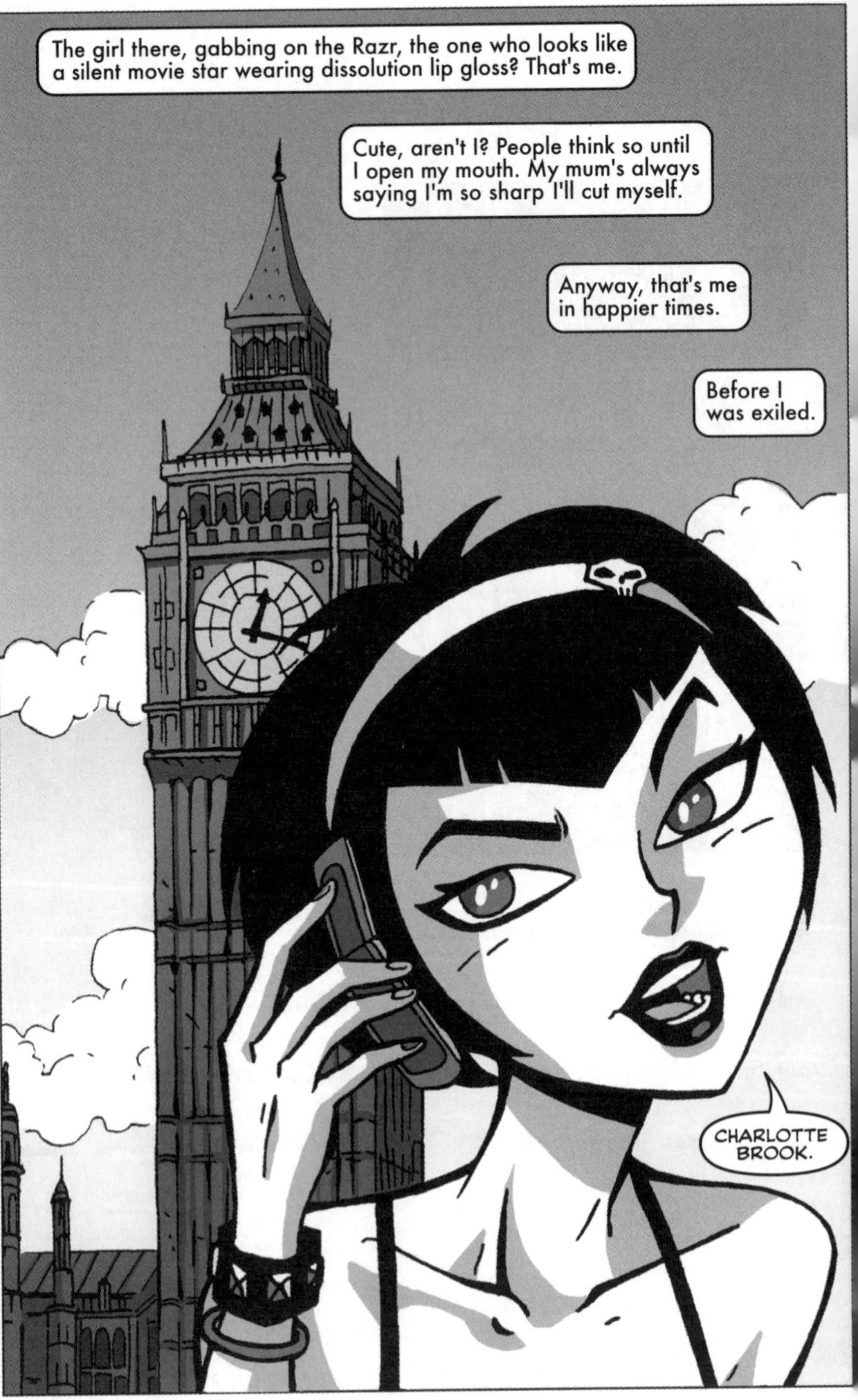

The girl there, gabbing on the Razr, the one who looks like a silent movie star wearing dissolution lip gloss? That's me.
Cute, aren't I? People think so until I open my mouth. My mum's always saying I'm so sharp I'll cut myself.
Anyway, that's me in happier times.
Before I was exiled.
CHARLOTTE BROOK.

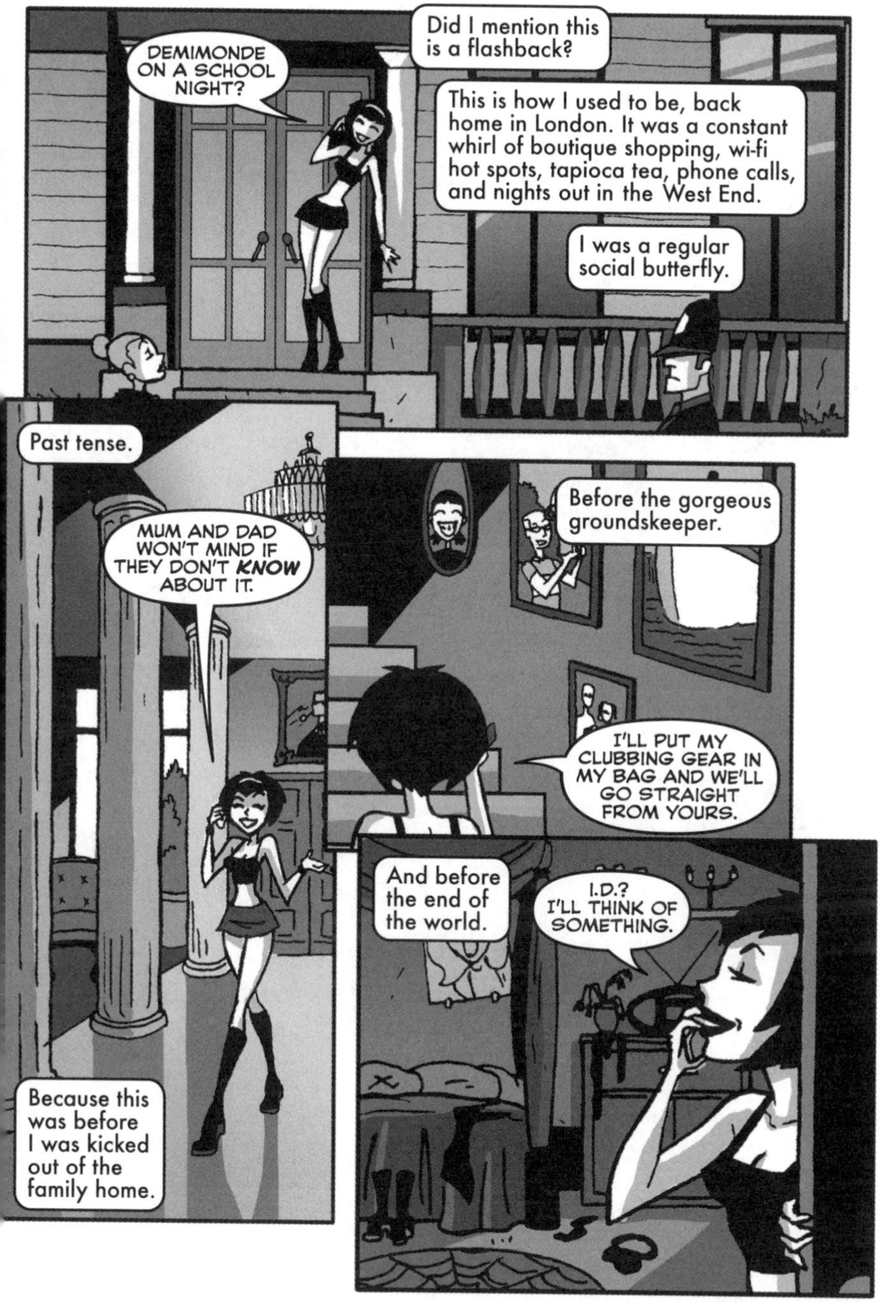

DEMIMONDE ON A SCHOOL NIGHT?
Did I mention this is a flashback?
This is how I used to be, back home in London. It was a constant whirl of boutique shopping, wi-fi hot spots, tapioca tea, phone calls, and nights out in the West End.
I was a regular social butterfly.
Past tense.
MUM AND DAD WON'T MIND IF THEY DON'T KNOW ABOUT IT.
Because this was before I was kicked out of the family home.
Before the gorgeous groundskeeper.
I'LL PUT MY CLUBBING GEAR IN MY BAG AND WE'LL GO STRAIGHT FROM YOURS.
And before the end of the world.
I.D.? I'LL THINK OF SOMETHING.

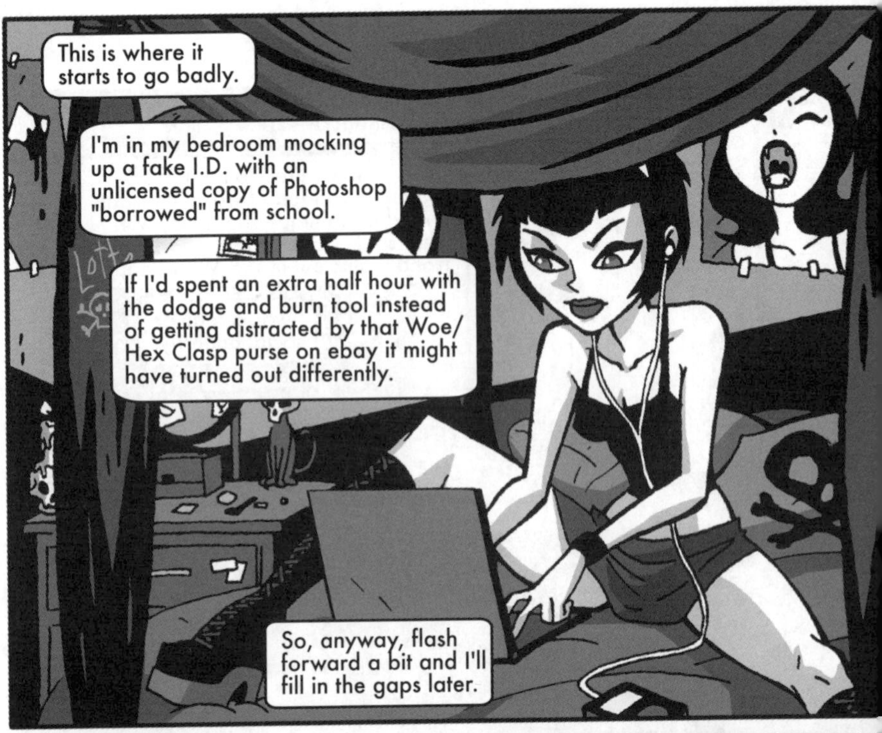
This is where it starts to go badly.
I'm in my bedroom mocking up a fake I.D. with an unlicensed copy of Photoshop "borrowed" from school.
If I'd spent an extra half hour with the dodge and burn tool instead of getting distracted by that Woe/Hex Clasp purse on ebay it might have turned out differently.
So, anyway, flash forward a bit and I'll fill in the gaps later.

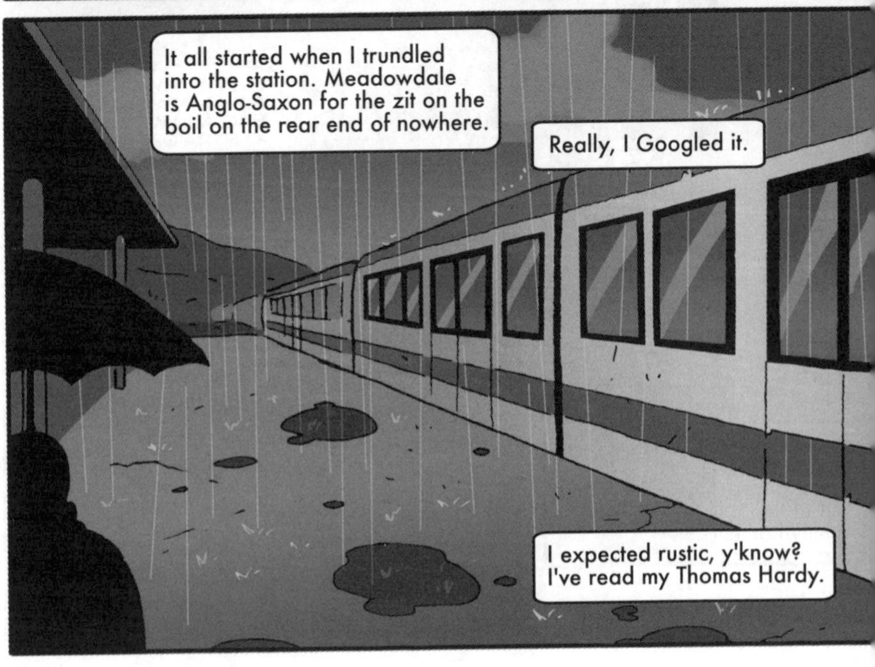
It all started when I trundled into the station. Meadowdale is Anglo-Saxon for the zit on the boil on the rear end of nowhere.
Really, I Googled it.
I expected rustic, y'know? I've read my Thomas Hardy.

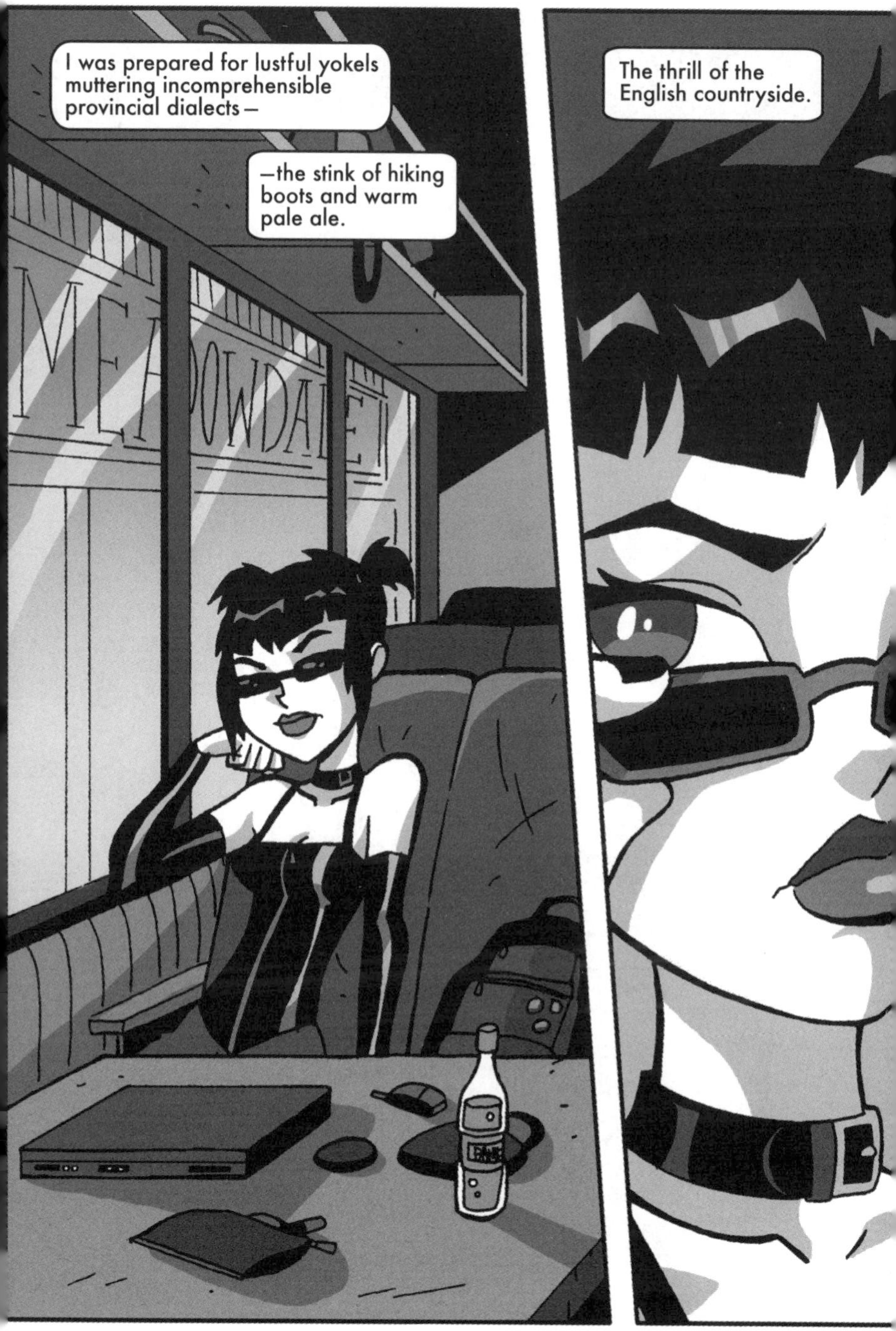
I was prepared for lustful yokels muttering incomprehensible provincial dialects –
–the stink of hiking boots and warm pale ale.
MEADOWDALE
The thrill of the English countryside.

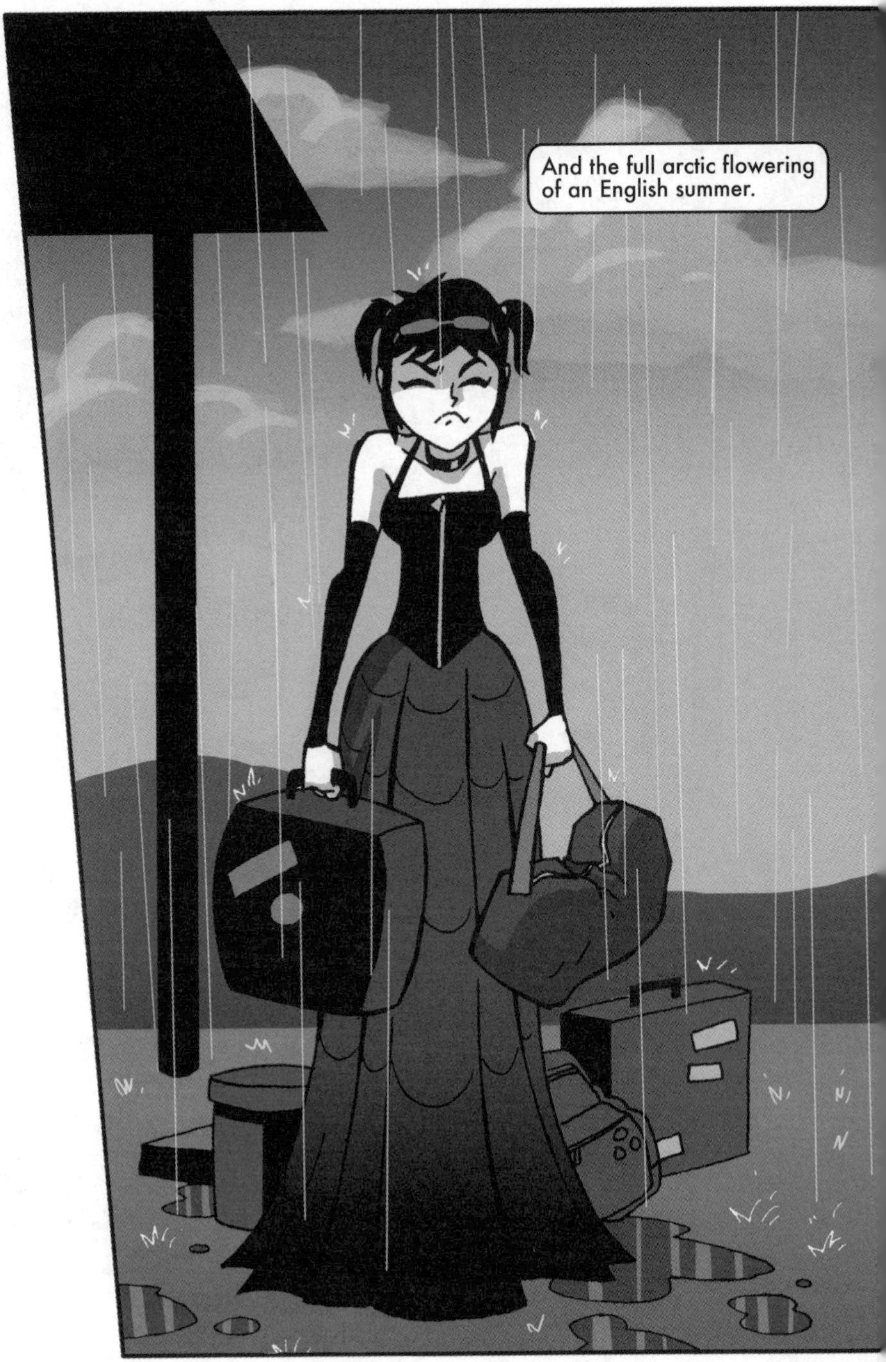
And the full arctic flowering
of an English summer.

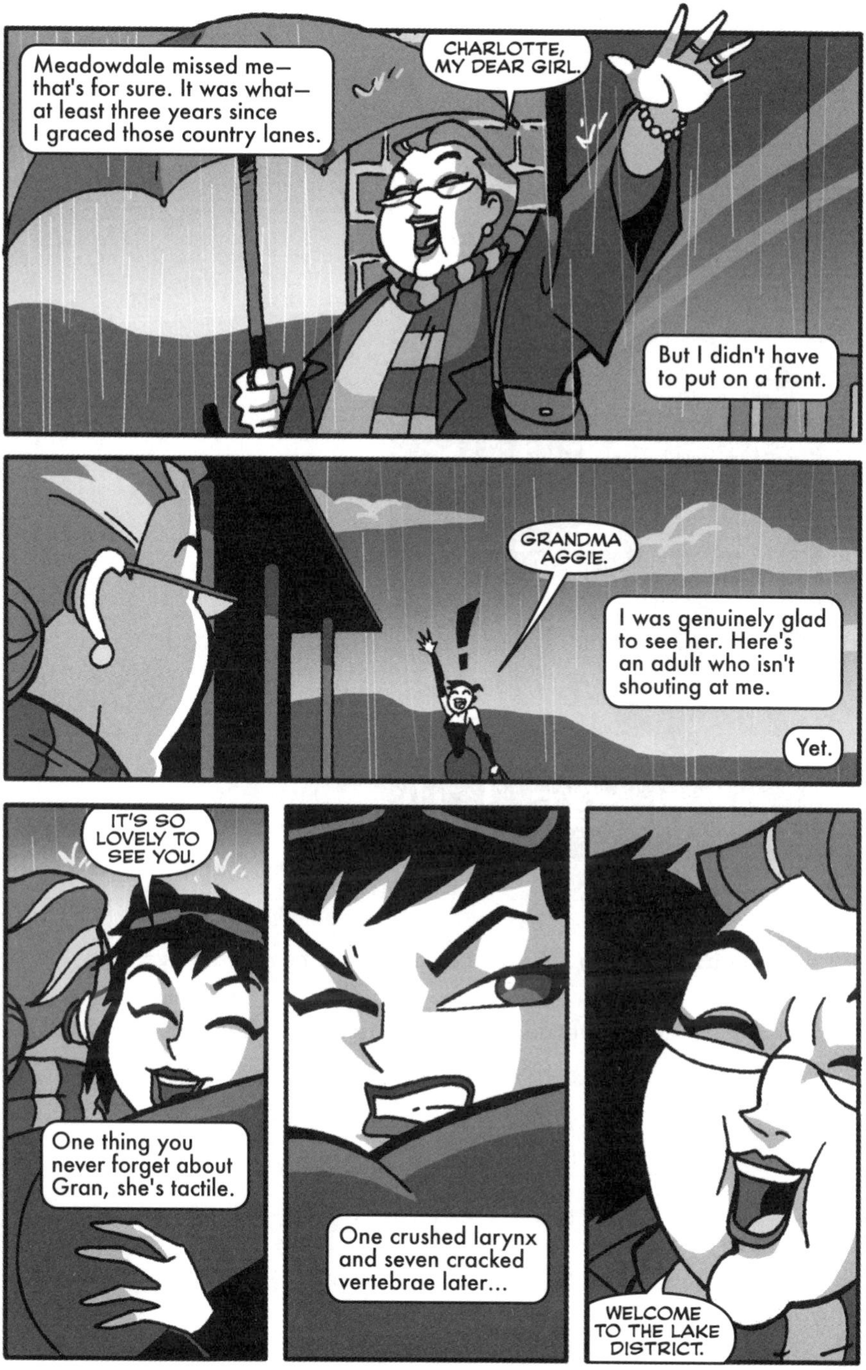
Meadowdale missed me—that's for sure. It was what—at least three years since I graced those country lanes.
CHARLOTTE, MY DEAR GIRL.
But I didn't have to put on a front.
GRANDMA AGGIE.
I was genuinely glad to see her. Here's an adult who isn't shouting at me.
Yet.
IT'S SO LOVELY TO SEE YOU.
One thing you never forget about Gran, she's tactile.
One crushed larynx and seven cracked vertebrae later...
WELCOME TO THE LAKE DISTRICT.

Derek Kirk Kim & Jesse Hamm

Good As Lily

What would you do if versions of yourself at ages 6, 29 and 70 suddenly became part of your already complicated high school life?

COMING IN SEPTEMBER 2007 ■ Read on.

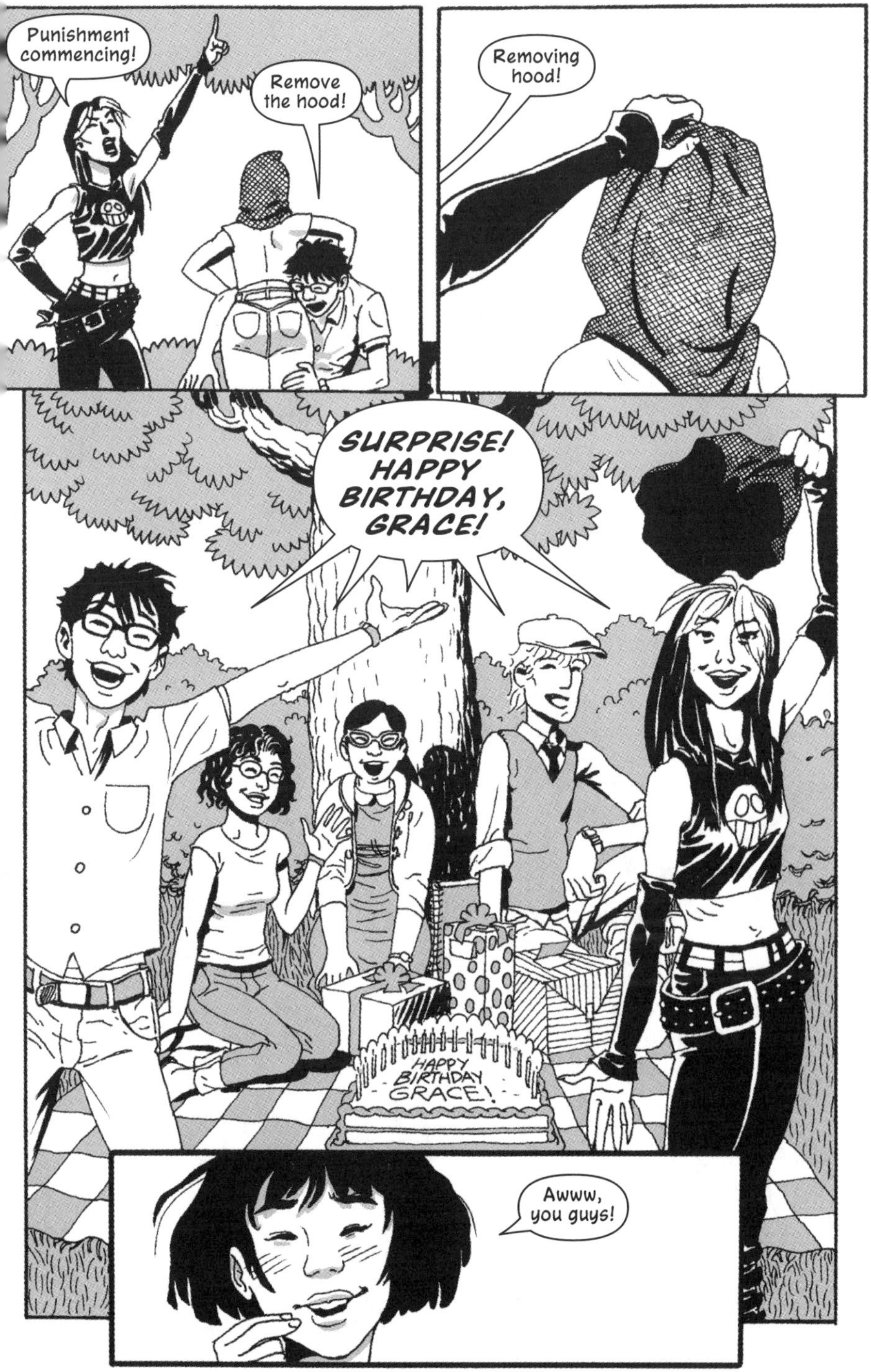
Punishment commencing!
Remove the hood!
Removing hood!
SURPRISE! HAPPY BIRTHDAY, GRACE!
HAPPY BIRTHDAY GRACE!
Awww, you guys!

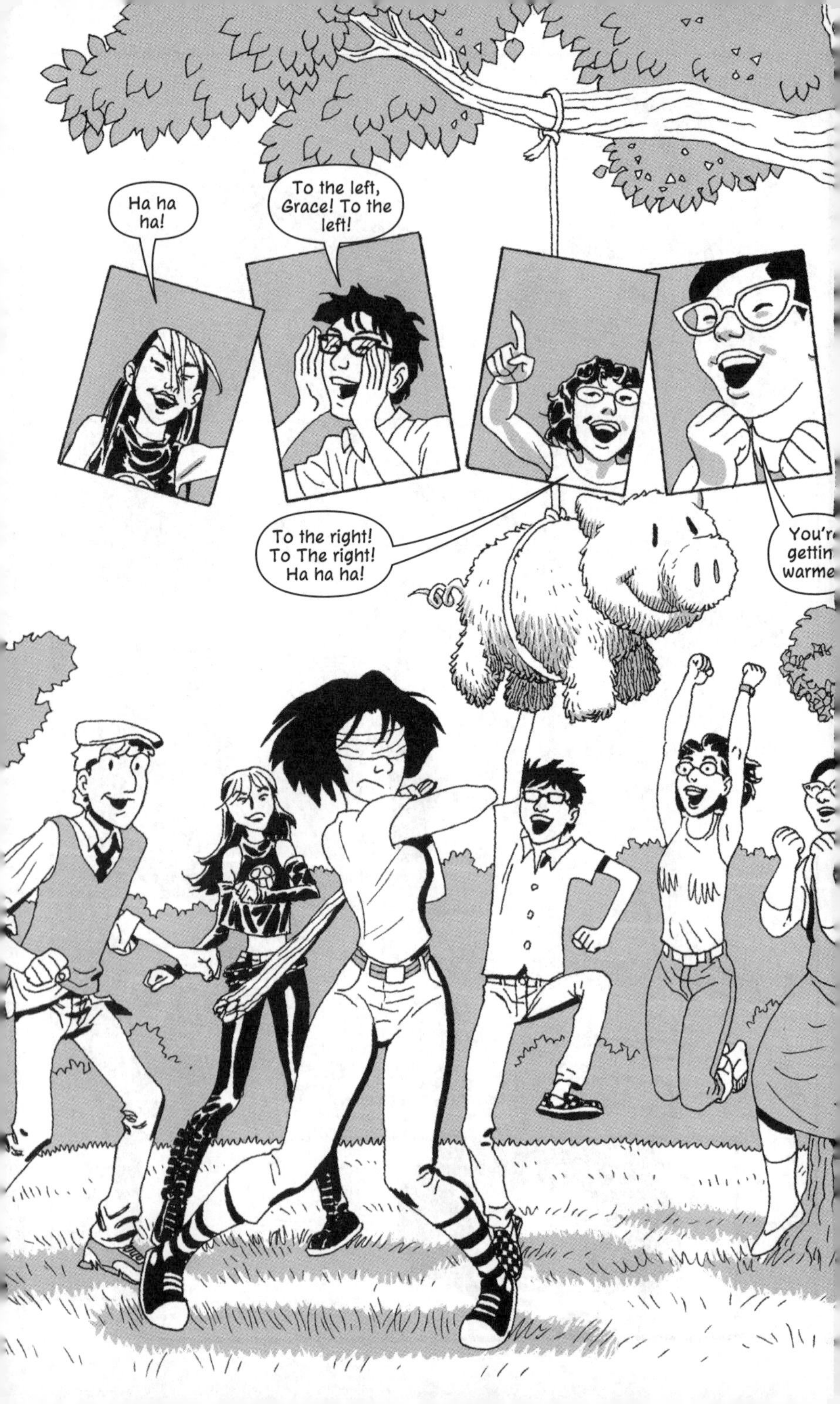
Ha ha ha!
To the left, Grace! To the left!
To the right! To The right! Ha ha ha!

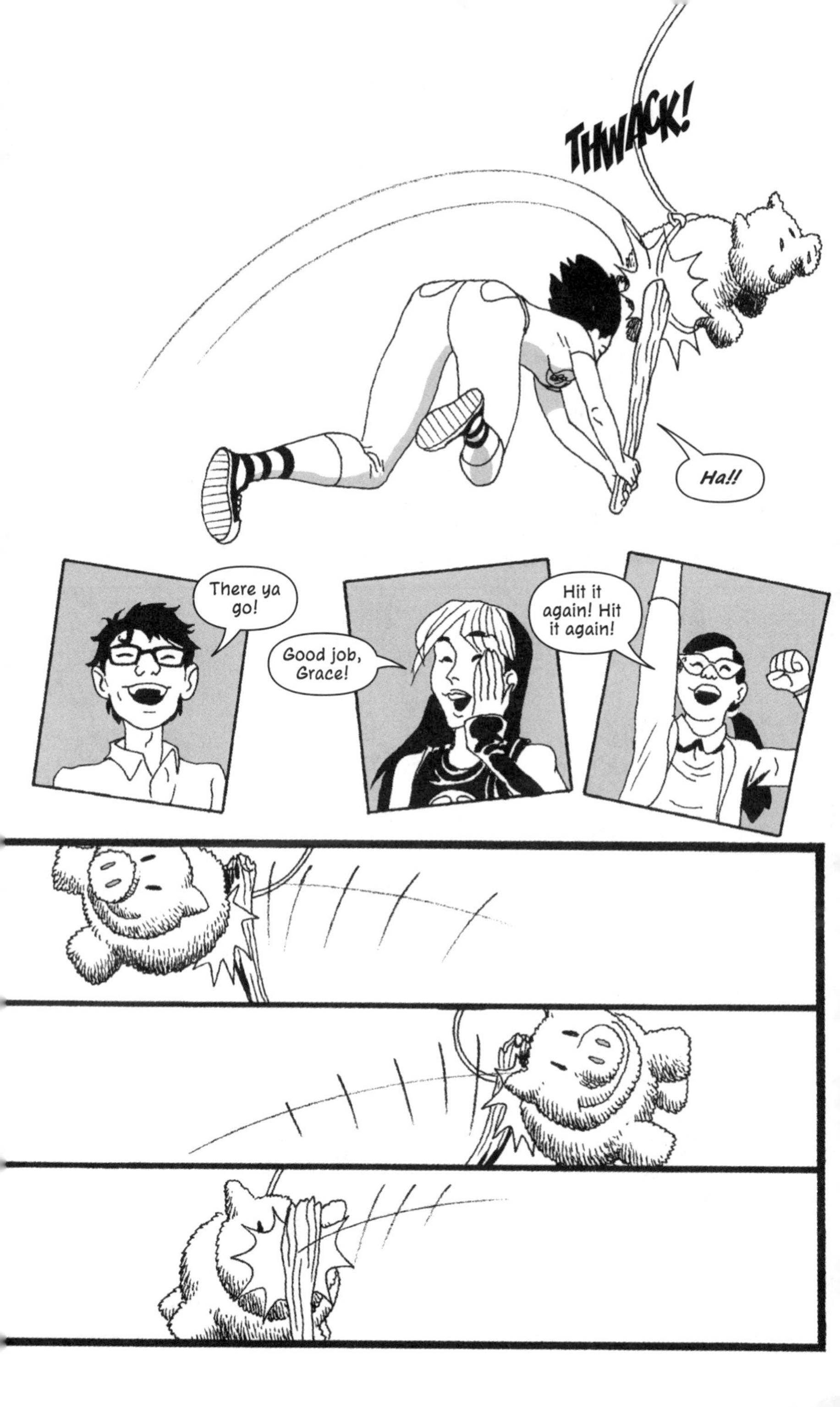
THWACK!
Ha!!
There ya go!
Good job, Grace!
Hit it again! Hit it again!

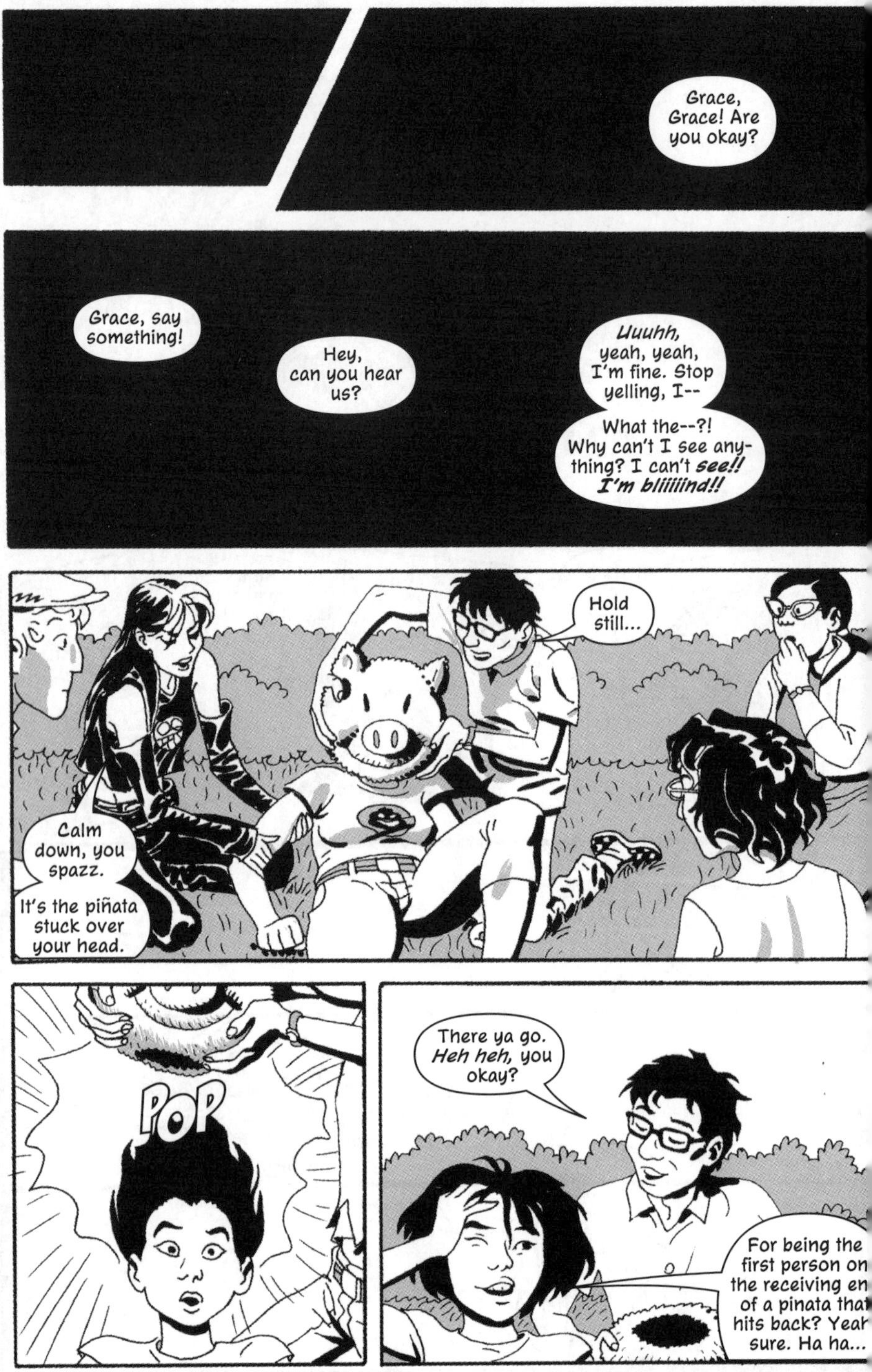

Grace, Grace! Are you okay?
Grace, say something!
Hey, can you hear us?
Uuuhh, yeah, yeah, I'm fine. Stop yelling, I--
What the--?! Why can't I see anything? I can't ***see!!*** ***I'm bliiiiind!!***
Hold still...
Calm down, you spazz.
It's the piñata stuck over your head.
POP
There ya go. *Heh heh,* you okay?
For being the first person on the receiving en of a pinata tha hits back? Yeal sure. Ha ha...

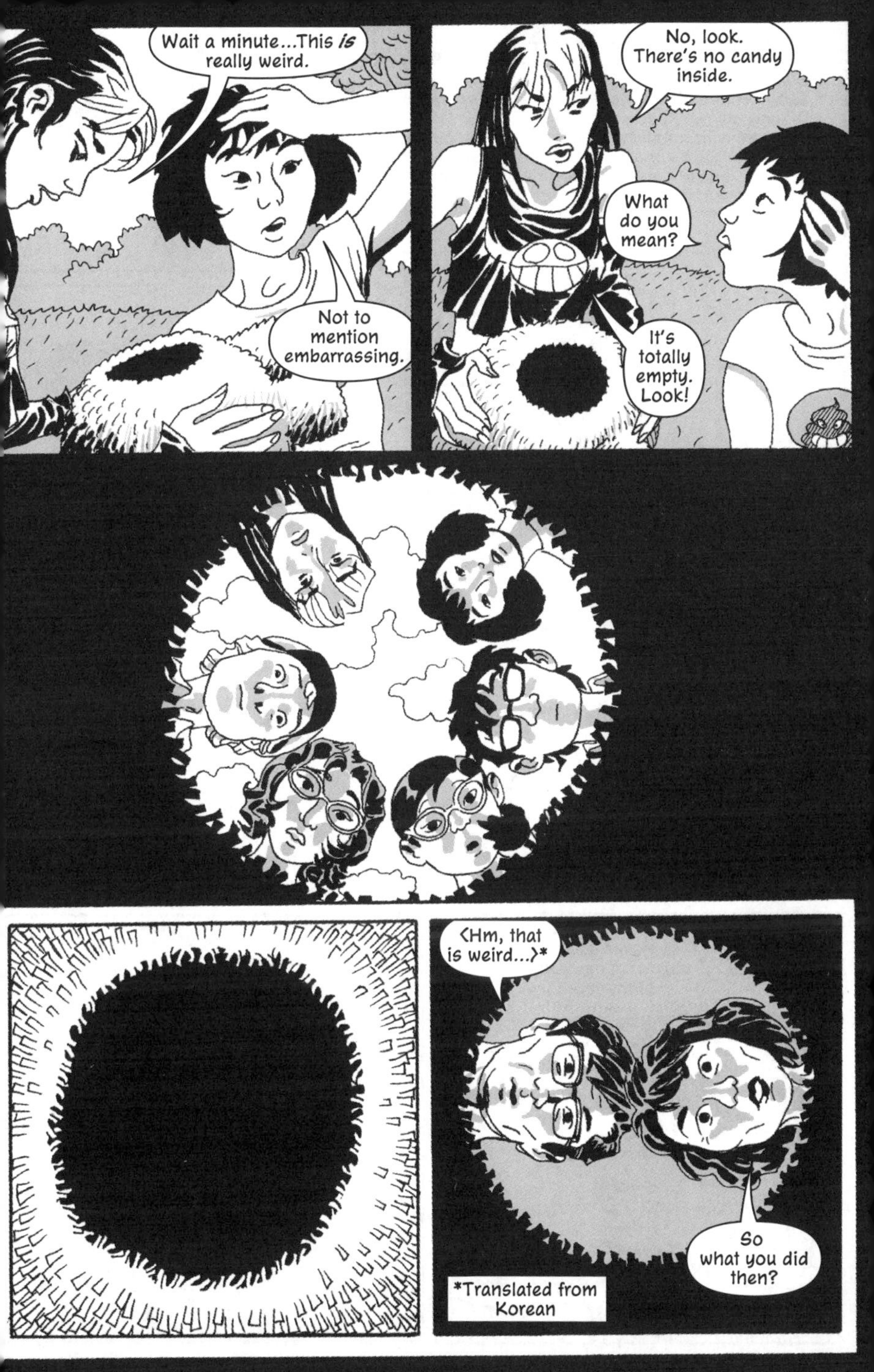

Wait a minute...This *is* really weird.
Not to mention embarrassing.
No, look. There's no candy inside.
What do you mean?
It's totally empty. Look!
<Hm, that is weird...>*
So what you did then?
*Translated from Korean

So there I was, about to blow my stack. But as I looked at the three of them, I suddenly started to feel dizzy. The total craziness of what was before me was hitting me full force again. There I was, standing in my room with... myself... at the age of 6, 29, and 70. I felt like I was in a dream, surrounded by distorted mirrors in an impossible funhouse.

...I can't stop staring... My room... My old room...

Okay, I wanna know one thing. What happened on your 18th birthday after you got hit on the head with the piñata?

I never had a piñata on my 18th birthday...

Yeah, what piñata?

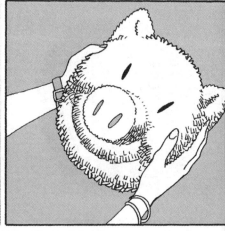

Don't miss any of the upcoming  books of 2007:

CONFESSIONS OF A BLABBERMOUTH
By Mike and Louise Carey and Aaron Alexovich
October

When Tasha's mom brings home a creepy boyfriend and his deadpan daughter, a dysfunctional family is headed for a complete mental meltdown.

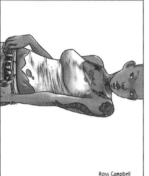

WATER BABY
By Ross Campbell
November

Surfer girl Brody just got her leg bitten off by a shark. What's worse? Her shark of an ex-boyfriend is back, and when it comes to Brody's couch, he's not budging.

KIMMIE66
By Aaron Alexovich
December

This high-velocity, virtual reality ghost story follows a tech-savvy teenager on a dangerous quest to save her best friend, the world's first all-digital girl.

Go to
www.titanbooks.com
for exclusive interviews
and bonus artwork!

The Face of Modern Fiction